AF654088

ANCIENT INDIAN TRADITION & MYTHOLOGY

Translated by
A BOARD OF SCHOLARS

Edited by
Dr. G.P. BHATT
Late Prof. J.L. SHASTRI

VOLUME 64

ANCIENT INDIAN TRADITION AND MYTHOLOGY SERIES

[PURĀṆAS IN TRANSLATION]

Volumes Released

ŚIVA 1-4
LIṄGA 5-6
BHĀGAVATA 7-11
GARUḌA 12-14
NĀRADA 15-19
KŪRMA 20-21
BRAHMĀṆḌA 22-26
AGNI 27-30
VARĀHA 31-32
BRAHMA 33-36
VĀYU 37-38
PADMA 39-48
SKANDA, PARTS I-XXI, 49-69

Volumes Under Preparation

SKANDA, PARTS XXII-XXIII, 70-71
VĀMANA 72-73
BHAVIṢYA
BRAHMAVAIVARTA
DEVĪBHĀGAVATA
KĀLIKĀ
MĀRKAṆḌEYA
MATSYA
VIṢṆU
VIṢṆUDHARMOTTARA

THE SKANDA-PURĀNA

PART XVI

Translated and Annotated by

DR. G.V. TAGARE

MOTILAL BANARSIDASS PUBLISHERS
PRIVATE LIMITED • DELHI

Reprint: Delhi, 2010
First Edition: Delhi, 2002

© MOTILAL BANARSIDASS PUBLISHERS PVT. LTD.
All Rights Reserved

ISBN: 978-81-208-1841-5

MOTILAL BANARSIDASS
41 U.A. Bungalow Road, Jawahar Nagar, Delhi 110 007
8 Mahalaxmi Chamber, 22 Bhulabhai Desai Road, Mumbai 400 026
203 Royapettah High Road, Mylapore, Chennai 600 004
236, 9th Main III Block, Jayanagar, Bangalore 560 011
Sanas Plaza, 1302 Baji Rao Road, Pune 411 002
8 Camac Street, Kolkata 700 017
Ashok Rajpath, Patna 800 004
Chowk, Varanasi 221 001

UNESCO COLLECTION OF REPRESENTATIVE WORKS—*Indian Series*
This book has been accepted in the Indian Translation Series of the UNESCO Collection of Representative Works, jointly sponsored by the United Nations Educational, Scientific and Cultural Organization (UNESCO) and the Government of India

Printed in India
By Jainendra Prakash Jain at Shri Jainendra Press,
A-45 Naraina, Phase-I, New Delhi 110 028
and Published by Narendra Prakash Jain for
Motilal Banarsidass Publishers Private Limited,
Bungalow Road, Delhi 110 007

PUBLISHER'S NOTE

The purest gems lie hidden in the bottom of the ocean or in the depth of rocks. One has to dive into the ocean or delve into the rocks to find them out. Similarly, truth lies concealed in the language which with the passage of time has become obsolete. Man has to learn that language before he discovers that truth.

But he has neither the means nor the leisure to embark on that course. We have, therefore, planned to help him acquire knowledge by an easier course. We have started the series of Ancient Indian Tradition and Mythology in English Translation. Our goal is to universalize knowledge through the most popular international medium of expression. The publication of the Purāṇas in English Translation is a step towards that goal.

Acknowledgements

It is our pleasant duty to put on record our sincere thanks to Dr. R.N. Dandekar and the UNESCO authorities for their kind encouragement and valuable help in the publication of the volumes in this series.

CONTENTS

SKANDA PURĀṆA
Book VI: NĀGARA KHAṆḌA

ABBREVIATIONS

Common and self-evident abbreviations such as Ch (s)—Chapter(s), p—page, pp—pages, v—verse, vv—verses, Ftn—Footnote, Hist. Ind. Philo.—History of Indian Philosophy are not included in this list.

AGP	S.M. Ali's *The Geography of Purāṇas*, PPH, New Delhi, 1973
AIHT	*Ancient Indian Historical Tradition*, F.E. Pargiter, Motilal Banarsidass (MLBD), Delhi
AITM	*Ancient Indian Tradition and Mythology* Series, MLBD, Delhi
AP	*Agni Purāṇa*, Guru Mandal Edition (GM), Calcutta, 1957
AV	*Atharva Veda*, Svādhyāya Maṇḍal, Aundh
BdP	*Brahmāṇḍa Purāṇa*, MLBD, Delhi, 1973
BG	*Bhagavadgītā*
BhP	*Bhāgavata Purāṇa*, Bhagavat Vidyapeeth, Ahmedabad
Br	*Brāhmaṇa* (preceded by name such as Śatapatha)
BsP	*Bhaviṣya Purāṇa*, Vishnu Shastri Bapat, Wai
BVP	*Brahma Vaivarta Purāṇa*, GM, 1955-57
CC	*Caturvarga Cintāmaṇi* by Hemādri
CVS	*Caraṇa Vyūha Sūtra* by Śaunaka, Com. by Mahīdāsa
DB	*Devī Bhāgavata*, GM, 1960-61
De or GDAMI	*The Geographical Dictionary of Ancient and Medieval India*, N.L. De/Dey, Oriental Reprint, Delhi, 1971
DhS	*Dharma Sūtra* (preceded by the author's name such as Gautama)
GP	*Garuḍa Purāṇa*, ed. R.S. Bhattacharya, Chowkhamba, Varanasi, 1964
GS	*Gṛhya Sūtra* (preceded by the name of the author such as Āpastamba)
HD	*History of Dharma Śāstra*, P.V. Kane, G.O.S.
JP	*Purāṇa* (Journal of the Kashiraj Trust), Varanasi
KA	*Kauṭilya Arthaśāstra*
KP	*Kūrma Purāṇa* Veṅkaṭeśvara Press Edn., Bombay; also Kashiraj Trust Edn., Varanasi, 1971

LP	*Liṅga Purāṇa,* GM, 1960; also MLBD, Delhi, 1981
Manu	*Manusmṛti*
Mbh	*Mahābhārata,* Gīta Press, Gorakhpur, VS 2014
MkP	*Mārkaṇḍeya Purāṇa*
MN	*Mahābhārata Nāmānukramaṇī,* Gītā Press, Gorakhpur, VS 2016
MtP	*Matsya Purāṇa,* GM, 1954
MW	M. Monier-Williams' *Sanskrit-English Dictionary,* MLBD, Delhi, 1976
NP	*Nāradīya* or *Nārada Purāṇa,* Veṅkaṭeśvara Press, Bombay
PdP	*Padma Purāṇa,* GM, 1957-59
PE	*Purāṇic Encyclopaedia,* V. Mani, English Version, MLBD, Delhi, 1975
PR or PRHRC	*Puranic Records on Hindu Rites and Customs,* R.C. Hazra, Calcutta, 1948
ṚV	*Ṛg Veda,* Svādhyāya Maṇḍal, Aundh
Śat Br	*Śatapatha Brāhmaṇa*
SC or SMC	*Smṛti Candrikā* by Devanna Bhaṭṭa
SkP	*Skanda Purāṇa*
SP	*Śiva Purāṇa*
VāP	*Vāyu Purāṇa*
VdP	*Viṣṇudharmottara Purāṇa*
VmP	*Vāmana Purāṇa*
VP	*Viṣṇu Purāṇa*
VR	*Vālmīki Rāmāyaṇa*
VrP	*Varāha Purāṇa*

SKANDA PURĀṆA

Book VI: NĀGARA KHAṆḌA[1]

CHAPTER ONE

The Birth of the Liṅga[2]

Obeisance to Śrī Gaṇeśa.

Oṁ obeisance to Śrī Puruṣottama.

Henceforth the sixth book called Nāgara Khaṇḍa of the Skanda Mahāpurāṇa begins:

Vyāsa said:

1. May the matted tresses of hair (twisted on the top of the head) of Dhūrjaṭi (Śiva) be conducive to your success—the matted hair in which Gaṅgā (with her stream of whitish water) creates the illusion of a streak of grey hair.

Sages enquired:

2-3. O highly wise one! How is it that the Liṅga (Phallus) of Hara is particularly adored to the exclusion of other organs (of his body) by Suras and Asuras? It behoves you to explain properly and thoroughly why it is so, O mighty-armed Sūta. An intense curiosity has been aroused in us now.

---

1. *Nāgara Khaṇḍa*: This Khaṇḍa describes the sacredness and glory of Hāṭakeśvara Kṣetra, the area around Vadnagar (Ahmedabad Dist., Gujarat). It is called by various names out of which Camatkārapura is more common. Dr. R.N. Mehta, former head of the Dept. of Archaeology, M.S. University Baroda, informs me that human habitation in that area dates back to the 1st century B.C.E. His article: "Vadnagara: A Study" in Journal of the M.S. University, Baroda, Vol. XVII, April 1968, throws some light on some incidents in this Purāṇa

2. *Liṅga*: The word is derived from two roots: √*lī*- "to dissolve" and √*gam*- "to go". The term means 'that from which the universe "comes" i.e. is created, and that in which it "dissolves", 'I have shown in my Marathi book *'Śaiva Darśana'* (pp. 2-17) that Liṅga-worship represents the worship of sacrificial fire. But the original Vedic identification of Rudra and Agni was forgotten long before this Purāṇa came to be finally redacted and here Śiva-liṅga is wrongly taken as 'Śiva's phallus.'

Sūta said:

4. Enormous indeed is the burden involved in answering the query raised by you. I shall, however, recount in details after bowing down to the Self-born Lord.

5-9a. In the land of Ānarta (Northern Gujarat) there is a forest resorted to by saintly people. It is charming unto all living beings. It consists of trees bearing fruits in the course of all seasons.

There is a beautiful penance grove therein. It is resorted to by gentle animals. It is full of sages and hence resounding with the sound of the Vedic Mantras chanted by them. There are various types of sages practising diverse kinds of austerities.

There are sages (some of whom were) *Abbhakṣas* (who took in water only for subsistence), *Vāyubhakṣas* (subsisting on air only), *Śīrṇaparṇāśins* (eating dry, withered leaves); Brāhmaṇas called *Dantolūkhalas* (who use their teeth as mortars for separation of grains from husk); some are *Aśma-kuṭṭakas* (who use stones for separating husk and pounding the grains to powder). The sages are engaged in holy baths and Homas; they are intent on Japas and self-study of the Vedas; there are *Vānaprasthas* (those who retired to the forests after active life of householders), *Tridaṇḍas* (recluses with three staffs), *Haṁsas* (sages of exalted position) and *Kuṭīcaras*[1] (recluses staying in huts), *Snātakas* (those who have concluded their student life), *Yatis* (ascetics), *Dāntas* (persons with full self-control) and *Pañcāgni-sādhakas* (sages practising austerities in the midst of five fires).

9b-11. After some time, the Lord, the Slayer of Tripura who was distressed due to the bereavement of Satī came to that forest in the course of his wanderings.

The forest was resorted to by gentle animals; there delighted mongooses played with serpents; lions with elephants and cats with mice. The crows played with flocks of owls without animosity.

12. On seeing the penance-grove, Lord Rudra who was nude, entered it for the purpose of begging for alms with a skull in hand.

---

1. '*Kuṭīcaka*' is the correct form and not *Kuṭicara.*

13-15. On seeing his handsome physical features never seen by anyone before, all the ascetic women became completely overwhelmed by the god of Love. They left off their domestic chores. The ceased to attend to the elders. Gathering together in groups at different places, they engaged in mutual discussions with comments like: "Only that lady is blessed who can freely and confidently embrace all the organs of the noble-souled sage."

16-18. Others in excessive enthusiasm ran about in all directions. They appeared staring at him with wide open eyes. Some of the women had applied the unguents only partly over their bodies. Some had applied collyrium only in one of their eyes. Others had tied up their tresses partially. Some of them had even abandoned their children. Being viewed thus by the ladies Maheśvara wandered through the highway uttering "Give me alms."

19. Those sages who saw him thus without clothes on, thereby provoking the lustful predilection in the women, spoke thus with their eyes reddened due to anger.

20-21. "O sinner, since this penance grove of ours has been defiled by you, may this penis of yours fall on the ground at once." Instantly his penis fell on the ground; piercing the surface of the earth, it entered Pātāla.

22. Bereft of his penis, the bashful Lord Maheśvara went into a deep pit and stayed there in the form of a foetus.

23-24. On account of the fall of the penis, O excellent Brāhmaṇas, there arose terrible bad omens that caused terror in all the three worlds. The peaks of mountains tumbled down; even during day, meteors fell down. All oceans overflowed their limits slowly.

25. All the groups of Devas were terrified in their minds. With Śakra and Viṣṇu as their leaders they went to the place where the Grandfather of the worlds was present.

26-29. After eulogising with prayers, originating from the excellent Śruti, they bowed down and said: "O Lotus-seated One, O Lord, what has happened! What is it, O god, that everything is going on in a topsy-turvy manner. Why is it so? Why has the whole range of the three worlds become agitated and vexed. O Lotus-born One, signs of the ultimate annihilation appear as it were. Will there be an untimely destruction now? You are an expert in the use of Mantras. You are the grandfather of all the worlds. You are the goal and refuge of all Suras, Daityas and human beings who are distressed and terrified with trembling bodies."

30-34. On hearing the words of those Devas the Four-faced Lord meditated for a long time and understood through his divine vision. Thereupon he spoke: "O excellent Suras, this is not the time for the ultimate annihilation. Listen to the reason for which the evil portents have arisen. In the country called Ānarta the noble-souled sages, for (the protection of their wives) have cursed (Lord Śiva); the Liṅga of the god of gods, the Trident-bearing Lord, has been made to fall. It is therefore that the entire range of the three worlds including mobile and immobile beings has become utterly upset. Hence we shall go to the place where Lord Maheśvara is present. At our instance, he may replace the penis quickly. Otherwise there will be untimely destruction of the entire range of the three worlds. What I have uttered is true."

35-36. Thereupon all the groups of the Devas, Ādityas, Vasus, Rudras, Aśvins and Viśvedevas with Brahmā and Viṣṇu as their leaders hurriedly went to that place where Lord Maheśvara was sleeping in the interior of the pit, overwhelmed with great shame.

The Devas said:

37. Obeisance to you, O Lord of the chiefs of Devas, O bestower of freedom from fear on your devotees, Obeisance to you, O support of the universe, O Lord with the crest embellished with the moon.

38. You are Yajña. You are Vaṣaṭkāra. You are the (great element called) Water. You are the Earth, O Lord. This entire region of the three worlds including mobile and immobile creatures is created by you.

39. O most excellent one among Suras, you protect as well as annihilate (the world), You are Viṣṇu. You are the Four-faced One (Brahmā). You are the Moon. You are the Sun.

40-41. Without you, O great Lord, nothing exists here. O Lord, even after committing a great sin on the earth, a man who glorifies your name and calls 'Mahādeva' repeatedly goes to heaven.

42. Crores of the sins of Brāhmaṇa-slaughter and crores of sins of aberrations get annihilated by glorifying your name 'Mahādeva'.

43. You are established in the overlordship of all the Devas even as a Brāhmaṇa is established in the overlordship of men and the great ocean of the rivers.

44. You are established in the overlordship of all the Devas even as the Moon is established in the overlordship of the stars and the Sun of all the luminaries.

45. You are established in the overlordship of all the Devas even as gold is established in the overlordship (i.e. the most excellent one) of all minerals and Nārada of Gandharvas.

46. You are established in the overlordship of all the Devas even as food-grain is established in the overlordship of medicinal herbs and the golden mountain (Meru) of all mountains.

47-48. Hence, O most excellent one among Suras, do this favour to us and to all human beings. O Lord, reinstate your penis once again. If not, O Lord, all the three worlds will face ruin. O Lord, if this penis stays fallen on the ground, the three worlds shall fall.

Sūta said:

49. On hearing their words, the Bull-emblemed Lord became all the more ashamed and spoke to them all as they bowed down to him:

50. "O excellent Suras, this penis has been abandoned by me under the pretext of the curse of the Brāhmaṇas, because I have been overwhelmed with distress due to separation from Satī.

51-52. In all the three worlds, who is competent to cause this fall of my penis, be he a Deva or Brāhmaṇa? You all do know this clearly. Hence I will not take this penis back from the ground. Now that I am without a wife, what will I do with this?"

The Devas said:

53-54. O excellent one among Suras, your beloved named Satī who died formerly, is reborn with the name Gaurī from the womb of Menakā through Himālaya. O Slayer of Tripuras, she will become your own wife again. Hence take back your penis and bring about the welfare of Heaven-dwellers.

Devadeva (Śiva) said:

55. If Devas and Brāhmaṇas are ready to worship my penis from now onwards assiduously, I shall reinstate it.

Brahmā said:

56. O Śaṅkara, I shall myself worship your penis. So also shall all the Devas. Why not then human beings on the earth?

57. Thereafter the Grandfather of the worlds entered Pātāla along with Devas and himself performed the worship of the penis (Liṅga) with devotion.

58. Thereafter Viṣṇu worshipped it with his mind sanctified by faith. So also all the Devas beginning with Śakra fully endowed with faith.

59. Thereat Mahādeva became pleased and he spoke these words to Pitāmaha as well as to Vāsudeva who stood bowing down with modesty:

60. "I am pleased with both of you. Hence, O mighty ones, may any desired boon be accepted from me."

Both of them said:

61. If, O Lord of Devas, you are pleased, give us both place of rest by a third part of the Liṅga so that all of us shall resort to one place.

Sūta said:

62. After promising "So it shall be", the Lord retrieved the Liṅga adored by all the Devas and reinstated it at its proper place.

63. Thereafter Pitāmaha took gold and made a Liṅga of the same shape joyously and installed it there itself.

64-67. Even as all the Heaven-dwellers (Śaṅkara and others) were listening, O Brāhmaṇas, he caused reverberation in all the three worlds through his well-modulated voice and said: "This first Liṅga has been made of gold (Hāṭaka) by me. In the whole of Pātāla it will become well known as Hāṭakeśvara[1]. Similarly, the men who with devotion make Liṅgas of gold etc. embellished with jewels, pearls and excellent gems and worship it thrice a day, will attain the great goal. They should avoid clay and base metals (like iron) too."

68. After saying this the Four-faced Lord, Brahmā', went to heaven along with all the heaven-dwellers. The Moon-crested Lord went to Kailāsa.

69. For this reason, the Liṅga is specially adored here by the Suras and Asuras excluding the other excellent organs of Śiva.

70. Ever since then Brahmā himself and Lord Vāsudeva stayed in that Liṅga. Hence it is auspicious and worthy of being worshipped.

71-72. If a person worships Śivaliṅga always with the mind full of faith, it is as though all the three, viz. the Three-eyed Lord, Acyuta and Brahmā are worshipped by him. Hence one should worship Śivaliṅga assiduously, touch it with deference, have a view of it always and glorify it, O excellent Brāhmaṇas.

CHAPTER TWO

Dialogue between Triśaṅku and Vasiṣṭha

Sūta said:

1. When that Liṅga was extricated from the ground, O excellent Brāhmaṇas, the water of Jāhnavī flowed out of Pātāla through that path. It is destructive of all the sins of men and it accords all desired things.

2. Even as I relate listen, O excellent Brāhmaṇas, to what naturally happened there formerly, causing surprise unto all the worlds.

3. A great king named Triśaṅku who had attained the state of a Cāṇḍāla had his bath there and regained his body befitting a king.

1. Hāṭakeśvara: The editor of the Sanskrit Text informs in a footnote that this Hāṭakeśvara is in Badnagar in Gujarat; near this town is another town called "Uṁjhā" which is famous for the shrine of Umā.

The sages said:

4. O Sūtanandana (son of a Sūta), how did the excellent king Triśaṅku attain the state of a Cāṇḍāla? Do recount all this in detail.

Sūta said:

5. I shall recount unto you all, this ancient story that pertains to Triśaṅku, that is very sacred and that destroys all sins.

6. Once, formerly there was a tiger among kings well-known as Triśaṅku. He was born in the Solar race and was valarous like a tiger.

7-10. He was a disciple of Sage Vasiṣṭha. He was a performer of Yajñas. The Lord had great interest in making gifts. *Makhas* (Sacrifices) beginning with Agniṣṭoma were performed by him always every year with the full complement of *Dakṣiṇās*. All kinds of *Dānas* were given by that noble-souled one to the distinguished ones, particularly to those who were poor. *Vratas* were duly performed. Those who sought refuge in him were protected. Common people were fondled by him as though they were his own sons. Enemies were killed. He had wandered all over the world visiting all the Tīrthas and shrines. He gave to ascetics the desired wealth in accordance with the wish expressed by them.

11. After some time, once, while the holy Sage Vasiṣṭha was present in the assembly, he duly bowed to him and said:

Triśaṅku said:

12. O holy Sir, now I wish to perform that Yajña whereby one can immediately go to heaven along with the physical body.

13. Hence do me the favour. Gather together all the requisite things quickly for a due performance of that Yajña and also invite competent Brāhmaṇas for the same.

Vasiṣṭha said:

14. There is now such *Kratu* (Sacrifice), O king, whereby one can go to heaven along with the present physical body. I

am telling you the truth.

15. Agniṣṭoma and other Yajñas were prescribed formerly by the Self-born Lord; but, O king, Svarga is obtained due to the performance of those Yajñas only with another body.

16-17. If, O king, you have seen or heard about a king, Brāhmaṇa, Vaiśya or any other person on this earth who attained heaven along with this physical body, do mention it (his name).

Triśaṅku said:

18. O Brāhmaṇa-Sage, I know really that there is nothing which you cannot achieve. Hence do me the favour and get my desire fulfilled.

Vasiṣṭha said:

19. No falsehood has been uttered earlier by this tongue even in playful joke. Hence in fact there is no Yajña of the type you wish to perform.

Triśaṅku said:

20-21a. O tiger among Brāhmaṇas, if you are incapable of performing a Yajña, on my behalf, that can accord Svarga along with this physical body, of what avail is your Brāhmaṇical power of penance, O efficient one?

21b-22. Further, listen to this statement of mine made clearly in the presence of the groups of sages and others who may witness, O excellent Brāhmaṇa. In spite of my repeated request, if you do not carry out my behest, I shall make another Brāhmaṇa my preceptor and get that Yajña performed.

Sūta said:

23. On hearing his words, the holy sage Vasiṣṭha told him laughingly, "Do so, O Lord of the earth."

CHAPTER THREE

Hariścandra Coronated as King

Sūta said:

1. Thereafter, he bowed down to the eminent sage Vasiṣṭha once again and went to the place where his (Vasiṣṭha's) sons numbering a hundred were present.

2. To them also the king mentioned the same topic after bowing down (in courtesy) to them. Everything that Vasiṣṭha had said earlier was repeated by them to him.

3-5. Thereupon he told them again: "Your father who is now unable to take me to heaven along with my physical body, has been abandoned by me. So if you do not perform the Yajña on my behalf, I will abandon you too and quickly make another person my preceptor who will lead me to heaven by the power of the Yajña, along with this physical body, O sons of the preceptor."

6-7. On hearing his words, all those exellent sages became excessively angry and spoke to him these harsh words: "Since the preceptor who has been your benefactor is abandoned by you, you are a sinner. Hence, O evil one, be a Cāṇḍāla now, censured by the world."

8-10. Immediately at the end of those words, the king became one with a form of a low-born (Śūdra) having the body of hideous features. His waist resembled a barley grain. The neck was lean, the eyes became tawny-coloured and the nose very crooked. His body and his limbs were dark in complexion. He was stinking awfully. The king observed himself having become ugly and deformed with the characteristics of a Cāṇḍāla and instantly he stood with down-cast face due to shame.

11-14. He was repeatedly scolded with words, "Go away; get away." All round he was pestered by dogs unleashed and let loose. He resembled crows and cuckoos (in complexion) and was clad in rags. Thus overwhelmed with great misery he began to think worriedly, "What can I do? Where shall I go? How can there be peace? Is this the rare position desired by me so foolishly? With it even my traditional practice has become upset. Shall I enter a water pond or burning fire? Shall I take in poison? How can I bring about an end of my life?"

15-24. "With this defiled body, how dare I look at my wives with whom I earlier sported about in my previous excellent physical form? How can I look at my sons, grandsons, friends, relatives and kinsmen? How can I look at the other attendants too? Formerly I had conquered many enemies in battle. All of them will be joyous now on hearing about such a transformation of me. They will cease to be afraid of me. The Brāhmaṇas having great mastery over the Vedas who had been propitiated by me through gifts will become miserable now on hearing that I have fallen into this plight. Similarly, what will be the state of those beloved friends of mine who are always engaged in acts beneficial to me? On seeing me in this situation they will be really miserable. I have numerous elephants of the Bhadra class aged sixty years and blind in the state of rut. Without me, who will engage them in mutual duels? My horses of variegated colours have been broken and rendered tractable by experienced trainers. Without me who will engage them in diverse types of gallops and trots. My servants of good nobility are irrepressible in their spirit for battle. In case they are distressed, to whom will they go in my absence? My treasury contains many gems and jewels and it is immeasurable. It has been well-preserved by me. When I am not present who is going to enjoy it? My storehouses of foodgrains, my sheds of cattle and goats, are also vast and innumerable. They have been well-looked after by my loyal servants. But what will be their state in my absence?"

25. Lamenting thus in various ways, the king in his misery wended his way on foot towards the city.

26-27a. He reached his city at night when it was practically devoid of people. Stopping at the gate he summoned his son along with the ministers and told them everything arising from the imprecation.

27b-28. Standing far off, he repeated the thunderbolt-like words of the sons of the noble-souled Vasiṣṭha. On hearing them they became grief-stricken. They cried with tears dimming their faces:

29-31. "O Lord, O great king ever fond of pious rites, how can we, the miserable ones, be alive in your absence? Is this proper on the part of those evil-minded sons of Vasiṣṭha? They have cursed one for whom they are bound to perform Yajña and particularly one who is very polite. O tiger among kings, we too shall renounce our household effects. Undoubtedly, along with you we too shall accept the state of being a base-born one."

Triśaṅku said:

32-34. If you have unrestrained devtion to me be the ministers of my son now. This is Hariścandra, my eldest son and my dearest one. Without delay and unhesitatingly appoint him in my place. As for me, I shall proceed ahead in doing what I have decided in my mind. Either I will die or I will go to heaven along with this physical body.

35-36. After saying thus and leaving all of them the king went away through the forest slowly on foot.

Those good ministers soon installed his honoured son as king with proper rites accompanied by intrumental and vocal music.

CHAPTER FOUR

Viśvāmitra Performs a Yajña for Triśaṅku

Sūta said:

1-2. After deciding thus, Triśaṅku thought about the great sage Viśvāmitra for a long time and then came to this conclusion: 'Barring Viśvāmitra there is no one else in all the three worlds who can save me from this terrible misery.'

3. Then he set off towards Kurukṣetra. As he went on enquiring about the way, he became very tired and distressed due to hunger and thirst.

4. In due course the king ultimately reached Kurukṣetra where he assiduously enquired about the hermitage of Viśvāmitra.

5-7. Even as the king went on enquiring thus, he saw a cluster of blue trees at a far-off place. Through aquatic birds like swans, cranes, Āṭis and Madgus, the thirsty king guessed that there was water nearby. He became delighted as the cool watery breeze removed his fatique. He proceeded hastily.

8-10. He found the hermitage situated on the banks of a river Nandinī(?). Gentle tame animals frequented it. It was a charming place and conducive to dispel mental grief. It reverberated with sweet warbling sound of excellent birds. There were mongooses sporting about with serpents and owls with crows. Cats were playing with mice and tigers with deer of diverse kinds.

11-12. Then on the banks of the river he saw Sage Viśvāmitra of great self-control engaged in the recitation of Vedic Mantras and surrounded by groups of ascetics. Thanks to the power of his penance and splendour, he appeared like a blazing fire. He was clad in bark garments and was sitting under a Śāla tree.

13-14. The eminent king proceeded ahead. He bowed down from a great distance. Announcing his name he prostrated before him and the disciples too with great faith. He bowed down to them one by one and stood by with palms joined in reverence.

15-18. On seeing the king with all the limbs soiled with dust, they thought him to be a Cāṇḍāla through the signs on the body. They rebuked him with harsh words and shouts of 'Fie upon you! 'Fie upon you!' They repeatedly told him: 'Go away; go away'. 'Who are you, O sinful one?' They said: 'Who are you? Why have you come to this excellent hermitage of sages, filled with the chanting sounds of Vedic Mantras, inaccessible even to pious people? Get away quickly lest some sage should curse you and deprive you of your very life.'

Triśaṅku said:

19-20. I am a king of the solar race named Triśaṅku. I have been cursed by the sons of Vasiṣṭha and turned into a Cāṇḍāla. O excellent Brāhmaṇas, for the sake of relief from the imprecation I have sought refuge in Viśvāmitra, the friend and well-wisher of the whole world. There is no other refuge unto me.

Viśvāmitra said:

21-22. You are the *Yājya* (one on whose behalf a Yajña is

performed) of Vasiṣṭha and hence particularly so of his sons. So why did they put you in an evil condition like this? O excellent king, what offence did you commit against them?

What crime have you perpetrated against them? An attempt on the life or outraging the modesty of their wives?

Triśaṅku said:

23-27. A Yajña was requested of the excellent sage Vasiṣṭha for the sake of going unto Svarga along with this body. He (Vasiṣṭha) replied: "There is no Yajña whereby it is possible to go to Svarga with this body, O king. It is not possible without taking another body." On hearing his words he was told further by me: "If you do not take me to Svarga along with this physical body immediately by the power of a Yajña, I will adopt another sage as my preceptor. There is no doubt about it." On realizing this the sage said: "Do what is conducive to your welfare." Thereupon, being thus forsaken by him, I went to his sons, who proved to be more ruthless, and told them whatever I told Vasiṣṭha before.

28-30. Then O excellent sage, I was cursed by them who too were grief-stricken. I have been reduced to this miserable plight of being a Cāṇḍāla. So I have thought of you cherishing a very great hope, O eminent sage. I have come down to Kurukṣetra from a great distance. O sage, in all the three worlds, there is nothing which you cannot achieve, So, do help me and dispel my misery.

Sūta said:

31-35. On hearing his words the great sage Viśvāmitra out of rivalry with Vasiṣṭha spoke out in the midst of the other sages: "O king, on behalf of you I shall perform that Yajña whereby you will go to Svarga soon after its performance. O king, you have been rendered to this state of a base-born one by the sons of Vasiṣṭha. Undoubtedly it is my duty to make you a king once again. Hence come on along with me, on a pilgrimage. By the power of the Tīrthas, you shall once again be pure and deserving enough for performing the rite of the Yajña after getting rid of your Cāṇḍāla state. There is no such sin that will not perish due to the holy plunge into a Tīrtha."

Sūta said:

36. After resolving thus, Viśvāmitra, the son of Gādhi, who was closely followed by Triśaṅku proceeded ahead for performing a pilgrimage.

37-40. They visited various places, viz. Prabhāsa Sarasvatī in Kurukṣetra, Kurujāṅgala, Pṛthūdaka, Gayāśīrṣa, Naimiṣa, the three Puṣkaras, Vārāṇasī, Prayāga, the big river Śravaṇa (Śoṇa), Kedāra, Śravaṇanada, Citrakūṭa, Gokarṇa, Śāligrāma, Acaleśvara, Śukla Tīrtha in Surājya (Saurāṣṭra), the auspicious Nada Dṛṣadvatī and many other meritorious Tīrthas and holy shrines. Thus the king wandered for a long time along with that noble-souled sage all over the world.

41-45. O Brāhmaṇas, despite the holy baths taken severally in the Tīrthas thus, he was not rid of the sinful Cāṇḍāla state. In due course he came to the Arbuda (Mt. Abu) mountain and climbed on to the top of that sin-destroying great mountain. Lord Acaleśvara, the deity, was visited and when the great sage came out of the shrine he saw Mārkaṇḍa, the excellent sage. On seeing the eminent sage Viśvāmitra, a friend and well-wisher of the worlds, he asked: "O great Sage, whence did you come here now? Who is behind you with the hideous features of a base-born class? Do tell me these things, O excellent Sage even as I ask."

Viśvāmitra said:

46-50. This is the famous tiger among kings, Triśaṅku. The sons of Vasiṣṭha, when their anger was roused, have reduced him to the state of a Cāṇḍāla. I have promised to take him round the earth consisting of the seven continents till he regains purity (capacity to perform Yajña). I have wandered over all the Tīrthas and shrines on the earth. He has not gained purity. I am now tired. I have become ashamed. Lest I should be laughed at by the sons of Vasiṣṭha. I intend to leave off the entire earth, all the continents and oceans. I shall go beyond since I have not kept my promise. What I say is true.

Śrī Mārkaṇḍeya said:

51-57. If it is so, O tiger among sages, do as I say. Do not go anywhere else leaving off the earth consisting of the seven continents. To the south-west of this mountain in the land called Ānartaka, there is the holy shrine named Hāṭakeśvara. There the very first Liṅga made of gold was installed by the excellent Suras. That Liṅga in Pātāla is glorified as Hāṭakeśvara. When his Liṅga (Penis) was retrieved by Śaṁbhu, the waters of Pātāla Jāhnavī surged forth from Rasātala, O excellent one among twice-borns. Let the king enter Pātāla with effort and take his holy bath in the waters of Jāhnavī faithfully. Thereafter let him visit that Hāṭakeśvara Liṅga. Thereby he will become pure and rid of the Cāṇḍāla state. You too shall regain your glory of realizing your objective cherished by you in your heart. If you perform penance there, you will get something more too.

Sūta said:

58-60. On hearing his words, Viśvāmitra, the leading sage, went there immediately accompanied by Triśaṅku. Through the Devamārga (divine path) he entered Pātāla and made Triśaṅku take his holy bath in accordance with the injuctions laid down. No sooner did the king take his holy bath and visit Hāṭakeśvara than the king became rid of the Cāṇḍāla sate and attained a lustre like that of the Sun.

61-63. The sage said to the king who bowed down to him and was bereft of all his sins: "O leading king, fortunately you are freed from the Cāṇḍāla state now. Luckily you have regained the power of penance and great splendour. Hence perform the Sattra with the requisite Dakṣiṇā as laid down, whereby you will attain the Siddhi that has been cherished in your heart for long. I shall myself go to Pitāmaha and plead to him on your behalf.

64. The primordial Lord of all the Devas shall partake of his share in the Yajña. By the time I return from Brahmaloka, get together all the requisite things of the Sattra. Fetch them here."

65-68. "Yes, Yours Holiness" said he. The sage of perfect holy vows approached Pitāmaha, bowed down and spoke these words: "O Prapitāmaha, I am performing a Yajña on behalf of Triśaṅku, the king, so that he will attain your region along with his human body. Hence, O Pitāmaha, do come to the sacrificial chamber along with all the groups of Suras with Śiva and Viṣṇu as leaders. Accept your share of the Yajña with your own hand in due form so that, with your favour, he may go to heaven along with his body."

Brahmā said:

69-71. Svarga is not obtained along with one's body, by means of Yajña rite. O Brāhmaṇa, excepting through change of body, it cannot be obtained. So do not persist in what you say to me. All of us have Agni as our mouth through whom we accept *Havis* in a sacrifice in accordance with what is laid down in the Vedas for the perfect welfare of the householder. So, O Brāhmaṇa, let him put the *Havis* in Agni. Thereby, with your favour, he will attain Svarga.

CHAPTER FIVE

Performance of a Satra for Triśaṅku

Sūta said:

1-2. On hearing the words of Brahmā, Viśvāmitra became furious. He said to Pitāmaha: "See the power of my penance. I will perform a Yajña with the due Dakṣiṇā on behalf of Triśaṅku. Even as you watch, O Pitāmaha, I shall bring him here through the power of that Yajña."

3. After saying this, Viśvāmitra hastened to the earth and made preparations for the Yajña on behalf of the noble-souled Triśaṅku.

4. At the time proper for commencement of the Yajña and in that very auspicious forest, he invited Brāhmaṇas who were masters of Veda (and expert in sacrificial rites) and got him (Triśaṅku) initiated.

5-8. That intelligent sage himself became Adhvaryu in the sacrificial rite. Sage Śāṇḍilya was Hotṛ. Gautama was Brahmā. The sage named Cyavana was Āgnīdhra. Maitrāvaruṇa was Kārmika. Yājñavalkya was Udgātṛ and Jaimini Pratihartṛ Śaṅkuvarṇa was Prastotṛ. Gālava was Unnetṛ. Pulastya was Brāhmanācchamsin. Eminent sage Garga was Hotṛ. Atri was Neṣṭṛ and Bhṛgu himself was Acchāvāka. Triśaṅku endowed with great faith, made all these the Ṛtviks.

9-10. Triśaṅku adorned the Ṛtviks with garments, armlets and coronets. He got his hair cut and clad himself in the skin of a black antelop. He engaged himself in *Payovrata* (vow of taking in only milk) and held horn of a deer. Thus he engaged all of them for the purpose of *Dīrghasattra* (Yajña of long duration).

11-12. When that *Dīrghasattra* got started in a befitting manner, divine Brāhmaṇas who had mastered the Vedas and Vedāṅgas came there. So also Tārkikas (Logicians), curious householders, poor people, blind ones, those in wretched state, dancers and actors etc., assembled there.

13-14. In the entire sacrificial premises, the following words were heard always: "Let this be given to these quickly; let this be given. O people, may you be pleased to eat. Do eat. Do us this favour" etc. Nothing else was heard.

15-17a. Huge mountain-like heaps of foodgrains were seen kept ready. So also were heaps of gold and silver and of gems and jewels in particular. There were innumerable cows for the sake of being given over to the Brāhmaṇas. Similarly there were well-tamed horses, and huge elephants in the height of their rut were kept all round. They appeared like mountains.

17b-18. When this elaborate Yajña went on and Devas were invoked to partake of their shares, they never turned up. It was their resolve that they would take in the Havis only through the sacred fire.

19. Thus twelve years passed off even as the king continued his Yajña. But the benefit that he had cherished in his mind was not attained.

20-21. O excellent Sages, Triśaṅku took the *Avabhṛthasnāna* (valedictory bath) at the conclusion of the *Sattra*. The Ṛtviks were propitiated with Dakṣiṇā due to them and duly sent off. So also all those who had assembled went away; kinsmen and friends also took leave and went away.

22-28. The king, still bashful and ashamed, humbly bowed down to the great sage Viśvāmitra and said: "With your favour the entire benefit of the *Dīrghasattra* not easily accessible to all men, has been obtained by me. So also, O excellent sage, the caste lost by me has been regained. O Brāhmaṇa-Sage, *Cāṇḍālatva* (the state of being a Cāṇḍāla) has been dispelled with your favour. But one sorrow is lurking like a dart thrust into my heart, since Svarga was not attained by me along with this body. O Sage, sons of Vasiṣṭha will laugh at me on hearing that my efforts have been in vain and that I have not reached Svarga. Vasiṣṭha's words that going to heaven in this physical body, was not attained through Yajña, proved to be true. Hence I shall go to forest now and perform penance. I will not rule the kingdom already given over to my son."

CHAPTER SIX

Attainment of a Boon by Viśvāmitra

1-3. On hearing the words of Triśaṅku, Viśvāmitra the eminent sage, became a little ashamed and spoke these words: "O king, grieve not on this account. I shall take you to heaven along with your physical body. I shall carry out the different rites for the sake of heaven, O king. I shall either accomplish your desired object or face my personal destruction."

4-5. After saying thus, the sage became all the more furious with the Heaven-dwellers. Within the direct presence of the king he spoke: "Just as the status of a Brāhmaṇa was forcibly achieved by my own effort, so also I will undoubtedly cause my own creation."

6. Thereafter viewing the Moon-crested Lord Śaṅkara the great sage duly bowed down with devotion and eulogized him.

Viśvāmitra said:

7-8. Be victorious, O lover of Pārvatī; be victorious, O Lord beyond the pale of thought or mind. Be victorious, O Kṛṣṇa, the Lord protector of the universe and the preceptor of the world. O incomprehensible one, be victorious. O immeasurable one, be victorious. O infinite one, be victorious. O unswerving one, be victorious. O immortal one, be victorious. O unconquerable one, be victorious. O immutable one, O Lord of Suras, be victorious.

9-14. Be victorious, O omnipresent one, O Lord of all. Be victorious, O Lord worthy of being meditated upon by all, be victorious, O destroyer of the sins of all. You are the creator and the dispenser; you are the creator and the protector of the groups of living beings of four types, O Śaṅkara, O Lord of Devas. Just as oil is present in gingelly seed or ghee in curds, so also you invisibly are present in the entire universe on which you preside. You are Brahmā; you are Hṛṣīkeśa; you are Śakra; you are Hutāśana (Fire god); you are Yajña; you are Vaṣaṭkāra. You are the Moon. You are the Sun. Or, of what avail is a eulogy of thine, O Lord, in too many words? I shall briefly mention your glorious power as recounted by Śruti. Whatever is mobile and immobile in all the three words, O Lord, is pervaded by you, like fuel by fire."

Śrī Bhagavān (Lord) said:

15. Welfare unto you, O excellent sage, I am pleased with you. Request for your boon; whatever has been present in your heart for long, I shall undoubtedly grant to you.

Viśvāmitra said:

16. 'O Lord of Devas, if you are pleased, if a boon has to be given to me, O Maheśvara, let me have the great ability of creation with your favour.

17. After saying "Let it be so" the holy Bull-emblemed Lord vanished from there along with all the Gaṇas (attendants).

18. Viśvāmitra stationed himself there with due meditation. Rivalling with Brahmā, the Lord moving about on his Swan, he began the creation of four types.'

CHAPTER SEVEN

Triśaṅku Attains Svarga

Sūta said:

1. With a keen desire, he entered water and began to meditate. Then he created two *Sandhyās* (Twilights). O Brāhmaṇas, they are to be seen even today.

2-3. Thereafter all the groups of the Devas were created by that noble-souled one. Persons travelling in aerial chariots, stars and planets, human beings, serpents and Rākṣasas, creepers and trees; the seven sages (Great Bear), Dhruva and others (Pole Star etc.) and sky-walkers were created.

4-5. After creating these, the angry sage Viśvāmitra employed them in his own work. At that time two suns and two moons rose up in the sky simultaneously. There were two sets of planets. Two sets of stars along with the Great Bear came up, O Brāhmaṇa.

6. Thus they competed with one another and were seen doubled causing chaos and confusion in the minds of the people.

7. In the meantime Śakra accompanied by all the heaven-dwellers went there where the Lotus-seated Lord was present.

8. O Brāhmaṇas, he along with the Suras, eulogized him with Vedic hymns, bowed down and stood with palms joined in reverence.

Then he said:

9-10. O most excellent one among Suras, creation of human beings, Yakṣas and Serpents, of Devas, Gandharvas and Rākṣasas has been brought about by Viśvāmitra. Hence do go and restrain him yourself, O Pitāmaha, lest the entire range of mobile and immobile beings should be pervaded by his creation.

11-12. On hearing his words Vidhi (Brahmā) in the company of Śakra went to the eminent sage Viśvāmitra, the friend and well-wisher of the world, and said: "O Brāhmaṇa-Sage, at my instance check this lest all the Devas including Vāsava should perish."

Viśvāmitra said:

13. If the excellent king Triśaṅku goes to your world along with the same physical body, I shall then desist from creation.

Brahmā said:

14-15. Let this king go to heaven along with me, O great sage. He shall go there along with his physical body, with your favour, stop your creative effort. No one else could have done this. What has never been done by anyone in the world has been achieved by you.

Viśvāmitra said:

16-17. O Lotus-born Lord, O grandfather of all the worlds, may this creation of mine (of a new world) carried out in rage by me be forgiven by you. With your favour, may this creation of mine be everlasting. O Lotus-born One, I will not repeat this again.

Brahmā said:

18. O Brāhmaṇa, what has been already created by you shall certainly come to stay. But they will never be eligible to share Yajña and all other rites.

19. After saying thus and taking Triśaṅku with him, the great Grandfather went to Brahmaloka. The delighted sage stayed there itself.

CHAPTER EIGHT

Killing of Vṛtra

Sūta said:

1-4. O excellent Brāhmaṇas, when Triśaṅku, the best of kings, reached Svarga thus, by the effort of Viśvāmitra, that Tīrtha became very famous in the entire range of the three worlds thereafter.

It became the bestower of virtue, wealth, love the salvation on all the people. It was untouched by the defects of Kali and also by minor sins. By the power of the Slayer of Tripuras, the sins of Brāhmaṇa slaughter etc. also never defiled it. One who casts off his life there with a mind filled with faith shall attain liberation even if the man happens to be great sinner.

5. Worms, birds and insects beasts, birds, and lower animals that die there, undoubtedly go to Śivaloka.

6. Those who take their holy bath there, with a mind sanctified by faith, will go to Svarga like Triśaṅku even if they happen to be irreligious.

7. Those who are distressed due to heat and those who are overwhelmed by thirst and plunge into the waters there shall go to the great place where Lord Maheśvara dwells.

8. On becoming aware of the excellent greatness of that Tīrtha, Viśvāmitra too left off Kurukṣetra and started to reside there.

9. Other quiescent sages abandoned their Tīrthas (of residence) which were far off and came there. Making their hermitages there, ultimately they attained the greatest region.

10-14. Similarly men from far-off lands, who had committed hundreds of sins hastened thither, had their holy bath and attained Svarga as a result due to the efficacy of the Tīrtha, O excellent Brāhmaṇas. In this manner, as the people attained heavenly abode easily, all the holy rites such as Agniṣṭoma etc., became defunct. No man cared to perform Yajña; no one wanted to observe vows and restraints. No on made gifts by way of Dāna; no one resorted to the holy Tīrthas. Everyone attended only to the holy bath in Liṅgabheda. Thereby he sat on excellent aerial chariots and went to Svarga.

15. Thereby, O Brāhmaṇas, the heavenly worlds became filled with human beings who competed with Brahmā, Viṣṇu Śiva, Indra and other excellent Suras.

16. At that all the groups of Devas, who were thus deprived of their shares of the Yajñas underwent a great deal of suffering. They took counsel with one another.

17-18. "The heavenly world is filled completely, due to the greatness of Hāṭakeśvara, by the people of raised hands competing with us. Hence step should be taken to wipe out this Tīrtha named Hāṭakeśvara from the surface of the earth."

19. Thereupon, at the behest of Śakra the Saṁvartaka Wind (the destructive storm at the time of the ultimate annihilation) filled the entire holy spot with dust particles, O excellent Brāhmaṇas.

20. When thus that Tīrtha became ruined and bruied all the rites associated with *Kratus* became revived.

21. After a lapse of long time an anthill rose up in that holy spot and it gradually reached down to Pātāla.

22-23. Thereafter, serpents came into the mortal world out of curiosity, through that path and wandered over the earth, where they enjoyed all human pleasures as they pleased and then went back to their own abode through the same path.

24. Thererore, O excellent Brāhmaṇas that anthill became well known all over the earth as Nāgabīla (Serpent-hole) due to the to-and-fro movements of serpents.

25-26. After some time the Lord, the Slayer of Pāka (i.e. Indra) incurred the sin of Brāhmaṇa slaughter and became lustre-less. Thereafter, by the command of Pitāmaha, he entered Pātāla through that path and visited Hāṭakeśvara.

27. Instantly he became rid of sins, as a result of that visit. Regaining his splendour he went back to heaven.

28. Having thus become aware of the power of that Liṅga of the Trident-bearing Lord named Hāṭakeśvara, he became afraid of danger from human beings.

29-31. 'If some man, like king Triśaṅku were to adore that Liṅga faithfully and become sinless, he will be sure to oust me from the heavenly abode. Hence I shall fill up this path to Pātāla.' Hence he hurriedly prepared for the same. Śatakratu himself hurled the excellent mountain Raktaśṛṅga[1] (Red-peaked) into that hole.

The sages said:

32-33. How did Devendra incur the sin of Brāhmaṇā-slaughter? When did that noble-souled Devendra incur that sin?, O Sūta, describe all this in detail to us. What is this mountain Raktaśṛṅga that was hurled there by him? Who was that particular group of men of whom the Consort of Śacī had the great fear?

Sūta said:

34-37. Formerly, O excellent Brāhmaṇas, the daughter of

1. *Raktaśṛṅga*: A mythical mountain, son of Himālaya. It was used by Indra to close the passage from the earth to Hāṭakeśvara Liṅga in Pātāla.

Hiraṇyakaśipu named Ramā was married by Tvaṣṭṛ. The lady was rich in beauty and other excellent qualities but for a long time she was not blessed with a son. Getting disgusted and detached, she performed a penance for the sake of a son. She began to meditate on Maheśvara, the Lord of Devas, the overlord of Suras. With perfect faith she offered oblations and other offerings and adored. She had perfect control and her diet was regulated. She had her holy baths regularly and performed Japa duly. To excellent Brāhmaṇas she offered different kinds of Dāna.

38-40. At the end of a thousand years, Maheśvara became pleased with her and said: "I shall grant you a boon you wish. Do choose it." She pleaded: "O Holy Lord, with your favour, let a son be born to me. Let him be heroic adopting the from of a Brāhmaṇa and Dānava. He should not be killed by means of weapons. He should have studied the Vedas fully and always be active in sacrificial rites. Due to his splendour and fame he should be well-known among all the embodied beings."

The Lord said:

41-42. There is no doubt about this. Your son will be learned and strong. He cannot be killed by any weapon. He will be endowed with great splendour. He will perform Yajñas and make gifts. He will be heroic with full mastery of the Vedas and Vadāṅgas. He will perform all the holy rites enjoined in the Brāhmaṇas. He will be invincible in battle unto all the Suras and Asuras.

43-44. Having said this the Lord of Devas vanished. After the next menstrual cycle she duly conceived from Viśvakarman. In the tenth month she gave birth to a splendid son marked with all characteristic features and splendorous shining like twelve suns shining together.

45. On the twelfth day, the father honoured excellent Brāhmaṇas and gave to him the well known name Vṛtra.

46. The boy grew up like the Moon in the bright half delighting the father and the mother. He was duly fondled by all the kinsmen.

47-48. Then the excellent Brāhmaṇa Śukra, formally initiated him in the Vrata of celebacy (Brahmacarya) befitting a Brāhmaṇa though he (Vṛtra) was a Dānava. Vṛtra was a favourite of his preceptors. Establishing himself in the holy Vrata of a celibate (religious) student Vṛtra studied by heart all the Vedas along with Vedāṅgas.

49. Attaining prime of youth, he conquered all the kings and brought the whole Earth under his control; thereafter he conquered Pātāla also.

50. Ambitious of conquering Indra, he went to the abode of Suras and routed the Devas including Indra in the course of a battel.

51-58. The Thunderbolt-bearing One fought eighteen battles with him but in none of them did he win, O excellent Brāhmaṇas.

Along with the surviving Suras who were wounded and maimed in all their limbs, the frightened Lord Śakra started from heaven and went to Brahmaloka.

Vṛtra occupied position of Śakra and enjoyed the entire range of the three worlds after destroying all the obstacles thereto.

The mighty one employed the power-arrogant Dānavas in the different positions of the Devas facilitating their partaking of the shares in the Yajñas.

O excellent Brāhmaṇas, thus he attained the suzerainty over all the three worlds, yet he was not contented because he had an eye on Brahmaloka.

Thereupon he summoned Śukra along with four of his ministers. Bowing down humbly, he spoke these sweet words:

Vṛtra said:

O leading member of the family of my preceptor, Śakra has gone to Brahmaloka in fright. Tell me how one has to gain access thereto, so that I can kill Śakra, Viriñci and everyone else. I shall grant you Brahmaloka and enjoy Svarga myself.

Śukra said:

59. O excellent one among Dānavas, you will have no access thereto. So, it behoves you to be contented with the dominion of the three worlds.

Vṛtra said:

60-61. As long as Sutrāmā (Indra) is alive, I will not be

happy. Hence, O excellent Brāhmaṇa, I shall endeavour for the state of full riddance of all obstacles.

O scion of the family of Bhṛgu, how did Śakra get an entry therein? O highly intelligent one, tell me why it will not be possible for me.

Śukra said:

62-64. Formerly a penance was performed by him in the Naimiṣa forest, O excellent Dānava. He had been meditating on Śaṅkara for a period of one thousand years. By the power thereof, he has free access thereto forever along with his servants and followers. There is no other reason for that.

Another person who performs a similar penance in the Naimiṣa forest shall also have undoubtedly the access to Brahmaloka.

Sūta said:

65-70. On hearing it, he hastened to Naimiṣa the excellent Tīrtha, and performed a very severe penance meditating on Maheśvara. Earlier he had assigned the protection of the three worlds to excellent Danujas who had great power and who were superior to even Śakra in valour.

During rainy season he remained under the open sky. During Hemanta (winter) he resorted to water-ponds. During summer he practised his holy rite in the midst of fires. He sustained himself by the intake of air only.

He continued the penance for hundreds of years. Therefore, Devas with Brahmā and Viṣṇu as leaders became frightened.

They could only take counsel together for destroying him. They tried to find loopholes and vulnerable points, but they could not. They became miserable.

Ultimately Viṣṇu decided in his mind, after giving deep thought for a long time to the means of destroying Vṛtra. He joyously said:

Viṣṇu said:

71-77. O Śakra, now I have found out a means to slay him certainly. There is no other means. Listen to this and act on it immediately.

He has been made immune to the fatal attack of all weapons by the Trident-bearing Lord. Hence for slaying him get the *Vajra* (thunderbolt) prepared out of bones.

Indra said:

O Lord, how is this Vajra to be created? What is that animal whose bones are to be used? Elephant? Śarabha(?) (eight-footed fabulous creature) or any other? Tell me.

Viṣṇu said:

O Lord of Suras, the bone should be hexagonal in shape and a hundred Hastas (cubits) in length. It should be thick at the sides and thin in the middle. It shall have frightening features.

Indra said:

O Lord of Suras, such an animal or being is not seen in all the three worlds from the bones of which the Vajra of these features can be created.

Viṣṇu said:

There is a Brāhmaṇa named Dadhīci. He is performing a severe penance in his hermitage on Sarasvatī. He is twice as long as the one we require. Go quickly and request him. He will give you his bones. Once he is requested he has nothing which he cannot give.

78-81. Then, O excellent Brāhmaṇas, Śakra went to his hermitage along with the Suras. His hermitage was at a Puṣkara on the banks of Prācīsarasvatī (modern Raunākṣī).

On coming to know that the Devas had come to his hermitage, Dadhīci became delighted and he hurried to meet them.

The excellent Sage bowed down to Indra and others and adored them with *Arghya* etc., thereafter. Then he stood by with humility after bowing down to Indra repeatedly. He said joyously:

Dadhīci said:

82. Why have Devas come here? May my duty be told quickly

O slayer of Bala, I am blessed indeed, to whose house you yave come.

Śakra said:

83-86. O excellent Brāhmaṇa, all of us have been defeated by Vṛtra. By the power of the boon, he cannot be killed by any weapon. Hari says that he could be killed by means of a Vajra created out of a bone a hundred Hastas in length. There is no such being excepting you, O excellent Brāhmaṇa. So give us your bones so that a Vajra capable of killing him (Vṛtra) may be made. O excellent Brāhmaṇa, do this much to quell the distress of Devas. Otherwise all the Devas will be utterly annihilated.

Sūta said:

87. On hearing it, the holy sage Dadhīci joyously cast off his life for the sake of the welfare of the Heaven-dwellers.

88. Then the delighted Devas gathered all the bones and made a great Vajra in the manner explained by Viṣṇu.

89-93. Śakra took it with him and went towards Naimiṣa.[1] He had fear still lurking in his mind and he trembled awfully. Immediately after nightfall, the Lord of Devas standing far away struck Vṛtra who was in meditation, by means of the Vajra. Having done it he fled.

Vṛtra, a tiger among Dānavas, was reduced to ash due to the blow with the Vajra, like a fire-fly that falls into fire.

Still in his fright, Śakra fled to the middle of the Sea and climbed on to a mountain with high peaks, which could not be scaled easily.

He still was not sure that Vṛtra had been killed by the blow of the Vajra. He stood there watching the path by which Vṛtra could possibly come.

1. Here the story of killing of Vṛtra by Indra is different. In *Mbh, Śānti.* 281.13-30, Indra fights with Vṛtra. But in this Purāṇa, Indra is a coward. Indra hurls his Vajra at Vṛtra while he was absorbed in meditation and instead of waiting for the effect of Vajra on Vṛtra, he immediately runs away and conceals himself in a cave in a far-off sea. Brahmahatyā closely followed him and overpowered him. When Bṛhaspati and Devas traced him, he was found as a leper, a victim of Brahma-hatyā.

94-97. In the meantime the Devas saw that Vṛtra had been slain. They experienced horripilation due to joy and eulogized Indra.

They were unware that out of fear he had disappeared on the mountain in the sea. They began a search and with very great difficulty they got at him after some time.

The saw him sitting inside an inaccessible cave in the mountain. He was lustreless and a dejected state. Evidently he was overwhelmed by the sin of Brāhmaṇa-slaughter. All the ten quarters were filled with the offensive smell from his body.

98-100. On seeing Śakra thus the Four-faced Lord stood aloof suspecting the sin and said to the groups of Devas: "O excellent Devas, this is Śakra overwhelmed by the sin of Brāhmaṇa-slaughter. He should be kept at a distance. Otherwise you will also contract the sin. See, all the signs of the sin of Brāhmaṇa-slaughter are evident on his limbs. They are clearly visible. We shall go to heaven."

101-103. The Lord of Suras had seen the Devas with Pitāmaha as the leader come there. But all of a sudden they were going away with faces turned. At this he was dismayed.

In great confusion he said: "O Suras, why do you go away. Even after seeing me, you go away without speaking to me. I hope everything is all right at home. Was that Dānava killed with my Vajra? I hope the wicked fellow is not on the lookout for me to fight with me."

Brahmā said:

104-111. O Śakra, the Dānava has already been killed by the Vajra. The sinful fellow is under the control of the god of Death. You need not fear at all. But due to his slaughter the despicable sin of Brāhmaṇa-slaughter has overcome you, O Śakra. You have become unworthy of being touched. We will not touch you.

Indra said:

Many Dānavas have been killed by me formerly but this sin of Brāhmaṇa-slaughter did not overtake me. How is it so now?

Brahmā said:

O Vāsava, they were killed by you in battle abiding by the

duty of a Kṣatriya. All of them were pure Dānavas. Therefore no sin overtook you. But this fellow had been invested with the sacred thread. Moreover he was peforming a penance. O Śakra, you killed him treacherously. So you have become a sinner.

Indra said:

O Four-faced One, I am conscious that my body has become foul and sinful through the symptoms of the sin of Brāhmaṇa-slaughter. Hence tell me the means of purification whereby the sin due to Brāhmaṇa-slaughter may be dispelled quickly and I can be worthy of being touched by Devas, O Prapitāmaha.

Brahmā said:

O excellent one among Suras, for that purpose you have to undertake a pilgrimage. Without it your sin cannot be eradicated completely.

Sūta said:

112-123. Then, at his instance Śakra undertook the pilgrimage. He wandered over the entire earth taking a holy plunge in all the well-known Tīrthas, Nadīs and Nadas. The Thousand-eyed Lord went to Vārāṇasī, Prayāga, Prabhāsa, Kurujāṅgala and other holy places but did not get rid of his sin.

Utterly dejected thereby, he thought thus: 'I have taken holy bath in all the Tīrthas on the earth. But I have not got rid of the sin. What shall I do now? Should I fall down from the peak of a mountain? Would I drink poison. Divested of the eminence of the kingdom of the three worlds, I am not eager to live.'

Thus in his utter disgust and dejection Vāsava climbed on the top of a mountain. In his resolve to die he was about to hurl himself down, when, O excellent Brāhmaṇas', a divine voice arose.

"Do not be rash, O Sákra, in your desperate state of mind. You have yet to reign for the period of eight Yugas in the heavenly kingdom. Hence, O Śakra, listen attentively to the means of expiation for the sin. Carry it out quickly. Otherwise there shall be no purification.

Formerly you had closed down a hole in the holy spot of

Hāṭakeśvara by means of dust particles. It is a place where Lord Hara is present himself. O Lord of Devas, through an anthill there a serpent hole has been made which was used by serpents to come to the earth and return. Through that very path you should go to Hāṭakeśvara. Take your holy bath in Pātālagaṅgā and worship Maheśvara. Thereby you will undoubtedly be rid of sins. You will regain your dominion of the heavenly kingdom free from all obstacles."

Sūta said:

124-132. On hearing the aerial voice, Śakra hurriedly went to the place where the serpent-hole (*Nāgabila*) was. Through it he entered Pātāla and took holy bath in the (Pātāla) Gaṅgā water. He then adored the Liṅga named Hāṭakeśvara. In an instant his body became free from impurities. The offensive small disappeared and the rediance increased.

In the meantime Suras led by Brahmā and Viṣṇu came there and joyously spoke to the king of Devas rid of all sins: "O Śakra, you have attained purity. You are freed from the sin of Brāhmaṇa-slaughter. So come on , we shall all go to heaven together. O Śakra, fill up this serpent hole with dust particles once again. Otherwise human beings may pass through this and attain Siddhi easily. They will take the holy bath in the waters of Gaṅgā, worship this Liṅga and attain the greatest goal even though they may be great sinners."

Thereafter all the Devas and Śatakratu bowed down to the Lord and went to the heavenly abode. There in heaven the festivities connected with the slaughter of Vṛtra were celebrated, O excellent Brāhmaṇas, when Śakra regained his status as the overlord of the Devas.

Sūta said:

133-134. Thus everything connected with the glory of Hāṭakeśvara has been recounted to you all. The greatness thereof, O excellent Brāhmaṇas, is destructive of all sins. One who recites this with devotion, one who listens to this with devotion, one who listens to this with attention shall go to the greatest region devoid of old age and death.

CHAPTER NINE

Filling up the Nāgabila

Sūta said:

1-2. Śakra summoned the Saṁvartaka wind and said: "You know that there is a great serpent-hole in the holy spot of Hāṭakeśvara. Rush to the place at my bidding and fill it up with dust-particles whereby no one of mortal features can have access to it.

Vāyu said:

3-6. At your behest I had earlier filled up that hole when the Slayer of Puras (Śiva) cursed me for polluting the Liṅga: "Since my Liṅga has been covered with dust particles, you shall be an indiscriminate blower of all sorts of odour. Due to my words (curse) even as you are the sole wafter of the fragrance of camphor, so you will also undoubtedly be the carrier of unpleasant odour of rubbish and filth too."

Understand this, O Lord of Suras, and spare me. Do me the favour and depute someone else for this task. I am afraid of the Slayer of Puras.

7-15. Thereafter, the Lord of Devas, pondered over the work of filling up the Serpent-hole and did not look into anything else.

Thereupon the preceptor of Devas himself said to Śatakratu: "O Lord of Devas, why are you so worried in this matter? There is the chief of all mountains well-known as Himālaya. He begot three sons. Listen to the details about them. Maināka is said to be the first and Nandivardhana is the second. Raktaśṛṅga is glorified as the third mountain.

O Śakra, afraid of you, Maināka has sunk into the ocean where he continues to be safe with his pair of wings intact.

At the bidding of Himācala as well as Sage Vasiṣṭha the hole (tunnel) around Vasiṣṭha's hermitage has been entirely filled up by the second one glorified as Nandivardhana. At the bidding of Himālaya and Vasiṣṭha he has left the celestial ground and has gone there in a hurry.

The third one who is remembered as Raktaśṛṅga still stands by, O Thousand-eyed One. Bring him here and get the Serpent-hole filled up.

O Lord of Devas, this hole cannot be closed by filling up otherwise, except through that excellent mountain. What has been said by me is the truth."

Sūta said:

16-17. On hearing the words of Bṛhaspati, the one venerated by the celestial beings, the Lord of Devas (Indra) rushed to the place where Himālaya was present. He approached Himālaya, the excellent one among mountains, resorted to by Siddhas and Cāraṇas and said:

Indra said:

18-21. There is a great Serpent-hole in the holy spot of Hāṭakeśvara. Even those men who are engaged in committing sins will go through the hole and adore Lord Hāṭakeśvara in Pātāla, O excellent one among mountains. Thereby they will be in a position to compete with me. Hence, O Himālaya, do despatch this son of yours named Raktaśṛṅga by whom it may be possible to fill up the Serpent-hole.

O Mountain, I am a guest come to your abode. Render the hospitality due to me by this gift of your own son; you will thus gain supramundane glory.

22-24. "Yes, it will be so", said he after worshipping the Lord of Devas.

Thereafter, Himālaya spoke to his son Raktaśṛṅga: "Dear son, the Thousand-eyed One (Indra) has come to me for getting your service. Hence hasten to the place where the *Nāgabila* is situated. At my bidding fill it up and completely fulfil the desire of Śakra. Be happy along with him as well as with other excellent Suras."

Raktaśṛṅga said:

25-29. I will not go there at any cost. It is the land of mortals where rugged thorny trees bereft of fruits are in plenty. Neither Siddhas nor Gandharvas, neither Devas nor Kinnaras live there.

No charming Tīrthas and no rivers with crystal-clear waters can be found there. Further, the men there are devoid of decency and decorum; they are prone to commit sinful deeds. All of them are evil-minded. Even the brutes are no better. Also, O excellent one among Mountains, my wings have been clipped off by Śakra himself. That has deprived me of the ability to go there even with great difficulty. So let the Thousand-eyed One exclude me from this matter and think about some other means. What has been uttered by me is the truth.

Śakra said:

30-34. I had wounded you. So I shall myself carry you there holding you up by the hand. There too excellent trees shall grow on you. So also there will be meritorious Tīrthas and shrines of deities. All round you there shall be the hermitages of sages. At my instance your power and prestige, if you stay there, will be a crore times more than what you possess staying here. Further the men though sinful, shall become free from sins by seeing you. Therefore, O son of the Mountain, hasten there in my company. Otherwise (This is no vain threat), I shall smash you into a thousand pieces with a blow of my thunderbolt.

Sūta said:

35-37. On hearing these words of his, Raktaśṛṅga became frightened. He hastened there and entered the Serpent Hole filling it up. O excellent Brāhmaṇas, he got sunk down therein up to the tip of his very nose with all his fascinating tall peaks entirely overspread with trees, creepers and twining vines, whereon charming birds perched.

After establishing thus that mountain, the son of Himācala, Śakra joyously said to him, "May a boon be received from me."

Raktaśṛṅga said:

38. O Sureśvara, this alone is a great boon to me that you are pleased with me. What shall I do with a boon? I am happy, thanks for your favour.

Indra said:

39. O son of the Mountain, seeing me even in a dream shall not go in vain. What then when you have actually seen me and particularly when you have accomplished my task?

Raktaśṛṅga said:

40. O Lord of all the Suras, if of necessity, a boon has to be granted, let all my rich products always be for the use of Brāhmaṇas, O Lord.

Indra said:

41-46. There shall be a king known as Camatkāra. On you he will establish a city for the sake of Brāhmaṇas. There these tigers among Brāhmaṇas, masters of the Vedas and Vedāṅgas, shall enjoy your rich products fully.

O son of the Mountain, on the fourteenth lunar day in the dark half of the month of Caitra, I shall personally come here along with all the groups of Devas, Kinnaras and Guhyakas. On the most important peak of yours I shall worship the Lord of Devas named Hāṭakeśvara.

On that one day, Hara too, very pleased with you, shall stay on you along with us. Thereby your power and prestige in all the three worlds shall be great. Welfare unto you. I shall now go to the heavenly abode.

Sūta said:

47-48. After saying thus, the Thousand-eyed Lord went back to heaven. Raktaśṛṅga pervaded the entire Serpent-hole and stayed behind. Very important Tīrthas and shrines came to flourish on it along with hermitages of sages.

CHAPTER TEN

King Camatkāra Cursed

Sūta said:

1-5. In the meantime the king well known as Camatkāra, the overlord of Ānarta (Northern Gujarat) came to the forest there to hunt deer.

Far away he saw a doe assured because not expecting danger from anywhere and therefore fearlessly suckling her young one motionlessly.

Immediately the delighted king fixed an arrow of crooked point, drew the string upto his ear and hit her in a vulnerable spot.

She was presently hit by that arrow to which vulture's feathers had been fixed. In her excruciating pain she looked around.

Seeing the king holding the bow not very far off, the doe, fond of her young one, with her face dimmed with tears spoke thus:

The doe said:

6-8. O king, what you have done now is very improper. I who was suckling my young fawn, have been hit with an arrow of crooked point. O king, it is not the destruction (death) of my own body that I bewail; I bewail this wretched fawn eager to suck the udder.

Since such a cruel deed has been committed by you, you will be immediately afflicted with the foul disease of leprosy.

The king said:

9. This is the regular practice and duty of kings to hunt and kill deer. So it does not behove you to curse me when I only carried out my duty.

The doe said:

10-14. O king, what you spelt out is true. Deer have been created by the Self-born Lord for being hunted and killed by

Kṣatriyas, but the injunction laid down by him also may be heard attentively even as I explain it.

A man is defiled by sin if he kills a deer that is asleep, that is eager to drink water, that is engaged in suckling (her young) or that is indulging in mating.

It is for this reason that the curse was pronounced on you, O king, not out of fanciful wish, nor of death. I vouch for it by a solemn promise.

After saying this in great agony the doe cast off her life. The king became overwhelmed by the foul disease of leprosy.

15-20. On seeing his own body defiled by leprosy the king summoned his servants and said to them in great misery: "I shall perform a penance. I shall worship Śaṅkara till the disease of leprosy is eradicated.

Whatever happiness men seek in all the three worlds can be entirely achieved through penance. Hence penance should be performed by me. I shall now roam about regularly over the earth begging for alms, staying under a tree everday.

Giving up everything that I like or dislike, my stay will be on bare ground covered with dust or a deserted house or at the root of a tree.

I shall eschew everything both pleasant and unpleasant. I shall be impartial towards enemies as well as friends. I shall see a lump of clay, a stone or a piece of gold impartially. Thus I will spend my life till the end of time (my death)."

21-24. After saying thus and dismissing his servants, the king set out on a pilgrimage and wandered over the earth. After a long time he listened to the advice of a Brāhmaṇa and arrived at Śaṅkhatīrtha of great efficacy in the holy spot of Hāṭakeśvara.

This is well known in all the three worlds as destructive of all diseases. This is filled with clear water. Merely by his holy bath there, the excellent king became rid of his leprosy. He shone with great splendour.

CHAPTER ELEVEN

Gift of a City to Brāhmaṇas[1]

The sages said:

1-3. O sage born of Sūta, how was King Camatkāra rid of leprosy? In what way did he perform penance? How long was it performed by the king? Who were those Brāhmaṇas by whom Śaṅkha Tīrtha was recommended for the purpose of the riddance from the ailment of the miserable noble-souled king? What is this Śaṅkhatīrtha? Where is it situated? What is its efficacy. Do explain in detail without leaving anything.

Sūta said:

4-7. I shall recount to you all, this fascinating story, O Brāhmaṇas, of King Camatkāra. It is destructive of all sins.

He wandered over all the Tīrthas beginning with Prabhāsa. He was a confirmed ascetic observing restrictions in his diet. He lived on cooked food received as alms.

For the sake of curing the disease, he used to consult leading physicians about medicinal herbs frequently and the knowers of Mantras about the curative incantations.

He did not get any desired (effective) Mantra or medicine or a holy spot whereby the tiger among kings could eradicate the foul disease.

8-11. Hence the excellent king became extremely disgusted. In a holy place of great merit shining (teeming) with all sorts of living beings, he continued to stay alone for a long time with his mind and soul under perfect control.

His food intake consisted of withered leaves and fruits. At night, he used to lie down on bare ground. Everyday he resorted to a new tree for the sake of food and rest. He fully eschewed pride and arrogance.

After roaming about a few days, the king saw many excellent Brāhmaṇas who were on their pilgrimage.

---

1. King Camatkāra of Ānarta built and gifted a city to Brāhmaṇas. The city was named "Camatkārapura" after the name of the donor. It is called "Ānandapura" and "Nāgara", synonyms of modern Vadnagara. It is the home of Nāgara Brāhmaṇas of Gujarat.

When those Brāhmaṇas sat down for rest near the hermitage of Viśvāmitra, he bowed down to them with great humility and requested:

The king said:

12-15. O excellent Brāhmaṇas, I am a king of the Solar race, Camatkāra by name, the ruler of Ānarta. I have been affected by leprosy. Is there any remedy, divine or human, any medicine or Mantra, whereby leprosy can be cured?

O excellent Brāhmaṇas, take pity on me and do tell me. My body defiled by this foul disease, leprosy, suffers a great deal. Or if you do not know (any remedy) I will enter fire or water and cast off my life or will take in poison to put an end to it.

16-20. On hearing his words, all the excellent Brāhmaṇas were moved with pity and they spoke to the Lord of the Earth: "O tiger among kings, not far from this place there is a holy place well known as Śaṅkhatīrtha. It is conducive to the destruction of all ailments.

Those men who are suffering from a disease, blind ones, those who have squints, sluggish ones, those deficient in limbs or those who have superfluous limbs, hideous ones, those who have deformed faces—all these should take their holy bath and observe fast at the beginning of the dark half of Caitra when the Moon is in the constellation Citrā.

We have seen hundreds of such persons who instantly became free from ailments and became endowed with refulgence of twelve Suns and handsome features like Kāmadeva (god of Love)."

The king asked:

21. How is this Śaṅkha Tīrtha to be known by me, O excellent Brāhmaṇas? How did it originate? Tell me in detail.

The Brāhmaṇas said:[1]

22-28. Formerly there was an excellent sage on the earth

---

1. Śaṅkha and Likhita are two ancient Smṛti-writers. The legend how Śaṅkha's arms were cut and were restored is found in Mbh, *Śānti* 231.16.36. The difference between the legend in Mbh and this Purāṇa is as follows: (i) Likhita himself cuts the arms of Śaṅkha in this Purāṇa while in Mbh

named Likhita. He was son of Sage Śāṇḍilya and was fully endowed with the power of penance and energy.

A younger brother of his was born. His name was Śaṅkha. He later became well conversant with scriptural texts. He perpetually performed penance with bulbous roots, roots and fruits for food.

After some time, he went to the hermitage of Likhita. On being afflicted with great hunger, Śaṅkha wanted to taste some sweet fruits. He entered the vacant hermitage of the noble-souled Likhita. Considering that the fruits belonged to him as well, he took many sweet fruits and ate them. In the meantime, Likhita came there along with his disciples.

On coming to know that Śaṅkha had already plucked the fruits, he said angrily: "O sinful one, you have yourself plucked the fruits not offered by me. Why did you take them like a thief? Why did you not wait for permission?"

Śaṅkha said:

29-33. O excellent Brāhmaṇa, what you have spoken is true. The fruits have been plucked from your hermitage when there was no one here. Hence give me punishment due for the act of theft, so that my life in this world as well as in the other one may be happy.

Thereupon he caught hold of the hands of Śaṅkha instantly. In his great rage, though he was prevented by the ascetics, he cut off the hands. Śaṅkha who got his hands amputated, performed a severe penance after going back to his own hermitage.

After some time Mahādeva became pleased with him. Appearing before him, he spoke to the eminent sage Śaṅkha:

Maheśvara said:

34. O sage of great inherent strength, you have done a very difficult job. Receive from me any boon conceived of in your mind.

Likhita lodges a complaint with king Sudyumna who ordered the amputation of the arms.

(ii) Śaṅkha regained his arms after bath in River Bāhudā (the granter of arms), modern Burha Rapti or Dhumila (De p. 6). This Purāṇa gives the credit to a Tīrtha at Camatkārapura obviously for the glorification of this holy place. The Tīrtha came to be known as "Śaṅkha Tīrtha".

Śaṅkha said:

35-37. O Lord, if you are pleased, if you wish to grant me a boon, O excellent one among Suras, may two hands similar to the former ones, spring up again. Further, O excellent one among Suras, let this Tīrtha bear my name and be well known in all the worlds as destructive of all sins of men. If one has deficiency or superfluity in one's limbs, if one is afflicted with any foul disease and if one takes one's holy bath here, one shall become fresh (normal) once again.

The Lord said:

38-45. O eminent Brāhmaṇa, this Tīrtha will become well known after your name. It shall be destructive of the sins of embodied beings from today. Any person having deficiency of superfluity of limbs, who takes his holy bath here in the bright half of Caitra when the Moon is in the constellation of Citrā and observes fast, shall undoubtedly become perfect in every limb and very brilliant. O leading Brāhmaṇa, if he has any desire and then meditates, he will attain handsome features.

If he has no desire he will attain the great region of Śiva of great auspiciousness. If Śrāddha is performed here, O Brāhmaṇa, on the fourteenth lunar day when the Moon is in the constellation of Citrā, the Pitṛs will attain the most excellent satisfaction.

O tiger among Brāhmaṇas, today we have the excellent period of the close (last day) of the bright half of Caitra. In the afternoon the Moon will be in conjuction with constellation Citrā. Then you take your holy bath and observe fast. Instantly you will have the perfect pair of hands as before.

After saying this the Lord vanished. Śaṅkha performed the holy ablution in the *Kutapa* (about noon) period. Instantly his hands sprang up as before. They resembled a red lotus and shone well. They were marked with piscine signs.

The Brāhmaṇas said:

46-48. It was thus, O excellent king, that by the power of the Moon-crested Lord of Devas that auspicious Tīrtha came into being on the surface of the earth.

Hence you too, O leading king, do take your holy bath there on the fourteenth lunar day in the bright half of the month of Caitra when the Moon is in the constellation Citrā.

There is no doubt about this that you will be rid of all ailments. We shall show it to you when the time arrives as mentioned.

Sūta said:

49-52. A few days thereafter the day previous to the dark half of Caitra arrived, when the Moon was in the contellation Citrā, the fourteenth lunar day. Presently those Brāhmaṇas, the well-wishers of the king, took the king towards the Śaṅkhatīrtha.

Then he deeply meditated on the utter eradication of the foul disease of leprosy and duly took his holy bath with great faith.

He came out of the water completely rid of leprosy, dazzling with the lustre of twelve Suns. He was extremely delighted.

53-57. Afterwards he bowed down to all those Brāhmaṇas who had mastered the Vedas. With palms joined in reverence, he spoke these words:

"It was indeed due to your favour that, O excellent Brāhmaṇas, I have become rid of the foul disease of leprosy which had made me despicable unto all embodied beings for a long time.

Therefore, O excellent Brāhmaṇas, I will no longer rule the kingdom. I shall perform great penance for ever here at this Tīrtha. Let excellent Brāhmaṇas take over this kingdom, this whole land, whatever I have, the elephants, horses etc., for blessing me, the wretched one devoted to them. As a favour to me let them take great pity on me now that I have become completely detached."

The Brāhmaṇas said:

58-63. O excellent king, we are incapable of protecting the kingdom. Then why should we take it up when it is going to become utterly chaotic?

Formerly the earth was given to us by Rāma, the son of Jamadagni, after exterminating the Kṣatriyas twenty-one times. But, O excellent king, more powerful Kṣatriyas slighted us and easily seized it.

The king said:

O excellent Brāhmaṇas, I will protect your interests though I will continue to perform the penance. In this matter none of you need have any fear.

The Brāhmaṇas said:

Of course, if you have faith in making munificent gifts, build an excellent city in this highly meritorious holy spot and give it to leading Brāhmaṇas, equipping it with ramparts, moats etc., then we can stay there comfortably taking the holy baths in the different Tīrthas, carrying on our duties as householders and proceeding with our study of the Vedic texts.

Sūta said:

64-70. On hearing it, the king became delighted. He accepted their suggestions and constructed a vast city at that holy spot. It was surrounded by lofty ramparts, a deep moats etc. It was charming. Its diameter extended to a Krośa. Triangular and quadrangular market-places shone splendidly. Banners fluttered. Big palaces glittered with fresh whitewashed walls, ornamental gates and attics. Buildings had many floors and good people praised the structures. The king filled the houses with gold, jewels, pearls and various articles of household utility.

He washed the feet of the excellent Brāhmaṇas well-versed in the Vedas, having perfect control over the senses, in accordance with the injunctions in the scriptural texts with due regard for the age and excellence of each and offered those houses to them.

CHAPTER TWELVE

Advice to the Sons

Sūta said:

1-5. Thus the king set up a city on a par with that of Indra (i.e., Amarāvatī) in accordance with his capacity and gifted it to the Brāhmaṇas.

Excellent houses shone displaying in various ways the glitter of pearls, corals, lapis lazuli and gold like the firmament displaying that of the clusters of stars.

The city had many palatial buildings made of crystal, comparable to the peaks of Kailāsa mountain. They were rendered all the more splendid by the divinely refulgent banners fluttering all round. Thousands of festoons of pure splendour and golden colour added to its charm. It had all the requisite things such as parks, wells, mechanical devices, large tanks resplendent with steps set with jewels. After dedicating this city to the leading Brāhmaṇas he became contented that he had done his duty.

6-15. He continued to stay near Śaṅkhatīrtha. He summoned his sons, grandsons and servants regularly and advised them thus:

"This city has been built by me and dedicated to the Brāhmaṇas. At my instance, you all should assiduously protect it so that the Brāhmaṇas shall be happy and delighted in their minds.

All of you should protect and maintain it. A king or any one else who is devoted to them and offers them succour shall obtain excellent refulgence on the earth.

He shall become invincible to all the enemies, valorous and endowed with flourishing prosperity. There is no doubt about this that one will become prosperous by protecting the Brāhmaṇas.

With the favour of the Brāhmaṇas and by my words (blessing) he shall be long-lived, free from ailments and endowed with sons, grandsons and loyal servants.

On the other hand, he who hates these tigers among Brāhmaṇas and causes them distress will fall into hell. He will meet with misery, suffer many humiliations, face separation from beloved ones and rebuke from others. In addition to the destruction of his family line he will pass on to the abode of Yama.

Hence with all endeavour this city has to be guarded by you if you desire your own welfare and specially because I say so."

Thus that king advised all of them and resumed his austerities. They too did what he had advised.

CHAPTER THIRTEEN

Glory of Acaleśvara

Sūta said:

1-6. Having advised his sons thus and handed over the kingdom to them and the city to the Brāhmaṇas, the king built an Āśrama (hermitage) for himself there and continued to worship Maheśvara, the Lord of Devas, with greatest faith.

The king spent a hundred years subsisting himself on fruit diet. He spent the same period of time with great concentration with dried and withered leaves for his intake. Thereafter, for a hundred years, he continued his penance taking in only water. A further period of a hundred years he spent taking in only air, after which Mahādeva became pleased and appeared before him even as he continued his penance with the intake of only air.

The Lord said "I am pleased. Request for whatever you wish from me. I shall grant you even what is inaccessible to Devas."

The king said:

7-15. This meritorious holy place that contains many Tīrthas, is conducive to the destruction of all sins due to the greatness of Hāṭakeśvara. So let it become still more sanctified by your residence here. O Lord, if you are pleased grant me this wish.

O Śarva, O Lord of the immortal beings, this distinguished city has been built by me and dedicated to Brāhmaṇas with the mind purified by ardent faith. As per my appeal you should always be pleased to stay steadily and permanently here, whereby it shall have the full complement of all good features.

Bhagavān said:

Acala (permanently abiding) I shall become in this holy spot, O Lord of the earth. I shall become well-known in all the there worlds by the name Acaleśvara.

If a man devoutly visits me stationed here, all his riches and powers shall always be unshakeable and permanent.

If a devout man equipped with great faith performs the rite of *Ghṛtakaṁbala* (Coating with ghee) to my Liṅga on the fourteenth lunar day in the bright half of the month of Māgha, all the sins committed by him in early childhood, youth or old age will vanish like darkness at the time of sunrise.

Hence, O Lord of the earth, install my Liṅga here itself so that I can stay here remaining steady for ever.

Sūta said:

16-27. After saying thus the Lord of Devas vanished. The king soon built a very charming, palatial shrine and devotedly installed there the Liṅga of the Trident-bearing Lord endowed with all the (auspicious) characteristics.

By seeing, touching, meditating and worshipping it, a man becomes rid of all the sins committed ever from birth to death.

Thereafter the king began to think (anxiously): 'Will the Lord steadily abide here in the Liṅga?'

In the meantime there arose an aerial voice of excellent distinct tone delighting King Camatkāra: "O lion among kings, do not become worried and anxious in this matter. I shall permanently stay here itself in this Liṅga. To convince you I shall further say another thing also, O king. On listening to it you shall feel relieved and will see carefully that the shadow of this Liṅga of mine shall always be steady solely remaining behind (the Liṅga) and not in different directions."

Sūta said:

Then he noted the shadow of the Liṅga of the same form and steady too when the sun was in that direction.

Thereupon the excellent king considered himself blessed.

In his great delight he bowed down to him (Śivaliṅga) on the ground.

Even today the shadow is seen in the same form always. This feature of the Liṅga, O leading Brāhmaṇas, caused great surprise.

There is another convincing proof. If anyone is destined to die within six months, he will never see the shadow.

Sūta said:

28-33. Thus the Lord remained for ever in the form of Acaleśvara at Camatkārapura. In the midst of sixty-eight holy places the Lord of Devas, Maheśvara, resides there at his request. Therefore, that holy shrine is glorified as one that accords all desires and liberation unto all embodied beings.

Further, O excellent Brāhmaṇas, I shall describe another incident pertaining to its power. May it be heard.

Due to the greatness of Acaleśvara all the men in that holy place attain all their desired benefit. Some get the heavenly pleasures, others salvation, a few wealth, foodgrains and sons. Whatever one keeps in one's mind and worships Lord Acaleśvara, one obtains it immediately without great effort.

34-40. The Thousand-eyed Lord observed that in his presence all sinful men on the earth go to heaven or attain salvation.

Thereupon, O excellent Brāhmaṇas Indra himself secretly called anger, passion, greed, hatred, fear, lasciviousness, delusion, vice, rivalry and attachment . . . all in their personified forms . . . and eagerly told them: "Any devotee, whether a man or a woman, if he or she is found going towards Camatkārapura, should be restrained by you all. Further, if one is residing there, he should be restrained from visiting Lord Acaleśvara. This should be done at my special request."

They promised, "So it will be and went there at the bidding of Śakra and rendered the greatness of the shrine ineffective and defunct.

Thus the narrative that is destructive of all sins has been recounted to you entirely.

Thus the story of the greatness of Lord Acaleśvara who always resides in that holy spot has been completely narrated.

CHAPTER FOURTEEN

Efficacy of Circumambulating Camatkārapura

Sūta said:

1-7. O excellent Brāhmaṇas, I shall describe to you what another miracle happened there, which abides in my heart as a secret.

There was a man in Camatkārapura. He was born in the Vaiśya caste. He was poverty-stricken and dumb too.

In view of the fact that he was oppressed by poverty, he looked after the cattle of all the people so that he could maintain his family. He was satisfied with whatever he earned.

Even as he continued looking after the cattle in forest regions, a beast (a cow) strayed away from the herd because it was covetous of plenty of grass elsewhere.

O excellent Brāmaṇas, it was on the fourteenth day of the dark half of the month of Caitra. The cow that had slipped away casually was not noticed by him. When the dumb cowherd reached home, the owner of the cow came there rebuking him: "O sinful one, how is it that one of my cows has not come back yet? Certainly it has been killed, concealed somewhere or sold by you. So fetch my cow back immediately. Hurry up even if you have not taken your food."

8-12. On hearing it, the dumb cowherd became very much frightened. Without taking food he started from his house with a stick in his hand. After reaching the forest, he surveyed all round carefully. In a certain place he saw a footprint of the cow clearly, as he was wandering about and recognised it fully.

Following the footprint, O excellent Brāhmaṇas, he went from forest to forest around Camatkārapura. Thus his act of search for the cow in the midst of herds incidentally resulted in a circumambulation of Camatkārapura on the part of the cowherd as well as the cow, O excellent Brāhmaṇas.

13-18. At the conclusion of the circumambulation, the cow was found out. Towards the close of the night, he took the cow home and returned her to the owner.

In the meritorious month of Caitra on the fourteenth lunar day in the dark half, all the Devas arrive at the Tīrthas of the sacred holy spot.

Thus on the holiest day both the cowherd and the cow completed the circumambulation though unwittingly. It was incidental, O excellent Brāhmaṇas. The cowherd observed fast and remained silent though he did not take his holy bath. The cow was of course silent though she had her food.

After a lapse a some time, as a result of their respective Karma, when the life period came to a close, both of them died separately.

The cowherd was reborn as son of the ruler of the country called Daśārṇa (Eastern Malwa). Due to the power (of his meritorious action) he could remember the previous birth.

19-29 That cow was born as a his minister, O excellent Brāhmaṇas. He could also remember the previous birth like the king. He was always honoured by the king.

At the end of every year that leading king in the company of that minister used to come to that city on the fourteenth lunar day in the dark half of the month(of Caitra) and used to circumambulate (Camatkārapura). He observed silence and refrained from taking food. He was fully endowed with great faith. He used to walk the whole distance on foot, O excellent Brāhmaṇas.

Once some holy sages of esteemed vows came there to the meritorious Viśvāmitratīrtha destructive of all sins. They were Yājñavalkya, Bharadvāja, Śunaḥśepa, Gālava, Devala, Bhāguri, Dhaumya, Kaśyapa, Cyavana,Bhṛgu and others of esteemed noble-souls devoted to life-long celibacy. In the course of their pilgrimage to various holy spots, they came to that place too.

On seeing them the king bowed down to them with palms joined in reverence. With great devotion he honoured them with due consideration for their seniority in age and eminence in achievement.

Then the king sat amongst those sages. He was duly congratulated by them too. In the presence of the king those sages held divine discourse about the activities of noble-souled important sages. They discussed the pious practices of old saintly kings obeying the injunctions of scriptural texts, which made that saintly king happy, O excellent Brāhmaṇas.

At the end of the discourse the great sages gave the king great blessings as enjoined by the Śruti passages. With their curiosity aroused, they asked the king thus:

The sages said:

30-32. O king, every year you assiduously come here alongwith your minister and circumambulate this city. O excellent king, there are many excellent Tīrthas in this holy place. So also there are many famous shrines, O king, but you seem to have not very great respect for them. In this we are excessively curious. If it is no secret, do narrate.

Sūta said:

33-35. On hearing their words the king became humble with the head bent down. He felt slightly shy too and said: "O excellent Brāhmaṇas, what I have been asked just now is worthy of being kept secret. It has never been revealed to anyone on the earth.

But your behest should be certainly obeyed. O excellent sages, do listen even if it be a much hidden secret.

Sūta said:

36. Thereafter, O excellent Brāhmaṇas, he narrated the incidents of the previous birth to those leading sages.

37-42. He told them how the cow was lost, how she was searched out, how it resulted in the circumambulation of Camatkārapura, how the power of remembering the incidents of the previous birth was acquired due to its efficacy, how he acquired whatever he desired every now and then, how he acquired the kingdom and gained prosperity.

On hearing this, all the sages were delighted. They showered blessings on him and said, "Excellent ! Excellent!"

Thereafter, with great faith and devotion, all of them circumambulated that city in accordance with the injunctions laid down. Due to its power, they attained great Siddhi that is really difficult to attain in the ordinary course by doing Japa, performing Yajña, offering monetary gifts, resorting to Tīrthas and similar things.

The king and his minister became gods moving about in aerial chariot. Even to-day, they are seen in the firmament in the form of stars.

CHAPTER FIFTEEN

Efficacy of Circumambulating Camatkārapura (Continued)

The Sages said:

1-8. O Sūta, even by circumambulating this city once, great welfare and glory is attained. What is the reason thereof ? O highly intelligent one, tell us everything in detail. We are eager to hear and you know everything fully.

Sūta said:

O excellent Brāhmaṇas, welfare is attained by the power of the excellent mountain well-known as Raktaśṛṅga.

Brahmā, Viṣṇu, Śiva and others always resort to it on the fourteenth lunar day in the dark half of the month of Caitra.

All the Devas, all the Tīrthas, all the shrines, all the rivers and oceans and whatever is held sacred are present on that mountain Raktaśṛṅga on that day as per the behest of Śatakratu.

When that mountain was brought by Indra to that place, it was told so: "On this day the Devas will come to you. All the Tīrthas in the world, all the meritorious shrines, will come to you."

Camatkārapura stands on its chief peak. Therefore by circumambulating it once welfare and glory is achieved.

9-15. O Brāhmaṇas, whatever is gifted with respect and high regard on that day has everlasting benefit as long as the moon and the sun shine.

A man who feeds Brāhmaṇas with sweet milk food with excellent devotion with the Pitṛs in view, shall attain the benefit of (a visit to) Gayā.

If anyone thinks of any desire and then circumambulates the city, he attains the desired object.

One without any desire shall attain salvation. One who gifts a cow with appurtenances to an excellent Brāhmaṇa attains the full benefit of the gift of the entire earth. Thus everything that I have been asked, O excellent Brāhmaṇas, as to how welfare is acquired by circumambulating by men, is narrated to you all.

Hence the rite circumambulating should be assiduously carried out around that city on the fourteenth lunar day in the dark half of Caitra by persons of great concentration and mental purity. They should strictly observe fast and the vow of silence. They should be mentally and physically pure and wear white clothes They should be free from attachment and hatred.

16-19. Since he was dumb, the cowherd was per force silent, O excellent Brāhmaṇas. As for the cow, it is naturally mute. Fast was observed by the two though without the ardour of faith. As for the cowherd, it was due to his dread of his master attached to the cow and not spontaneous faith. While he wandered in search of the cow, it resulted in a circumambulation just incidentally.

In spite of all this, the benefit was excellent in the case of both.

So if a man with great faith observes fast and silence and circumambulates he shall become an aerial chariot-rider in heaven like the ruler of Daśārṇa.

CHAPTER SIXTEEN

Merit of Residing near Raktaśṛṅga

Sūta said:

1-9a. Hence with all endeavour, the vicinity of Raktaśṛṅga should be resorted to by all sensible persons after eschewing all other rites.

Of what avail is Dāna ? Of what use are rituals ? Of what purpose are Yajñas ? Of what avail are Vratas (religious observances) even ? One should devoutly resort to that holy spot of (i.e. associated with) Hāṭakeśvara.

As compared to that holy spot, Yajñas beginning with Agniṣṭoma performed with the full complement of all monetary gifts, do not deserve even one-sixteenth fraction thereof. (Expiations like) Cāndrāyaṇa, Kṛcchra and Sāntapana do not deserve even one-sixteenth part of that holy spot.

Tīrthas beginning with Prabhāsa as well as rivers beginning with Gaṅgā do not deserve even one-sixteenth fraction of that holy spot.

All types of gifts (such as) of plots of land, all the righteous activities of compassion etc., do not deserve even one-sixteenth part of that holy spot.

Formerly many saintly kings had attained Siddhi here. Animals, birds, serpents, lions, tigers, deer etc., that died there in due course of time had also attained heavenly abode.

A person devoid of Vratas, one engaged in agricultural activities, who lives there and dies shall go to heaven, O Brāhmaṇas.

9b-11. What is the use of talking again and again, O excellent Brāhmaṇas ? Let the great secret connected with that holy spot be heard. (Other holy spots and Tīrthas sanctify men when they stay there. But the holy spot of Hāṭakeśvara sanctifies by its mere thought. What to say, O Brāhmaṇas, of visiting and touching (i.e. staying here) in particular!

CHAPTER SEVENTEEN

Vidūratha Goes Ahunting[1]

The sages said:

1-2. O highly wise one, the origin of the city of Camatkāra has been heard from you. Do narrate to us the dimensions of that holy spot. Also narrate to us all the meritorious Tīrthas and holy shrines thereof along with their efficacy.

Sūta said:

3-6. The holy spot extends to five Krośas, O excellent Brāhmaṇas, In length and breadth. That is the extent of the excellent Camatkārapura. To its east is Gayāśīrṣa. Viṣṇupada is

1. This king Vidūratha is different from king Vidūratha mentioned in Mbh, *Adi.* Chapters 185, 218. This king belongs to the Haihaya dynasty. This and the following chapters describe how King Vidūratha became a goblin after death, miseries of goblinhood, and the means to be adopted to get redemption from that state such as Gayā Śrāddha.

Like other Sthala Purāṇas, this Purāṇa claims all important holy places at Camatkārapura (Vadnagar).

to the west. To the south and north the deity is called Gokarṇeśvara. The holy spot (Kṣetra) has been called Hāṭakeśvara since earlier days, O excellent Brāhmaṇas. This holy spot is famous in the world as destructive of all sins.

Even since that holy spot was gifted to Brāhmaṇas by that noble-souled king, Camatkāra, it become famous after his name.

The Brāhmaṇas said:

7. O son of Sūta, recount to us in detail the greatness of what has been called by you Gayāśiraḥ to the east thereof.

Sūta said:

8-14. Formerly there was a Lord of Haihayas named Vidūratha. He was a master-donor, very efficient and capable of destroying hosts of enemies.

Once that king surrounded by his army went to a forest infested by beasts of prey and overgrown with different kinds of trees and creepers.

He went there for hunting deer. There with his arrows comparable to serpents, he killed hundreds and thousands of deer, buffaloes, boars, hyenas, Śāṁbaras, antelopes, lions, tigers and elephants in their rut.

Then, one of the deer hit by him with an arrow having a crooked point did not fall on the ground. It fled quickly alongwith the arrow (sticking to it). Overwhelmed by curiosity he pursued it riding his excellent horse having the speed of mind or wind.

Leaving his army behind, in his eagerness to capture the deer, the king reached a dreary forest that could inspire fear in any one's mind.

It was full of thorny Badarī shrubs, overgrown with Śālmalī trees as well as other rough and rugged thorny trees.

15-18. There the entire ground was hard and waterless. Full of birds like owls, vultures and Cīrikās (herons)it was utterly dark. There was no shade over the head.

It was the height of summer and the Sun was in the middle of the sky. Fascinated by the deer and riding an excellent horse and armed with a spear, the king covered a long distance. All his followers and servants and their mounts were tired and overwhelmed with hunger and thirst. They took shelter in different places.

Those who fell down unconscious were devoured by the lions, tigers and other animals. Those who were conscious were unable to move.

19-22. The king too was distressed with hunger and thirst. Observing this calamity for himself along with the servants, the king wanted to find the ultimate end of the forest. For that purpose he hit his excellent horse of good breed with the whip.

The horse with the speed of wind carried the king very far away along the impassable path devoid of all animals. Ultimately the galloping horse was utterly weary and it fell on the ground. He too fell down from the horse.

CHAPTER EIGHTEEN

King Vidūratha in a Hermitage

Sūta said:

1-8. The king fell down on the ground utterly overwhelmed with hunger and thirst. He got up and walked on foot further into the forest.

Above in the sky, he saw three *Pretas* (ghosts) of terrible features. Their hairs stood up (erect). Their eyes were red, teeth black and bellies lean.

On seeing them, the king was extremely frightened. Losing all hopes of remaining alive he spoke these words with great difficulty:

"Who are you, O ghosts of hideous features. Beings like this have never been seen by me before,wandering everywhere in the moral world.

I am Vidūratha, a leading king, now excessively afflicted with hunger and thirst. I was eager to capture a deer and have reached this desolate forest."

Thereupon Māṁsāda (Flesh-eater), the senior-most ghost bowed down humbly with palms joined in reverence. He replied:

"O great king, we are ghosts living in this forest in extremely miserable condition due to the defects of our own misdeeds. I am *Māṁsādaka* (Flesh-eater) by name; this second one is *Vidaivata* (Godless) and the third one is *Kṛtaghna* (Ungrateful), the most sinful of all the three."

The king said:

9-11. All embodied persons are named by their parents. What is the reason for your having been named by yourselves ?

On hearing it Māṁsāda said: "O king, these names based on our actions were given by ourselves to designate us. Listen attentively to the several activities which resulted in our ghosthood.

12-17. By birth we are Brāhmaṇas. O king, we were born in the house of a noble-souled Brāhmaṇa Devarāta in the city called Vaidiśā (Vidiśā).

We were atheists breaking all social conventions. We were always enamoured of other men's wives. We were devoid of auspicious rites; we indulged in sinful activities. Due to gluttonousness meat was eaten by me always. Hence my name become fixed as *Māṁsādaka* as based on my activity.

This fellow standing before you,O great king, used to take food always without worshipping the deities. As a result thereof he has acquired this ghosthood. This second great sinner has become notorious by the name *Vidaivata.*

This third fellow has always practised ingratitude. O excellent king, in view of that evil habit, he is called *Kṛtaghna.*

The king said:

18-28. All creatures maintain their existence through food. What constitutes your food, may kindly be told in detail.

Māṁsāda said:

(Food suitable for ghosts)

If a quarrel arises among womenfolk at the time of taking food, ghosts partake of the food there, even if it consists of medicinal herbs or it is consecrated by means of *Mantras.*

O king, if food is taken by men without performance of the Vaiśvadeva rites, or without offering a part of the cooked food, ghosts partake of the food there.

O tiger among kings, if Śrāddha is performed at night or if the rite of Dāna is performed without reference to a *Parva* (festival or ritual) the entire thing becomes food of *Pretas.*

If no regular sweeping is performed in a house, if no plastering or white-washing is carried out, if no auspicious rite is performed or no hospitality is offered, *Pretas* partake of the food there.

If a broken utensil is not abandoned in a house, or if no Vedic chant occurs in a house *Pretas* partaka of the food there.

If Śrāddha is unaccompanied by monetary gifts, if it is bereft of the sacred rites or if (the food) is looked at by women in their monthly course, then that belongs to us, O king.

If Brāhmaṇas invited for Srāddha have deficiency or superfluity of limbs, or if they have kept Vṛṣalīs (Śūdra women) as their mistresses, the Śrāddha belongs to us.

At the advent of Śrāddha hour, if a guest comes but is compelled to go away unhonoured, then that Śrāddha accords satisfaction to Pretas.

Or, why elaborate it? Listen to a brief statement (of the food we get), O king. Our permanent food consists of what you will despise on (mere) hearing. That food which is defiled by hairs, urine, bone, phlegm and other things, that which is touched by persons of low caste, belongs to us.

The king said:

29. O Māṁsāda, even as I ask, do tell me everything in detail. What are those activities that result in ghosthood in the case of men.

Acts Leading to Ghosthood (vv30-39):

Māṁsāda said:

30-39. A man who is petty-minded and indulges in slandering and calumny and is addicted to flesh diet becomes a *Preta.*

A man who takes food without performing the worship of deities and offering libations to Pitṛs and without giving to servants, is born as a *Preta.*

A man enamoured of other man's wives, one who steals other's wealth and one who revels in slandering others becomes a *Preta.*

One who, out of greed for money, gives away his daughter in marriage to an old man, or a base one, an ugly person or one of foul habits becomes a *Preta*

A man who forsakes his righteous wife born of a noble family, modest and polite, brought up in comforts and free from faults, becomes a *Preta*. .

A man who takes away money belonging to a deity, woman and preceptor and does not return it, particularly one who appropriates the assets of a Brāhmaṇa, becomes a *Preta*.

A man who is pleased with the griefs and sufferings of others, an ungrateful wretch, a defiler of preceptor's bed and one who censures Devas and Brāhmaṇas becomes a *Preta*.

A great sinner who begins to put in obstacles when money is being gifted to Brāhmaṇas, becomes a *Preta*.

A Brāhmaṇa may be conversant with all the six Vedāṅgas but if he dies when the food offered by a Śūdra is still in his stomach, becomes a *Preta*.

A man who forsakes duty befitting his family and the native land and follows another avocation out of lust or greed, becomes a *Preta*.

40. Thus, O excellent king, everything has been narrated to you regarding the actions as a result of which a man becomes a *Preta*.

The king said:

41-48. O Māṁsāda, relate to me in detail those activities by doing which a man does not become (averts the possibility of becoming) a *Preta*.

Māṁsāda said:

A man who looks at other men's wives like his own mother, other men's properties like a piece of clod and all the creatures like his own self never becomes a *Preta*.

A man who is always devoted to making gifts of food, who is especially fond of guests and who has adopted the *Vrata* of self-study of the Vedas never becomes a *Preta*.

One who is equally disposed towards an enemy and a friend, who equally views a piece of clod, a stone and a piece of gold one who maintains equanimity when honour or insult is accorded to him, never becomes a *Preta*.

One who encourages persons engaged in making munificent gifts and performing pious actions and those who follow the righteous path, never becomes a *Preta*.

A man who looks after all living beings, even creatures like lice, bugs, flies etc., like his sons never becomes a *Preta*.

A man who always performs the rites of Yajñas, who always likes to go on pilgrimage to Tīrthas and who patiently listens to discourses on scriptural texts never become a *Preta*.

A man who gets tanks, wells and lakes dug, who plants gardens and parks and who makes drinking-water sheds always, never becomes a *Preta*.

49-51. Thus everything kept as great secret has been recounted, O lord of the earth. We have become vexed and fed up with our *Preta* state. Do be our liberator.

Do go to the meritorious Gayāśiras and perform the rites of Śrāddha for all the three of us severally so that the terrible state of being a *Preta* may end with your favour. Otherwise there is no liberation by any means whatsoever unto us.

The king said:

52-61. You have such a bright recollection of previous birth, in the state of a *Preta*! You have the power to move in the firmament! You have sound knowledge of piety and impiety. Then why do you despise it?

Māṁsāda said:

O king, this birth and state of a *Preta* is termed as the ninth divine clan. It has only three good features. All other defects are present in full. These three good features are present only in this *Preta* state: the first is *Jātismṛti* (ability to remember previous birth); the second is *Khecaratva* (ability to move about in the firmament) and the next one is *Dharmādharmaviniścaya* (decisive knowledge of piety and impiety). Thus, O excellent king, the three good feartures in the *Preta* state have been mentioned. I shall mention the defects also. Listen attentively.

O king, if we move away from this forest we shall immediately be hit by unseen *Mudgaras* (iron rods).

Righteous religious rites have been prescribed in the case of human beings, not of *Pretas* or *Devas* or any beings other than human.

O king, we see vast expenses of water when the Sun is in Taurus. Weary and tormented by thirst if we go near those water ponds we are immediately struck by unseen *Mudgara* strokes.

Similarly from far-off we see kitchens and cooking chambers in the houses of householders, full of cooked foodstuffs and delicacies of various kinds. We see also trees with plenty of juicy fruits surrounded by chirping birds. They are extremely splendid and shady. But we do not get the opportunity to resort to them.

62-68. Of what avail is too much talk? Whatever is despicable and irksome comes to us by itself. Our life does not go on without holes (vulnerable things). We have no water, no shade, no cart, no vehicle. For this reason we wander incessantly for seeking holes (vulnerable points) (in others) when night falls, O king, neither at dawn nor during day time.

O king, you seem to praise our ability to move about in the firmament. It is also futile. There is no benefit thereby. Listen to the reason thereof. By means of this ability what righteous action is done for certain? No salvation is achieved thereby. Similarly the ability to remember previous birth and similar powers are also futile. Hence, O king, although these are glorified as good features, they are only defects. By resorting to them, *Pretas* do not achieve any Siddhi. Only grief results from these good features, O king. Due to our associaton with *Pretas*, we are incapable of doing any righteous act.

The king said:

69-73. If ever I go home from this great forest I shall perform the Gayā Śrāddha for all of you undoubtedly.

With my effort I shall redeem all of you from all sins. Even if it becomes necessary, I shall sacrifice myself for this cause. This I promise. Since the doubt in my heart has been removed by you all, I shall help you on return after reaching Gayāśīrṣa.

Māṁsāda said:

Not very far from this place there is a water pond. It is

extremely delightful to the mind. There are plenty of trees there. From there go northwards where those aquatic birds are seen going through the sky in all directions.

Sūta said:

74-82. The great king got up and set off slowly towards the northern direction. He was extremely miserable.

As he proceeded thus in his distress due to hunger and thirst, not far off was seen a blue cluster of trees with cranes, swans and *Madgus* (waterfowl) moving about here and there.

It was as though the king was beckoned by the cool wind wafting from the surface of the pond. He hastened thereafter

Then he saw a charming hermitage resorted to by tame and gentle animals. It was on the banks of a wherlpool and there were ascetics all round.

The trees were in full bloom and laden with fruits. They were seen all round with excellent birds of various kinds chirping sweetly. There he saw the quiescent, excellent sage Jaimini attended upon by groups of ascetics. He was seated beneath a tree eagerly performing auspicious rites. The great king approached the sage and bowed down to him as well as to his disciples. He fell down on the ground in the act of humble prostration.

On seeing that king whom they had not met before, they decided that he should be a king because he had all the characteristics of a king, although his limbs were rendered grey with dust particles like a mountain covered by ashes. As soon as they decided that he was a king they spoke sweet words, with words of blessings preceding them. Their eyes beamed with delight and dismay they experienced.

83-93. "From where have you come to this desolate forest? You are alone and have come on foot. Tender in you limbs, you have become distressed due to fatigue. The signs of a king are seen in plenty in you, but we do not know anything for certain. Do tell us the reason for your coming this way."

The king said with difficulty: "I am tormented by thirst. Give me water. After drinking it I shall tell everything."

They pointed out the water present already near the king. He plunged himself into the water and drank it to his content.

Ripe fruits had fallen beneath the trees. All those sweet fruits were gathered together and eaten by him. Fully satisfied thereby he went near Jaimini. He bowed down again to him as well as to the other sages in due order and sat there.

With palms joined in reverence, he described the details about himself on being asked by all those sages in the height of their surprise and curiosity.

"I am king Vidūratha and Māhiṣmatī is my capital. Desirous of capturing deer I had entered the terrible forest along with my soldiers. Even as I strayed from them all, the men of the army disappeared from view being hidden by thickly grown hedges and bushes. I do not know where they are now.

I was riding a splendid horse equipped with all good characteristics. Unfortunately he has died.

Since I am destined to live more, I have come here in the course of further wanderings. Do tell me, what is this place? How far is my city?"

94-102. Then those sages said: "We do not know of any city. We do not know you, O king, nor your kingdom. We do not know what this place is called. We have nothing to do with kings and emperors nor with kingdoms and cities. We are perpetual wanderers of forest but eager to propitiate Śiva. In order to sustain the body we eat withered leaves, flowers and fruits of trees. We rarely come into contact with men, nor do we converse with them. We do not even look at them. We go elsewhere far away. It is our practice to stay under a tree only for a day or two, lest we should be swayed by a sense of possession for them. Because of you, O great king, we shall pass this night under this tree. At dawn we shall go to another forest. We take pity on you because you are alone, roaming about on foot. You do not have your weapons with you and you are extremely tired. We thought, 'How will this lonely king pass the night in this forest?'and so decided to stay here itself. We shall all stay here together for this night. Getting up in the morning, all of us shall go away."

103-108. Even as they were saying thus, the sun set behind the western mountain. He appeared like a mass of saffron powder. Bowing down to those sages, the king said, "O excellent sages, dusk has set in now. Hence let us all perform the rites to be observed at twilight"

Thereupon all those sages and the king performed the rites of the evening as laid down by the ancients.

Then night arrived—night that was eagerly desired by lovers, lovely women, those considered as near and dear ones particularly by women of ill repute, that is welcomed as an ocean of nectar by owls and considered by Cārvāka birds as a poisonous tree at the same time.

It was the night which is sought by owls, Rākṣasas, thieves, lovers, courtesans etc. eagerly like an excellent shower of rain desired by farmers.

CHAPTER NINETEEN

Greatness of Pitṛkūpikā Tīrtha

Sūta said:

1-6. In the meantime the attendants (those who survived) of that king arrived there after a few had been unfortunately half-swallowed by the beasts of prey. They were extremely distressed due to hunger and thirst. They were extremely miserable. They came to the footpath by which the king had gone.

On seeing the king they said Oh! it is our good fortune; it is our good fortune" and joyously fell at his feet.

They told the great king the miseries the army suffered, as experienced by them, seen personally and also heard by them.

Thereafter all the sages, the king and all his attendants spread leaves beneath the tree on the ground and slept. Even as those noble-souled ones slept soundly the night passed off blissfully.

7-11. Then the king got up early in the morning and duly performed the rites of the forenoon. After bowing down to the sage and repeatedly taking leave of him, he started towards his city Māhiṣmatī along with his attendants proceeding slowly and viewing various things.

They reached the city and the king took rest in his abode for some time. Then he proceeded to the meritorious Gayāśiras. There he took his holy bath, wore clean white clothes. With the mind sanctified by faith, he performed the Śrāddha for Māṁsāda.

While he was a sleep at night, the king saw him in his dream. He had smeared his body with divine unguents and was clad in divine clothes. Divine garlands had been worn and he was seated in an excellent aerial chariot. He was surrounded and eulogized by Kinnaras.

Māṁsāda said:

12-16. O king, with your favour, I have been liberated from the state of *Preta*. Hail unto you! I shall now go to heaven.

Getting up early in the morning, the delighted king performed a befitting Śrāddha for Vidaivata i.e. (with Vidaivata in view). He too appeared before the king in a similar form in dream and after saying similar words (as those by Māṁsāda) went to heaven.

Thereafter on the third day, the king performed as before, the Śrāddha for Kṛtaghna with the mind sanctified by faith. He too came before the king in his dream in the form of *Preta*. He was extremely miserable.

Kṛtaghna said:

17-23. O great king, I have not been blessed with liberation. I had committed many sins. I had stolen cash and spoilt the lake and been ungrateful. Hence, O excellent king, be truthful to your promise. Do something to enable me to attain salvation.

Truth alone is the great Brahman. Truth alone is the greatest penance. Truth alone is the greatest wisdom. Truth alone is the greatest learning. The wind blows in accordance with truth. The Sun blazes in accordance with truth. The ocean does not transgress the boundary in accordance with truth. Resorting to the Tīrthas, performing penance, making gifts by way of Dāna, self-study of the Vedas, service unto the preceptor–all these are futile in the case of one devoid of truthfulness. Formerly out of curiosity Devas put all the Dharmas (pious rites) on one pan in the balance and truth on the other pan and it was found that truth was weightier. Hence redeem me, O highly intelligent one, keeping truthfulness before you. This shall be conducive to the greatest welfare unto you and to your penance.

Vidūratha said:

24. O *Preta,* tell me quickly how your liberation can be effected so that I can do accordingly even if it be very difficult to perform.

The Preta said:

25-32. O king, in the holy shrine Hāṭakeśvara in the city of Camatkāra there is the Tīrtha Gayāśiras covered with dust particles because it is frightened of Kali. Beneath a Plakṣa tree, the place is overgrown with dark-coloured vegetables appearing like Darbha grass. There are many gingelly plants of the wild variety. There are some spaces where Darbhas too grow. Do go there quickly and perform Śrāddha with those *Śākas* (vegetables), gingelly seeds as well as Kuśa grasse. By this my salvation can be brought about.

On hearing the words of the wretched *Preta* the compassionate king went to the place where the Plakṣa tree grew. On seeing the vegetables, gingelly plants and Darbha grass as mentioned (by the *Preta),* the king got that place dug up for the sake of water. A small well was dug thus. Thereafter he brought excellent Brāhmaṇas who had mastered the Vedas and Vedāṅgas and performed the Śrāddha mentioned before with Kṛtaghna in view. No sooner was the Śrāddha performed than a being assuming a divine form spoke to Vidūratha. He was then seated in an excellent aerial chariot: "O Lord, due to your favour, I have been liberated from the terrible state of *Preta.* Hail unto you! I shall now go to the abode of Devas."

Sūta said:

33-37. Ever since then, that Kūpikā (small well) has become well known. The Kūpikā dug up in Gayaśīrṣa is the sustainer of Pitṛs always. One who performs Śrāddha there on a New Moon day, in the Pitṛpakṣa (the dark half of Bhādrapada) with the dark *Śākas,* the wild variety of gingelly plants and well-cut Darbha grass shall be blessed with excellent faith, O leading Brāhmaṇas. He will attain the full benefit from Kṛtaghna Preta Tīrtha. The following groups of Pitṛs are always present there: Agniṣvāttas, Barhiṣads, Ājyapas and Somapas. Hence one should assiduously perform Śrāddha there for the sake of permanent satisfaction of Pitṛs whether the time be proper or otherwise.

CHAPTER TWENTY

Greatness of Bālamaṇḍana Tīrtha[1]

Sūta said:

1-8. O excellent Brāhmaṇas, Rāma, the son of Daśaratha, who had undertaken the vow of exile in forest, was wandering over the earth in the company of Sītā and Lakṣmaṇa.

In the course of his peregrinations, he came to the place where there was Pitṛkūpikā. Weary and distressed with thirst, he sat down on the ground.

In the meantime, O excellent Brāhmaṇas, the Lord of the day came to the mountain of sunset. He appeared like a Japā flower.

After completing the religious rites of the evening, he spread leaves on the ground beneath a Plakṣa tree. There (on them) the scion of the Raghu family had his sleep.

There in his dream, he saw Daśaratha with a very delighted mind. He was eager to speak in affectionate words, as before.

When the day dawned clearly and the solar disc came up, Rāghava summoned some Brāhmaṇas and told them everything (about the dream):

"O Brāhmaṇas, in the course of a dream to-day my father was seen by me wearing white garlands and unguents. He was excessively delighted in his mind and he was eager to speak pleasing words. Therefore, tell me, O excellent Brāhmaṇas, the result of this dream. I have a great curiosity in this respect."

---

1. The legend herein is a glaring example of how in their exaggerated enthusiasm in gloriyfing a particular Tīrtha (here a well called Pitṛ-kūpikā) the Purāṇa-authors get insensitive to the defamation of respectable persons. Here Lakṣmaṇa is shown to have planned Rāma's murder and abduction of Sītā as wife. Any reader of VR knows the great sacrifice made by Lakṣmaṇa for Rāma, who immortalised himself as the ideal of brotherhood.

The Brāhmaṇas said:

9-18. O king, we have heard that Pitṛs who yearn for a Śrāddha or who foresee prosperity appear to their sons.

Gayā Tīrtha is present itself in this Kūpikā. Therefore, your father who yearns for a Śrāddha was seen by you in the dream.

Hence, O excellent one among the descendants of Raghu, do perform the Śrāddha in the prescribed manner. You can perform it with Nīvāra rice, *Śākas* (greens), roots as well as gingelly seeds from plants grown in forest.

Presently the most excellent one among the descendants of Raghu, invited the Brāhmaṇas.

"You may be pleased to grant me your faithful favour in the Śrāddha rites."

They assented saying "So it shall be." The excellent Brāhmaṇas then went for their bath towards their hermitages with very great delight.

When those Brāhmaṇas had gone the most excellent one among the descendants of Raghu said to Lakṣmaṇa who was standing with modesty at his side:

"O son of Sumitrā, fetch greens, roots and fruits quickly for the sake of the Śrāddha. The splendid lady Vaidehī will cook them herself."

On hearing it Lakṣmaṇa went to the forest immediately. He soon brought various kinds of fruits for the sake of the Śrāddha. There were mangoes, embilic myrobalan, *Iṅguda, Cirbhaṭa, Karīra,* Kapittha and many other fruits in plenty.

At the behest of Rāma, the modest lady, the chaste daughter of Janaka, cooked them for the sake of Śrāddha.

19-27. When the appointed *Kutapa* hour arrived the excellent Brāhmaṇas endowed with great devotion of Rāma, came there after duly concluding their routine rites.

In the meantime Sītā stood behind the Plakṣa tree and hid herself. Rāghava could not see her.

He repeatedly called "Sīta, Sītā." Then he thought that she was probably in her monthly period and said to Lakṣmaṇa: "Dear Lakṣmaṇa, it behoves you to attend to the Brāhmaṇas, as required by the Śrāddha rite, for washing their feet etc."

Saying "Yes", Lakṣmaṇa of auspicious characteristics did everything like an efficient woman.

Thus the Śrāddha was duly concluded and the Brāhmaṇas went away. Immediately thereafter the chaste daughter of Janaka appeared.

On seeing Sīta then, Rāghava became furious with reddened eyes. He rebuked her repeatedly in harsh words:

"O sinful woman, tell me where you had gone leaving me far behind at the time of the Śrāddha when the Brāhmaṇas had come. This is not proper on the part of a woman of noble family especially here in forest, to be going about far in the desolate land. Now, O daughter of the king of Mithilā, you deserve to be abandoned."

28-38. On hearing his words, the daughter of Janaka became frightened. Trembling in limbs and faltering in her speech, she said: "O excellent one among the descendants of Raghu, you do not deserve to despise me in this matter. Listen, why I went away from this place. Your father Daśaratha was seen directly by me stationed in the body of a Brāhmaṇa. The grandfather was stationed in the body of a second Brāhmaṇa and the grandfather of the father in the body of a third Brāhmaṇa. Three others on a par with kings were seen in the bodies of three other Brāhmaṇas by me. They were highly delighted. I think that those three were maternal grandfathers evidently. I disappeared due to bashfulness on seeing the assembled fathers in-law. Your father by whom various kinds of sweet foodstuffs to be chewed, sucked, licked etc. were enjoyed before, (I thought,) will not find it proper to eat these bitter and estringent things given (served) by me with my own hands. O Lord, it was for this reason that I disappeared from your presence although the time for Śrāddha had come. I promise that this is the truth."

On hearing this, the lotus-eyed Rāma became highly pleased in his mind. He embraced her frequently and said "Well! Well!" Thereafter in the company of Lakṣmaṇa, Rāma took his food.

In the evening he performed the requisite rites and said to Lakṣmaṇa: "Dear one, spread the leaves on the ground and prepare our bed. Bring good water for washing the feet."

39-48. Then the son of Sumitrā became extremely angry and said to Rāghava: "I will not spread the bed (leaves). Nor will I fetch water for washing the feet, I will not at all do any other bit of work, O Lord. Due to this slavery I have been tormented much. I will leave you and go somewhere. This is the truth I speak. Why don't you ask Sītā to do anything? Even the meanest bit of work, why do you compel me to do?"

Even though his words were foul, the intelligent Rāghava smiled slightly to himself and kept quiet. He got up and arranged his own bed as well as he could. He got his feet kneaded by Sītā and thereafter went to sleep.

With his eyes burning red with anger, Lakṣmaṇa went to the root of a tree farther away and thought thus lying down for sleep:

'Rāghava is asleep. I shall kill him and make Sītā my wife and then go to my abode or to some far-off alien land.'

O Brāhmaṇas, Lakṣmaṇa went on thinking thus and the night rolled by with some difficulty. He did not come to any decision regarding what he proposed to do. Only, he did not get any sleep due to the anger and he heaved hot sighs frequently.

The day dawned clearly. Rāma concluded his rites of the morning and taking Sītā with him went towards the south.

49-58. Lakṣmaṇa fitted an arrow to the well-strung bow and closely followed him watching for a loophole to strike.

Rāghava went to Gokarṇa and bowed down to Maheśvara and set off.

Then the son of Sumitrā came there with the face drooping down due to shame and with the eyes turned turbid due to tears.

He bowed down to Rāma in great sorrow and said: "O Lord, I have been disloyal. Give me the punishment for the same, O excellent one among the descendants of Raghu. I am a big sinner, wicked and ungrateful. I have made antagonistic retorts many times. Without any guilt on your part I thought of the means of killing you."

Thereupon Rāma embraced his brother. With tears drenching his face he said: "Dear brother, I have forgiven you. I know fully well that you have no one dearer than I. Hence come on. Let us go along our path. It may be late."

Lakṣmaṇa said:

O Lord, if you do not execute me now, I will take away my life. I will cast myself into fire for the sake of purifying the soul.

Even as Rāma and Lakṣmaṇa were thus conversing together in the forest, the excellent sage remembered as Mārkaṇḍa, happened to come there. Thereupon Rāma in the company of Sitā and Lakṣmaṇa bowed down to him and said, "Welcome to you, O excellent Sage. Whence do you come now?"

Mārkaṇḍeya said:

59-69. O Raghunandana, I am coming now from Prabhāsa. I shall now go to my hermitage situated here itself in this holy spot. O Rāghava, Great-Grandfather (Brahmā) has been installed by me. His Yātrā (religious festival)which is to be held this day, is remembered as bestowing great welfare. Hence do come with me quickly. From my hermitage you can view Lord Pitāmaha. Thereby, O one foremost among the descendants of Raghu, you shall be unapproachable unto all your enemies.

If the eldest son takes his holy bath with great concentration there on the full-moon day in the month of Jyeṣṭha, he need not be afraid of death.

To-day happens to be the full-moon day in the month of Jyeṣṭha. The constellation too is Jyeṣṭhā. It behoves you to take the bath.

On seeing Rāma who had already started.

Lakṣmaṇa said:

O Lord, execute me first and then go to the Tīrtha.

Rāma said:

Dear Lakṣmaṇa, this tiger among sages being present here, it is not proper on my part to do something by way of punishment. Do request him.

Lakṣmaṇa said:

O holy Sir, give me that expiatory rite which is to be observed when betrayal of master has been perpetrated. Thereby my body shall become purified.

Mārkaṇḍeya said:

There is an excellent Tīrtha named Bālamaṇḍana near my

hermitage. If those who were engaged in treachery towards the master, take their holy bath there, they are liberated from their sins.

O most excellent one among the descendants of Kakutstha, formerly Śakra had killed the foetus of Diti. She was careless as she was his own mother. But he became free from sins by taking the holy bath there

Hence, O highly intelligent one, go there quickly and take your holy plunge. Thereby you will become rid of the sin arising from committing treachery unto the master. Moreover there is no sin in you. You have committed the sin only mentally.

70-81. This is the opinion of learned men that mind becomes purified by repentance. In respect to Rāma, your disloyalty is only mental. From such a sin you are now purified, O Lakṣmaṇa, due to your mental repentance.

Listen to another statement of mine. O sinless one, really you are not at fault. The power of this holy spot excludes fraternalities. O Lakṣmaṇa, there is no brotherly affection in persons staying in the holy spot extending to five Krośas. A man is friendly, a man speaks tender words as long as he does not tread on the holy spot of Camatkāra with his feet. The animals, birds and beasts that live here are utterly devoid of friendliness. They are mutual rivals. No one has any fraternal feeling towards anyone else. Hence it is not your fault. This is the nature of the Kṣetra. Still if any lurking suspicion persists in your mind, go to that excellent Tīrtha and take your holy bath.

It was there that Śakra had become rid of sins after committing the terrible act of treachery in the form of destroying the foetus of Diti who had been confident and careless.

On being told thus, O excellent Brāhmaṇas, the son of Sumitrā became pure through his holy plunge in the Tīrtha that had been resorted to by Śakra.

Rāma too hastened to the excellent hermitage of Mārkaṇḍeya, duly had his holy bath and visited Pitāmaha. Thereafter he went in the southern direction, in the company of Sīta and Lakṣmaṇa.

It was by the power of that holy spot that he could kill great Rākṣasas like Khara and Rāvaṇa, the terrible one, along with Meghanāda(?)[1]

---

1. According to VR Lakṣmaṇa killed Meghanāda.

CHAPTER TWENTYONE

Glory of Bālasakhya Tīrtha

The Brāhmaṇas said:

1. When was Prapitāmaha installed by Mārkaṇḍa there? Tell us where the sage built his hermitage.

Sūta said:

2-8. There was an excellent Brāhmaṇa named Mṛkaṇḍa. He was the greatest among the masters of Vedic knowledge. He was in the Vānaprastha stage of life and lived very near Camatkārapura. He was quiescent and fully observed the restraints. He performed a great penance. Even as he was continuing in the Vānaprastha stage, a splendid son was born to him in that advanced age. He was fully characterized with all the auspicious features. He resembled the full moon in his lustre. The boy was named Mārkaṇḍa by the father himself. In that excellent hermitage, the boy grew up excellently like the moon in the sky in the bright half of a month. Five years passed thus and the boy continued to be interested in child-like plays and games on the lap of his father. After some time a certain scholar came there. He was fully conversant with the Science of Sāmudrika (Physiognomy). He looked at the child from the tip of his nail to the hair on top of the head. With his eyes beaming with wonder, he smiled slightly.

9-17. On seeing the learned man with beaming smile on his face, Mṛkaṇḍa joyously but politely said:

Mṛkaṇḍa said:

How is it, O tiger among Brāhmaṇas, that you were observing my son for a long time; first you appeared to be surprised, then you were smiling. Why?

Sūta said:

On being asked thus by him many times, the excellent Brāhmaṇa disclosed the reason for his smile.

The Brāhmaṇa said:

O excellent sage, on the limbs of this child certain signs are visible which show that the man shall be devoid of old age and death. But, this child will die within six months from this day. There is no doubt about it. The truth has been spoken by me.

After learning this, O excellent Brāhmaṇa, do everything possible for his welfare in this world as well as in the other world, at the bidding of mine in regard to this boy.

After saying this, that leading Brāhmaṇa went away in the direction he wished. Though it was premature, Mṛkaṇḍa thought of something in his mind and performed the rite of *Mauñjīnibandhana*(the rite of tying the girdle of Muñja grass as a part of the sacred thread ceremony) for his son. The sage who knew the reason said to his son the reason thereof: "O son, whomsoever you see, a wandering excellent Brāhmaṇa to be sure, you should politely pay obeisance to him."

18-28. Accordingly the boy continued his Vrata and regularly made obeisance to eminent Brāhmaṇas. There remained only three days to complete the stipulated period of six months. In the meantime the seven sages eagerly desirous of visiting Agni Tīrtha came to the place where Mārkaṇḍa with the Muñja girdle was present. On seeing the sages, the son of the sage bowed down to them. They also severally blessed him saying "Be long-lived". Urged by the fancy for the child-like simplicity of the religious student, the eminent sage Vasiṣṭha said these words: "This child had been (sincerely blessed) by all 'Be long-lived'. But on the third day from to-day he will undoubtedly cast off his life. In that case, O Brāhmaṇas, our statement would be improper. Hence do something whereby he shall really be long-lived." They had mutual consultations. Then the eminent sages said: "Except resorting to Pitāmaha there can be no way longevity. Hence let this boy whose life is nearly extinct be taken there so that he can be long-lived by his (Lord's)words." They took the Brahmacārī immediately to Brahmaloka without depending on the efficacy of the Tīrtha. They then bowed down to the Lord, O Brāhmaṇas, reciting the Vedic hymns. After eulogizing, they sat in his vicinity. After them the boy too bowed down to Pitāmaha. Then boy was told by the Self-born Lord, "Be long-lived".

29-35. Thereafter when all the sages had their rest the

Lotus-born Lord asked them: "Whence have you come now? What for? What should be done unto you now, may be mentioned. You have come to my house. Who is this boy of excellent holy rites?"

The sages said:

In the course of our pilgrimage, we went to the earth, O Pitāmaha, and came to a place near Camatkārapura. O Lord, we were duly bowed down to by this boy there and he was blessed by all one by one, "Be long-lived." But only three days of his life remain. O excellent one among Devas, we became ashamed thereby. Thereafter, we have now come to you, taking the boy with us. The boy was blessed by you too, "Be long-lived". Hence, O Lotus-born Lord, do that whereby we can become truthful along with you. So we have come here.

Sūta said:

36-41. On hearing the words of those sages the Lotus-born Lord took (to him) the boy and said laughingly: "This boy shall be free from old age and death by my blessings. He will undoubtedly become efficient in the Vedic lore. Hence, at the outset, O excellent sages, go to the earth. Take this boy to his abode itself. O excellent Brāhmaṇas, go there before his aged father yearning to see his son, meets with his death along with his virtuous wife." Then all the excellent sages came to the earth and left the boy in Agni Tīrtha in the vicinity of his hermitage. After speaking to him they hastened to the other places for pilgrimage.

42-47. In the meantime the Brāhmaṇa Mṛkaṇḍa, fond of his son, failed to see his son. He became extremely sad and lamented: "Where is my dear son? How is it that he cannot be seen now? Has he fallen into a well? Has he been swallowed by pythons? My little son has made me and his mother distressed by this long journey that he has undertaken. Fate has become adverse in its action. See, O Brāhmaṇa lady, I have committed sins. I am a sinner. I could not see the face of my son who has set off to the abode of Yama. Earlier the learned, noble-souled man had already warned me, 'This son of yours will give up his life in six months.' Now, grief-stricken for the loss of my son, we shall get together in the funeral pyre lest, O lady of excellent countenance, the fire of grief should burn my body."

The Brāhmaṇa lady said:

48-49. Indeed my opinion too is this alone that has been uttered by you. Then, O holy Sir, why do you delay. Fetch the wood so that I can enter the pyre along with you. For us grief-stricken due to the loss of the son that is the only way for quelling the misery.

Sūta said:

50-53. Even as the couple were discussing thus, O excellent Brāhmaṇas, the delighted boy came near them. On seeing him, the Brāhmaṇa and the Brāhmaṇa lady were equally pleased. With tears of joy welling in his eyes he rushed at the child. Embracing him repeatedly the Brāhmaṇa and the lady asked him: "O dear child, where had you gone from the hermitage? Why have you come after such a great delay? Hereafter, O dear son, do not cast us, an old man and his wife, into the ocean of distress. Do not do such a thing again."

Mārkaṇḍeya said:

54-56. O dear father, to-day some sages had come here. Remembering your advice, I made obeisance to them by turns. On seeing me but a child yet one who has undertaken Vratas they were surprised. I was blessed, "Be long-lived" by those surprised, excellent Brāhmaṇas. Thereafter Vasiṣṭha, the sage in their midst, spoke to all those sages laughingly about me.

Vasiṣṭha said:

57-64. O leading sages, this boy who has been told (blessed) by you, "Be long-lived" will meet with his death on the third day.

Thereupon the sages became afraid of being untruthful. Instantly they took me to the place where Brahmā was present. I was blessed, "Be long-lived" by that Lotus-born Lord to whom I bowed down. I was also asked, "From where have you come here?" Then all details were mentioned to him by the sages. They told him (about their predicament) arising from the benediction and said: "Therefore we have come here. O Lord Pitāmaha, it behoves you to do something so that this boy becomes really long-lived with your favour." Then, dear father, I was made free from old age and death by Brahmā and despatched home immediately alongwith them. Those sages have left me here in the vicinity of the hermitage and have gone to the splendid whirlpool for having their holy plunge.

On hearing his words, Mṛkaṇḍa became joyous and he hurried to the place where the sages were present.

65-68. He bowed down to all those sages and stood there with palms joined in deference:

He said:

With your favour, my family has flourished. O excellent-sages, certain preceptors have resorted to good people well-known in all the three worlds and have made this excellent statement: "A sight of good people is meritorious. Good people are like Tīrthas; but a Tīrtha yields its benefit in due course, though contact with good people yields fruits immediately." Hence you all come to my house as my guests. O excellent Brāhmaṇas, may this be mentioned: In what way shall I offer hospitality?

The sages said:

69. O sage, this alone is a crorefold hospitality unto us that your son who was destined to be short-lived has become free from death.

Mṛkaṇḍa said:

70-72. O lords of sages, by saving our son from the clutches of the god of Death the entire family has been saved and redeemed by you all. Expiation has been laid down by great men in the case of a Brāhmaṇa-slayer, imbiber of liquor, thief and violator of vows, but there is no atonement for an ungrateful one. Hence, O leading sages, whatever you all do should be such as averts the sin of ingratitude on my part. There is no doubt about it.

The sages said:

73-80. O excellent Brāhmaṇa, if you agree to do some good thing in return, then, at our instance, make a shrine unto Lord Parameṣṭhin by whom your son has been made free from the eventuality of death. Hence instal Lord Prapitāmaha by the side of the Tīrtha.

Later you along with your son will propitiate him day and night. We too shall worship Lord Pitāmaha along with you. So also shall worship other excellent Brāhmaṇas. Since there had been a *Sakhya* (companionship) with your son here this Tīrtha will become famous by the name *Bālasakhya.* The Tīrtha glorified by others thus shall be conducive to the welfare of children who may be distressed due to ailments or fear at our instance. If people bathe a child distressed due to illness or fear or one afflicted by Planets etc., in this Tīrtha, he will be rid of all defects, O Brāhmaṇa, at our instance and with the favour of Pitāmaha.

O Brāhmaṇa, those men who are endowed with faith and are free from desire and take their holy bath here, will attain the greatest goal.

81-83. After saying this, all those sages of esteemed Vratas took leave of the sage and hurriedly went to another Tīrtha. In the month of Jyeṣṭha when the Moon was in the constellation Jyeṣṭhā, Mṛkaṇḍa and his brilliant son established joyously (an image of) Lord Pitāmaha at that spot. Along with his son endowed with great faith, he propitiated the Lord without lethargy day and night. He thereby attained the greatest goal.

Sūta said:

84-86. Ever since then that Tīrtha, remembered as *Bālasakhya,* sanctified all creatures and destroyed the ailments of children. O Brāhmaṇas, a boy who takes his holy bath there on the Jyeṣṭhā constellation day in the month of Jyeṣṭha never becomes afflicted for the whole year. He becomes immune from the attacks of malefic Planets, spirits, ghosts and particularly Śākinīs. So also from other evil agents.

CHAPTER TWENTYTWO

Greatness of Bālamaṇḍana Tīrtha[1]

The sages said:

1-3. You just now said something regarding the Tīrtha pertaining to Śakra and that in the Tīrtha thereof Lakṣmaṇa was rid of the sin arising from treachery to his master.

How did Śakra originally get himself released from the very same sin arising from treachery to the master. When did it happen, O Sūtaja?

On what account was such a misdeed committed by Mahendra in regard to Diti? Why was the foetus destroyed by him? Say everything in detail.

Sūta said:

4-8. Dakṣa, the patriarch, was born of the right big toe of Brahmā. He begot fifty splendid daughters. He gave ten of them to Dharma and thirteen unto Kaśyapa. Dakṣa then gave twenty-seven of his daughters to Indu (Moon) through the divine rite.

Diti and Aditi two of the wives of Sage Kaśyapa were the important ones, O excellent Brāhmaṇas. They were dearer to him than even his very life always.

He begot of Aditi Devas with Śakra as their leader and of Diti, Daityas of very great power.

For the domination of the realm of the three worlds, a great series of battles ensued between them. There in the battle, Daityas were overthrown by Śakra.

9-12. Thereupon the grief-stricken Diti performed an excellent Vrata for the sake of son. In this very holy place, she observed restraints and regulations with very great concentration.

Then at the end of a thousand years, Maheśvara was pleased with her and said, "I am pleased, request for the desired boon."

1. This Tīrtha absolves a person from the sin of ungratefulness. This is illustrated by the redemption of Indra from the sin of clandestinely entering Diti's womb and cutting up the foetus in forty-nine parts (now known as Marut gods, the allies of Indra). The second instance of Lakṣmaṇa is noted in *suprs* Chapter 20.

She said: "If you are pleased with me, O Moon-crested Lord, then give unto me a son superior to all the Devas in strength. He shall be one partaking of the main shares in Yajña and a destroyer of the arrogance of the Devas. He should not be killed in battle by any of Devas including Vāsava."

"So it shall be", he said and vanished.

13-19. Diti conceived from Kaśyapa, the leading sage. Śakra was frightened on coming to know of the conception of the foetus reported by Nārada, the noble-souled chief of sages.

With an evil intention of destroying the foetus, he attended upon her day and night without lethargy. He was keenly watching for the least of opportunities, but nine months passed off, O Brāhmaṇas, and he did not get at any vulnerable point. Then, when the tenth month arrived and the time of child-birth was imminent, she was once lying asleep in sheer weariness due to the advanced stage of pregnancy. It was the beginning of the night and she was having her head turned in the southern direction.

Śakra was gently pressing her feet and the pleasure thereof lulled her into a deep slumber blissfully unaware of everything else.

On noticing that she was unconscious, Śatakratu left massaging the feet and entered her stomach holding his sharp weapon in his hand. With that the King of Devas split the foetus into seven. He thereupon saw before him seven boys of fullgrown limbs. Thereat he chopped off each of those seven into seven pieces.

20-26. There itself forty-nine children were born. On seeing them growing up, Śatakratu became afraid and came out of the belly quickly without being noticed by Diti.

When the day dawned clearly, Diti gave birth to seven times seven boys. The Thousand-eyed One (Indra) was shrouded in filth of stinking odour. He was lustreless and pallied in the face. Due to shame he stood near her with face looking down.

On seeing Śakra in such a state, agitated in mind due to fear and standing bowing down nearby, Diti asked him tenderly: "O Śakra, why are you so depressed? You have lost all your refulgence? Why does a stinking odour issue from your body? Was any Brāhmaṇa, a child or any preceptor or any woman killed by you, whereby the lustre of your limbs has vanished?

Have you been sprinkled with water from nails or assailed by wind from a winnowing basket? Are you defiled by dust raised by a broom or hoofs of a she-goat?"

Śakra said:

27-29. O well-esteemed lady, this is true? What you said in regard to me is a fact now. At night when you were asleep, I entered your belly and therefore I am a sinner. O fair lady, your foetus was split into forty-nine pieces. Hence so many boys are born of you. I made my exit in sheer fright, O fair lady, without being noticed by you. That was why, O uncensured lady, this loss of lustre.

Diti said:

30-39. O Lord of Devas, since the truth is confessed by you to me, you can choose any boon desired by you from me.

Śakra said:

O fair lady, while being split by me with the sword, these sons of yours were gently prevented by me from crying, "Do not cry repeatedly" (*mā-rudantu*). Hence let them become well-known in all the three worlds by the name 'Maruts.' Let them be devoid of the nature of Daityas. Let them be dear and subservient to me. All of them shall partake of their shares in Yajñas along with me.

Since this Tīrtha was embellished by me with many *Bālakas* (children) of yours it will be famous as *Bālamaṇḍana.*[1]

A pregnant lady who devoutly takes her holy bath here shall have her womb free from damage of any sort. One who drinks the water of this Tīrtha when the time of delivery is imminent, will give birth to a son easily.

Diti said:

O Lord of Devas, Hara was earlier requested by me for your annihilation. "Grant me a son who will exerminate all the Devas",

1. The author is fond of giving popular etymologies e.g. *Bālamaṇḍana* here *Marut* from *Mārud.*

I had said, but that has been cut into forty-nine pieces. Since you have spoken the truth what you say will take place.

Sūta said:

Ever since then they became the Maruts on a par with Devas. They could partake of their shares in Yajñas at the behest of Diti and Śakra.

Thereafter the Thousand-eyed One (Indra) asked Bṛhaspati, the preceptor of Devas: "How will the sin arising from the treachery committed unto the mother perish?"

Bṛhaspati said:

40-48. For the sake of the eradication of the sins, O Devendra, perform a penance here itself at this Tīrtha which is destructive of all sins and where the sin was committed by you. Neither through Yajñas, nor through Dāna nor by resorting to other Tīrthas can the sin arising from treachery unto the mother perish, O Purandara. Thus this Tīrtha of the Mother should be your resort to eradicate this sin.

Sūta said:

Thereafter, O excellent Brāhmaṇas, Sahasrākṣa (Indra) quickly installed a Liṅga named Sahasrākṣeśa. He performed the adoration thrice a day with flowers, incense and unguents as well as with other things of oblation and offering, songs and dances of diverse kinds.

Then at the end of one thousand years Maheśvara became pleased with him and said, "O Śakra, I am the bestower of boons. Request for whatever is desired by you."

Śakra said:

O Slayer of the Three Puras, let my sin arising from the treachery committed into the mother perish and also similar sins of other men who are blessed with faith and worship you with concentration devoutly after taking their holy bath.

Sūta said:

Hara assented, "So it shall be", and vanished. Śakra too, rid of his sins went to the heavenly abode. It was thus that the Tīrtha named Bālamaṇḍana came to be there.

There men become liberated from the sin arising from treachery and disloyalty to the master.

Thus, O excellent Brāhmaṇas, everything connected with the origin of Bālamaṇḍana has been explained to you. Now listen with due veneration to the greatness thereof.

49-56. A person should perform Śrāddha there during the period beginning with the tenth lunar day in the bright half of Āśvina and ending with the fifteenth day. He gets the benefit of the bath in all the Tīrthas. Or, O Brāhmaṇas, by performing the Śrāddha itself one gets the benefit of a horse-sacrifice.

At that time the Thousand-eyed One (Indra) comes down to the earth in order to partake of his shares on the earth offered by human beings.

As long as Śakra stays thus on the earth, O excellent Brāhmaṇas, all the Tīrthas stay in this Tīrtha.

Hence all the devotee should assiduously take their holy bath in the auspicious Tīrtha and worship Śakreśvara.

In this context there are two verses sung by Nārada, the celestial sage. I shall recite them. May the sages listen.

"A man who takes his bath in Bālamaṇḍanaka and visits Śakreśvara during the *Śrāvaṇa Pañcaka* in the month of Āśvina shall be rid of all sins committed ever since birth and till death on the earth. By the power of that Tīrtha this happens. This is the truth, O excellent Brāhmaṇas."

CHAPTER TWENTYTHREE

Greatness of Mṛga Tīrtha

Sūta said:

1. To the west thereof is the excellent Mṛga Tīrtha which is well-known as the most meritorious on the entire earth.

2-3. Men with perfect faith who take their holy bath on the fourteenth lunar day in the bright half of Caitra, when the Sun is in the middle of the sky, are never born as lower creatures even though they are sinful and are defiled by all faults.

4. Even those who are ungrateful, atheists, thieves and transgressors of conventional restrictions and who take their holy bath in the excellent Tīrtha, attain the greatest goal, being seated in an excellent aerial chariot and eulogized by Kinnaras.

The sages said:

5. O Sūtanandana, how did the Mrga Tīrtha originate there? What is its power? Do tell us. We are very eager to know.

Sūta said:

6-12. Formerly it was a great forest full of different kinds of animals and birds and abounding in different kinds of trees. To that forest came excessively terrible hunters armed with bows. They began to roam about here and there. Those dark-complexioned hunters appeared like the messengers of Yama. In the meantime a herd of deer was seen beneath a tree. O excellent Brāhmaṇas, they were taking rest without worry then. But when they saw the hunters from afar they fled from the place soon. The frightened deer afflicted by arrows saw a vast expanse of water nearby and entered it. By the power of the water of the lake, all the deer that entered it were transformed into human beings.

Then the hunters asked the deer (now in the form of human beings): "Just now a herd of deer had come by this way. By which way has it escaped? Tell us quickly."

The men said:

13. We ourselves are those deer that have attained the rare status of human beings, by the power of this Tīrtha. This is the undoubted truth.

14. On hearing this, the hunters were surprised. They soon cast off their bows and arrows and took their holy bath there.

15. Merely on account of this holy bath, they were transformed into excellent kings endowed with divine limbs and having divine garlands and unguents.

The sages said:

16-17. This is extremely wonderful, O Sūta; what has been

narrated by you is surprising. Merely by taking their bath, the hunters attained such wonderful bodies! So also in the case of the deer that have attained human form and features by plunging into the water! How did such a Tīrtha come into existence on the surface of the earth?

Sūta said:

18-21. Earlier it was recounted to you that water issued from the Liṅga when it was pierced. This was entirely overspread with dust particles by Vāyu at the bidding of Śakra. The water then came out through the holes in the anthill. It was only a very little quantity and that too issued forth in the course of a long time.

It was here that King Triśaṅku had his holy bath and eschewed the state of Cāṇḍāla. He regained divine form.

It was for this reason that all the deer and all the hunters became rid of their sins after taking their bath and they attained great form.

CHAPTER TWENTYFOUR

Origin of Viṣṇupadī Tīrtha

Sūta said:

1-4. O excellent Brāhmaṇas, at that auspicious Tīrtha. there is another Tīrtha named Viṣṇupada which is destructive of all sins.

In the course of the southern transit of the Sun, one should adore it with concentration and mental purity. With great faith he should dedicate himself. Even if he were to die in the course of Dakṣiṇāyana, he shall attain the greatest region of Viṣṇu by the power of the Tīrtha, O excellent Brāhmaṇas. There is no doubt about it.

Similarly a person who duly adores in the course of Uttarāyaṇa and dedicates himself duly and devoutly with great concentration, also attains the meritorious region of Viṣṇu and becomes happy.

The Sages said:

5-6. How did the *Pada* (foot, region) of Viṣṇu of unmanifest origin come into existence? How is it that in either Ayana, Ātman is dedicated perfectly there? O Sūtaja, what is the benefit that is obtained by men when it is seen or touched? We are very eager. Describe everything.

Sūta said:

7-17. When Bali was bound by Viṣṇu, the powerful one, the three worlds, including the mobile and immobile beings were covered by the three steps (of his).

The first step was placed on the Hāṭakeśvara Kṣetra. The second step was placed on Maharloka then by the noble-souled one. When the Discus-bearing Lord attempted the third one, O excellent Brāhmaṇas, the whole Cosmic Egg became split up and too small. When the Cosmic Egg became split up by the tip (toe) of the foot, pure water dripped down to the earth, slowly through the tip of the big toe.

The sacred water, clear like crystal, flooded the entire Brahmaloka. Its lustre resembled that of a jasmine flower and the moon. Fishes, tortoises and herds of crocodiles abounded therein. Ever since then she is remembered as Gaṅgā, Viṣṇupadī, in the world. She rendered the spot already sacred, still more sacred. It was thus, that the foot of Viṣṇu came to be present there, O excellent sages. Then Viṣṇupadī is remembered as destructive of all sins.

One who has faith in the river, takes his holy bath in the manner mentioned and touches that foot of Viṣṇu attains the greatest region.

One who has perfect faith, takes his holy bath in the waters of Viṣṇupadī and performs Śrāddha there, shall obtain the benefit of Gayā Śrāddha. A man who gets up early in the morning in the month of Māgha and takes his holy bath there, shall always obtain the benefit of pilgrimage of Prayāga. Or a man who stays here for a whole year with devotion and takes his holy bath there, shall attain liberation.

18-27. Even a man of sinful activities, if his bones are thrown into the water there, attains the greatest goal. Even birds and locusts, animals, worms and beasts that enter her waters distressed with thirst but without devotion, shall be rid of sins. At the time of death, they attain the extremely rare region of the Discus-bearing Lord, which is devoid of death and old age. All the moves in the case of persons endowed with faith who make Dāna to Brāhmaṇas well-versed in the Vedas, O Brāhmaṇas.

There is a Gāthā (traditional song) sung formerly by the great sage Nārada after seeing the power of Viṣṇupadī that is destructive of sins.

"As long as the waters of Viṣṇupadī are present on the earth, of what avail is the observance of *Vratas* and *Niyamas,* the performance of austerities and different kinds of sacrifices!

One man may take the holy bath in all the Tīrthas and another may take his holy bath in the waters of Viṣṇupadī: The benefit of both is the same.

One may gift away all the things to Brāhmaṇas and another may take his holy bath in the water of Viṣṇupadī: The benefit attained by both is the same.

One may perform austerities in the midst of five fires during summer, he may stay beneath the open sky during rainy season and then resort to a waterpond in Hemanta. Another may take his holy bath in the waters of Viṣṇupadī and touch the foot of Viṣṇu. Both of them have been spoken of as excellent persons on a par with each other.

28-31. One may throughout his life observe fast on alternate days and one may take his holy bath in the waters of Viṣṇupadī. Both derive the same benefit.

One man may observe fast of three days (duration) and continue it for a hundred years. One may take his bath in the waters of Viṣṇupadī. Both attain the same benefit."

Sūta said:

Thus, O excellent Brāhmaṇas, Nārada, the excellent sage, spoke (sang the Gāthā) frequently before many sages and then stopped. Hence he who wishes for his own welfare should assiduously take his bath there and touch the foot of Viṣṇu.

The sages said:

32-36. You said that in the course of the two Ayanas the northern and the southern, devotee should dedicate himself to the foot of Viṣṇu. But what is the procedure thereof? O Sūta, mention it quickly along with the Mantras pertaining to it, so that we shall also perform it with devotion.

Sūta said:

In the course of Dakṣiṇa and Uttara Ayana a devotee should worship Viṣṇu's foot and utter this Mantra: "If death overtakes me suddenly within six months, it is your foot (place-Vaikuṇṭha?) that is my refuge. I am your servant."

After saying this, he should worship Hari and then Brāhmaṇas. Then he should take food along with them. Thereby he attains the good goal.

CHAPTER TWENTYFIVE

Greatness of Viṣṇupadī Gaṅgā (Continued)

Sūta said:

1-8. I shall recount to you a miracle that happened earlier due to the greatness of Gaṅgā.

Formerly there was a Brāhmaṇa of esteemed religious rites in Camatkārapura city. He was well-known as Caṇḍaśarman. He was blessed with handsome features and good qualities like liberal-mindedness.

During his youth, he had a passion for courtezans. Though he was a Śrotriya (well-versed in the Vedas), he had been afflicted by the rashness of youth.

Once he got up at mid-night distressed much with thirst. He requested the courtezan, "I wish to drink water."

Mistaking a bowl of liquor for waterpot, she handed it over to him who was already overcome by sleepiness. The moment the liquor got into his mouth he became furious. He repeatedly rebuked the courtezan with words like "Fie upon you" etc.

"What is this? What is this, O sinful woman? A despicable act has been committed by you by pouring the filthy and offensive liquor into my mouth. By imbibing liquor my Brāhmaṇical status has been ruined. Undoubtedly I will have to undergo expiation for regaining the purity of the self."

9-18. After saying this, he sadly left the house. Going to a lonely spot, he lamented piteously.

In the morning, he had bath with the clothes on. O excellent Brāhmaṇas, he had got all the hairs on his body removed and arrived at a place where an assembly of leading Brāhmaṇas was being held. All of them were poring over scriptural texts and the Upaniṣads completely.

He bowed down and said to the excellent Brāhmaṇas loudly, "Mistaking it to be water, I drank liquor. Mete out the punishment to me."

Then they pondered over the scriptural texts repeatedly. Then all those Brāhmaṇas said to him, who was waiting to hear their decision on atonement:

The Brāhmaṇas said:

Whether knowingly or unknowingly, if a Brāhmaṇa drinks liquor he can get purified by drinking clarified butter having the lustre of fire. So if you wish for self-purity, do drink clarified butter (hot) like lustre of fire. The quantity shall be the same as that of the liquor taken in. This shall be conducive to purity

Saying "So it shall be", he took some quantity of ghee and made it hot (so as to be like fire), O excellent Brāhmaṇas.

By that time, his father and mother who had heard the news came there sadly proclaiming. "What is this? What is this, O son." His eyes were filled with tears and the wretched man faltered in his speech choked with tears.

Thereupon he narrated to him all the events of the night and the befitting expiation suggested by the Brāhmaṇas.

19-29. Then that excellent Brāhmaṇa (his father) spoke to all those Brāhmaṇas: "Discuss the scriptural texts and ponder over them repeatedly. Let another means of expiation be offered to my son. On behalf of my son, I shall give everything I possess."

Then, O excellent sages, all those Brāhmaṇas thought over the topics dealt with in the ethical treatises with great deliberation and spoke to him: "In the case of imbibing liquor, there is no other atonement for Brāhmaṇas excepting Mauñjī Homa (Homa with Muñja grass). Therefore do what is proper."

Thereupon, the Brāhmaṇa said to his son: "It does not behove you to do like this. Make liberal gifts to Brāhmaṇas. Undertake pilgrimage. Thereby subjecting yourself to rigorous discipline, you will attain purity in due course through the observance of various Vratas. I am speaking the truth. The atonement suggested by the Brāhmaṇas cannot contribute to the purity."

The son said:

The highly esteemed ones mention Vratas etc. Hence, dear father, Mauñjī Homa should be performed by me undoubtedly. It behoves you to pardon everything done by me due to childishness.

Sūta said:

Seeing the tenacity of the son, the father, fond of his son, became angry. Having resolved to die he gave away everything he possessed. His chaste wife who too had decided to die, gave away the house etc. Looking at her son, she said:

30-37. "If you have any consideration for me and your father, dear son, this Mauñjī Homa should be performed by you after both of us have entered fire."

Then the joyous couple got ready to die and came near the fire. So also their son.

In the meantime, O excellent Brāhmaṇas, the sage named Śāṇḍilya who had mastered the Vedas, came to that place in the course of his pilgrimage.

On hearing the news of what had happened there, he became angry. His eyes became red. Rebuking the Brāhmaṇas repeatedly, he told them thus:

"Alas, you are utterly deluded and foolish! For nothing have these three Brāhmaṇas been compelled to die when there is an easy way of expiation.

May all the Brāhmaṇas as well as this youth who wants expiation, listen to the words uttered by the noble-souled Kātyāyana in this respect: "Cāndrāyaṇa, Kṛcchra, Sāntapana and other expiatory rites are prescribed where there is no Gaṅgā. But, O excellent Brāhmaṇas, there is Viṣṇupadī Gaṅga in that holy spot. Let this youth take his holy bath there. He will attain purity thereby.

38-46. If Mauñjī homa is valid and authorized by the statement of a sage, so also this is the statement of sage Kātyāyana."

Thereat all the Brāhmaṇas were extremely delighted. They said: "Excellent! Excellent! This is true, O sage." Then the excellent Brāhmaṇas wakened (enlightened) the Brāhmaṇa and took him to the place where Viṣṇupadī Gaṅgā was flowing.

There, as soon as the Brāhmaṇa took a mouthful of the Gaṅgā water, he became purified. The entire water came out of the belly, O excellent Brāhmaṇas, and he entered the splendid waters.

At that time a majestic voice arose from the firmament. "Due to a direct contact with Viṣṇupadī the Brāhmaṇa has become pure. The holy bath and the ritualistic sipping of water has rendered him pure. Let him go home."

Then all the Brāhmaṇas including Caṇḍa Śarman went to their respective homes, exclaiming, How fortunate! How fortunate!

Sūta said:

O Brāhmaṇas, this Viṣṇupadī Gaṅgā has such an efficacy and it is situated near the western border of the holy spot. It is destructive of all sins.

Thus everything regarding the greatness of Viṣṇupadī has been narrated to you, O excellent Brāhmaṇas. It is destructive of all sins.

CHAPTER TWENTYSIX

Greatness of Gokarṇa Tīrtha[1]

Sūta said:

1-7. I have already recounted what is between the eastern and western borders. Now I shall recount what is between northern and southern borders.

There is a great city named Mathurā on the earth. It is situated on the banks of Yamunā and many Brāhmaṇas reside there.

There was an excellent Brāhmaṇa well-known as Gokarṇa. He had acquired mastery in the study of the Vedas. He was well-versed in all scriptures.

Another Brāhmaṇa of the same name but of very advanced age also lived in that city. He was also very excellent and a master of all lores.

Some time Yama asked his servant who was hideous and terrible with hairs standing up and whose eyes were red and teeth black: "O messenger, go to the city of Mathurā now. Be quick. There is a Brāhmaṇa named Gokarṇa in that city. Bring him here. At midday today his life span comes to an end. There is another similar Brāhmaṇa there itself; he is of great longevity and so should be left alone.

8-17. The messenger hurried to that city at the bidding of Yama. But due to utter confusion, he brought Gokarṇa of great longevity.

Yama, with rage overpowering his soul, said to the servant: "O sinful one, fie upon you! This man of longevity has been brought here by you. What have you done? Take him back to the same place before his kinsmen burn his body with well-kindled fire on account of their grief."

---

1. This Tīrtha is different from Gokarṇa Mahābaleśvara in Kanara district of Karnatak, Here Gokarṇas are the Brāhmaṇas who got Siddhi at a Tīrtha in the Hāṭakeśvara area. The chapter gives a terrible description of the Narakas (21 according to this Purāṇa). The object is to make people lead a moral life by such deterrence.

The Brāhmaṇa said:

I will not return there. It is my fortune that I have come to your presence. Afflicted by poverty I have always been desiring death.

Yama said:

If any man has yet to live even a minute (lit. wink of the eye) more, I will not fetch him here from the earth. O leading Brāhmaṇa, if anyone's life span is full, I will not leave him too. That is why I am called Dharmarāja. I am equally disposed to all the creatures. I eschew partiality.

Hence, O Brāhmaṇa, go home before the body is burnt by your kinsmen who are grief-stricken. Nor can you stay here now. But, O excellent Brāhmaṇa, request for anything desired in your mind as your boon. No embodied beings should see me unnecessarily (i.e. prematurely).

The Brāhmaṇa said:

O Lord, if it is compulsory (essential) that I should go home, then tell me what I ask for. It shall be my boon. Terribly hideous Narakas are seen where men of sinful activities go. Tell me which of those Narakas are attained by men and what the act is whereby it is attained.

Yama said:

18-28. O Brāhmaṇa, the Narakas are innumerable just like the groups of living beings on the earth. They cannot be completely enumerated even in the course of hundreds of years.

O excellent Brāhmaṇa, I shall enumerate them in accordance with their importance. They are twenty-one in number and have been specially created for sinning folk.

(THE LIST OF HELLS:)

The first Naraka, O excellent Brāhmaṇa, is *Raurava* by name. There creatures are cooked (burned) in pots of boiling oil.

"Alas mother ! O father ! Ah son !" They make very fearful cries, the petty sinners who seek the cooked food of others and misappropriate the money of others.

O leading Brāhmaṇa, the second one (hell) is called *Mahāraurava.* It is resorted to (as punishment) by ungrateful ones and those who defile the preceptor's bed. These sinners cry out utterly distressed by heat. They are roasted in fire and cut into many pieces by means of sharp weapons.

The third Naraka named *Andhatamas* is extremely terrifying. O excellent Brāhmaṇa, I shall tell you who those persons are who go here. Those base men by whom other men's wives were looked at with evil eyes, get their eyes, pricked into by birds with steely beaks.

The fourth Naraka is called by the name *Pratapta.* After undergoing tortures here, they become pure once again. The sinners so destined are those who censure preceptors, gods and saints. Their tongue is uprooted frequently here, even as it comes up again and again.

This is another well-known Naraka, the fifth one named *Vidāraka.* Persons who had been guilty of treachery to friends are cut and pared by means of saw-blades.

29-38. The sixth Naraka is known to all as *Nikumbha.* It is terrifying unto all the people. It is filled with heated sands and fire is perpetually burning here. Those men who had tortured other living beings without any fault of theirs earlier in their lives, are roasted here in heaps of (hot) sand.

The seventh foul Naraka is well-known as *Bībhatsu.* Urine, filth and rubbish abound therein. It is on the whole very despicable. Those men of evil souls who had indulged in calumny of the royal personages are kept here with their mouths filled with rubbish.

O Brāhmaṇa, the eight base Naraka is known all round as *Kutsita.* It is filled with offensive odour of phlegm, urine etc. Those who had taken food without offering it to the preceptors, deities and guests and more particularly to their own servants, are lodged here. O excellent Brāhmaṇa.

The ninth Naraka is named *Durgama.* It is full with sharp thorns and infested with serpents and scorpions. Those people who take food without first offering it to a fellow traveller of the same caravan unit, who shows symptoms of fatigue and languishes with hunger, are lodged in the Naraka.

This tenth Naraka is also known all round by the name *Duḥsaha.* It is surrounded with pillars of heated iron. Those sinners who are attached to the wives of others and are fond of tasty meat dishes are compelled to embrace red hot iron pillars in this Naraka.

39-49. Another Naraka here, the eleventh one, is called by the name *Ākarṣa.* O tiger among Brāhmaṇas, it is full of red-hot tongs and pincers. Those men who had misappropriated the wealth of a woman, a Brāhmaṇa, the preceptor and the deities are dragged here with heated tongs and pincers.

This twelfth Naraka is called *Sandaṁśa.* Base men who had eaten with relish prohibited foodstuffs are munched and crunched here by vultures with steel-like teeth and beaks.

This thirteenth Naraka is very well known as *Niyantraka.* It is fully infested with insects. The bondages here are firm and fixed. Sinners who misappropriate trust properties are kept in bondage here. They are eaten by worms, insects, scorpions etc., O excellent Brāhmaṇa.

The fourteenth Naraka is named *Adhomukha.* It stands topsy-turvy. This is the most terrifying in form among all the Narakas. Those men who kill Brāhmaṇas are kept suspended from branches of trees, with their faces kept down and burned with fire.

This great Naraka, the fifteenth one, named *Bhīṣaṇa* is fully infested with lice, flies, bugs, etc., O excellent Brāhmaṇa. I have allotted this Naraka to men indulging in perjury, false statements and other evil activities.

This sixteenth Naraka is called *Kṣudrada* by name. It is filled with men distressed with hunger all round, O excellent Brāhmaṇa. Those Brāhmaṇas of great sin who had eaten tasty meat-dishes remain here. When distressed with hunger they eat their own body.

50-62. This seventeenth Naraka is remembered by the name *Kṣāra.* It is scattered with *Sukṣāras* (acid particles). It frightens all living beings. Those great sinners who violate their holy vows, heretics, etc. come here. They are crushed and pounded here with sharp weapons.

This eighteenth Naraka is noted by the name *Nidāghaka.* It is filled with burning coals. It is very difficult to be approached in the case of all embodied beings. O Brāhmaṇa, those men who censure and defile scriptural texts, good epics, Brāhmaṇas and virgins are placed under burning coals here.

This nineteenth Naraka is known very well as *Kūṭaśālmali,* O excellent Brāhmaṇa. It is filled with sharp thorns all round. Atheists, breakers of conventional curbs, slayers of Brāhmaṇas—all these men climb up and fall down in this Naraka.

This is the twentieth Naraka, O excellent Brāhmaṇa, named *Asipatravana.* Men of evil souls finds this very difficult to approach and resort to, O excellent Brāhmaṇa. Men who watch for vulnerable points of others, those who are engaged in deceitful actions and those who sell scriptural texts go to this hell.

This twenty-first one is the river named *Vaitaraṇī.* All people should pass through this, whether they are righteous or not. Those men who make gift of a cow when death is imminent, shall easily cross the river by holding her tail. Those who do not gift a cow and die, O excellent Brāhmaṇa, cross this impassable river by means of their hands etc.

Thus, O excellent Brāhmaṇa, everything that you asked me regarding the nature of the Narakas has been recounted to you in detail, out of love for you. Hence do go home quickly before the body is burned by the kinsmen who are distressed with grief. Do take with you whatever wealth you desire.

The Brāhmaṇa said:

63-70. O Lord, if it is decided that I should go back to my abode, then tell me what those acts are whereby a man can avoid going to Naraka.

Yama said:

A man who is always eager to undertake pilgrimage, who worships deities and guests, who is well disposed towards Brāhmaṇas and who deserves to be sought refuge in, can avoid going to Naraka.

One who is always eager to help others, one who is keen in performing Japa, and one who is engrossed in the study of the Vedas can avoid falling into Naraka.

O Brāhmaṇa one who is always engaged in digging wells, tanks and lakes and erects shrines for deities does not see Naraka.

One who offers warmth through fire during winter, one who

offers water during summer and one who offers shelter during rainy season never sees Naraka.

A man who regularly observes holy vows and fasts, whose soul is quiescent (peaceful), who has conquered the sense-organas, who practises celibacy always and one who is constantly engaged in meditation does not go to Naraka.

A man who gifts foodgrains and one who particularly offers gingelly seeds and one who practises non-violence as a rule, does not see Naraka.

One who has done regular study of the Vedas, one who is devoted to the scriptures, one with sweetness of speech and one who always gives religious discourses, does not see Naraka.

The Brāhmaṇa said:

71-80. Even a fool knows that a person regularly doing righteous acts does not fall into a Naraka and one who is engaged in sinful activities does not go to Svarga. Hence tell me how and by what means can a person of unrighteous acts dispell sin with a little effort and thereby attain Svarga.

O excellent one among Suras, tell me that Vrata or Niyama, Tīrtha, Japa or Homa that is contributory to the happiness of all the worlds.

Yama said:

In this context, O excellent Brāhmaṇa, I shall reveal to you a very great secret. At my instance it should be kept confidential always. It is a rite by performing which even a person defiled by great sins, can avert going to Naraka that causes pain.

In the land of Ānarta there is a splendid, auspicious and beautiful holy spot called Hāṭakeśvara which is destructive of great sins. It consists of all the Tīrthas. One who with devotion worships Hara there even for a fortnight, is honoured in Śivaloka even though he may be defiled by all sins.

Hence, go there quickly and propitiate Śaṅkara, whereby you will attain liberation along with ten members (generations?) of your family.

Sūta said

After hearing the advice of Dharmarāja he joyously proceeded towards his abode. By that time the messenger arrived there with the second Gokarṇa. He presented him to Dharmarāja quickly.

81-89. Dharmarāja joyously said to the messenger on seeing the other Gokarṇa: "Since this Brāhmaṇa has been brought here by you after a delay, take him away quickly and leave him there." Thus both the Brāhmaṇas of the name Gokarṇa were simultaneously released.

They assumed their respective bodies and the first Brāhmaṇa Gokarṇa who was benefited by Yama's advice told everything in detail to the second one. Both the Gokarṇas left their homes and visited all holy centres abounding in holy shrines.

On the southern and northern borders two Liṅgas were installed by them. They reached Hāṭakeśvara Kṣetra and soon engaged themselves in penance. After performing the requisite penance and propitiating Śiva, they attained heaven along with their bodies, O excellent Brāhmaṇas.

On the fourteenth day in the dark half of Mārgaśīrṣa, they kept awake. One who devoutly does so, goes to Śiva's abode. One without a son gets sons, one who seeks wealth attains wealth and a man with no desire attains salvation undoubtedly.

Sūta said:

90-98. Thus, O excellent Brāhmaṇas, everything concerned with the border has been narrated to you. The extent of the holy spot in all the four directions has been recounted.

Excellent Brāhmaṇas and men engaged in agricultural activities within the limits of these attain the great goal. In the case of persons of restrained souls, quiescent and self-controlled, persons who have conquered their sense-organs all the more so. Even insects and worms, animals, birds and beasts dying in that holy spot go to the heavenly world undoubtedly. Men who undertake fast unto death have still greater chances of doing so.

Those who have renounced and are endowed with faith in Janārdana in their heart will definitely attain salvation.

Hence with all effort that holy spot should be resorted to especially in Kaliyuga full of sins. All the Tīrthas sanctify through holy baths and Dāna rites but Hāṭakeśvara Kṣetra does so through mere residence there.

A man taking his bath in wells, tanks, lakes etc. and wherever there is water, O Brāhmaṇas, should be rid of all sins.

Of what avail are Yajña, Dāna, Vrata and Japa! It is better that people who desire heaven simply stay there.

This is sacred, conducive to longevity and auspiciousness and destructive of sins of those who listen to the greatness of Hāṭakeśvara Kṣetra.

CHAPTER TWENTYSEVEN

Characteristics of the Four Yugas[1]

The sages said:

1-7. O Sūtaja, do tell us fully the general characteristics of Caturyuga (the group of four Yugas), its greatness and the extent thereof. We are extremely interested in it.

Sūta said

This very same topic was asked by Vāsava from Bṛhaspati. I shall tell you all, O leading Brāhmaṇas, what Bṛhaspati told him.

Formerly Śakra, the noble-souled one, was seated in the assembly along with Devas and Śacī. Suras served him. So also did Gandharvas, Apsarās, Vidyādharas, Guhyakas, Kinnaras, Daityas, Rākṣasas, serpents, (units of time like) Kalās, Kāṣṭhās, Nimeṣas, Constellations, Planets, the Vedas with their ancillaries in their personified form. The holy Tīrthas and sacred shrines also were present there.

They discussed diverse stories of the Devas, Dānavas, Rākṣasas, saintly kings and particularly of old Brāhmaṇa-sages.

---

1. This topic is popular with other Purāṇas also. It describes continuous deterioration of the span of life, living conditions and morals in the course of time. The sinfulness and wretchedness of the people is probably the result of the unsettled condition of India after ancient foreign invasions like those of Greeks, Scythians and Huns.

Curiously enough the description of the Kali age is applicable in toto even today.

In a certain context, the Lord of Devas politely asked Bṛhaspati, the most excellent Brāhmaṇa:

8. "O holy Sir, I wish to hear the extent of the Yugas, their greatness and special characteristics. It behoves you to recount duly."

Bṛhaspati said:

9. I shall expound to you the greatness of the Yugas, their extent and special features Listen attentively.

[*KṚTA YUGA*]

10-18. Kṛta Yuga is said to consist of seventeen lakh twenty-eight thousand years, when Janārdana remains white in colour, and Dharma has all its four feet intact. (Then) the earth is full (in all respects). The people are devoid of lust and anger, fear and hatred. All people are long-lived with quiescent souls and full control over the sense-organs. They are as tall as five Tālas (Palms). They are brilliant and well-informed. Men's childhood extends to sixteen thousand years. Thereafter the youth extends to thirty-two thousand years. It is only thereafter that old age befalls men slowly. The ultimate life span is one lakh years. In certain cases it extends even beyond that. All living beings, animals, birds and beasts speak the divine language. They are not mutually inimical. Serpents sport about alongwith mongooses, cats along with mice, deer with lions, and owls with crows. Even without being cultivated, the earth (though not ploughed) produces much vegetation consisting of cereals, pulses, barleys etc. They are tasty and able to accord strength and nourishment. The trees bear fruits in all the seasons with excellent flowers and fruits, good leaves etc. They are devoid of thorns and they resemble Kalpa trees.

19-29. Cows yield the desired tasty milk at all times. The butter and ghee produced from it is enormous. No woman becomes a widow there, nor an unfortunate wretch. There is no Kākavandhyā (a woman with but one child) there bereft of sons. There is no woman without virtue (all women are virtuous). Birth and death befall men in due order. A father never sees death of his son. People who die do not become ghosts. No one is compelled to stay in Naraka. No one suffers pain due to sickness. All Brāhmaṇas are well-versed in Vedānta. They regularly study their Vedic Mantras. They are delighted in expounding the Vedas and well-versed in the knowledge of Brahman.

Kṣatriyas make one of them the king with great devotion and loyalty. They enjoy the earth righteously following his behests.

Vaiśyas are engaged in the various activities befitting the Vaiśya community such as breeding of cattle, buying and selling of commodities etc.

O most excellent one among Suras, Śūdras are extremely faithful. They do not do anything except service unto Brāhmaṇas and twice-born ones.

No one is base-born there nor is there anyone of mixed caste. No impure one and no one of the fifth caste is to be seen there on the earth.

Men there perform Yajña (Fire-worship), Yājana (Yajña on behalf of others), Dāna, Vrata, Niyama etc. and pilgrimage without any expectations of personal benefit thereof. O Thousand-eyed One, of this sort is the first Yuga named Kṛtayuga that is conducive to the happiness of all the worlds.

[*TRETĀ YUGA*]

30-42. Thereafter the second Yuga named Tretā begins to function. It consists of twelve lakh ninety-six thousand years.

The Lord of the world resorts to Śvetadvīpa. The Garuḍa-emblemed Lord assumes red complexion at that time. Dharma has only three legs intact then. One leg is that of Sin. Thereby mutual rivalry is generated among the people of all Varṇas.

People begin to desire the benefits accruing from pilgrimages. Vrata and Niyama are observed with the motive of residence in heaven etc.

Overpowered by lust all men become deluded. Delusion leads to hatred which induces them to commit sins.

Then, O Lord of Devas, Yama himself devises Raurava and other Narakas which are twenty-one in number.

Base men resort to them in accordance with their Karmas. Others attain the worlds of Mahendra etc., and still others salvation.

There are three types of men: excellent, mediocre and base ones. O King of Suras, they do three types of acts. They are one

Tāla (palm tree) in height. They possess lustre and virility. Vaiśyas are engaged in agricultural activities motivated by their desire for food and foodgrains. They sow seeds only once in field but they reap seven times. The trees bear fruits and flowers in accordance with the seasons. They become very beautiful with the foliage in accordance with the seasons.

Thousands of Agniṣṭoma and other Yajñas are performed by excellent kings and Brāhmaṇas vying with one another in their eagerness to attain the heavenly world. Men desirous of the other world undertake pilgrimage and observe Vrata, Dāna, Niyama, Saṁyama etc.

43-54. There the youth of men extends to one thousand years and old age to about five thousand years.

On account of mixture of castes the following (sub) castes are born: *Rajaka* (washermen), *Carmakāra* (cobbler), *Naṭa* (actor), *Buruḍa, Kaivarta* (fishermen), *Meda, Bhilla, Cāṇḍāla* and *Śūdra* etc., in that Yuga.

There are other inferior people who are more censured than these (above-mentioned castes) but their number is less.

Indra said:

O excellent Brāhmaṇa, how do these base-born ones (castes) originate? Do tell me duly and entirely. My eagerness is great.

Bṛhaspati said:

On account of the defect of the source of origin eight types of mixed castes are born of these, O excellent one among Suras. I shall mention them clearly.

A son of a Kṣatriya born of a Brāhmaṇa's girl (woman) is called Sūta; one a Sūta begets is called Rajaka and one a Rajaka begets is called a Carmakṛt and the one a Carmakāra begets is called Naṭa. Thus these four are born of Kṣatriya in Brāhmaṇa wives.

A son of a Vaiśya born of a Brāhmaṇa girl is Māgadha, O most excellent one among Maruts. A son born of the semen of a Māgadha in a Brāhmaṇa girl is Buruḍa a Buruḍa begets a Kaivarta and a Kaivarta begets a Medaka. These five are born of Vaiśyas in Brāhmaṇa wives. They are despised in all holy rites. A Śūdra begets a Bhilla in a Brāhmaṇa girl, O most excellent one among Suras, and a Bhilla begets a Cāṇḍāla. These two are born of Śūdras in the wife of a Brāhmaṇa caste, O Overlord of all Suras. What I have mentioned is the truth.

Thus I have explained Tretā Yuga, O most excellent one among Suras. Listen attentively to the position of Dvāpara now.

[*DVĀPARA YUGA*]

55-63. That Yuga consists of eight lakh sixtyfour thousand years. There the Garuḍa-emblemed Lord becomes tawny-coloured, Dharma stands on two legs and Sin also stands on two legs.

At the end of a hundred years people become youthful and after lapse of five hundred years old age sets in.

There people, deities and kings are partially truthful and partially untruthful.

Women too are reputed to be so in their features, O excellent one among Suras.

Some come to a height of five Hastas and others four Hastas. They are neither very beautiful nor devoid of beauty.

Beasts, birds, and deer murmur indistinctly.

The trees do not bear too many flowers or fruits, O Lord of Suras. Vegetation is produced on being sown duly by farmers.

The clouds shower adequate rain. All medicinal herbs are grown.

Whatever knowledge or scripture is available, O excellent one among Suras, is of indifferent nature, neither true nor false.

In Dvāpara, O excellent one among Suras, the benefits of the Tīrtha, Dāna and the Makha (sacrifices) are in accordance with the ardour and faith.

Thus the Yuga called Dvāpara has been described to you, O Lord of Suras, as seen and heard by me.

[*KALI YUGA*]

64. Even as I describe further, listen attentively. Kaliyuga is indeed terrible. Janārdana is dark in colour then.

65-66a. Kaliyuga which is avoided by good people consists of four lakh thirty-two thousand years. Dharma stands on a single leg and *Pāpa* stands on three.

66b-67. (In) everything after the first half, sin asserts itself. Sons will not pay heed to fathers nor daughters-in-law nor brothers. Neither servants nor wives will pay heed to their elders. There shall be hatred for one another.

68. In the sixteenth year men turn grey in their youth itself. A girl begins to conceive even in the twelfth year.

69-72. O Lord of Suras, the maximum life expectancy of men is a hundred years. In the case of elephants and trees it is not more than that. Excellent horses live upto thirty-two years; ass and camel upto twenty-four. It is sixteen in the case of goats and twelve in that of dogs. Other quadrupeds live upto twenty-five years. Crows, vultures and owls live for a very long time. So also is the case of sinful persons and those in wretched conditions more particularly.

Trees are hard, thorny and devoid of fruits and flowers. They are resorted to by vultures and they do not give shade.

73. In this Yuga, O excellent one among Suras, Dharma is tormented by Adharma, truth by untruth and kings by thieves perpetually.

74. Preceptors are tormented by disciples and base men by women; masters are troubled by groups of servants and persons of deep learning by fools.

75-77. In Kaliyuga, righteous men, men dedicated to truth, persons of full control over the sense-organs, persons of discretion, quiescent ones and those devoted to the good of others—all these suffer.

Mental anguish, ailments, afflictions of mysterious origin—all are always prevalent in Kaliyuga causing misery to the good. Men become short-lived due to mixture of castes and those who survive are utterly miserable.

78-82. Cloud never showers rain at requisite period. Even if there is heavy rain, there shall not be the production of vegetation as desired by the farmer. Even well-bred cows do not yield ample milk. Even if they are guarded carefully, there is not plenty of cattle wealth.

People begin to relish and praise the milk of sheep and camels. People become lustreless and dirty. Ascetics become Śūdras and Śūdras become experts in Dharma-śāstra. Śūdras begin to discuss the Vedas and endeavour to peform Yajña rites.

Śūdras begin to receive monetary gifts and Śūdras become liberal donors. Śūdras become worthy of honour and Śūdras establish themselves in Tīrthas.

83. At the time of death men of beastly type begin to dig five pits with their head, pair of hands and pair of feet. Out of delusion they lose their consciousness.

84-89. Brāhmaṇas begin to sell the Vedas and are bereft of cleanliness. They give up regular study of the Vedas and always depend upon cooked food from Śūdras. Mostly they take gifts from the non-righteous. They turn into greedy and indiscrimate eaters addicted to tasty foods.

Heretics indulge in misdeeds. They subsist on the bounty of the wives of other men. Friendship develops only on the basis of bussiness dealings (i.e. self-interest). O Thousand-eyed One, it never depends on natural affinity. All the castes of the twice-born ones become barbarous in their tendency.

They lose interest in festivities; they are unrighteous and they cause mixture of castes. In the beginning of the Yuga, men reach the height of three and a half Hastas. From there they diminish in size even as Kali advances. Ultimately men become hole-dwellers.

90. On account of short and non-availability the people are incapable of doing domestic duites. Yajñas and Vedic Vratas are fruitless.

91. *Niyamas* and restraints too as well as the practice of spells and incantations are also ineffective. O Śatakratu, Tīrthas are defiled by the contact of Mlecchas. They lose their intrinsic nature and are also deficient in water.

92-95. Those who practise spells and incantations are despised. Ascetics too are despised. All the men become despised.

They forsake a bridegroom of noble birth and endowed with handsome features and youthful appearance and men offer their daughters to despicable persons due to greed of money.

Girls begin to give birth, virgins are eager to cohabit and virgins carry on intercourse with grown-up men.

Even women of noble families become unfaithful to their husbands. In all activities men of evil deeds are guarded carefully.

96. Ruthless kings will harass farmers. In that Yuga people will afflict undoubtedly blameless ones due to greed for money.

97-98. They will let off even one deserving to be killed, one who is defiled due to greed for money. They will let alone men who continue to harass living beings. They practise war like activities without caring for Kṣātradharma (rules of righteous war).

Bṛhaspati said:

99-101. Thus I have recounted everything connected with the Yugas and their features. O excellent one among Suras, the extent of the four Yugas also has been described. One who recites this always with concentration, is rid of his sins committed ever since his birth till death. One who listens to this with a mind purified by faith, becomes liberated from the sin of the day.

CHAPTER TWENTYEIGHT

The Refuge to All Tīrthas

Sūta said:

1-2. All the excellent Brāhmaṇas who were present in the assembly of gods, Prabhāsa and other Tīrthas in their personified forms heard these words (speech) of the preceptor of gods; it created great fear in their minds. They said to the Lord of Heaven (Indra):

3-7. "O Lord of chiefs of Devas, if the Yuga is to be so inauspicious, we are sure to be doomed. We cannot have any place in any of the three worlds. O Purandara, show us some place or haven of shelter. Whatever it may be, wherever it may be, indicate it clearly to us so that we can stay and pass the terrible Kali days there. The spot should be untouched by Mlecchas (barbarous people). O powerful one among Suras, it may be in Pātāla, heaven or mortal world, but it should be efficacious."

On hearing their words, Śatakratu became compassionate. He spoke again to Bṛhaspati, the most excellent one among Brāhmaṇas:

"O Bṛhaspati, mention a place untouched by Kali in any of the three worlds, if you know it. It should be a place of refuge to the Tīrthas."

8-15. On hearing the words of Śakra, Bṛhaspati thought for a long time and said, delighting the Tīrthas which were frightened:

"There is an excellent holy shrine named Hāṭakeśvara. It has been created by the fall of the penis of the Trident-bearing Lord of the chiefs of gods.

The intelligent Viśvāmitra, the noble-souled one, performed a penance at that Tīrtha, on behalf of king Triśaṅku.

Staying there king Triśaṅku became rid of his sins. He shook off the Cāṇḍāla-hood and went to heaven along with his physical form.

At the bidding of Śakra, the excellent Tīrtha was filled with dust particles by Saṁvartaka, the Raudra (terrible, pertaining to Rudra) wind.

There Lord Hāṭakeśvara guards the lower part and Lord Acaleśvara the upper part in Kali age.

An extent of five Krośa from Acaleśvara is not touched by Kali, due to the greatness of Hāṭakeśvara.

Hence, O Śakra, let all the Tīrthas go there with a part of theirs. Undoubtedly they will have no fear from Kali."

16-18. On hearing his words, all the Tīrthas went instantaneously to the Kṣetra called Hāṭakeśvara, O excellent Brāhmaṇas.

They occupied that Kṣetra creating a spot for themselves to the extent of Yajñopavīta (i.e. 96 *Aṅgulas*).

For this reason that holy spot became most meritorious. It is the Tīrtha of Lord Hāṭakeśvara and is extremely destructive of major sins.

The sages said:

19-21. O Sūta, what has been narrated by you is highly wonderful. You have glorified the confluence of all the Tīrthas in that Tīrtha.

How do those holy spots get so much power? O highly intelligent one, describe all those Tīrthas in detail to us, as regards their names, places occupied and the efficacy, O highly esteemed one. Our curiosity is great indeed.

Sūta said:

22-26. O excellent Brāhmaṇas, the number of the Tīrthas amounts to three and a half crores. They have pervaded the entire area of Hāṭakeśvara Kṣetra and have stabilized themselves.

Even in the course of hundreds of years, it is impossible to describe all of them. In the first Kalpa at the beginning of the Svāyaṁbhuva (Manvantara) all the Tīrthas resorted to that auspicious Tīrtha and took refuge therein. Due to passage of enormous time, O excellent Brāhmaṇas, many of these Tīrthas and holy shrines have been destroyed.

But what I know I shall entirely (alongwith their efficacy) narrate to you. Listen with attention.

O excellent Brāhmaṇas, a man is rid of sins by listening to them, meditating upon them, taking the holy bath therein, touching them and making liberal gifts (at them).

CHAPTER TWENTYNINE

Greatness of Siddheśvara Kṣetra

Sūta said:

1-8. When all the Tīrthas were stabilized thus, O excellent Brāhmaṇas, that holy place attained reputation over the entire earth.

The sages of esteemed holy vows resort to it, which is far away from everything. So also kings in their old age come to it for performing penance.

Similarly, the persons of great control over the sense-organs named 'Liṅgins' (persons wearing Liṅgas of Śiva[1]) who desire Siddhi, resort to that holy spot all round as it is the place of refuge to all Tīrthas.

O excellent Brāhmaṇas, there is a Liṅga named Siddheśvara. It yields Siddhi itself. It bestows all the Siddhis on men.

Śarva, the omnipresent Sadāśiva, became disgusted with the surface of the earth. The Lord stationed himself in this holy spot named Hāṭakeśvara.

Lord Hara himself manifested in the form of a Liṅga. By remembering him or seeing him, one always achieves all Siddhis. He is remembered as Siddheśvara because he was propitiated by

1. This shows that Liṅga-wearing was current among Brāhmaṇas in pre-Basava period.

a Siddha. In order to grant him a boon, Hara stationed himself here. One who visits him with excellent devotion, who remains pure and touches him, immediately attains the desired thing even if it be very rare to be achieved.

9-18. Formerly hundreds of persons have achieved Siddhi there by visiting and touching him. Other men have achieved perfection by making obeisance. If a devotee approaches Dakṣiṇāmūrti and performs the Japa of his six-lettered Mantra (*Oṁ namaḥ sivāya*) with great faith, his longevity increases. A man can prolong his life by as many days as the number of times he repeats the Mantra. There is no doubt in this respect.

The sages said:

O Sūta, what has been said by you, viz. that a man lives beyond the span of life allotted to him, is extremely surprising.

Sūta said:

I shall narrate to you what has been heard by me personally from the noble-souled Vatsa who narrated it.

Formerly, even as I was staying in my father's house, there in front, that sage of great lustre named Vatsa happened to come there.

He was in the prime of his youth. He had the lustre of twelve Suns. He was like another Kāmadeva endowed with comely features and limbs.

When seen by father, he was devoutly saluted by my father. After offering the *Arghya,* he was requested to take rest after which he was politely addressed: "O leading Brāhmaṇa, welcome to you. Where are you coming from? I may kindly be instructed what befitting service I may render."

Vatsa said:

O Sūta, if you are ready to attend upon me I wish to perform the Cāturmāsya rites (for the period of four months of the rainy season) in your hermitage.

Lomaharṣaṇa said:

19-29. O Brāhmaṇa, I shall certainly carry out your behest. I am blessed. I am obliged since you have come to my house, O excellent Brāhmaṇa.

After saying thus to him, my father told me, "Service to Vatsa should always be rendered by you."

Thereupon I humbly continued to do everything for him. During the nights, he used to tell me interesting stories of ancient saintly kings, Devas, Dānavas and Rākṣasas, islands and continents as well as of mountains, all of which he had himself seen.

Once at the close of the narration of these tales, O excellent Brāhmaṇas, I asked that Brāhmaṇa out of my curiosity, with my mind overwhelmed with surprise:

"O holy Sir, your body is tender. You are in the early stage of life, but you are narrating many tales of diverse nature pertaining to different continents. How were you able to visit the whole of the world including the various oceans in the world in this short span of life? Do narrate to me in full detail. It is impossible for ordinary men even to traverse mentally, over the continents, oceans, mountains etc., narrated by you. To be sure, you are a man whose statement is worthy of credence, but the words spoken by you appear to be unbelievable. Curiosity has been created (in me). Hence do tell me the truth.

Is this the result of your penance? Or the power of the Mantras practised by you? How could you, O leading sage, see the entire surface of the earth?

Perhaps it is divine favour or the result of the intake of some medicinal herb. O dear one, it is extremely meritorious. Do describe it in detail."

30-35. Then, O excellent sages, that sage said to me laughingly: "You have truly understood it. This is the power of my practice of Mantras. Always in the presence of Siva, I recite the six-lettered Śivamantra a thousand and eight times. I recite this thrice a day. As a result thereof, O sage, my youth has become permanently stabilized. I have the knowledge of the past and the future. My life has ever-flourishing happiness.

Many thousands of years, hundreds of thousands of years, I have spent thus, O highly esteemed one. Even now it appears as though I am still young.

In this context, O highly intelligent one, I shall explain to you how Siddhi has been achieved by me, due to the favour of Śaṅkara.

I am well-known all over the earth as the Brāhmaṇa named Vatsa. Formerly I was a master of the Vedas and had studied the different scriptural texts.

36-47. In the meanwhile, at the advent of spring season, Menakā, the excellent Apsarā (celestial woman), happened to come to the mortal world. In course of her wandering, she reached the excellent forest named Kāmyaka reverberating with the cooings of inebriate cuckoos. It abounded in charming trees.

It was there that the tiger among sages, remembered as Devarāta, stayed. He was richly endowed with the practice of holy vows and regular study of the Vedas. With regular penance, he had dispelled all sins.

In that longly forest he lived alone, practising the adoration of deities with excessive ardour and faith.

Once he was sitting on the bank of the river. The celestial damsel of excellent complexion was distressed due to the heat of the sun. Even as the sage was watching she disrobed herself revealing her exquisitely divine features and entered the water. On seeing the lady of excellent limbs diving into the watery expanse, instantly the leading sage involuntarily discharged his semen.

In the meantime an extremely thirsty doe came there. The water of the river with which the semen of the sage had got mixed was completely drunk up by her.

By the power of the sage whose semen could never be futile, the doe conceived a human foetus. Thereafter in the tenth month, the doe of brilliant limbs (body) gave birth to a girl with eyes like petals of a lotus. The child was delivered in the same meritorious water in front of the hermitage of Devarāta.

By means of his divine knowledge, the sage came to know that the girl was born of his own semen. With great compassion he took up the child and nursed her lovingly.

He performed all the solemn ceremonies for the child. He took all precautions to protect the child from the beasts of prey in the forest.

He himself went far into the deep forest infested with wild animals and gathered sweet fruits to be given to her.

48-56. Like the digit of the moon in the sky in the bright half of a month, she grew up there and became well known by the name of Mṛgāvatī.

Once while I was wandering, I chanced to see the fawn-eyed girl. Immediately I was struck in the heart by the darts of Kāma.

On enquiry I came to know that the maiden of fascinating smiles was of the same caste as I. Accordingly I eagerly went to the home of the sage and requested him respectfully: 'O holy sir, give unto me this daughter of yours as my wife. I shall look after her offering her requisite garments and food as though she is my very soul.'

Thereupon, the sage readily gave me the beautiful girl in accordance with the injunctions of the scriptural texts. It was on a day when the constellation was Uttarā Phālgunī, the deity whereof is Bhaga.

A few days after the marriage, that lady of pure smiles set out to gather fruits from the forest in the company of her maiden friends.

The forest was overgrown with creepers growing in a cluster. There was a serpent beneath the grass and the unfortunate girl (happened) to tread on the hood of the serpent.

On being bitten by it, she fell suddenly on the ground. The poison was too powerful and the beautiful damsel fell down dead. Her grief-stricken friends came to me and told me everything with tears in their eyes, O Sūta.

57-65. I hastened to the place where that lady (my wife) had fallen down. Seeing her on the ground, I, poor fellow, lamented much crying piteously.

'This lady of large wide eyes is my beloved wife like my own mind and the very vital breath. She is dead and lying down on the bare ground. Being bereft of her, I do not feel inclined to live.

I too shall accompany her to the other world. Of what avail is a life bereft of my beloved? What is the propriety (fruit) of having a life or a home bereft of one's beloved? The abodes of householders my be filled with sons, grandsons, daughters-in-law and a host of domestic servants; but, should they be devoid of the housewife, they do not shine at all.

If this maiden with long eyes extending upto the ears, of a slender body, sweet voice and large buttocks cannot be resuscitated, I will undoubtedly die.'

While I was lamenting thus, O scion of the family of Sūta, all the friends too assembled there. They too lamented in their grief.

We wept for a long time. With their help I arranged for a big pyre and placed her thereon. Fire was then applied to it.

Thereafter they took me with them with difficulty to my house. I was lamenting, faltering and fainting at every step. At the close of the night, I got up and hastened to the same forest. I was so overwhelmed by the grief at the death of my wife.

66-75. I was frantic and mad due to frustrated love. Lamenting grievously I wandered all over the desolate forest blurting out: 'O lady of large eyes, where have you gone? You have left me alone in this lonely, dreary forest. I will not go back home. It mercilessly enhances my grief.'

At the close of the night when the sun's rays at early dawn touch him, the Moon loses his lustre. It appears that like me, he too has been rendered morose and bereft of enthusiasm by adverse fate.

Here comes up the smaller orb of the Sun with red disc. Certainly he is going to bring me some tidings from you. Ere long the Sun will spread all over the sky and scorch me much externally. Kāma is scorching me internally. How am I to sustain my life?

Here comes a lordly elephant bearing the frontal globes on his forehead. They resemble her breasts. I shall go to him and ask him. He may tell something about my beloved.

Even as I lamented thus I fell into a deep swoon having already been distressed by Madana and now severely scorched by the rays of the Sun.

In my infatuation and delusion I began to ask the trees or living beings whichever I met while roaming over the great forest:

'O tusker, take pity on me. Tell me whether you have seen that maiden whose pair of thighs resemble your pestle-like tusk.

O jackal, if my beloved whose lips are on a par with a Bimba fruit is seen by you, do tell me. That will be conducive to your own welfare.

76-85. Or, O Bilva tree, do tell me whether you have seen my dearest beloved with breasts resembling Bilva fruits, wandering in the forest.

O Campaka, my wife of exalted mind has limbs (smooth) like your flowers. If you know anything about her, do tell me quickly.

O Madhūka, the splendid cheeks of my beloved are similar to your flowers. They have somewhat pallid lustre. On seeing you, I recollect her.

It is clear, O stump of plantain tree, that the thighs of the slender-limbed lady are more tender than you. I can aver it on the basis of my own experience.

O deer, have'nt you seen my wife here in this forest? Her collyrium-dyed eyes are like yours.

Even an animal feeding on grass, even if it is too old, even an animal brought up and bred in forest, can not divert itself for a moment, on being abandoned by its mate.

In order to excite the Flower-missiled Lord (god of Love) a being belonging to the class of birds, e.g. a peacock, spreads his plumes in front of his beloved.

This swan seen yonder seems to recollect his mate. His gait is not at all exquisite like that of my beloved.

This bird Cakravāka (ruddy goose) alone is blessed, for he will never leave off its beloved Cakravākikā even for a short while.

A sound is heard now. It causes some tremulous flutter in me. Has it originated from a cuckoo or from my beloved?

86-96. On seeing me this deer goes away and the female deer follows him closely behind. My beloved too used to run about following me like this formerly.

This tusker gently touches with the tip of his trunk his beloved who is following him out of fondness. Thereby he reminds me painfully of my beloved.

Alas my beloved! O fawn-eyed one resembling molten gold in complexion! How is it that you do not take notice of me even as I roam about in the forest?

Where is that former devotion of yours? Where is that love? Where is that deep satisfaction? Where is that compassion? Why don't you reply to me even as I speak to you pleading wretchedly?

Even as I was lamenting thus, all my friends who had been searching for me on the rugged paths of the forest, reached the place. O Sūtanandana, I was furiously rebuked by them with eyes blazing in anger: 'Fie upon you now, O lascivious fellow!' They scolded me thus with harsh words. 'O foolish one, why do you bewail? The life of human beings is not worthy of any bewailing. Others too may be bewailing you even as you go on bewailing thus.

All of us, all of you and all the other living beings on the earth—all are destined to die. Why weep over this?

After being out of your sight, this beloved of yours came to you. Now she has vanished from your sight. She does not belong to you nor do you belong to her. No one has an everlasting contact with anyone. Anyway you lament in vain, even in case of your own physical body; why should it not be futile in the case of others?

If one bewails what is dead or lost, one incurs more misery due to the previous misery. He thus courts two disasters.'

97-98. After admonishing me thus, they took me home from that extremely terrible forest. Staying at home, I constantly remembered my beloved. This kindled in me, O highly intelligent one, a great wrath for serpents.

99. Thereafter in my excess of anger, I solemnly took this vow against serpents. Understand how terrible it was.

100-101. 'From this day onwards if I do not hit with a stick and kill any serpent that comes into my sight, let there be sin befalling me surely: Let mine be the same sin as that of those who misappropriate trust properties and those who betray friends, if I do not kill a serpent that falls within the range of my vision.

102. Let the same sin be mine the sin that befalls one who censures good people or one who slays his own mother, if I do not kill a serpent that falls within the range of my vision.

103. Let me incur the same sin as befalls those who are enamoured of other people's wives or those who slaughter living being's if I do not kill a serpent that falls within my view.

104. Let me get the same sin as those who are engaged in the words of those who administer, poison if I do not kill a serpent that falls within the range of my vision.

105. Let me have the same sin as that of ungrateful persons and those who steal other people's wealth, if I do not kill a serpent that falls within the range of my vision.

106. Let mine be the same sin as that of the people who

manufacture weapons or commit arson, if I do not kill a serpent that falls within the range of my vision.

107. Let mine be the same sin as that which accrues when a vow is broken or a vow is censured, if I do not kill a serpent that falls within the range of my vision.

108. Let me get the same sin as that which accrues when a foetus is destroyed or as that of those who relish eating meat, if I do not kill a serpent that falls within the range of my vision.

109. Let mine be the same sin as of those engaged in felling trees or those manufacturing shafts and darts, if I do not kill a serpent that comes within the range of my vision.

110. Let me incur the same sin as that of heretics and atheists, if I do not kill a serpent that falls within the range of my vision.

111. Let mine be the same sin as that of those who are enamoured of meat and liquor, and that of those who are gluttonous and lascivious, if I do not kill a serpent within my view.

112. Let mine be the same sin as that of those who are engaged in baseless calumny and of those who seek vulnerable points in others, if I do not kill a serpent that falls within the range of my vision.

113. Let mine be the same sin as that of those engaged in giving false evidence and of those who hoard foodgrain, if I do not kill a serpent that falls within the range of my vision.

114. Let mine be the same sin as that of those who are engaged in hunting and spreading nooses and nets, if I do not kill a serpent that falls within the range of my vision.

115. Let mine be the same sin as that of those who subsist on liquor and smuggle the same out, if I do not kill a serpent that falls within the range of my vision.

116. Let mine be the same sin as that of those who have never seen the face of a deity or the Fire god (*Deva-vaktra*) and of those who subsist on fish, if I do not kill a serpent that falls within the range of my vision.

117-118. Let mine be the same sin as that of those who prattle something with partiality in the course of arguments either through fear, or through greed or through hatred or through whimsical desire, if I do not kill a serpent that falls within the range of my vision.

119. Let mine be the same sin as that of those who sell their daughters and associate with sinners, if I do not kill a serpent that falls within the range of my vision.

120. Let me incur the same sin as is cited in the case of those who sell their learning, if I do not kill a serpent that falls within the range of my vision.'

121. Thus I took my vow furiously, O Sūtaja. I armed myself with a big stick for the purpose of killing serpents.

122. Ever since then I began roaming about on the earth with a stick as my weapon. I forsook all Brāhmaṇical ways of life and went in search of serpents.

123. Many serpents were killed by me overwhelmed with wrath. There were highly poisonous serpents, huge pythons, middling ones and low and base ones too.

124. Once, armed with the stick, I came to a dense forest. I saw an old water-snake lying low.

125-128. Angrily I lifted up my stick resembling the staff of the god of Death and was about to strike the snake when it spoke thus: 'O excellent Brāhmaṇa, why do you angrily strike me, an old snake?' Thereupon I angrily told that water-snake as my anger was further aroused by remembering my wife Mṛgāvatī: 'Formerly my beloved wife was killed by a serpent. So, due to my enmity thereof I am destroying all great serpents. Today I shall despatch you also to the abode of the god of Death by striking with this huge stick of mine. So you had better remember what you like the best.'

129-130. Frightened very much the snake said to me further: 'Listen to my words and then do whatever you consider befitting, O Brāhmaṇa.

There are other serpents who bite human beings. But we are water-snakes without poison. Only, we appear like serpents.'

131. Although he spoke thus, I did not hesitate in my mind about killing him, O Sūta. I killed him with the stick.

132. But the moment the stick hit his body, the snake was transformed into a great being resembling twelve Suns in lustre.

133-134. On seeing that wondrous miracle, I was wonder-struck. With due veneration I bowed down to him and said: 'May I be excused. Who may you be? Wherefore had you assumed the serpentine form? Is it due to the curse of any Brāhmaṇa? Or is this one of your usual sports?'

135. Thereupon that man spoke with delight and humility. 'Listen attentively. I shall tell you my previous history.

136-138. O Brāhmaṇa, formerly I was in the excellent city of Camatkārapura. At that time I was in the prime of youth with great radiance. I was quite affluent and endowed with prosperity.

In the same city is a meritorious Śiva temple of Lord Siddheśvara. It is beautifully adorned with banners.

Once there was a great religious festival there. The sounds of the musical instrument to reverberated in the whole of the three worlds.

139-149. In order to view the Lord, hundreds and thousands of sages of esteemed holy vows, had come there. There were Śaivas, Pāśupatas, Kāpālikas; there were devotees of observance of holy vows with great veneration for Śiva.

Some sages were *Ekāhāra* (taking food once a day), *Nirāhāra* (taking in no food, observers of fast), other were *Vāyubhakṣas* (sustaining themselves by taking in air only), *Abbhakṣa* (living on water only), *Phalabhakṣa* (who ate fruits only), *Śīrṇaparṇāśins* (who ate only withered leaves).

After duly worshipping Maheśvara, the Lord of Devas, they sat down in front of the Lord and began the joyous narration of the tales of diverse kinds of ancient saintly kings, Lords of Devas etc.

They discussed the mercifulness, piety etc., of various others as well. Some of the devotees were dancing, some singing, Good men of devout nature were playing on musical instruments. Rich people endowed with faith were munificent in their charitable gifts unto the wretched, the blind and the impoverished ones, especially persons engaged in penance.

While these festivities were going on with great *éclat,* I entered the place along with many other persons in the height of our arrogance.

I was one who hated the very sight of Śiva. I was overwhelmed by the Tamas quality. Some of the other wicked people there, instigated me to create havoc in the course of religious festivity. I seized a very long water-snake with hideous appearance. It was lolling out its tongue frequently, though it was in the stage of old age.

I hurled it into the assembled congregation at which all the people became extremely afraid and they ran helter-skelter out of fear of death.

150-161. At that congregation there was an ascetic of esteemed holy rites, by the name Suprabha. He had the full complement of many excellent disciples. He was reputed as one who had burned all sins by means of his penance.

He was at that time in the state of Samādhi (meditation). His body was steady and firm. Straight and erect, it was neither in a tense state nor in complete relaxation and bent one. The neck was steady. He was looking at the tip of the nose avoiding the glances at any other direction. The steady tip of his tongue was resting in the middle of the palate. The eight-petalled prone-faced lotus of the heart was being steadily gazed at by him viewing the solar disc fixed at the pericarp in the middle thereof. He was also viewing in the course of his mental absorption, Maheśvara, the Lord of Devas, seated in Lotus-posture. The Lord was in human form of the size of the thumb. He was as dazzling as twelve suns blazing together. It was difficult for everyone to imagine his form adequately. It is this deity that the learned call *Akṣara* (imperishable), omnipresent, omniscient, uncensurable, unpierceable and devoid of death and old age. The sage in the Yogic slumber experienced horripilation in all his limbs. He was drenched in tears of joy. Controlling all the functions of all the sense-organs, he retained by means of his steady practice the five internal airs in the position of *Kumbhaka*. He showed the mystic gesture by joining together the thumb and the index-finger placed close to the chest.

While the noble-souled sage was sitting steady like this, the water-snake coiled itself around his body.

His disciple who was well-known as Śrīvardhana, and endowed with great austerity, having assiduously mastered the different scriptural texts, was also present there in the meantime. He saw his preceptor coiled around by the body of the snake. Seeing me not far from the place, he inferred that it was I who did it.

162-163. With the eyes turned red due to anger, he spoke these harsh words. With tears choking his speech and the lips throbbing. He said: 'If excellent penance has always been performed by me along with regular attendance upon my preceptor, if Maheśvara has been meditated upon by me with exclusive concentration, then on the basis of that truth, let this sinful and wicked, base Brāhmaṇa become immediately one with a body similar to that whereby my preceptor has been outraged.'

164. Even as all the people were watching and exclaiming 'Excellent! Excellent!' I immediately became transformed into the awfully hideous form of a serpent.

165. After concluding his meditation, the sage looked at the hideous form of the snake over his own body with full self-control.

166. Then he saw me in great misery in my new form of serpent and the people there standing aloof in great fear.

167-170. The sage then understood everything by means of his mind's eye and was evidently moved with pity. He said to his disciple Śrīvardhana out of tenderness: 'Dear disciple of mine, in doing thus, in cursing this wretched Brāhmaṇa you have not done anything pleasing to me. This is not good on the part of ascetics.

Equanimous towards honour and insult, and treating a clod of earth, a stone and a piece of gold equally as well as looking at a friend and an enemy with equanimity, an ascetic achieves perfection.

Hence, O dear one, It was unwittingly that this Brāhmaṇa has been cursed by you. It was mere childiness. It is my command that doing a favour to him is now due.'

171. Then Śrīvardhana bowed down to his preceptor. He was evidently angry but remained calm and stood with palms joined in reverence. He said:

172-174. 'Whether knowingly or unknowingly, whatever has been uttered by me cannot but be so, to be sure. Hence, O preceptor, it behoves you to be silent. O my preceptor, no lie has been uttered by me even playfully. Why should it then be for your sake? Hence kindly be silent over this.

The sun may rise in the west. The ocean may get dried up. Even Meru may become shattered. But my words cannot be altered.'

175-184. Then the preceptor addressed the disciple in pleasing words: 'I do know that your words cannot be otherwise at all. Even an elderly, mature disciple should be admonished assiduously. Then why not you, a mere young man!

Hence I tell you once again. None among sages wastes the pious merits hoarded previously. They will never have the plight of those bereft of piety and penance.

Forbearance alone has been cited as the bestower of Siddhis, particularly in the case of ascetics. Hence ascetics should always keep forbearance in view in their day-to-day life. One should never be a sinner towards another sinner. This is the eternal wisdom. One who commits sins is doomed due to himself alone. One who commits sinful crimes against another sinner is one bereft of perfect knowledge.

He tries to burn what is already burnt and kills what is already killed. One who retaliates upon a sinner by a sin (sinful act) is bereft of proper knowledge. Doing good to a benefactor is no virtue at all. Only he is glorified as an excellent man by common people who behaves in a good way towards those who illtreat him.'

After saying this to his disciple, sage Suvrata of esteemed holy rites with a feeling of great compassion spoke to me:

'O serpent, the words of my disciple cannot be altered. Hence do wait for some time in the body of serpent.'

The serpent said:

O excellent sage, what is that probable time when this curse on me will come to an end? I am a wretch completely ignorant about the extent of this curse.

Suvrata said:

185-195. O gentle one, it is impossible to reckon adequately the pious merit of that person who makes arrangement for music etc., in a temple of Śiva, even if it be of very short duration.

Similarly no one will be able to calculate the magnitude of the sin of that person who causes obstacles in religious festival even for a short while.

Hence though a Brāhmaṇa, you have become a sinner. You will never attain liberation by association with the occupations of Vaiśyas.

Hence, O evil-minded one, listen to my words. If anyone with ardent faith recites the six-syllabled Mantra of Śiva, his sin arising even from the slaughter of a Brāhmaṇa becomes destroyed.

A man washes off his sin by regular Japa of the six-syllabled Mantra. A sin committed on the day perishes after the Mantra is repeated ten times and that arising in the course of a whole year after the Mantra is repeated twenty times.

So staying under water you should repeat that Mantra with ardour and veneration whereby the sin committed in the course of the previous birth too may perish.

Even as you remain under water, a Brāhmaṇa named Vatsa will angrily strike you with a stick. You will attain release then. Hence, O serpent, hasten to a water pond and go away from this place.

The excellent sage then stopped. I said something pleasing to him. Thereafter I came to this water-reservoir with great sorrow. Ever since then I have been staying here repeating the six-syllabled Mantra everyday, O excellent Brāhmaṇa, I have been liberated due to your favour from the state of serpent.

What shall I do to please you? Do tell me quickly. There is no doubt about it that you are the person named Vatsa who was honourably referred to by Suvrata. See, this aerial chariot has come near me.

196-207. Then the serpent who had assumed a divine form was addressed by me: 'O holy Sir, give me some auspicious instruction whereby the misery caused by the disappearance of my beloved may end. There shall not be wretchedness due to poverty, nor ailment nor discomfiture due to enemies.'

Thereupon that excellent person who appeared to be very enthusiastic said to me again: 'O excellent Brāhmaṇa, a huge burden has been put on me by means of this series of questions and problems mentioned by you.

Since the aerial chariot has already come this cannot be explained in detail. O Brāhmaṇa, I shall therefore mention briefly.

The six-syllabled Mantra of Śiva dispels all inauspiciousness in the case of men. O Brāhmaṇa, that Mantra should be repeated day and night by you according to your capacity. Thereby you will attain undoubtedly whatever you desire mentally, be it heavenly pleasures or salvation.

You shall be rid of all your sins. A great sin was always

committed by me, still prosperous worlds have been obtained due to the greatness of the Mantra.

One may make all munificent gifts with great faith and ardour. Another may repeat the six-syllabled Mantra. The benefit of both of them is the same.

O Brāhmaṇa, a man may take the holy ablution in all the Tīrthas. Another may repeat the six-syllabled Mantra. The benefit of both is the same.

A person may perform Cāndrāyaṇa rites a thousand times in the most befitting manner. Another may repeat the six-syllabled Mantra. The benefit of both is the same.

One man perform penance for a hundred years, lying under the open sky during rainy season, staying in water during winter and standing in the midst of five fires during summer. Another man remaining pure and clean may perform the Japa of the six-syllabled Mantra day and night with faith. The benefit of both is the same.

208-220. One man may always perform Śrāddha in Gayā in the course of Pitṛpakṣa (the fortnight of the Manes i.e. the dark half of Bhādrapada). Another may repeat the six-syllabled Mantra. The benefit of both is the same.

One may make the gift of a thousand cows on the Kārttikī full-moon day in the holy city of Puṣkara. Another may perform Japa of the six-lettered Mantra. The benefit of both is the same.

A man may take his holy bath in Sannihiti Tīrtha when the Sun is in the grip of Rāhu (Solar eclipse). Another man may repeat the six-syllabled Mantra. Both are on a par with each other.

During a lunar eclipse on a Monday a man may visit Lord Somanātha. Another may repeat the six-syllabled Mantra. The benefit of both is the same.

One may visit Caṇḍīśvara in Uttarāyaṇa. Another may repeat the six-syllabled Mantra. The benefit of both is the same.

After visiting Lord Kedāra devoutly one man may perform the rite of Bhṛgupāta (hurling oneself from a precipice to court holy death). Another may perform Japa of the six-syllabled Mantra. The benefit of both is the same.

A person may gift away the entire possession at the outset and then perform self-immolation in the fire of dry cowdung. Another may repeat the six-syllabled Mantra. The benefit of both is the same.

One man may give up his association with everything and gain perfect knowledge. Another may repeat the six-syllabled Mantra. The benefit of both is the same.

O Brāhmaṇa, I have told you this greatest secret. It should not be revealed to an atheist or one devoid of devotion.

Further, O excellent Brāhmaṇa, I shall mention another thing out of consideration for your welfare. If you desire the greatest goal, you must carry out my instruction.

Abstention from injury to others is the greatest piety. It has been glorified in all the Vedas. Particularly it concerns a Brāhmaṇa. Hence give up killing serpents.

A ruthless one who attacks non-violent timid beings, falls into awful Naraka and remains there untill the annihilation of the entire universe.

One who accords succour from fear to all the beings, mobile and immobile, shall be happy always enjoying all pleasures here and in heaven.

221-230. There is no other Lord on a par with Bharga (Śiva); there is no river on a par with Gaṅgā. There is no sin like violent injury to others. There is no greater virtue than compassion.

On hearing his utterance I spoke to him: 'One who is distressed due to the fear of the other world accepts the virtue characterised by non-violence.

A statement of elders has been heard by me that a king does not incur any sin by killing a deer and other animals in forest.

Physicians who are masters of the science of medicine aver thus: Those who eat meat become well-developed and they live long.

Hence, in this matter, tell me what is the highest good. Whatever issues out of your mouth shall be faithfully carried out by me.'

Then he further told me, 'O excellent Brāhmaṇa, do not say so. This is the opinion of sinners who are never good and who are gluttonously covetous of meat.

These wicked souls without compassion, are deluded ones worthy of our pity. They are foolish enough to relish meat, the source of all defects.

Meat cannot be said to be the course of longevity, health or strength. This is not true to fact. Listen to an example.

Even meat-eaters are found distressed due to illness. They are also lean and weak as well as short-lived. Understand this and eschew meat from afar.

Many of those who abstain from meat in the world are seen free from illness, long-lived and stout-limbed. So one should avoid eating meat.

231-241. One who eats the meat of those living beings who yearn to live, falls into a hideous Naraka. Staying there, he is eaten by those very animals.

Meat does not originate from grass, wood or stone. Only when a living being is killed can there be meat. Hence one should avoid it.

This is an excellent instance for avoiding meat. Even one's limb pricked by a thorn is withdrawn immediately. Hence the cases of all living beings should be viewed on the basis of one's own reaction.

Learned ones should views themselves, and living beings alike. They should not be injured. They should be protected with all one's strength.

The following eight are *Ghātakas* (killers): (1) one who actually kills; (2) one who permits or abets (killing); (3) one who pares and rinds; (4) one who buys; (5) one who sells; (6) one who cooks and seasons it; (7) one who offers it, and (8) one who eats it.

Again slaughter is of three kinds: (1) one who buys it kills it by paying the price; (2) one who eats kills it by eating; and (3) one who slays it does it so by binding and striking.

One who does not injure any one physically, mentally or verbally, attains the greatest place devoid of old age and death.

One who invariably takes in vegetables, roots and fruits and maintains the vow of celibacy, attains the greatest place, If a man is devoted to violence, he does not get the benefit.

One man may perform a very severe penance for more than a hundred years. Another is compassionate and strictly follows the vow of non-violence. Of these two the compassionate one is better.

If a man is fully endowed with excellent compassion, he undoubtedly obtains whatever he desires even if it be a rarest thing.

One who offers freedom from fear to all living beings, goes to heaven by means of an aerial chariot that can go wherever he wishes to go. Surrounded by hundreds of celestial damsels, he rejoices like a Deva.'

242-253. O Sūtaja, after saying thus, that noble-souled one got into the excellent aerial chariot and went to heaven even as I stood watching.

It was due to the greatness of the six-syllabled Mantra. Gandharvas sang in praise of him and Kinnaras eulogised him.

When he went away to heaven, misery overtook me on remembering the serpents killed by me earlier. All my limbs were shattered to pieces as it were.

Afraid of my own Karmas, I began to lament in the great forest: 'Alas, I have been wicked! Many living beings were killed by me. Even Lord Mahādeva was censured by me. Surely I will become distressed in Naraka.

So, I shall abstain from violence, and perform great penance. Adopting Śiva Dīkṣā, I shall worship Maheśvara.

Whatever happiness men may covet and pray for in all the worlds, can be achieved through penance. Hence I shall perform penance.

I shall roam about in these hermitages. I shall silently go on begging for alms. I shall go alone and take shelter under trees everyday for this purpose.

I may be covered with dust particles. I will resort to empty houses or I may have the roots of trees as my abode. I shall eschew everything pleasing or otherwise.'

After lamenting thus, O scion of the family of Sūta, I assiduously adopted the vow of Śiva Dīkṣā with great devotion.

Thrice a day I perform Japa of the six-syllabled Mantra ten thousand times in the vicinity of Siddheśvara.

O Sūtaja, by its power, I have attained the steadiness of the prime of youth, knowledge of the other world and ability to move about in the sky.

254-259. At the close of Dvāpara I will go to Siddheśvara Sadāśiva. This is the truth that I say.

Thus O Sūtaja, everything that accords salvation, the greatness of the six-syllabled Mantra that is destructive of all sins, has been narrated to you.

A man who listen to this always, with perfect faith, shall be rid of all sins. Acquired in the course of the life from birth to death.

O highly esteemed one, you too should repeat this Mantra always. You will obtain all desires cherished in the mind.

Sūta said:

This greatness of the six-syllabled Mantra that has been expounded to you was heard by me from my preceptor.

It is conducive to affluence, renown and longevity. It can bring about destruction of enemies. It accords all desires and freedom from fear to those who read and listen.

CHAPTER THIRTY

Manifestation of Siddheśvara

The sages said:

1. By which of Siddhas was Lord Siddheśvara propitiated there? O Sūtanandana, describe all this in detail to us.

Sūta said:

2-5. Formerly there was a Lord of Siddhas by the name Haṁsa. He was without any child for a long time.

Worried on account of this, he went to Bṛhaspati, the great Brāhmaṇa, the priest of Devas and son of Aṅgiras, and asked him: "O holy Sir, I am issue-less and old age has overtaken me. Hence do tell me a means whereby I can have progeny. Be it pilgrimage to a holy place, a holy vow or a Śāntika rite (expiatory observance), O excellent Brāhmaṇa. O Bṛhaspati, with your favour let there be the birth of a child soon."

6-7. Bṛhaspati meditated for a long time and told the Siddha thereafter. "Go to the holy spot Camatkārapura to perform a penance there. Thereby you will get a good son, splendid and capable of redeeming the race. O Lord of Siddhas, I do not see any other means of acquisition of a son that will be conducive to auspiciousness."

8. Then that Siddha endowed with great faith arrived at that holy spot and worshipped the Liṅga himself in accordance with the prescribed manner.

9. Without any lethargy, he propitiated day and night, offering oblations, adoration and presents, singing songs and playing on musical instruments.

10. O excellent Brāhmaṇas, he propitiated Śaṅkara by observing Kṛcchra Cāndrāyaṇa, Parāka and monthly fasts.

11. After two thousand years, he (Śiva) manifested himself to him as seated on the bull along with Umā and he spoke:

12. "O Haṁsa, I am now pleased with you. So, request for anything desired by you. Certainly I shall grant you even what is very difficult to acquire."

Haṁsa said:

13-14. O Lord, O most excellent one among Suras, for a long time this propitiation was undertaken by me for the sake of a child. Hence, do grant me sons capable of redeeming the family. Further, at my request and for the sake of the welfare of all the worlds, you should undoubtedly be present in this Liṅga.

Śrībhagavān (The holy Lord) said:

15-17. As per your request there shall be my presence in this Liṅga from now onwards, O Lord of Siddhas. What has been said by me is true. I will grant every benefit cherished in the heart by a man who devoutly worships me who am present herein. If the devotee sits on the southern side of my Liṅga and repeats the six-syllabled Mantra, I shall grant him longevity besides sons.

18. After saying this Mahādeva vanished from that place. Haṁsa went home and begot sons.

19-20. Hence, O Brāhmaṇas, that Liṅga should be sought after with great effort, touched, worshipped and assidiously bowed down to. It should be glorified by means of the six-syllabled Mantra repeated within one's capacity, by those who wish fulfilment of their cherished desires, very rare even in the case of Devas.

CHAPTER THIRTYONE

Greatness of Nāga Hrada[1]

Sūta said:

1-3. Similarly there is another excellent place Nāga Tīrtha there. One who takes his holy bath there, need not be afraid of serpents anywhere.

If a man takes his holy bath on the fifth lunar day in the dark half of the month of Śrāvaṇa, none in his family need be afraid of any serpent anywhere.

It was there that penance was performed by Śeṣa and other serpents afflicted by the curse of their mother for the sake of escaping from being burnt in fire.

4. Kaṁbala and Aśvatara, two serpents well-known on the earth, performed severe penance there and attained great Siddhi.

5-6. The following nine are the leaders of serpents referred to as Śeṣa and others. They are (1) Śeṣa, (2) Ananta, (3) Vāsuki, (4) the powerful Takṣaka, (6) Maṇikaṇṭha, (7) Airāvata, (8) Śaṅkha, and (9) the highly poisonous Puṇḍarīka.

7. These had their sons and grandsons. The entire surface of the earth is pervaded by their innumerable, unlimited wealth.

8. These crooked and wicked serpents used to torment people with the sheer multiplicity of their numbers, by their very touch. They ate people for no fault of theirs.

9-10. Thereupon all the subjects sought refuge in Brahmā: "O most excellent one among Sūras, we are all harassed. Save us immediately from these serpents lest the entire surface of the earth should become a void on being fully occupied by all these terrible and extremely poisonous serpents."

11-13. Thereupon, Brahmā spoke to these nine leading Nāgas beginning with Śeṣa: "These subjects are being eaten. Save them from your progeny." All those serpents promised: "It shall be so"

1. The story of Astika's birth from a Nāga woman, his successful intervention and stopping of the *Sarpa-Satra* (Sacrifice of serpents) of king Janamejaya is given in details in Mbh, *Ādi.* Chs. 13-58 (*Astika Parva*). The story is adopted here to glorify Nāga Hrada at Hāṭakeśvara.

and went away. There was no effective security due to the sheer numerousness of these Nāgas. Though restrained, they continued destruction of the subjects.

14-17. Brahmā became enraged. He called all the heads of the different families of Nāgas and the Devas. "Since these serpents devour the subjects for no fault of theirs, despite being restrained by me, I shall chastise them now. A king named Janamejaya shall be born on the earth. In his sacrifice Fire-god will consume those serpents. Due to the curse of their mother and particularly being dragged by excellent Brāhmaṇas through their Mantras, they will themselves fall into the well-kindled fire."

18. On hearing it, the nine leaders of serpents began to tremble. With palms joined in reverence they immediately bowed down and spoke to Pītāmaha:

19. "O holy Sir, our tribe was made crooked by you. Then why do you get angry when they follow their innate predilection?"

Brahmā said:

20. Granting that you were naturally made by me very poisonous indeed, why do you bite and eat these subjects without any offence on their part?

The Nāgas said:

21. O Lord of the Devas, make the line of demarcation between us and the human beings. Or do grant us a spot devoid of human beings.

22. Even as they get burned by the fire in the sacrifice of the son of Parīkṣit do ponder over some means of saving them.

23. It behoves you to do something, O Prapitāmaha, that will avert the total extinction our progeny in all the worlds.

Brahmā said:

24. Somewhere a Brāhmaṇa is to be born who will become famous by the name Jaratkāru. He will be in search of a wife all over the earth for the sake of progeny.

25. In your family a splendid girl called Jarat Kanyā will be born. That girl of excellent complexion should be given to him (in marriage).

26. The son born to both of them will save the remaining serpents of excellent conduct strictly adhering to the bounds of decency.

27. There are three nether worlds: Sutala, Nitala and Vitala. Your residence shall be in the fourth nether world beneath these.

28. Hence leave off the earth and go to that world of great charm full with all pleasures.

29. At my bidding go there quickly and enjoy all good pleasures in the company of sons and grandsons, the pleasures very difficult for Devas too to acquire.

The Nāgas said:

30. O Lotus-born Lord, we will not be able to stay there enjoying the pleasures . Hence do show us some spot on the earth. We shall stay there keeping up our restrained, elegant association with human beings.

Brahmā said:

31. This lunar date of Pañcamī (fifth) has been allotted to you on the earth. The other period has to be passed by you in Rasātala (Nether World).

32. When you go there, men devoid of defects should not be killed by you; as also those whose limbs have been safeguarded through Mantras and those who have faith in (i.e. use) medicinal herbs.

33. O excellent Nāgas, a permanent residence in the holy spot of Camatkārapura on the earth has been granted by me to prominent serpents of all the serpent races.

Sūta said:

34. On being told thus by Brahmā, the serpents immediately went to the Nether World. The prominent serpents of all the races established themselves at that holy spot.

35. A man who worships them on the fifth lunar day in the month of Śrāvaṇa attains everything desired due to their favour.

36. There shall be no fear of serpents in his family. There shall be no sin, on ailment, no natural calamity, nor the fear of evil spirits in his family.

37. A man without a son who performs Śrāddha there with a desire for son, will beget an excellent son, and become free. from indebtedness to the ancestors.

38-39a. A barren woman who takes her holy bath on the fifth day particularly in the dark half of Śrāvaṇa, soon begets a son capable of redeeming his race.

The son shall be free from all ailments, full of humility and handsome in features.

39b-40. A man ousted from his kingdom, who takes his holy bath there and worships Nāgas on the fifth day in the month of Śrāvaṇa, will be able to kill the hosts of his enemies and regain his kingdom.

41-42. Those who die due to serpent-bite cannot be rid of ghosthood unless and until Śrāddha is performed in that holy Tīrtha, O excellent Brāhmaṇas. Hence Śrāddha should be performed in that holy spot of serpents, with all efforts on behalf of one who die of a serpent bite.

[*Story of Indrasena*]

43. In this context I shall narrate unto you a splendid story regarding what happened formerly to a saintly king, Indrasena. The story is destructive of all sins.

44-45. Formerly there was a king named Indrasena who subdued the arrogance of his enemies. That noble-souled one had performed a thousand horse-sacrifices.

Once, by chance, he was lying on his splendid couch when he was bitten by a serpent which left him off immediately. King Indrasena was suddenly deprived of his life.

46. Thereafter, his beloved son performed all obsequies on his behalf with great devotion, as per injuctions in the Smṛtis.

47. He immersed the bones in Gaṅgā and performed sixteen Śrāddhas. Then he went to Gayā and performed the Śrāddha with great faith.

48. The king, his father, appeared in dream. In great sorrow, he spoke to his son whose eyes were turbid due to tears:

49-52. "Dear son, I have attained the state of a Preta (a ghost) due to the fact that I died of serpent bite. Therefore nothing offered by you has come within my reach. Hence do go to the holy spot of Camatkārapura immediately. There, dear son, on my behalf perform Śrāddha unto the serpents. Thereby I shall be rid of the terrible state of a Preta (ghosthood)."

He got up in the morning and remembered the words of the king in the form of a Preta. Distressed due to misery, he hastened to that Tīrtha. He then performed the Śrāddha on the fifth lunar day in the month of Śrāvaṇa.

53-58. With great faith, he took his holy bath after having given assignment to a priest. Again the king, distressed with misery in the form of Preta, appeared to him as on the previous occasion and spoke these words: "O dear son, nothing that was offered by you on my behalf in the form of the benefit of the Śrāddha has been received by me. Listen to the reason thereof. All the Brāhmaṇas hailing from Camatkārapura are worthy of the performance of Śrāddha. Persons of mutilated limbs etc., who are despised (and so excluded from) Śrāddha elsewhere, are not so (excluded) in the case of holy rite or Vrata or Dāna performed here. So also, in the case of other Brāhmaṇical rites such as Yajña etc. Though incomplete, these rites shall be perfect by their words. Those fully performed without their konwledge or presence may become manifestly futile. Hence summon Brāhmaṇas from this city and then perform the Śrāddha in my name, so that liberation can be ensured."

59. He (the prince) got up in the morning. Remembering the words of his father, he was overwhelmed with grief and entered the excellent city.

60. He went in search of deserving Brāhmaṇas for the rite of Śrāddha. In spite of his effort, he did not come across one because all the Brāhmaṇas were rich and affluent.

61. No one was distressed there. No one was impoverished and miserable there. No one was engaged in unholy activities. Nor was there anyone engaged in heresy.

62. Recitation of the Vedic passages was the pastime of the people in different places. They discussed the Smṛti topics. There were tumultuous festivities in every house.

63. The performers of Yajña rites were diligent and their utterances in the course of their rites could be heard everywhere. There was no trace of famine or ailment anywhere. Premature death was not heard at all. In fact in that city resorted to by the Brāhmaṇas, there was no death at all.

64. Clouds showered rains in the proper seasons. The

production of vegetation was superb. Cows yielded plenty of milk. Goats and sheep too produced good supply of milk.

65. The king requested some Brāhmaṇas to become the priests in his Śrāddha only to be rebuked angrily with harsh words. That was the case with everyone, he requested for.

66-67. "Fie upon you, O base Kṣatriya of sinful activities! Does any Brāhmaṇa partake of the food in a Śrāddha here and that too in one concerning a Preta? Hence go away from here before some Brāhmaṇa curses you or even kills you angrily, because you happen to be an obstacle in the path to heaven."

Sūta said:

68. Thereupon the king became distressed, frightened and excessively ashamed. He went out of that city of Camatkārapura.

69. The eminent king recollected that former state of his father and began to ponder: 'What shall I do? Where shall I go? How will my father attain liberation?'

70. Then he sent away all his ministers back home. Alone he stayed there in the same excellent city in the form of a mendicant.

71-72. He got the information that there was a Brāhmaṇa of esteemed holy vows named Devaśarman in that city there. Among all the leading Brāhmaṇas, he was the most endowed with civility. He was affectionate towards those who sought refuge in him. He had mastered the four Vedas and maintained the sacrificial fires. He strictly followed the path enjoined by the Smṛtis.

73. He got up very early in the morning and assumed the guise of a base-born labourer. With very great difficulty, he cleaned the part of the house where the toilet was situated.

74. The sweeper who regularly carried out the task of removal of faeces there, came there, with eyes reddened with anger and said:

75. "Wherefrom have you come with the intention of depriving me of my means of sustenance? Go away quickly."

76. In spite of the other man's protests, the king forcibly continued the task of cleaning the toilet of Devaśarman.

77. O excellent Brāhmaṇas, this went on for a year, at the end of which the Cāṇḍāla bowed down to the Brāhmaṇa from a distance and spoke to him at an opportune moment.

78. "O master, I am the regular sweeper of rubbish of your house. That work belongs to us. Then why is another one employed therein?"

79. On hearing his words, the excellent Brāhmaṇa said: "No other person has been directed by me to do this job reserved for slaves. The right thereof is yours. You carry on as before."

80. The next day, the Cāṇḍāla came there in excessive fury, armed with a weapon to kill the king.

81-82. On seeing him with the weapon lifted up in his hand with the intention of striking, the king playfully hit him on the head repeatedly with his fist. O Brāhmaṇas, his eyes were dislodged immediately. Much blood flowed down and he fell down dead.

83. On hearing that his servant, the Cāṇḍāla, was killed by him, Devaśarman arrived at the spot in great anger for chastising him.

84. With the help of his sons, grandsons and other kinsmen, he struck him with clods of clay and rebuked him frequently.

85. On being struck thus by repeated blows he was shattered and rendered disabled. Thereupon, he displayed his sacred thread and recited Vedic Mantras.

86. On seeing him engaged in the recitation of Vedic Mantras, all those Brāhmaṇas with Devaśarman at their head, became surprised.

87-89. He was asked: "How incongruous is this! Here is a job befitting only the base-born and there is the Vedic recital with clarity of tone and sweetness of voice! Could it be that you are an excellent Brāhmaṇa fallen through some curse? That may be the reason whereby you do this menial job despised even by base ones?"

Thereupon he laughingly said: "I am a Kṣatriya and a king well-known as Viṣṇusena hailing from the family of the Haihayas. It was for the purpose of propitiating the Lord that I came to this holy spot. A year has now been completed since I have been doing this work."

Sūta said:

90. On hearing his words, the Brāhmaṇa became very compassionate. Respectfully joining together his palms, he spoke

to the king:

91-92. "What is that purpose for which this despicable, menial job was performed by you? Do mention it so that I can fulfil your desire. O king, there is nothing inaccessible to me or impossible for me to accomplish. Hence I shall carry out what you wish to do even if it be very difficult to perform."

The king said:

93-94. My father was bitten by a serpent. He has attained the state of a *Preta*. If a Śrāddha is performed here in this Nāgahrada, he may attain salvation. Hence, in order to redeem him, kindly perform the duty of a presiding Brāhmaṇa priest. It is for this sake that this despicable, menial job was done by me.

Devaśarman said:

95. Do so, O excellent king. I shall myself officiate as the Brāhmaṇa priest in the Śrāddha of your father. So, perform the Śrāddha.

Sūta said:

96-97. Thereat, his friends, sons, grandsons and kinsmen said: "It is not proper for you to partake of the food in the despised Śrāddha. So, in case you eat in the Śrāddha, all of us and other excellent Brāhmaṇas as well, will leave you (excommunicate you)."

Devaśarman said:

98. Well! You as well as other Brāhmaṇas may leave me. I have promised to partake of the food in the Śrāddha of this king.

99. After saying thus, the leading Brāhmaṇa accompanied him to the Nāgahrada and partook of the food in the Śrāddha.

100. Immediately after he had partaken of the food, an unembodied voice said, delighting the king and making the entire world reverberate.

101. "Dear son, I have been rid of the state of *Preta*, by your effort. Hail unto you! I shall now go to heaven."

102-104. After concluding the rite, the delighted king bowed down to the excellent Brāhmaṇa and said: "Kindly do as I tell you, O excellent Brāhmaṇa. There is a city on the banks of Narmadā named Māhiṣmatī. O holy Sir, that is our hereditary capital city. I shall grant it to you, O Brāhmaṇa, along with the entire realm. I shall be your servant. Stay there, and do administer the kingdom free from all obstacles."

Devaśarman said:

105. This is not proper to say. No Brāhmaṇa is capable of ruling a kingdom. So, go back to your realm and rule.

Sūta said:

106. Being sent away thus by him, the king went back to his land with great delight, O excellent Brāhmaṇas. He considered himself blessed with his task fulfilled.

107. Devaśarmā was, of course, excommunicated by all the Brāhmaṇas of the city. He was an outcaste (according to them) in view of the defect inherent in that (kind of) Śrāddha.

108. Thereupon, he (Devaśarmā) built his abode at the Nāga Hrada. Remaining pure and clean, he engaged himself in self-study of the Vedas.

109. O excellent Brāhmaṇas! All the sons and the progeny of that Brāhmaṇa who had been excommunicated but continued to stay there were called *Bāhya-vāsins* (who stay outside the city).

110. Thus the greatness of Nāga Hrada has been entirely narrated to you, O excellent Brāhmaṇas. It is destructive of all sins.

111. If a person reads with great ardour or listens to this on a fifth lunar day. There shall be no fear arising from serpents in his family.

112. Similarly, O Brāhmaṇas, he shall undoubtedly get rid of sins arising out of indiscriminate intake of food unknowingly done. What I say is the truth.

113. Hence the excellent greatness of Nāga Hrada should be read and listened to assiduously by persons with due mental concentration.

114. A Brāhmaṇa who reads this at the time of Śrāddha obtains the complete benefit arising from Gayā Śrāddha.

115-117. Many defects have been mentioned in regard to Śrāddhas arising from the materials used, defects in the observance of holy vows and the Brāhmaṇas officiating therein. All these defects perish when the greatness of Nāgahrada is glorified by persons of great concentration and mental purity, during the Śrāddha. Similarly those who have been killed by cows, Brāhmaṇas or beasts of prey, attain the greatest goal when this is read in the course of a Śrāddha.

CHAPTER THIRTYTWO

Greatness of the Hermitage of Seven Sages

Sūta said:

1-3. There is one other place, O excellent Brāhmaṇas, in that auspicious holy region. It is the well-known hermitage of the seven sages. It fulfills all cherished desires.

One who takes his holy bath there on the full-moon day in the month of Śrāvaṇa with mental purity and concentration, shall obtain his desired object.

One who performs Śrāddha there with roots, fruits bulbous roots and greens, obtains the full benefit of Rājasūya and Aśvamedha Yajñas.

4-5. O leading Brāhmaṇas, a person should worship with ardour those sages on the fifth lunar day in the bright half of the month of Bhādrapada with flowers, incense and unguents in the following way. He should worship them in the due order: Oṁ obeisance to Atri; Oṁ obeisance to Vasiṣṭha; Oṁ obeisance to Kaśyapa; Oṁ obeisance to Bharadvāja; Oṁ obeisance to Gautama; Oṁ obeisance to Kauśika; Oṁ obeisance to Jamadagni; Oṁ obeisance to Arundhatī.

The Mantra for the worship:

"May the sages, the bestowers of all desires, whose bodies are sanctified by Gaṅgā and who are holding the garland of beads for doing Japa accept the *Argha* (materials of worship) offered by me."

The sages said:

6. At what time was that Tīrtha established by the seven sages? O Sūtaja, narrate it in detail. We are very eager.

Sūta said:

7. Formerly there was a great drought in the world extending to twelve years. All vegetations were destroyed. All the people were distressed due to that destruction.

8. People were reduced to mere skeletons. They lacked interest in everything. All pious rites, holy vows and religious activities were forsaken by them. They began to eat and drink all forbidden things.

9-10. Mothers abandoned their sons, men their wives and rich men dismissed their servants. What to say regarding other hangers-on? *Agnihotras* were set aside by Brāhmaṇas and even by those who sponsored Yajñas. O Brāhmaṇas, Vratas were discontinued by those who had regularly observed vows, even by the oldest among them and by those who had control over their sense-organs.

11. Wherever any shoot or sprout was seen somehow springing up, it was immediately seized and taken away by shameless men emaciated by hunger.

12. When there was a great dearth of foodstuffs and the whole surface of the earth was afflicted, the seven sages who were overwhelmed with hunger began to wander here and there.

13. They were: Atri, Vasiṣṭha, Kaśyapa of great penance, Bharadvāja, Gautama of esteemed holy Vratas, Kauśika, Jamadagni and the chaste lady Arundhatī (wife of Vasiṣṭha).

14. Caṇḍā was the female attendant for all of them and Paśuvaktra endowed with humility was the male servant.

15. Hungry and emaciated much, the sages came to the realm of King Vṛṣadarbhi of a country named Ānarta.

16. For the sake of alms, they wandered there from house to house, O excellent Brāhmaṇas, but did not get even a morsel of food.

17. A dead body of a boy was seen by them lying on the ground. They consulted one another and afterwards took it up for eating.

18. Overwhelmed with hunger, they began to cook it on fire. Presently King Vṛṣadarbhi who happened to hear about their act, came there.

Vṛṣadarbhi said:

19-20. O excellent sages, why is this despicable act done? Eating human flesh is a practice of Rākṣasas. I shall give you vegetables, cereals, barley grains and even villages. At my instance, do abandon this dead boy.

The sages said:

21. An expiatory rite has been laid down for the sin of eating human flesh but, O king, none for the sin of accepting a gift from a king even in emergency.

22. We shall perform a penance later on and destroy the sin arising from eating human flesh. Therefore we shall eat this.

Vṛṣadarbhi said:

23. Acceptance of gifts has been cited as uncensured means of sustenance for Brāhmaṇas. Hence it should be accepted by you all. You need not hesitate in this respect.

The sages said:

24. Accepting a gift from a king is a terrible thing. It is like poison. O king, it should be avoided by Brāhmaṇas, especially by those who are wise and learned.

25. A *Cakrin* (slanderer, informer) is on a par with ten *sūnās* (injury and killing involved in daily work such as grinding stone, broom-stick etc.). A *Dhvajin* (vendor of spirituous liquor) is on a par with ten informers and a *Veśyā* (prostitute) is on a par with ten vendors of liquor). A king is on a par with ten *Veśyās.*

26. (Acceptance of a) gift from a king is on a par with ten thousand Śūnās. Who will accept such a gift like a greedy Brāhmaṇa?

27. He (such a Brāhmaṇa) is cooked in all hells beginning with Raurava. Hence, O king, go home welfare unto you for ever.

28-29. We will go elsewhere. We will not accept your monetary gift.

After saying thus, all those sages of esteemed holy rites left the king as well as the dead boy. They went away in the direction of the holy place of Camatkārapura.

30. On being rebuked by them, the king became enraged, O excellent Brāhmaṇas. He did something to test them.

31. He filled some Udumbara fruits (of holy fig-tree) with gold pieces and scattered them on the ground on their path.

Sūta said:

32. The sages saw the Udumbara fruits fallen on the ground and took them up because they were distressed due to hunger.

33. Naturally the excellent sages found them too heavy. Atri broke one fruit and on seeing the gold pieces said:

Atri said:

34-35. O sages, we are neither ignorant nor too worried over household matters to take these Udumbara fruits after realizing that they contained gold. We shall cast away these Udumbara fruits filled with gold and go away. We are free from desires.

36. (On the one hand) There is a king wielding sovereignty (all over the world) and (on the other hand) there is a person free from desires. In any case the person without desires is always more fortunate between the two.

37. In the case of Brāhmaṇas amassing of wealth even for pious activities, is censured. Better to avoid mud from afar, than to wash it later.

38. If one avoids all hoardings, all tormenting worries disappear. No one possessing all wealth is seen free from worries.

39. In my opinion, if a sensible man weighs poverty and kingly possession in a balance, poverty becomes weightier.

Kaśyapa said:

40. O sage, collection of wealth is itself a disaster. One deluded in the mind due to prosperity and affluence becomes deprived of welfare.

41. Richness and affluence is conducive to delusion. Delusion is conducive to Naraka. Hence one who seeks lasting welfare should avoid filthy lucre.

42. Virtue achieved through wealth is well-known as transitory. What is achieved through penance is conducive to salvation. This is my opinion.

Bharadvāja said:

43. As one grows old, the hairs get decayed and fall off; the teeth grow shaky and fall off. So also the eyes and ears of a man. But thirst (covetousness) alone remains ever young.

44. Just as a needle puts a thread through cloth by means of its eye, so also the Ātman stitches the Cosmic thread through desire.

45. Just as a horn (of an animal) grows as the body grows up, so also, thirst (greed) increases as the riches grow.

46. Thirst (greed) is unlimited, difficult to be fulfilled and it involves hundreds of misdeeds. Hence one should eschew it.

Gautama said:

47. By whom can a man of contentment be agitated, even if he is deprived of the fruit? O Brāhmaṇas, all ordinary persons get involved in difficulties due to the cravings of the sense-organs.

48. To a man whose mind is contented there are riches everywhere. If one has protected one's feet with shoes, one will find the whole ground covered with leather.

49. Men of quiescent mind, pleased with the nectar of contentment have great happiness. How can people covetous of wealth who run about here and there, get that happiness?

50. Discontent is the greatest misery and contentment is the greatest happiness. Hence a person seeking happiness should always be contented.

Viśvāmitra said:

51. One may eagerly seek the fulfilment of one wish. If that wish is realized, another one of the same sort immediately arises in men.

52. Never does any passionate person feel contented with thousands of wishes fulfilled. His desires become increased just as a fire blazes when offerings of clarified butter are made.

53. A man cherishing more and more desires, out of delusion, never attains happiness, like a Kapiñjala bird (small Cātaka or Ṭiṭṭiri) that resorts to the shade of a tree on which vulture has its abode (nest).

54. A person viewing a piece of stone and a lump of gold as equals is more blessed and contented than a king who always enjoys the earth encircled by oceans.

Jamadagni said:

55. A base Brāhmaṇa who feels delighted after obtaining wealth, although it is something to be regretted, is a dullwitted person who pretending to be fearless does not see Naraka.

56. Persons who deserve gifts but who abstain from receiving them, will attain those regions which the donors themselves attain.

Arunddhatī said:

57. Just as many lotus-fibres occupy the stalk of a lotus, similarly beginningless and endless covetousness occupies the body of beings.

58. Happiness belongs to a person who eschews covetousness that is very difficult to forego for persons of wicked mind—covetousness that never fades away even if a person gets old and that is a veritable ailment ending only with the end of the life.

Caṇḍā said:

59. My Lords are afraid of wealth as though of serpents. Hence especially why should I have fear from it.

Paśumukha said:

60. A wise man who desires his own welfare should follow that which learned men devoted to piety adopt and practise.

Sūta said:

61. After saying this, all those sages of steady resolve

abandoned those fruits with gold pieces stuffed in and went away.

62. They entered the holy place of Camatkārapura thereafter. They saw a sage Śunomukha (Dog-faced) who arrived there accidentally.

63. Accompanying him they reached another forest region. They saw a charming lake too, beautified with lotuses.

64. Overwhelmed with great hunger, they collected a lot of lotus-stalks, placed them on the banks of the lake and took their holy plunge.

65. They emerged from the water and met together once again. Unable to see the lotus-stalks they spoke these words:

The sages said:

66. Who is that ruthless soul by whom all the lotus-stalks belonging to us have been taken away from this place?

67. Suspecting one another those sages of esteemed holy vows pledged their words awfully to clear themselves.

Kaśyapa said:

68. May the stealer of the lotus-stalks be an indiscriminate eater of all sorts of things always or one who misappropriates the deposit kept in trust or let him practises perjury.

69. May the stealer of the lotus-fibres be a hypocrite in the practice of piety; may he be a servile attendant of a king and may he always eat meat and drink liquor.

Vasiṣṭha said:

70. May the stealer of the lotus-stalks be one who indulges in sexual intercourse outside the period enjoined after the days of menstruation, or during the day time or during Parvan days. Let him be a mutual guest with another.

Bharadvāja said:

71. May the stealer of the lotus-stalks incur the sin of that person who, after getting instruction in the scriptural texts from a preceptor, does not give the prescribed fee.

72. May the thief of the lotus-stalks be a ruthless and wicked person; may he be one arrogant due to prosperity all round;

may he be inimically jealous; and may he be a slanderer.

Viśvāmitra said:

73. May the stealer of the lotus-stalks be one who enjoys by himself delicious dishes, or who indulges in boasting about himself or a person who sells the Vedic text.

Jamadagni said:

74. May the stealer of the lotus-stalks be one who gives a girl in marriage to an old man, who becomes the paramour of a Śūdra woman, or one who maintains himself by usary always.

Gautama said:

75. May the stealer of the lotus-stalks be one who accepts the gift of an ewe, one who sells horses or one who censures the preceptor.

Atri said:

76. May the stealer of the lotus-stalks be an evil-minded person who always insults his father and mother or one who consults a Śūdra in religious matters.

77. May the stealer of the lotus-stalks be one who incurs the sin of not making the gift of cows etc., to a Brāhmaṇa after having promised the same before.

Arundhatī said:

78. May the woman who steals the lotus-stalks be on a par with that woman of evil conduct who takes food or goes to bed before her husband.

Caṇḍā said:

79. May the woman who steals the lotus-stalks be on a par with a woman engaged in hating good people and pious activities as well as being antagonistic to her lord and master.

Paśumukha said:

80. May the man who steals the lotus-stalks be on a par with

a sinful man engaged in hating good people and acting treacherously against his master.

Śunomukha said:

81. May the stealer of the lotus-stalks be one who tells the truth always, who recites the Vedas properly and a householder who likes his guests.

The sages said:

82. The way in which you pledged the words is what is actually desired by the twice-born. Hence it is certain that the theft of our lotus-stalks is committed by you.

Śunomukha said:

83-84. O Brāhmaṇas, your lotus-stalks have been taken by me because I wanted to listen to the statement about Dharma. Know ye all that I am Purandara (Indra), O excellent Brāhmaṇas. I am indeed much pleased with the absence of covetousness in you all. Hence, all of you be pleased to accompany me to heaven quickly.

The sages said:

85-86. We are inclined towards the path of salvation. We are not enamoured of heavenly pleasures. So, we are going to perform penance here at this lake for the purpose of liberation. We are among those excellent sages who undertake pilgrimage all over the earth bounded by the oceans. Sustaining ourselves by means of lotus-stalks. Hence do go. Let this association do good to you.

Śakra said:

87. O sages of excellent vows, viewing me shall never be fruitless. Hence accept a boon whatever has been cherished in the heart for a long time by you.

The sages said:

88-89. O Śakra, may this hermitage be well-known on the

entire earth after our name. May it be the destroyer of all sins of men. O most excellent one among Suras, we shall stay here only for ever for the sake of penance. We shall maintain the purity of the soul. We shall be here until the achievement of salvation becomes certain.

Indra said:

90. Your hermitage will become well-known in all the three worlds. It shall fulfill the desires of all the people.

91. Whoever performs a Śrāddha here on the Full-Moon day in the month of Śrāvaṇa with any desire in the heart, shall surely attain it entirely.

92. A man devoid of any desire who performs Śrāddha or Dāna rite shall undoubtedly attain salvation.

93. Those who cast off their bodies in this splendid hermitage of yours will attain the greatest goal even if they are sinners.

94-95. One who performs Śrāddha with mental concentration and purity using Iṅgudas, Badaras, Bilvas and Bhallātakas (cashewnuts) with ancestors in view will attain the greatest goal inaccessible even to Devas. He shall be rid of all sins and be eulogized by Kinnaras.

Sūta said:

96. Saying thus the Thousand-eyed One vanished after being duly commended by them. Those excellent Brāhmaṇas stayed there itself.

97. In due course of time, by performing great and severe penance, they attained the greatest region bereft of old age and death.

98. The Liṅga of the Trident-bearing Lord of Devas was installed by them there. Merely by viewing it, a man is rid sins.

99. O excellent Brāhmaṇas, one who adores that Liṅga with devotion and offers flowers, incense and unguent shall certainly attain salvation.

100. This description of the hermitage of the Seven Sages is sacred, conducive to long life, and destructive of all sins. It has been duly narrated.

CHAPTER THIRTYTHREE

Greatness of Agastya's Hermitage

Sūta said:

1-4. There is another hermitage there, O excellent Brāhmaṇas, that of Agastya.[1] It is there that Lord Maheśvara himself, the immanent soul of the universe, abides.

On the fourteenth lunar day in the bright half of the month of Caitra, Sun-god himself comes there and worships Śaṅkara, the Lord of Devas. Hence anyone else who comes there and adores devoutly Śaṅkara on that day, goes to the place of the Lord.

If any one duly performs Śrāddha with ardour and faith, the Pitṛs become pleased with him as when Pitṛmedha is performed.

The sages said:

5. Why does Sun-god come to the hermitage of Agastya and perform the rite of circumambulation? Narrate this in detail to us.

Sūta said:

6. I shall narrate this story. Listen, O excellent Brāhmaṇas. There is a mountain on the earth well-known as Vindhya.

7. The rays of the Sun falling on the tops of the trees on this mountain are taken to be a mass of flowers by the confused Siddhaka, stationed beneath it.

8. Even during the nights of the dark half of the month, the inhabitants of the ridges of this mountain are never aware of darkness as it is dispelled by the lustre of the jewels.

9. When the trees drop down flowers on its ridges as the gusts of wind blow, they appear like clouds pouring down a flood of waters.

10. The different kinds of deer and other animals run about

1. This story is based on Mbh, *Vana,* chs. 101-105. Mbh does not mention Camatkārapura. But the Purāṇa author locates Agastya's hermitage here for the glorification of this place. Mbh, *Vana,* 87.20 locates the Āsrama near Nasik (Maharashtra).

here and there on that mountain and they appear like men covetously inclined to bring up and nurture their wives and children.

11. With their barks scratched off by the tusks of elephants, the trees there appear to shed tears under the pretext of the exudation that rendered all the quarters fragrant.

12. Other trees on its ridges are thought as though they are wailing through the cries of the crickets, when they are hit by trunks of elephants.

13. The mountain shone like a man adorned with white cloths etc., as it was sprayed by the waters of rivulets, flowing here and there in different directions.

14. Formerly a rivalry arose between it and Sumeru mountain. Hence Vindhya became highly enraged. He went to the Sun-god and said:

15. "O Bhāskara, why do you circumambulate Meru? Although I too am called a *Kulaparvata*, you do not go round me"

Bhāskara said:

16-17. We do not go round it because of any faith in that mountain. This has been ordained as our path by the being that created the universe. Further its lofty peaks have spread through the space. It is due to compulsion that the circumambulation is caused.

18. On hearing this Vindya Mountain became further enraged. He said: "O Bhānu (Sun-god), then you shall see my loftiness as well." He blocked the path of the sky by which the Sun used to go round.

19-21. On seeing his way blocked, the Lord of the Day thought within himself: 'What shall I do now? If I circumambulate this mountain also there shall be a disturbance of time in all the three worlds.

The months, seasons and the regions around shall become unsettled. Agniṣṭoma and other rites will become defunct. If Yajña and other festivities were stopped the Devas will be hurt much.'

22-23. After thinking thus in various ways, the Hot-rayed One (Sun-god) became afraid and thought of Agastya, the eminent sage.

'Excepting Agastya, the progeny of Mitra and Varuṇa, the most excellent one among Brāhmaṇas, no one else is competent to restrain this Vindya.'

24. The Hot-rayed One (Sun-god) then adopted the guise of a Brāhmaṇa and went to his (Agastya's) hermitage in the holy spot Camatkārapura.

25. At the conclusion of Vaiśvadeva Yajña (the Sun-god in the guise of a Brāhmaṇa) uttered Vedic passages and said, "O excellent sage, a guest has come to you."

26-27. Agastya was delighted. He said: "O great sage, welcome to you. One who has arrived at the conclusion of the rites performed in the sacred fire is like an ardent wish meditated upon. Hence tell me, O excellent sage, what thing wished by you shall I give you. There is nothing that you desire which cannot be given by me if I am requested at this time."

Bhāskara said:

28-30. O good sage, I am Bhāskara (Sun-god) come here in the form of a Brāhmaṇa in the belief that you are the only person in all the three worlds competent to accomplish any task. Formerly the ocean, the storehouse of waters, was drunk up by you for the sake of Suras. Similarly Daitya Vātāpi, a thorn unto the Brāhmaṇa community, was swallowed. Hence, O excellent sage, be our refuge now, because you are the sole shelter unto Devas and the different castes of people here.

Sūta said:

31. O Brāhmaṇas, on hearing his words the sage was exceedingly pleased. After offering Arghya to the Lord of Day, he respectfully said:

32. "A favour has been done to me. I am blessed because you came to my abode. Hence tell me; I shall completely carry out your wish."

Bhāskara said:

33-34. O excellent sage, due to his rivalry with Sumeru the principal mountain, this Vindhya Mountain is blocking our way. Hence avoiding further delay, restrain him by means of the different expedients like peaceful conciliation etc. Do bring about the cessation of the blocking of our path.

Agastya said:

35. I shall restrain that *Kulaparvata* that has begun to grow in size. Hence, O Divākara, go to your abode and relax.

36. Thus dismissed by him, Bhāskara, the hot-rayed (god), joyously went to his abode after duly taking leave of the lord of sages.

37-38. Agastya hastened to Vindhya and spoke respectfully: "O excellent mountain, at my request, do shorten your stature quickly. I am now feeling inclined to take the holy plunge in the southern Tīrthas.[1] All that depends on you. Hence do what is proper."

39. On hearing his words, Vindhya, the excellent mountain, became humble and stooped down immediately.

40-41. O Brāhmaṇas, after crossing over to its southern side, Agastya said to him: "You shall continue to stay thus till I return. No hesitation in this respect. Otherwise I am bound to curse you, whereby you will attain destruction."

42. Afraid of the curse that excellent Mountain promised, "It shall be so." He did not grow in size further in the expectation of his return.

43. Till now, O Brāhmaṇas, that sage has resorted to the southern region and so has not returned that way.

44. The Lord of sages brought Lopāmudrā there. He then called the Thousand-rayed One and eagerly said to him:

45. "O Hot-rayed One, my hermitage has been abandoned by me at your instance. It is in your interest that I should never return there again.

46. Hence, O Bhānu, at my instance, on the fourteenth lunar day in the bright half of the month of Caitra, the Liṅga that has been installed by me should be worshipped by you."

---

1. Agastya seems to be the first Aryan explorer to make his way through the Vindhya mountain. Hence this legend is repeated in several Purāṇas. Mbh, *Ādi* 215.3, mentions a lake and a Tīrtha (*Vana* 82.44) named after him. But both are in South India.

Bhāskara said:

47-48. O sage, I shall undoubtedly do thus at your instance. At the end of every year I shall myself worship that Liṅga. Any other man who worships that Liṅga on that day shall attain my world and then salvation.

Sūta said:

49-50. It is for this reason that the Hot-rayed Lord always presents himself there on the fourteenth day in the bright half of the month of Caitra.

Thus, O excellent Brāhmaṇas, everything that I have been asked has been narrated. If you have any other doubt in your heart do tell me.

CHAPTER THIRTYFOUR

Fight between Devas and Asuras

The sages said:

1-2. O Sūtaja, about that sage (Agastya) you have said: "For the sake of Suras the ocean, the storehouse of waters, was drunk by you (Agastya) formerly[1]." O highly intelligent one, describe in detail how the storehouse of waters was drunk up by that sage formerly.

Sūta said:

3. Formerly the foremost among Dānavas, famous by the name Kāleya, became the cause of the loss of vigour and enthusiasm of all the Devas.

4. On seeing the entire range of the three worlds trembled by their enormous powers, Lord Maheśvara was thus told by Viṣṇu the powerful one:

---

1. This legend viz. drinking up the Sea completely by Agastya is found in Mbh, *Vana* 105.3-6.

5. "O Īśāna, this entire range of the three worlds is tormented by Kālikeyas of great power. Hence, O Lord, we have to go to the earth now itself and carry on a great fight with them."

6. Thereupon Rudra, Viṣṇu and the Thousand-eyed One (Indra) armed themselves with sharp weapons and accompanied by Suras all of them arrived on the earth.

7. On coming to know that all the Devas had assembled together, all those Dānavas angrily came face to face with them quickly for fighting them off.

8. Then ensued a great fight between the Devas and the Dānavas, wherein the entire range of the three worlds trembled with fear and agitation.

9. Then, arrogant with his might a Dānava named Kālaprabha saw before him Śakra with the Vajra lifted up in his hand. He then laughed and said these words in a voice majestic like the report of thunder:

10. "It is after the passage of a long time that the Lord of heaven has fortunately come within our vision. O Thousand-eyed One, release your Vajra. Let me witness your manliness."

11. Thereupon, the enraged Śatakratu hurled the Vajra at him. The demon sportingly caught hold of it with his left hand.

12. Then aiming at Śakra he threw a huge club entirely made of iron. It was very terrific and appeared like another tongue of Yama.

13. On being struck by it, the Thousand-eyed One became unconscious. Drenched in a pool of blood he somehow remained on the chariot with the help of the flagstaff.

14. Mātali saw the Slayer of Bala (Indra) unconscious. Remembering the conventional duty of a charioteer he turned the chariot eastward (away from the battlefield).

15. Then, as the chariot of Śakra was turned away in the course of the battle, all the Devas became excessively frightened and they fled in all directions.

16. Ādityas, Vasus, Rudras, Viśvedevas, and the group of Maruts shamelessly (fled away). They were hit on their backs with sharp arrows and were shattered.

17. On seeing the army shattered by the Dānavas the Slayer of Madhu (i.e. Viṣṇu) immediately mounted Garuḍa and rushed against Kālaprabha.

18. Then all the Dānavas surrounded him roaring aloud

repeatedly. They covered him with sharp arrows.

19. Enveloped by them all round, Viṣṇu shone like another red (bloody) mountain with the boldly experiencing horripilation.

20. He then split the volleys of arrows by means of arrows fitted with feathers of heron, discharged from his Śārṅga bow and killed the Daityas.

21. Being annihilated by Murāri (Viṣṇu) all those groups of Daityas resembled deer oppressed by lions. They did not find any saviour.

22. In the meantime a Daitya remembered as Kālakhañja furiously rushed at Vāsudeva.

23. Striking Vāsudeva with five arrows very sharp and hard as rocks, he furiously hit Garuḍa with ten flat-jointed arrows.

24. Thereafter Mādhava discharged the discus Sudarśana for slaying that Daitya. It was encircled by a series of sparks of fire.

25. On seeing that discus that issued from Vāsudeva's hand coming towards him, the Daitya opened his mouth wide to swallow it and stood facing it.

26. The great Daitya did swallow it and said "Wait! Wait!" Then he discharged arrows aiming at Vāsudeva.

27. Being struck by the Daitya who had swallowed the (Sudarśana) discus, Vāsudeva along with Garuḍa experienced acute pain.

28-29. In the meantime the enraged Lord, the Slayer of Tripuras, saw Hari in the plight and Śakra with averted face. He then hit the son of Danu with his trident. he killed the others by means of the arrows discharged from his Pināka bow.

30. Lord Śaṁbhu slew Kālaprabhạ, Prakāla, Kālāsya, Kālavigraha and other leaders.

31. Then all those hideous Dānavas, despite their importance, became bereft of enthusiasm in the conquest of their enemies. They began to flee.

32. Then Śakra and Viṣṇu regained consciousness and took up again their weapons. They congratulated Mahādeva and stood ready for the battle on the field.

33. In the meantime all the Devas including Vāsava observed that the sons of Danu were smashed. They then began to exterminate them with hundreds of arrows and other weapons.

34-35. Most of the powerful Dānavas had been killed or were

being killed with sharp arrows by the Devas proud of their victory. They, therefore, entered the ocean which the Devas could not reach even mentally. Thus the Daityas became leaderless and miserable. All their limbs had been mutilated.

CHAPTER THIRTYFIVE

Installation of Citreśvara Pīṭha

Sūta said:

1-3. When those Daityas had been shattered and slaughtered by Lord Maheśvara, rendered free from danger by him alone, the excellent Suras with Śakra and Viṣṇu as their leaders became delighted in their minds. All of them eulogized Lord Maheśvara and bowed down to him repeatedly. Then they went to their respective abodes.

With their hopes thus shattered by the excellent Suras, the tiger-like Dānavas consulted one another for ways and means of bringing about the destruction of heaven-dwellers.

4-5. As they consulted one another and discussed thus, it was decided by them that except putting obstacles in the performance of religious rites, there was no other means for destroying Devas; hence ascetics, people interested in Yajñas and the virtuous ones should be killed at nightfall.

6. After deciding thus, they used to come out of the abode of Varuṇa (i.e. the ocean) always at nightfall and began killing people engaged in religious acts.

7. Wherever there was any Yajña, Sattra or religious festivities, they went there at nightfall and carried on annihilation of those people.

8. Many Yajñas were spoiled by them, Dīkṣitas (persons who were initiated for Yajñas) were struck down and Ṛtviks (priests) and ordinary good Brāhmaṇas were killed.

9. A thousand leading Brāhmaṇas were eaten up by those evil-hearted ones, in the hermitage of the noble-souled Śāṇḍilya, a leader of sages.

10. Hundreds and thousands of Brāhmaṇas were killed. Five

thousand followers of Viśvāmitra and seven thousand of intelligent Atri were destroyed.

11. At the same time, the entire surface of the earth was afflicted by the fear of Kāleya and all Yajñas and religious festivals became defunct.

12. No one on the earth dared to sleep during nights. People well-equipped with weapons stood by the ascetics.

13. A few virtuous people who confidentally took repose during nights (were killed) and only their bones were seen in the morning.

14. All the groups of Devas with Brahmā and Viṣṇu as their leaders, who were deprived of their shares in the Yajñas suffered the greatest distress.

15. In order to slay the enemies of Suras, they entered the ocean too but could not assail them even mentally because they were placed in a very difficult position.

16-18. Deeply grieved thereupon they consulted (each other) for drying up the ocean. (They thought that) 'the leading Dānavas could be killed when the ocean no longer existed. Without (the help of) Agastya, the ocean will not become dry. Hence we shall go to that leading sage and make a request to him in this matter. That excellent sage resides in the holy place of Camatkārapura.[1] So we shall go there itself and he will come quickly (to our help).'

19. After deciding thus, all of those Devas went to the hermitage of the son of Mitra and Varuṇa, the important sage.

20. On seeing all the excellent Suras gathered together before him, the good sage became delighted.

21. Seeing Brahmā and other Suras, the eyes of the sage gleamed with delightful surprise. With palms joined together in veneration, he spoke these words in a voice choked with excess of delight:

22-23. "Though already sacred and pure, this holy place Camatkārapura has become more sacred by your presence. Hence speak out ye all, what task should be carried out by me now. I shall carry it out even if it be very difficult."

---

1. The legend of Agastya's drinking up the sea is given in Mbh, *Vana* 105.3-6 but no Camatkārapura is mentioned there.

The Devas said:

24-26. The Daityas named Kāleyas who have survived a general slaughter by the Suras, are now taking shelter in the ocean and killing the performers of auspicious rites. If auspicious rites are defunct, the destruction of heaven-dwellers is certain. So, in order to facilitate their annihilation, do make the great ocean dried up. Thereby the leading Dānavas will be visible to our eyes. They then could be killed by Devas and *Makhas* (sacrifices) could be resumed here.

Agastya said:

27. O excellent Suras, by the end of a year I shall gain the *Vidyā* (magical lore) of Yoginīs and on the strength thereof I shall dry up the ocean.

28. Hence do ye all go to your abodes. A year will pass presently. At the end of the year, do certainly come back.

29. You can come along with me. After the ocean has been dried up, the wicked Dānavas by whom the world is being afflicted should be killed.

30. Thereafter all the groups of the Devas went to their respective abodes. Agastya carried on his endeavour for the acquisition of the Vidyā.

31. Then all the Pīṭhas (shrines of Mother Śakti) on the earth were brought together by the great sage through the power of his Mantras.

32-34. On the eighth and fourteenth lunar days, he devoutly worshipped the groups of Yoginīs and Kanyakās (Virgins) in particular therein.

Thus the Brāhmaṇa propitiated the Vidyā named *Viśoṣiṇī* (that which dries up). Further the Brāhmaṇa worshipped devoutly and with faith the Guardians of Quarters, the Kṣetrapālas (guardians of holy shrines) and the deity roaming through the skies with great faith. At the close of the year the deity became pleased and said: "Do tell me what should be done, O good sage. I have been won over by you."

Agastya said:

35. O goddess, if you are pleased, do enter my mouth

quickly. I shall restrain speech and dry up the ocean by means of that power.

36. That great Vidyā named Saṁśoṣaṇī said, "It shall be so" and entered his mouth presently as the sage had perfectly purified his soul.

37. In the meantime all the Devas including Vāsava came there joyously holding the weapons and ready for the battle.

38. Then the Brāhmaṇa who had kept his mouth dry set off with mental concentration and purity, towards the ocean in the company of all the Devas.

39. Being eulogized by the heaven-dwellers he approached the shore of the sea. Agitated by thirst very much, he spoke to the Devas:

40. "I am now going to dry up the ocean immediately. Be prepared for the act of annihilating the enemies of the Suras."

Sūta said:

41. After saying thus, the sage sportingly drank the entire vast expanse of water agitated by fishes and turtles and abounding in alligators.

42. The ocean came to be on a par with the bare ground and the Daityas were killed by the excellent Suras desirous of the ultimate victory everywhere by means of their sharp arrows.

43. After fighting to the best of their ability in the terrific battle, those who survived after most of them had been killed, pierced the ground and went beneath to the nether worlds.

44-45. After eulogizing the excellent sage, all the Suras said to him: "Give out the water again for filling up the great ocean. O Brāhmaṇa, bereft of the sea, the earth does not shine like a lady worthy of being adorned but bereft of property and possessions."

Agastya said:

46. The water has been drunk by the Vidyā named Praśoṣaṇī which had been propitiated by me. It has been digested too.

47. This ocean will get again filled up unfathomably with the waters of Gaṅgā free from impurities after being dug up.

48. There will be a king on the Earth named Sagara. His

49. There will be born in the same race a king named Bhagīratha. For the sake of his kinsmen, he will fetch Gaṅgā from the Cosmic Egg.

50. With her flooding waters gushing all round, the ocean will become perfectly filled up. The truth has been uttered by me.

The Devas said:

51. O excellent sage, the task of the Devas has been completed by you. Hence, O lordly sage, request for any boon you have cherished in your heart.

Agastya said:

52. O excellent Suras, all the Pīṭhas have been completely gathered together in the holy spot of Camatkārapura by the power of Mantras.

53. By the power of all the Yoginīs and the Mātṛs in particular, let the Pīṭhas stay there itself.

54. May a person endowed with ardent faith, who worships them on eighth and fourteenth lunar days, attain everything mentally desired.

The Devas said:

55-57. Since the wonderfully variegated Pīṭhas have been gathered together, they will constitute one Pīṭha named Citreśvara. A man who worships Yoginīs, Vidyās and Mothers in particular there, with any desire meditated upon, O great sage, will soon obtain that desire, due to this offer of the boon by us, even if he be a great sinner.

58-59. After saying thus, all the Suras took leave of the leading sage and joyously went to heaven. Agastya went to his hermitage.

Sūta said:

Thus everything about how the ocean was drunk up formerly by Agastya for the sake of Devas has been narrated to you.

CHAPTER THIRTYSIX

Greatness of Citreśvarī Pīṭha

The sages said:

1-4. Do describe to us the extent and the power of this Pīṭha named Citreśvara created by Sage Agastya.

Sūta said:

O Brāhmaṇas, it is impossible to describe the greatness of that Pīṭha in the course of a thousand years by ten thousands of mouths.

Hundreds and thousands of Yogins of esteemed holy vows, fully endowed with meditation, have attained Siddhi there.

Within a day Yogins certainly attain that Siddhi which is attained in other Pīṭhas after practice for a year.

5. One who, with ardent faith, performs the Japa of Atharvaṇa Mantras certainly attains the entire fruit stated in the Mantras.

6. A man who is desirous of a son and performs the Japa of *Pulliṅgas* (masculine names) shall obtain desired sons though he may be old.

7. A man desirous of sons should recite the *Grabhopaniṣad* there. He shall beget sons even by cohabiting with barren women.

8. If a devotee recites *Śatarudriya* with the aim of the destruction of enemy hosts in that Pīṭha, his enemies meet with destruction immediately.

9. A man who recites *Vāmadevya Sāman* for the sake of protection from evil spirits, ghosts and vampires and the like shall be rid of all torments.

10. A man who performs the Japa of the Ṛk beginning with *ko'dāt* While meditating upon a virgin of his choice shall undoubtedly obtain her.

11. If a devotee constantly recites *IMAM DEVĀ* for gaining favour of the king, he shall have the favour of the king unhindered.

12. O Brāhmanas, if a person recites the Mantra *TAM PATNĪBHIḤ* for getting his own wife's affection, his wife shall be a chaste lady with abundance of love for him.

13. If one performs the Japa of *Aditi* for obtaining the

blessings of people, he will have a profitable affection of the people.

14. O Brāhmaṇas, if a man seeking wealth repeats *Śrī Sūkta* there, riches will move unto him from all directions.

15. If a devotee performs the Japa of the Sāman Mantra *bhūmi* for the sake of realm there, that man shall certainly be the lord of earth even if he is of low birth.

16. If a man for the sake of vehicles performs the Japa of the *Rathantaram Sāman* there, he obtains splendid and swift vehicles.

17. O excellent Brāhmaṇas, if a devotee who seeks elephants repeats the Mantra *gaṇānām* etc. there, that man obtains elephants that flood the ground with their ichor.

18. If a man repeats the Mantra *na tadrakṣa* etc. for the sake of security, he will obtain it from everywhere when chances are favourable or adverse.

19. One who repeats with concentration and mental purity the excellent Ṛk beginning with *saptarṣayaḥ* for the destruction of ailments, is rid of ailments.

20. If people oppressed by malefic Planets perform the Japa of the Mantra beginning with *yadubhī* there, undoubtedly the Planets become favourable to them.

21. If a man assailed by the affliction of evil spirits repeats the *Bṛhat Sāman,* the evil spirits and even the god of Death becomes like a father unto him.

22. If a person repeats the *Śakuna* (pertaining to omens) *Sūkta* for successful conclusion of his journey, he shall accomplish it even if he is impoverished.

23. If a man recites the *Sarpa* (pertaining to serpents) *Sūkta* for the destruction of serpents, they do not at all enter his abode.

24. One who is endowed with ardent faith and performs there the Japa of the Mantra beginning with *uttiṣṭha* for the purpose of quelling poison, will find that the poison is immediately dispelled.

25. Whether poison arises from an immobile being or a mobile being or if it is artificial, it goes away even when his name is uttered, like darkness at the rise of the Sun.

26. If a devotee with ardent faith, performs there the Japa of *Vyāghra Sāman,* pythons, tigers etc., become gentle in regard to him.

27. If a devotee performs there the Japa of the Mantra *lāṅgalāni* etc. for prosperous increase in agricultural work, even when the whole world is without rain, cultivation will be achieved by him.

28. For the destruction of *Ītis* (natural calamities) a man should perform there the Japa of the Mantra *devavrata.* Thereby, mere utterance *Ītis* get destroyed.

29. When the world is affected by drought a devotee should perform there the Japa of *Pañcendra* Mantra. If Homa is performed by himself with his own hands repeating those Mantras, there shall be the coming in (supply) of water.

30. If a man afflicted by thieves and robbers recites the Mantra beginning with *daṁṣṭrābhyām,* never will he be tormented by thieves.

31. For success in argument, a devotee should perform there the Japa of the Mantra beginning with *saṁsṛṣṭam.* Even if he is a sinner, he will win the argument.

32. For the sake of driving away enemies a man should perform the Japa of *Rudraśiras.* Thereupon his enemies with crooked intellect will abandon that land and go away.

33. For the enchantment of the enemies, a devotee should perform the Japa of *Viṣṇusaṁhitā.* His enemies will certainly be deluded and enchanted.

34. For the purpose of captivating people, a man should perform the Japa of *Kūṣmāṇḍīḥ* Mantra. Even enemies will be under his control, to say the least about young women etc.

35. For the purpose of stunning and paralysing enemies, O excellent Brāhmaṇas, a man with ardent faith should perform the Japa of *Prājāpatya* and *Vāruṇa* Mantras. All his enemies become paralysed by means of these Mantras.

36. O Brāhmaṇas, for the purpose of drying up things a man should perform the Japa of the Mantra *kālī karālī* etc. Whatever the man thinks about, he can dry it up entirely.

37. This Mantra was repeated by the noble-souled Agastya then. By means of the power thereof the Lord of Rivers was dried up by him.

38. Such is the power of the Pīṭha that causes the Siddhi of Mantras. It yields worldly pleasures also. It has now been described unto you.

39. One who desires heavenly pleasures, O excellent

Brāhmaṇas, should perform there the rites of holy bath, Dāna and Śrāddha in particular.

40. If, on the other hand, one is detached and wishes for liberation from the ocean of worldly existence, let him be contented and free from all desires. Let that sensible man perform penance there.

The sages said:

41. The great efficacy of the Japa of the Mantras has been described by you. But, O Sūtaja, how does this Japa of the Mantras become fruitful.

Sūta said:

42. In this context I shall tell you what has been heard from my father (i.e. Lomaharṣaṇa). He was expounding this to Sage Durvāsas.

43. O Brāhmaṇas, formerly our father was asked by Durvāsas in regard to *Mantravāda*. This, you do listen, with great mental concentration.

Durvāsas said:

44. I have observed Vratas and am practising a certain desired Mantra. Do tell me the procedure as laid down in the Śāstras for its success.

Lomaharṣaṇa said:

45. O good sage, the practice of Mantras is painful and difficult affair unto all. It is likely to be obstructed and it is full of loopholes.

46. Hence, O Brāhmaṇa, if you desire fruitful result of the practice of Mantras, it behoves you to go to the holy spot of Camatkārapura.

47. Citreśvarīpīṭha thereof has been created by Agastya. It is said to be one that brings about achievement of the fruit of Mantras retained in the heart.

48. Due to the boon granted by all the heaven-dwellers, there is no possibility of any loophole there. There is no hindrance or impediment there, O Brāhmaṇa, nor lack of fulfilment.

49. That Pīṭha belongs to all the four Yugas. It accords Siddhi unto those who stay there, in accordance with the Yuga and that too instantaneously. Hence I speak so, Brāhmaṇa.

50. O excellent Brāhmaṇa, if a person wishes to practise (Japa) of any Mantra, he should at the outset perform the Japa of that Mantra a hundred thousand times.

51. Thereby he becomes a Siddha, a man of purity qualified for the Mantra. Then, O tiger among Brāhmaṇas, he should repeat it four hundred thousand times. A tenth of that is the number of Homas performed in a well-kindled fire.

52-53. Thereby the Siddhi originating from that Mantra is certain. In regard to gentle activities, the Homa is done by means of white mustards, Jāti flowers and the feeding of Brāhmaṇas.

O leading Brāhmaṇa, in regard to violent activities, it is done by means of red flowers along with *Guggula* (aromatic resin). Virgins should also be propitiated. Then the Homa shall be fruitful.

54. This mode of practising Mantras mentioned by me, O excellent Brāhmaṇa, is to be adopted in Kṛtayuga and by all Sādhakas (aspirants).

55. In Tretā Yuga, the practice of Mantras is reduced by a quarter. It should be performed to the extent of a half in Dvāpara and a fourth in Kali Yuga.

56. After attaining the Mantra-Siddhi there in that Pīṭha a man should employ it and accomplish any task.

57. He shall become equipped with capacity to curse or to bless. He shall be brilliant. He cannot be conquered by any living being. He will become one approved of by good people.

Sūta said:

58. On hearing all the speech of my father that good sage came to Citreśvara Pīṭha.

59. There with ardent faith, he practised (mastered) all the Mantras in the due order in accordance with the injunctions laid down in the scriptural texts.

60. After a successful practice of the Mantras thus, he went to Camatkārapura, O Brāhmaṇas, in order to request the Brāhmaṇas for the sake of plots of land.

CHAPTER THIRTYSEVEN

The Palace Called Duśśīla

Sūta said:

1-3. Then, O excellent Brāhmaṇas, he saw a group of Brāhmaṇas comparable to Devas. They were seated on the playground. Some were well-versed in the Vedas and they were ready for expounding the same. They were eager to defeat others and were angrily disputing with one another.

Others were well-versed in the science of Yajñas. They were busily discussing (the details of) Yajñas. There hundreds of Brāhmaṇas were seen expounding Brahman.

4. Others were tiger-like Brāhmaṇas expert in Vedāṅgas. Standing in front of the groups of people, they were clearing the doubts.

5. O excellent Brāhmaṇas, still others were busy in reciting Vedic passages loudly. They were making the quarters reverberate.

6. Others were full of curiosity. They asked one another questions about difficult passages. Still others laughed at the person engaged in the (exposition of) passages.

7. Others were engaged in discussing the Smṛtis. Still others were reciters of the Veda. Others asked and clarified the doubts pertaining to the Smṛti texts.

8. Other excellent Brāhmaṇas were expounding the Purāṇa to elders. They were seated in the midst of the assembly.

9. On seeing those Brāhmaṇas of esteemed vows, the sage humbly bowed down to them and said respectfully:

10-11. "O tigers among Brāhmaṇas, I am feeling inclined to erect a temple of Śaṁbhu. Hence let a suitable place be pointed out. I shall build an excellent mansion of Śaṁbhu, the Lord of Devas. I shall propitiate the same Bull-emblemed Lord there."

12. Although he repeatedly said so energetically, he did not get from them any reply good or otherwise.

13. The sage became excessively furious. He cursed those excellent Brāhmaṇas in a loud voice so that all could hear.

Durvāsas said:

14. The pride of learning, that of affluence and the third

one arising from nobility of birth: In the case of arrogant persons these are inebriating factors; but in that of good people, they are means of self-control.

15. Everyone of you appears to be inebriated. Hence only such inebriate ones will be born in your families.

16. In this city all fathers will be devoid of friendliness or affection for sons, still more so in the case of other kinsmen?

17. O excellent Brāhmaṇas, feeling insulted by the Brāhmaṇas, the eminent Brāhmaṇa Durvāsas said this and turned away.

18. Among them there was a wise elderly Brāhmaṇa well-known as Suśīla. He was a master of the Vedas and Vedāṅgas.

19. He saw the sage going away furiously after being insulted. He quickly followed him saying "Stop! Stop!"

20-22. By this time the sage had gone very far. But the Brāhmaṇa overtook him. He bowed down to him and said: "O Brāhmaṇa, on my request, please forgive the Brāhmaṇas. These were busy in the recitation of their respective Vedic passages and so did not hear your words. Therefore they did not reply. This is the truth I am telling you. So, for the sake of a mansion dedicated to Śaṁbhu a plot of land is offered by me to you. In this spot, O excellent Brāhmaṇa, it behoves you to build a temple."

23. On hearing his words, Durvāsas became delighted. O excellent Brāhmaṇas, he hailed him for the gift of the plot. Afterwards in accordance with his word, he built a palace (shrine) there.

24-32. Those Brāhmaṇas came to know that a plot of land was given to the sage by Suśīla for erecting a temple. All those Brāhmaṇas became very angry with Suśīla.

Coming upto him they said: "A piece of land has been given by you for the sake of a palace to be dedicated to that wicked-minded one by whom we have been cursed. Hence you will be excommunicated by us. Though your name is Suśīla, you will be proclaimed Duśśīla by learned ones.

This wicked ascetic intends to build a Śiva temple. Even in hundreds of years, he will not realize his wish.

Those who earn reputation in the world are glorified by men. So also those who see things correctly, but not this evil-minded one.

This palace shall be named Duśśīla after your name. It shall be a mansion only in name. But it will never be completed.

Since we Brāhmaṇas have been made bereft of friendliness (for our sons) and associated with three kinds of arrogance along with our entire line of descendants, therefore this sinful person too shall be erascible (prone to be angry), thereby while he goes on performing penance, his penance will become futile."

33. After saying thus with eyes reddened with anger, those Brāhmaṇas left Duśśīla there and entered their city.

34. Excommunicated by the residents of the city like Devaśarman before, Duśśīla built his house outside the city.

35. Those who were born in his family were proclaimed "Outsiders". They were excluded from all the holy rites of all the citizens.

Sūta said:

36. After the departure of those leading Brāhmaṇas after cursing thus, Durvāsas said to Duśśīla angrily with eyes turned red:

37-38. "Mantras from the Atharvaveda and other three Vedas capable of annihilating enemies have been mastered by me. I shall destroy the entire city along with animals and birds therein like a ruthless (king) razing down the city of the enemy."

Duśśīla said:

39. O excellent one among men, this is not at all proper to do against the Brāhmaṇas particularly by a Brāhmaṇa.

40. Whether they kill, curse or speak harsh words, Brāhmaṇas should always be worshipped by those who wish for divine worlds.

41. One who considers himself victorious when Brāhmaṇas are vanquished (by him) is cooked in the terrible Narakas beginning with Tāmisra.

42-43. O excellent Brāhmaṇa, one who desires a permanent residence in heaven shall endure his own discomfiture at the hands of a Brāhmaṇa. Your Mantras have attained Siddhi in the holy spot of these leading Brāhmaṇas. How can you then cause their destruction?

44. Atonement has been enjoined by good people in the cases of a Brāhmaṇa-slayer, one who drinks liquor, a thief and

one whose *Vrata* has been broken. There is no atonement for an ungrateful person.

45. Hence those who stay in this holy spot should not be angry. O excellent sage, be compassionate towards me and forgive me.

Sūta said:

46-48. He promised "It shall be so", performed penance and stayed there. Thereby he attained the greatest Siddhi inaccessible even to Devas.

That place (mansion of Śiva) became well known after the name Duśśīla all over the earth. Merely by visiting it, a man is rid of his sins. A man who always visits the Liṅga within it on the eighth day in the bright half of a month and meditates for a moment, never sees Naraka.

CHAPTER THIRTYEIGHT

Greatness of Dhundhumāreśvara

Sūta said:

1-3. A Liṅga was installed there itself by king Dhundhumāra after erecting a very charming palace full of all kinds of jewels.

He built a hermitage there and performed a severe penance. It was, due to its power, that the Lord stationed himself in that Liṅga.

A tank near it was constructed by that noble-souled one, filled with water free from all impurities and very auspicious, comparable to all the Tīrthas.

4. An excellent man who takes his holy bath there and visits Dhundhumāreśvara, never sees the impassable Narakas in the abode of Yama.

The sages said:

5. In which race was King Dhundhumāra born? At what time was the penance performed by that very noble-minded one?

Sūta said:

6. A powerful son of Bṛhadaśva was born in the race of the Sun-god. He is well known as Kuvalayāśva as well as Dhundhumāra.

7. The great Daitya Dhundhu was killed by him in Marujāṅgala. Hence he is remembered as Dhundhumāra. He became renowned in all the three worlds.

8. Towards the closing days of his life, he went to the great holy spot Camatkārapura and performed a penance meditating on Maheśvara.

9. After installing the great Liṅga in the palace studded with jewels, he adored it along with oblations, offerings flowers, incense and unguents.

10. Thereupon Maheśvara, the great Lord, himself appeared before him seated on his bull and accompanied by Gaurī and the attendants.

11. The Lord said: "I shall bestow a boon. Request for anything desired by you. I shall grant you everything even if it be rare."

Dhundhumāra said:

12. O Lord of all the Suras, if a boon has to be granted to us, O Bull-emblemed One, you should station yourself in this Liṅga.

Śrī Bhagavān said:

13-14. O excellent king, undoubtedly I shall always be present on the fourteenth lunar day in the bright half of Caitra along with Gaurī. A man who takes his holy plunge in the tank there and worships me present in the Liṅga shall go to my world, O king.

Sūta said:

15. After saying this the Lord vanished. Delighted in his heart the king stayed there and attained salvation.

CHAPTER THIRTYNINE

Greatness of Yayātīśvara

Sūta said:

1-2. There is an excellent Liṅga installed by King Yayāti to the north of Dhundhumāreśvara. There is another Liṅga installed by Devayānī and Śarmiṣṭhā, his wives. It is the bestower of all cherished desires.

3. O excellent Brāhmaṇas, when he was completely satisfied with all worldly pleasures, he entrusted his son[1] (Pūru) with the kingdom and gave back his youthful form.

4. He took back the old age of his physical form. Accompanied by his two wives, he went to the excellent Sage Mārkaṇḍa and requested him humbly:

5. "O holy Sir, describe unto us the most important and holiest of all the Tīrthas and holy spots."

Śrī Mārkaṇḍeya said:

6. It appears to us that the holy spot of Camatkārapura which is adorned by all the Tīrthas is the most important of all holy spots.

7. O excellent king, Viṣṇupadī Gaṅgā, the destroyer of the sins of all creatures, and the gods including Hara, are themselves present there.

8. O excellent king, similarly all other Tīrthas stationed on the earth are present there permanently.

9. For the delight of Brāhmaṇas, a big rocky slab fifty-two Hastas in extent has been left there by Pitāmaha.

10-11. Whereas an auspicious rite performed elsewhere yields fruit (benefit) in the course of a year, O Lord of the earth, the same does there in a single day.

So, O Lord of the earth, go there quickly and perform a penance there in the company of your wives. By it you will attain the worlds cherished in your heart.

---

1. Purū accepted his father's old age. As a reward, he became the ruler of the whole of Yayāti Kingdom (Mbh, *Ādi*, 24.27-37)

12. On hearing his words, the king, the son of Nahuṣa, went to the holy place of Camatkārapura accompanied by both of his wives.

13. He installed the Liṅga of the Trident-bearing Lord of Devas and propitiated it well with the utmost faith.

14. Then, by its power, the king accompanied by his wives went to heaven riding in an excellent aerial chariot.

15. Kinnaras sang about him and Cāraṇas eulogized him. Emulating Devas he had the lustre of twelve Ādityas.

CHAPTER FORTY

Greatness of Citraśilā

The sages said:

1-2. O Sūtaja, it has been mentioned by Your Holiness that a great rock (Slab) pertaining to Brahmā is present there. It accords salvation unto all the creatures and destroys sins. How was it installed there? What is its power? Do narrate this completely. We are not fully satisfied.

Sūta said:

3. Brahmā, born of the Unmanifest One was stationed in Brahmaloka. Formerly he became very anxious to do pilgrimage.

4-8. "All the Devas have their own Tīrthas on the earth except me. Therefore, I shall have to make a Tīrtha on the earth that I can resort to in the mortal world and perform Sandhyā prayers thrice a day. Further like deities Śiva and others, I can also perform other virtuous rites conducive to welfare. Here in Svarga, there is no right to perform holy rites. Only the fruit of auspicious rites is enjoyed. Hence for the sake of regular performance of the rites of the three Sandhyās, I must go to that place on the earth where this rocky slab falls."

9. After saying thus, a large slab from his seat was hurled by Pitāmaha to the surface of the earth.

10. That slab consisting of all jewels fell on the earth on the holy spot of Camatkārapura, The most prominent of all holy places.

11. Thereupon the Lord of the worlds himself came to the earth and surveyed that holy place surrounded all round by Tīrthas.

12. On noticing that the rocky slab came to rest at a very meritorious place he became delighted. Thereafter he said:

13-14. "Oh! There is no one more blessed than I in all the three worlds because the slab has come to rest in a holy spot full of all Tīrthas. Since no holy rite can be efficacious without water, a big tank full of pure water should be created here by me."

15. Then he thought of his daughter, River Sarasvatī, that flows beneath (the earth) in the nether worlds because it is afraid of contact with lay people.

16. Thereat the great river came into view piercing the ground and flooding the slab all round with her sacred water.

17. Assuming a visible form she asked Prapitāmaha, "Why am I remembered, O Lord. May the command be pronounced."

Brahmā said:

18-19. You must always stay here near me on the slab so that I can perform the holy rite in all the three Sandhyās by means of your water. So also, men who perform their holy bath with your water shall attain the greatest Siddhi inaccessible unto even Devas and human beings.

Sarasvatī said:

20-21. O excellent one among Suras, I am a virgin flowing through the nether worlds. Since I am afraid of contact with lay people, I do not come up to the surface of the earth. It does not behove me to do contrary to your behest. Considering this aspect, O excellent one among Suras, do what is proper.

Brahmā said:

22. For your sake I shall make a great tank here itself in the holy spot. It shall be unapproachable to all mortals. It behoves you to stay there.

23. After saying thus the Lord of Devas dug up a big tank there. Then Sarasvatī made it her place of residence.

24-25. Then Pitāmaha ordered serpents who can kill by mere looking (at a victim): "At my bidding all of you should always stay in this tank. O excellent serpents, you must carry out your task in such a manner as to prevent men from touching her."

Sūta said:

26. After establishing Sarasvatī thus in that holy spot and that Citraśilā (wonderful slab) in the middle, he went to the world of Brahmā.

27. Once thereafter a great sage of esteemed holy vows, named Maṅkaṇaka, came to that holy place. He was an expert in the science of poisons.

28. He went round that holy spot well-guarded by serpents. They coiled round the sage and bound him as though with cords.

29. By the power of his Vidyā, he rendered all the serpents devoid of poison. He took his holy plunge there and sanctified himself. After offering libations to the Pitṛs, he came out of water joyously feeling blessed and contented.

30. As the sage gathered together Kuśa grass the tip of his hand got pricked.

31. From that wound of his a large quantity of vegetable juice issued forth. On seeing it he was surprised but all the more delighted.

32. Knowing that he has become a Siddha, tears of joy flooded in his eyes. He climbed on the slab of Brahmā and then began to dance[1].

33. As the noble-souled sage danced thus, the entire universe too consisting of mobile and immobile beings danced gracefully.

34. The entire Camatkārapura became shattered. The excellent Brāhmaṇas were destroyed. As the mansions crumbled down there was a great cry of "Hā! Hā!".

35. On seeing his action all the groups of Devas pleaded unto the Bull-emblemed Lord for restraining the dance.

36-37. "O Lord of Devas, while he is dancing, the whole universe too consisting of mobile and immobile beings dances. Hence do go and get it stopped.

1. This legend of sage Maṅkaṇaka's exultation and dance at the exuding vegetable juice and Śaṅkara's show of superior power, is based on Mbh, *Vana* 83.115-131.

O Īśāna, O most excellent one among Suras, no one else is competent to forbid (and stop) the sage. Hence do what is good unto the universe."

38. On hearing their words, the Bull-emblemed Lord adopted the guise of an eminent Brāhmaṇa and approached him.

39. He said, "O sage, why do you dance now? Speak out your intention at once. We have great curiosity."

40. O excellent Brāhmaṇas, on being asked by Śaṅkara thus, the leading Brāhmaṇa showed his hand covered with vegetable juice.

41-42. "O Brāhmaṇa, don't you see that a large quantity of vegetable juice has come out of the opening in the wound? Hence Siddhi has come to me. It is for this reason that I dance, O Brāhmaṇa. O most excellent one among Siddhas, I am delighted as a result of the Siddhi gained."

43-44. Even as he said this, the Bull-emblemed Lord struck his thumb with the tip of his figure. Instantly sacred ash resembling snow and crystal issued forth from the opening of the wound causing great surprise (to the Brāhmaṇa).

45-47. Then, O excellent Brāhmaṇas, the Lord said to the Brāhmaṇa: "O excellent sage, from the tip of my thumb grey ash has issued forth. Still I am not eager to dance. Why then do you dance merely at the sight of the vegetable juice? Stop this despicable dance. O leading Brāhmaṇa, by dancing and singing the power of the penance of a Brāhmaṇa gets wasted."

48. On seeing the feat of the discharge of ash from a wound, he became ashamed. Stopping his dancing activity, he bowed down to him.

49. Then he said, "I think you are none other than Lord Maheśvara. Do this favour unto me. Let there be no wastage of my penance."

The Lord said:

50. With my favour the power of your penance will increase day by day. I shall always stay with you in this holy spot.

51. O sage, since I have been requested by you in a blissful mood, I will become well known all over the earth by the name Ānandeśvara. After my name, this city too will be called Ānanda (modern Vaḍnagar in Gujarat).

52. After saying thus, Mahādeva vanished from there. Maṅkaṇaka, the leading sage, began to perform penance.

53-54. Then the serpents bowed down to the leading sage and said: "O holy Sir, all of us have been deprived of our poison by your holiness. Do a favour unto us so that the terrible poison may come back. Otherwise, we will be subjected to great discomfiture by all the people."

Maṅkaṇaka said:

55. Untruth has never been uttered by me even for the sake of a joke. Hence you will all continue to be like this as water-snakes.

Sūta said:

56. Ever since then all of them remained as water-snakes on the earth—two-tongued serpents in form but devoid of poison.

57. Then men began to take their holy plunges in that auspicious Sārasvata Tīrtha. After touching that Citraśīla (wonderful slab) they attained the greatest goal.

58. Accompanied by Yama, the terrified Thousand-eyed One (Indra) went to Lord Pitāmaha and spoke these words:

59-60. "O Pitāmaha, men take their holy bath in the Sārasvata Mahātīrtha created by you and go to heaven. Men merely visit the Lord and go to heaven. Even persons of sinful conduct, men excluded from all righteous rites, take their bath there, touch the slab and attain the greatest goal then itself."

Yama said:

61. A careful scrutiny of the auspiciousness and inauspiciousness of all embodied beings has been the duty assigned to me, O Lord. That has become invalidated now.

62. Hence, O Lord , remove one of us—either me or that excellent Tīrtha. By its power my Narakas have become devoid of people.

63. On hearing the words of Yama, Prapitāmaha said to Śakra who was standing nearby, "Destroy that Tīrtha."

64. Thereupon Śakra went to that tank and filled it with dust

particles, O Brāhmaṇas, both the Sārasvata Hrada as well as the Citraśilā.

65. Even today, a man who establishes himself perfectly in that holy spot and performs penance shall attain Siddhi soon.

66-68. That leading Brāhmaṇa Maṅkaṇaka stays there even today along with Lord Śaṁbhu. The Liṅga installed by Maṅkaṇaka and filled with dust particles is still there. It brings great prosperity, O excellent Brāhmaṇas. Men who touch it are rid of sins. A man who worships it on the fourteenth lunar day in the bright half of the month of Māgha is honoured in Śivaloka even though he may be defiled with sins.

CHAPTER FORTYONE

Manifestation of Jalaśāyin

Sūta said:

1-4. There is the holy spot of Lord Jalaśāyin (one who lies down in the waters i.e. Lord Viṣṇu) on the northern side (of Ānandeśvara Liṅga).

It is well-known and is destructive of all sins. One who observes fast and worships there at the time of *Śayana* (going to asleep by the Lord on the eleventh day in the bright half of Āṣāḍha) and Bodhana (waking up on the eleventh day in the bright half of Kārttika) of Hari, with great devotion, shall go to the place of Viṣṇu.

The Dvitīyā (second lunar day) of the dark half (of Āṣāḍha) when the Lord of Devas is asleep, is liked well by the Lord. It is called *Aśūnyaśayanā* (not being levoid of lying down).

On that day, if a devotee worships Lord Jalaśāyin in accordance with the injunctions laid down in the scriptural texts, he goes to Hari's place.

The sages said:

5. O Sūtanandana, how did Jalaśāyin come to that place? What is the procedure whereby he is worshipped? Mention everything in detail.

Sūta said:

6. Formerly there was a very powerful king of Dānavas named Bāṣkali. He could not be defeated by all the Devas, Gandharvas, Uragas and Rākṣasas.

7. This powerful Dānava brought the entire earth under his control and then proceeded to the abode of Devas along with groups of Daityas.

8. A fight took place between the furious Devas and the Dānavas. The great war caused the destruction of both the Devas and the Asuras.

9. Everyday there occurred terrible fight and it lasted for ten thousand years. It produced muddy slush mixed with blood and a huge mountain of bones.

10. When ten thousand years were completed the Thousand-eyed One (Indra) was defeated by him along with his armies and followers.

11. He left heaven along with all the groups of Devas and sought refuge in Viṣṇu seeking shelter in Śvetadvīpa.

12. It is there that the Lord lies down in his Yogic slumber on the couch of Serpent Śeṣa with his feet massaged by Lakṣmī.

13. Then, all the Devas including Vāsava, who are good devotees of that Lord, eulogized him all round by means of Vedic Sūktas.

14. Then the Lord of the universe got up and spoke to the Slayer of Bala: "O Thousand-eyed One, I hope everything is quite all right now in all the three worlds. Wherefore have you yourself come here along with the groups of Devas?"

Śakra said:

15. There is a king of Daityas named Bāṣkali. He has become very mighty through the boons acquired from Hara. He is invincible to all the Devas in battle. I have been defeated by him in the battle.

16. Now, O Slayer of Madhu, he has established himself in heaven. Therefore, O most excellent one among Suras, I have sought refuge in you along with the Devas.

17. We, the Devas, were formerly saved by you from the danger from Hiraṇyākṣa and Hiraṇyakaśipu and also from other wicked-minded ones.

18. Hence, O Lord of Devas, save us from this mightier Dānava, Bāṣkali also. Excepting you, we have no other greater resort.

Śrī Bhagavān said:

19-20. O Śakra, I shall myself overpower him when the proper time comes. Till that time, perform a great penance, O Vāsava, whereby through the power of penance, you will get the needed strength for slaying that Daitya, Bāṣkali, who is very mighty.

Śakra said:

21. O Lord of the universe, in which holy place should I perform the great penance for the destruction of that Daitya? Do tell it unto us.

Sūta said:

22. On hearing it, Lord Viṣṇu, after thinking in his mind for a long time about holy spots and shrines, spoke to Purandara:

23. "O Śakra, the holy spot Camatkārapura is one that accords Siddhi. Hence hasten to that place and perform penance for slaying him."

Śakra said:

24-25. O Keśava, we are mortally afraid of Bāṣkali, the king of Dānavas. So, without you, we will never go elsewhere. Hence, O Lord of Suras, you too do come there yourself, so that I can perform the great penance under your protection.

Sūta said:

26. Then Lord Viṣṇu said: "It shall be so." Accompanied by Śrī and the Suras, he came over to the holy spot Camatkārapura.

27. All the delighted groups of the Devas went there. Having resolved to perform penance, they built separate hermitages.

28. Vāsudeva remembered his big Ocean of Milk and brought it quickly to that ancient tank.

29. As in the Śvetadvīpa before, he lay down there even as all the Suras humbly eulogized him all round.

30. At the advent of the auspicious second lunar day in the dark half of Āṣāḍha Bṛhaspati himself spoke these gentle words to the Thousand-eyed One whose eyes became turbid due to tears.

Bṛhaspati said:

31. O Purandara, today it is the Dvitīyā (second lunar day) named *Aśūnyaśayanā.* It is very dear to Viṣṇu who is asleep in the watery expanse.

32-33. On being worshipped on this day for four months and meditated upon in the mind always, Viṣṇu fulfills all desires.

The Thousand-eyed One observed perfect Vrata in accordance with the injunctions of the scriptures. For four months, he adored Hari, the Jalaśāyin, on the Dvitīyā day and became endowed with brilliance.

34. On seeing (Indra) endowed with brilliance, Janārdana became pleased. He said: "O Śakra, go this day along with all the groups of Devas for killing that Daitya Bāṣkali. You will be victorious."

Śakra said:

35. O Lord, I am afraid of that evil-minded king of Dānavas. Without you, I dare not go even in the company of all Suras.

Śrī Bhagavān said:

36. O Thousand-eyed One, this discus of mine, Sudarśana, will go with you for the destruction of the enemies of Suras.

37. After saying thus, Hari released the discus Sudarśana along with Śakra for killing the leaders of Dānavas.

38. After going in the company of the discus Śakra exterminated all the Dānavas in the course of the battle.

39. Bāṣkali too was cut up entirely. He fell on the ground like a mountain struck down by thunderbolt.

40. There were many other heroic Dānavas arrogant due to their might. After killing them too, the discus Sudarśana once again returned to the hand of Hari.

41. Śakra and other Devas were delighted. All their suspicions and fears vanished. They approached Viṣṇu again,

bowed down to him and said:

42.43. "O Lord of Devas, by your might all the enemies of Amaras (Devas) have been killed. The kingdom of the three worlds has been regained with all the thorns removed. So tell me my duty that shall be conducive to welfare, O Lotus-eyed One, and also still fear into the enemies."

Śrī Bhagavān said:

44. O Vāsava, for the sake of the welfare of all the worlds I have to remain in this form for ever in this pool, the store-house of meritorious waters.

45. O Consort of Sacī, you should also come here and observe *Aśūnyaśayana Vrata* for the duration of the four months.

46. Thereby no one will dare to be antagonistic to you, O Thousand-eyed One. With my favour you will undoubtedly obtain the benefits desired.

47. Any other man who adores me with devotion here will gain all those regions inaccessible even to Devas.

48. Hence, do go back, O Thousand-eyed One, Rule over heaven. O Lord of Devas, here again I should be seen if there be an occasion for my action. I should be visited undoubtedly as at Śvetadvīpa.

Sūta said:

49. Sátakratu (Indra) bowed down to him and went away. Vāsudeva stationed himself there for the sake of the welfare of the worlds.

50. Thus, O excellent Brāhmaṇas, Jañardana, the great Lord, stationed himself there as Jalaśāyin for the sake of the welfare, of all the worlds.

51. One who is endowed with great ardour and faith and who devoutly worships him particularly in the course of the four months attains the greatest goal.

52. It was converted into Dvārakā by all the groups of Devas. Men who worship there during the four months go to the heaven.

53. On other occasions too a man shall attain the desires cherished in the heart. Hence that Dvārakā should be assiduously worshipped by men at all times and during the Cāturmāsya particularly.

54. Thus the narrative of Jalaśāyin, the Lord of Devas, has been recounted to you in full. It is meritorious and destructive of all sins.

CHAPTER FORTYTWO

Menakā Meets Viśvāmitra[1]

Sūta said:

1-3. O excellent Brāhmaṇas, there is another splendid Kuṇḍa (holy pit) pertaining to Viśvāmitra, situated there. It yields all desires.

If holy bath is taken there on the third lunar day in the month of Caitra, O excellent Brāhmaṇas, a man becomes endowed with divine form like another Kāma himself.

On taking the holy bath there, a woman with ardent faith becomes pregnant. She will be a most covetable one on the earth and endowed with all conjugal felicity.

The sages said:

4. O Sūtanandana, at what time was the Tīrtha of that sage established? How is it free from all impurities? Do tell us without dropping anything.

Sūta said:

5. O excellent Brāhmaṇas, there was formerly an ordinary waterfall there falling down on the ground and endowed with greatness.

6. The divine river Gaṅgā herself is present therein. A person who takes the holy bath there is immediately rid of all sins.

7. If a person remains pure and performs a Srāddha there with the Pitṛs in view, it becomes everlasting in benefit giving satisfaction to the Pitṛs.

1. This is a strange story. Here Menakā falls in love with Viśvāmitra. He is not tempted, for which she curses him and Viśvāmitra retaliates with counter-curse of old age. Both became free from old age after taking a bath in Tīrtha near which Viśvāmitreśvara is installed (Chs. 42-44).

8. Whatever is given as religious gift in that excellent Tīrtha, O Brāhmaṇas, will have lasting benefit of unlimited nature. Homa and Japa performed there too is similar (in benefit).

9. Once upon a time, a doe hit by the arrow of a hunter, entered the water there and died.

10. O excellent Brāhmaṇas, it was also the third lunar day in the bright half of the month of Caitra. It was a Sunday with the constellation Bharaṇī. The time was midday.

11. Due to the great power of that holy water she was transformed into an Apsarā of the Lord of the Devas. She was a lady full of charming smiles shedding lustre all round.

12. Remembering the efficacy of that Tīrtha the lady of excellent complexion used to come there regularly with great devotion and take her holy bath on the third lunar day in the bright half of the month of Caitra when the constellation happened to be Bharaṇī and the day Sunday.

13. Once, on that day, an eminent sage possessing the power of penance and well-known by the name Viśvāmitra came there in the course of his journey.

14. She too who had come there for visiting the deity, concluded the adoration and was about to return to heaven.

15-17. She happened to see the sage who was roaming about here and there. He was in the prime of his youth with handsome features as though he was another Lord of Love wielding the five arrows. He was endowed with the radiance born of the greatness of the Vratas performed by him. He was as brilliant as the sun with refulgent rays. He had burnt all his sins by means of the penance he had performed ever since the days of his childhood.

Merely at his sight, she became afflicted by the arrows of the god of Love. In the height of her delight, she came to the vicinity of the sage for the purpose of sexual dalliance.

18. On seeing the lady hitherto unseen, he hastened to her vicinity with a pleased mind. He stood in front of her as though he wanted to enquire about the way.

19. Apparently enquiring about the land, he spoke about the duties of women in particular.[1] "O fair lady, may you acquire auspiciousness mentally, verbally and physically.

1. VV 19-41 describe "Strī-dharma", "Duties of an ideal wife"

20. Let there be unswerving devotion unto Vāsudeva for ever. I hope, O daughter, you are devoted to the feet of your husband and equipped with chastity and humility and always speaking pleasant things.

21. I hope you always endear yourself to your husband making gifts to his kinsmen and circle of friends and praising them whether in front of him or behind his back.

22. O lady of excellent complexion, I hope, you always go to sleep after the husband is asleep and, I hope, you get up even before he gets up.

23. I hope, you get up early in the morning and do the sweeping at home, O beautiful woman. All embellishments and beautifications thereof too you yourself do.

24. I suppose, you bow down to the deities and then to the elders. I hope, you give food and water to others in accordance with your capacity and then take your food.

25. I believe, O beautiful lady, that you never take cooked food after the Sun has set. I hope, you never take food before offering it to your servants and in particular to saintly people.

26. I hope, you always drink water after filtering it seven times with a thick cloth thus protecting the water-borns(?)

27. I hope, you are so kind-hearted as to preserve like your sons even lice, bugs and flies that afflict your limbs awfully(!)

28. I hope, you always hear straight from the mouths of good people, the *Śivadharma* (auspicious religious acts or devotional acts pertaining to god Śiva) with great devotion. O fair lady, I hope, you respectfully follow them too.

29. I believe that you do respectfully adore the scripture, the expounder and the person who reads it after listening to it.

30. I hope, you copy in beautiful handwriting the Purāṇas and the Śāstras composed by eminent people and then give away those manuscripts to good people.

31. One who listens to all the Śāstras but does not give the prescribed fees should be considered as Śāstra-thief. He never attains the fruit thereof.

32. I hope that you make due arrangements within your capacity for dances, songs, musical instruments and the like in the temple of Śiva. I hope, you make the customary oblations, offerings etc., within your means.

33. I hope, O excellent lady, that you offer shawls, blankets etc. to good people after respectfully bowing down to them.

34. O lady of wide eyes, I hope you avoid straying into the abodes of others unnecessarily without any work always, especially after nightfall.

35. I hope, O fair lady, you never take food while your husband is hungry. I hope, you take care to avoid disobedience to his command.

36. I hope, you never retort when the husband is angry. I hope, you speak pleasant things to dispel his anger.

37. I hope that when your husband is away from home you wear dirty clothes and become distressed, lean and pallid in face.

38. I hope that you never keep broken vessels in the backyard of the house or the remnants of food taken in by the people, though they may be of use.

39. I hope, you never wander at night even for religious vigils and discourses, in streams, isolated places, forests and sand banks.

40. O splendid lady, I hope, you never contract friendship with courtezans, nurses, a gardners's wife and a washermen's wife.

41. I hope, you always keep your face brightly coloured with saffron, hairs decorated with flowers and the eyes darkened by collyrium."

CHAPTER FORTYTHREE

Dialogue between Viśvāmitra and Menakā

Menakā said:

1. O Brāhmaṇa, the women for whom the code of virtuous conduct you have spoken (prescribed) so far are different. We are, on the other hand, courtesans of Heaven-dwellers, who wander freely according to our sweet will.

2. Anyway, O highly esteemed one, tell me what is that land from which you have come? Even in this Tīrtha, the resort of virtuous ones, you are the captivator of my heart.

3-4. O highly fortunate one, your personal form is on a par with that of Kāmadeva. On seeing you I have become tormented by the arrows of Kāma. I experience horripilation all over my limbs.

So accept me and enjoy me. I am attached to you. If you do not, I will be doomed. Already scorched by the arrows of Kāma, O ascetic, I will die in front of you. Thereby you will incur the sin of the murder of a woman. There is no doubt about it.

The Tāpasa (Ascetic) said:

5. O lady of excellent eyebrows, we are persons with holy vows, strictly adhering to the vow of celibacy. O fair lady, of course we are fools (totally ignorant) in the matters of love as we abide by the *Śivaśāsana* (Śaiva Śāstra).

6. *Brahmacarya* (celibacy) is cited as the root of all holy vows and restraints, especially in the case of devotees of Śiva. Hereafter you will do what is proper bearing this in mind (I am not a sex addict. Don't court me—Editor's footnote).

7. A man of vows may perform penance for more than a hundred years. But sexual dalliance even once brings about utter destruction of his Pāśupata vow.

8. O timid lady, why do you speak as though you are enamoured of me, a follower of Paśupati (Lord Śiva). Such a highly sinful activity as this is condemned in *Śivaśāsana.* (Śaiva Śastra or Paśupatism).

9. A man of the holy vow of Pāśupatism, who enjoys a woman, becomes a false Pāśupata. Along with ten earlier generations of his family, he will be cooked in Naraka.

10. O lady of excellent countenance, leave alone sexual union or even touch of a lady, even conversation with a woman leads to a great sin in the case of a Pāśupata.

11. Hence, O beautiful lady, go away from this place. It behoves you to go there where your desires can be fulfilled.

CHAPTER FORTYFOUR

Greatness of Viśvāmitreśvara

Menakā said:

1-2. O highly lustrous one, you are not an expert in sexual acts indeed. That is why you restrain me, a loving woman, by means of words like these.

Sūta said:

On being told thus, Viśvāmitra who never desired to accept her as his wife, became very angry and he said thus:

Viśvāmitra said:

3. You may live or court death. I will not carry out your words. The sin originating from the violation of one's holy vow, is worse than that from the murder of a woman.

4. Expiation has been prescribed by learned men in regard to men of holy vows when the murder of a woman is committed but not when they come into carnal contact with them. Hence you may go away.

5. It is not that only men who have adopted holy vows incur sin from physical intimacy of women. Even men outside the pale of holy vows face downfall if they are attached to women.

6. Even at the time of the first meeting under the pretext of circumambulating the sacred fire (in marriage ceremony) a woman indicates transmigration (coming and going) in Saṁsāra.

7. Hence a wise man who desires his own welfare should avoid conversations with women, let alone physical, intimate contact.

8. A woman is like a smouldering, charcoal. A man is like a pot of ghee. Avoiding the contact he remains strong (compact); by the contact he becomes ruined (melts).

9. Women are at the root of all disasters and adversities of all the living beings on the earth. Hence they should be kept off at a safe distance, because they are obstacles to the attainment of heaven.

10. Women of noble families commanding great affluence

and having their own husbands begin to love someone else. They are very fickle.

11. By coming into contact with women, people wander about in the worldly existence. Hence no one other than women contributes anything to sin on the earth.

12. Women attend to a base man who serves them in isolated places even if he be ugly and base-born.

13. Women of uncontrolled nature abide by the conventional decorum with their husbands only because they are afraid of the servants and danger from other men.

Sūta said:

14. Thus rebuked by him Menakā became very angry. With her lips throbbing much through anger, she cursed that excellent sage.

15-16. "O highly evil-minded one, by avoiding the sexual dalliance (with me) you have abandoned me though I am sexually excited. So, take this curse from me. Be now itself one with wrinkles and grey hair, one with the limbs shattered by old age, one of dim vision and bereft of colour, O evil-minded one."

Sūta said:

17. Immediately after these words had been uttered, the excellent sage came to be one as imprecated by her.

18. He too became highly furious and attempted to curse her. With eyes reddened due to distress, he took water from the waterpot.

19. "O basest courtezan, although I am blameless I have been cursed by you. So you too shall become one with the limbs shattered due to old age."

20. At his words she too became one of that type of physical form as that of the excellent sage with the body covered with wrinkles and grey hairs.

21. Then, along with such a hideous form she took her bath in the Tīrtha whereat she got transformed into her original form.

22. On seeing that great miracle, he took in a very great haste, his bath there and became transformed as before.

23. Thus, by the power of the Tīrtha both of them became endowed with handsome features, beauty and exalted virtues. They joyously took leave of each other and went to the place they desired.

24. By coming to know the greatness of the Tīrtha in this manner, the holy sage installed the Liṅga of the Trident-bearing Lord of Devas.

25. The holy lord performed very great penance at that excellent Tīrtha. By means of the blades of Kuśa grass, he made the lake very wide.

26. A man who takes his holy bath there and worships the excellent Liṅga well-known as Viśvāmitreśvara shall go to Śiva's palace.

27. Even today the water seen there is on a par with the water of Gaṅgā, meritorious, destructive of all sins and yielding all cherished desires.

28. One who takes his holy bath there with the mind sanctified by faith, shall attain the world of Devas and rejoice along with the Pitṛs.

29. Ever since then that Tīrtha earned a great reputation that it bestows exalted handsomeness on men all over the earth, the nether world and the heavenly region.

30. Thus, O excellent Brāhmaṇas, the greatness of Viśvāmitreśa, that is destructive of all sins and about which I had been asked, has been completely narrated to you all.

CHAPTER FORTYFIVE

Greatness of Tripuṣkara[1]

Sūta said:

1-2 O excellent Brāhmaṇas, there itself is the highly meritorious group of three Puṣkaras where penance was performed formerly by the king of Ānarta. One who takes his holy bath there at midday in the month of Kārttika when the Moon is in the constellation Kṛttikā (i.e. on the full-moon day) attains the greatest goal.

The sages said:

3. O son of Sūta, do tell us how the highly meritorious group of three Puṣkaras happened to be there? At what holy spot should it be identified? What are the signs thereof.

Sūta said:

4. I shall describe unto you how the intelligent sage Viśvāmitra saw (recognized) the group of the three Puṣkaras formerly by what indicators.

5. Formerly when the excellent sage Viśvāmitra was staying there, the meritorious Kārttikī (full-moon day in the month of Kārttika) arrived when the constellation was Kṛttikā.

6. The storehouse of penance, the son of Gādhi, realized that the holy spot consisted of all the Tīrthas. Then he thought thus in his mind.

7-9. 'It happens that today is the highly meritorious Kārttikī with the Kṛttikā constellation. On this day, if men take their holy bath in the waters of Puṣkara, welfare is attained by them. The primordial Puṣkara is very far off. It is not possible to go there now. So, I shall take the holy bath in the Tīrtha situated here.'

After resolving thus with the mind sanctified by ardent faith,

1. Puṣkara lake is near Ajmer in Rajasthan. It is glorified in Mbh and other Purāṇas. God Brahmā performed a sacrifice here. This Purāṇa claims the existence of this holy place at Camatkārapura as well.

he began to search for the Puṣkaras all round. Due to the multiplicity of the Tīrthas, he could not come to a decision.

10. Wherever he saw a pool of water, he took his holy bath there. Wandering here and there he became tired.

11. He came to the root of a tree. Standing there on the ground and remaining pure he faithfully eulogized Tripuṣkara:

12. "Svarga is within a Yojana from the middle Puṣkara and half a Yojana from the least (smallest) one. Splendid souls have proclaimed that Svarga is within the reach of a hand from the greatest Kuṇḍa (holy pit).

13. Other Tīrthas indeed sanctify the devotees undoubtedly who take holy plunge and perform Dāna. But, one is rid of sins merely by a visit to Puṣkara.

14. After arriving at the forest region of Puṣkara if one feeds a single Brāhmaṇa with greens, roots and fruits, it is as effective as though a core of Brāhmaṇas are fed.

15. It is very difficult (to get the opportunity of) having a holy plunge in Puṣkara; penance at Puṣkara is rarely achieved. Residence at Puṣkara is also very rare. Everything in Puṣkara is rarely achieved.

16. A man who takes his holy bath in Puṣkara on the occasion of Kārttikī along with the Kṛttikā constellation is instantly rid of sins incurred ever since birth and till death.

17. A man who takes but a single holy plunge in the morning in the biggest Puṣkara, at midday in the middle Puṣkara and after sunset in the smallest Puṣkara shall attain Svarga.

18. Sin abides in the bodies of the embodied beings only until they take their holy bath in the waters of Puṣkara.

19. Just as darkness touched by the rays of the sun gets dissolved, so also sin vanishes quickly after coming into contact with the waters of Puṣkara.

20. Even after committing Brāhmaṇa-slaughter and other sins on the earth, a person becomes free from defects (sins) if he bathes in Puṣkara on the Kārttikī day.

21. Of what avail is Dāna? Of what importance is Homa? Of what avail is elaborate Yajña? The benefit of all these is achieved through a holy baths in Puṣkara on the Kārttikī day.

22. If this statement perfectly uttered by me is true, let Puṣkara be seen immediately."

23. Even as the intelligent Viśvāmitra was saying thus, O

excellent Brāhmaṇas, there arose an unembodied voice from the sky.

24. "O Viśvāmitra, O most excellent one among sages, my perpetual residence is in the sky excepting the single occasion of Kārttikī accompanied by the Kṛttikā constellation.

25. Therefore on this day I certainly come to the earth in this very meritorious forest. Therefore you perform the rite of holy bath."

Viśvāmitra said:

26. We hear that this place is a supporting base in the case of all Tīrthas. O Lord of all the Tīrthas, how can I identify you stationed here itself.

27. Then, O excellent Brāhmaṇas, a loud voice originating in the aerial space rose up once more, delighting Viśvāmitra, the most excellent one among sages:

28-31. "Not far from this forest there are (three) watery expanses (lakes). In one of them there is a lotus with face stooping down. In the second it has the face lifted up. In the third the face is turned sideways. Among them the Jyeṣṭha Puṣkara (the greatest Puṣkara) should be identified through the lotuses with faces lifted up.[1]

O excellent Brāhmaṇa, the identification mark of the middle one is the lotuses with faces turned sideways. The smallest Puṣkara should be identified through the lotuses with faces downwards. O excellent Sage, after identifying them through these signs do perform your holy bath."

On hearing it the sage got up and went away quickly.

32-35. Those lakes were seen with such lotuses. On seeing them the sage endowed with ardent faith performed the holy bath in due order. Then he offered libations to the Pitṛs in accordance with injunctions. Thereby, O excellent Brāhmaṇas, he performed in accordance with the injuctions the rite of Śrāddha through greens, roots and Nīvāra rice-grains together with fruits. Thereafter he stood on the bank itself and began to look around with mental concentration. He was keen to see the

1. *Puṣkara* means a lotus. The association of Lotuses with the Tīrtha is significant (PE p. 622).

signs of identification of the conjunction of Kṛttikā constellation with the Kārttikī day.

The Brāhmaṇas said:

36. Of what nature is the sign in the greatest Puṣkara on the Kārttikī day when there is the conjunction of Kṛttikā constellation. Describe everything to us quickly.

Sūta said:

37. On the Kārttikī day when the Moon comes into contact with Kṛttikā constellation, an excellent lotus comes up from the middle of water.

38. Within it a being of the size of thumb is seen by the people endowed with ardent faith, who have taken their holy bath duly. Thereafter, a devotee obtains the merit of pilgrimage to the Tīrtha.

39. It was for this reason that the great sage Viśvāmitra strenuously looked around for the expected sign after his holy bath.

40. Even as the intelligent Viśvāmitra was watching thus, King Bṛhadbala, the overlord of Ānarta, came there.

41-42. He was extremely tired after hunting herds of deer, bears, boars, stags and *Sambara* bucks, lions tigers, wolves and other wild beasts of prey. He reached that place at midday along that path.

43. Near a tree he saw Viśvāmitra, the leading sage. He was seated there after his holy bath keenly watching the lake before him.

44. The king got down from the horse and bowed down to the sage. The excellent king was excessively tired and so entered the water of the lake.

45. In the meantime that lotus came up from the water. It had a thousand petals and its lustre was similar to that of twelve Suns.

46. On seeing that large wonderful lotus, the king was curious and he caught hold of it with his left hand.

47. O excellent Brāhmaṇas, hardly had the lotus been touched when a loud report was heard which filled the entire universe.

48. On hearing that sound, the king swooned and fell into

the water. The lotus vanished.

49. With very great difficulty, he was pulled out of the water by his attendants miserable and grief-stricken uttering cries of "Hā! Hā!"

50. After reaching the banks, he regained consciousness with great difficulty. As he glanced over his body he found it affected by leprosy.

51. The nose, the hands and the feet were badly affected and decayed. His voice was gruff. He became sad and gloomy.

52. Approaching Viśvāmitra, the king uttered wretched, feeble words choked with tears.

53-54. "O holy sage, see how despicable my body has become all of a sudden as I went into the water. O leading sage, could it be any defect of the water or the soil beneath, that my body has suddenly attained this serious mal-transformation?"

Viśvāmitra said:

55. This is a solar lotus. Within it Lord Sun himself is present. But you touched it with an *Ucchiṣṭa* (impure) body.

56. O king, when in the month of Kārttika the Moon comes into conjunction with Kṛttikā constellation, this comes up from the waters of the Puṣkara.

57. This Puṣkara is the Jyeṣṭha (greatest) which you got into on being weary. Today is the Full-Moon day in the month of Kārttika and there is the conjunction of Kṛttikā constellation.

58. After seeing this a man with ardour and faith should take his holy bath. He shall attain the greatest goal.

59. It was only to pluck it out, O king, that you touched the lotus and that too when you were *Ucchiṣṭa* (impure). Therefore this is the result.

Bṛhadbala said:

60. O excellent sage, how can I get rid of this fell disease of leprosy? Could it be through penance, observance of restraints and holy vows?

Viśvāmitra said:

61. Propitiate the Thousand-rayed Lord in this holy spot,

O king. You will attain good result, ease and comfort arising from the destruction of (perfect cure from) leprosy.

62. On hearing the words of the sage, King Bṛhadbala immediately installed an idol of Sun-god.

63-64. With great ardour and faith, he regularly adored the idol in accordance with the injunctions with flowers, incense and unguent. On Sundays he conducted special worship after observing fast. He faithfully adored with red flowers along with red sandalpaste.

65-66. At the end of a year, the king experienced complete relief from the disease of leprosy. He regained the refulgence of twelve suns. Thereafter, he went back to his kingdom and enjoyed many pleasures. On death he attained the world of the Sun-god.

Sūta said:

67. O excellent Brāhmaṇas, it was thus that the intelligent Viśvāmitra made the three Puṣkaras manifest and accessible to all the people of the world.

68. A man who takes his holy bath there on days with Kṛttikā constellation, or on the full-moon day in the month of Kārttika goes to Brahmaloka.

69. A man who visits Bhāskara (the Sun-god) installed by Bṛhadbala on all Sundays for a period of one year celebrating great festivals therein, shall be rid of all ailments he may be suffering from.

70. A man without ailments immediately attains whatever he desires mentally with the favour of the Hot-rayed One. One without desires attains salvation.

71. One who performs the rite of Vṛṣotsarga (ritualistic releasing of a bull as dedication unto the deity) on the Kārttikī day when there is the conjunction of Kṛttikā constellation in the highly meritorious Puṣkaras, shall get the merit of a horse-sacrifice.

72. One should desire to beget many sons so that one may go to Gayā, one may perform a horse sacrifice or one may ritualistically dedicate a 'blue' bull.

73. All the Tīrthas or all the Dāna rites may be put on one pan of the balance and in the other one, the dedication of a bull. Both are on a par with each other.

74. One who listens to this always or reads with ardent faith, attains all desires and is honoured in Brahmaloka.

CHAPTER FORTYSIX

Greatness of Sarasvatī Tīrtha

The sages said:

1-3. O highly intelligent one, do narrate all the other Tīrthas that may be present there.

Sūta said:

There is another very splendid Tīrtha there, named Sārasvata Tīrtha. Even one who is dumb and mute but takes his holy bath there, shall become an expert in speech. O excellent Brāhmaṇas, he gets all human and heavenly objects desired by him and also the worlds ending with Brahmaloka etc.

4. Formerly there was a very famous king named Balavardhana. He enjoyed the ocean-girdled earth acquired through the might of his own arms.

5. A son was born to him. He was endowed with all good features. On the twelfth day the father invited excellent Brāhmaṇas and clearly named him Aṁbuvīci.

6. Fondled lovingly by the king, the boy grew up properly but due to dumbness he could not even lisp words.

7. While the boy was running his seventh year, Balavardhana was attacked by his enemies in battle and killed.

8. Thereupon, in the absence of another son, that boy, although he was dumb, was crowned as the king of the kingdom by the ministers of the king.

9. Even as the sluggish king, not yet out of childhood, was thrust on the kingdom, there was a great revolt in the realm.

10. The practice (Nyāya) of acquatic beings (called *Mātsya Nyāya:* 'Might is right') then prevailed on the earth. And strong men oppressed all weaker people.

11-12. Thereupon those ministers spoke to Vasiṣṭha, their priest: "O great sage, find out some means to restore the power of speech to this king. See, the entire surface of the earth has become a void due to the defect of this king. Do something that is proper in this connection."

13. He meditated for a long time and then spoke to the distressed ministers, all of whom were extremely grief-stricken even as the king himself was listening:

14. "In the holy spot of Hāṭakeśvara, there is Sārasvata Tīrtha that grants all desires to men. Let this king go there and have his holy bath."

15. At his instance, the king immediately rushed to the Tīrtha. Thanks to the holy bath in that Tīrtha, he became one with sweet voice.

16-21. Having clearly understood the power of Sarasvatī, the king equipped with great ardour and faith meditated upon Sarasvatī. He took some clay from the river-bank and himself made an image of Goddess Bhāratī having four arms.

In her right hand she held a very charming lotus. In the other hand there was an Akṣamālā (rosary of beads) that surpassed the stellar lustre. In another (third) hand she held a waterpot filled with divine water. Similarly in the left (fourth) hand she held the book containing all lores.[1]

He then placed that image on a sanctified slab assiduously and devoutly worshipped it through incense, garlands and unguents. Afterwards the king stood before the image with bodily and mental purity. With the mind purified by ardent faith, he began to eulogize in a loud voice.

The prayer of Sarasvatī

22. O goddess, whatever there is *Sat* (manifest) and *Asat* (unmanifest), the place of bondage and that of liberation—all these are pervaded by you in a concealed form in the same manner as fuel is pervaded by fire.

23. You are stationed in the heart of everyone in the form of Siddhi (fulfilment), in the tongue in the form of speech and in the eye in the form of *Jyoti* (light, sight).

24. O goddess of Devas, One devoted to favour the wretched and the distressed who seek refuge in you, you alone are accessible

---

1. The famous icon in the Sarasvatī temple at Bikaner (Rajasthan) is like this.

and comprehensible through devotion in all the three worlds.

25. You are the goddess dwelling in all living beings. You are *Kīrti* (renown); you are *Dhṛti* (fortitude). You are *Medhā* (intellect). You are *Bhakti* (devotion). You are remembered as *Prabhā* (refulgence). You are *Nidrā* (slumber). You are *Kṣudhā* (hunger). You are *Kīrti* (reputation).

26. You are *Tuṣṭi* (satisfaction), *Puṣṭi* (nourishment), *Vapus* (physical form). *Prīti* (love), *Svadhā, Svāhā, Vibhāvarī* (night), *Rati* (enjoyment), *Prīti* (affection), *Kṣiti* (Earth), *Gaṅgā, Satya, Dharma* and exaltedness of mind.

27. You are *Lajjā* (bashfulness), *Śānti* (peace), *Smṛti* (memory), *Dakṣa* (efficient), *Kṣamā* (forgiveness), *Gaurī, Rohiṇī, Sinīvālī, Kuhū, Rākā, Deva-mātā* (Aditi) and *Diti.*

28. You are *Brahmaṇī, Vinatā, Śivā* the daughter of *Dakṣa, Gāyatrī, Sāvitrī, Kṛṣi* (cultivation), *Vṛṣṭi* (shower), *Śruti* (Veda), *Kalā* (Art).

29. You are the nerve vessel called Balā, Tuṣṭikāṣṭhā (acme of satisfaction), Rasanā (tongue), Sarasvatī. In fact, you are everything in all the three worlds not enumerated because of multiplicity.

30. Whatever is intended or not intended is your form, O goddess of Suras. Gandharvas, Kinnaras, Devas, Siddhas, Vidyādharas, Uragas,

31. Yakṣas, Guhyakas, Bhūtas, Daityas, Vināyakas—all these attained Siddhi, with your favour.

32. Others too not mentioned due to multiplicity are also propitiated (by me) and worshipped with strenuous effort elaborately. Let those deities remove the sin. Thus you are glorified.

33. On being eulogized by that king the highly pleased goddess of Devas, Bhāratī, immediately manifested herself and spoke.

Sarasvatī said:

34. O king, I am pleased with this prayer of yours and the steadfest devotion. So choose your boon as you desire.

The king said:

35. From now onwards, at my request you shall undoubtedly

stay in this idol as long as my fame is steady throughout the three worlds.

36. If any devotee, urged by me, adequately propitiates you staying in this, you should immediately grant him everything befitting his devotion.

Sarasvatī said:

37-40. If any man takes his holy bath here in the auspicious waters on eighth and fourteenth lunar days and worships me present here, O king, I shall grant him all the cherished desires.

Sūta said:

Thus, from that day onwards, the greatest goddess Sarasvatī became stationed there herself for the sake of the welfare of all the worlds. A man who observes fast on eighth and fourteenth lunar days and worships her with white flowers and unguents, shall become very intelligent and eloquent always in every birth.

41. He may have frequent rebirths. With the favour of Sarasvatī, no fool will be born in his family.

42. A man who listens to pious discourses in front of her, resides in heaven for three Yugas by her power.

43. A man endowed with ardent faith who makes the gift of learning in her shrine shall obtain the merit of a horse-sacrifice.

44. One who offers to a leading Brāhmaṇa a book on religious conduct shall obtain the full merit of a horse-sacrifice.

45. One who stands before her and recites the Vedas shall obtain the full merit of an Agniṣṭoma Yajña.

CHAPTER FORTYSEVEN

Greatness of Mahākāleśvara

The sages said:

1. O highly intelligent Sūtaja, tell us in detail the greatness of Mahākāla, because you know everything.

Sūta said:

2. Formerly there was a king hailing from the family of Ikṣvāku. He was well-known as Rudrasena. He was the destroyer of all his enemies.

3. In majesty he was like the ocean; in gentleness he resembled the moon. In vigour he was on a par with the Thousand-eyed One (Indra); and in handsome features he was like Kandarpa (god of Love).

4. A city endowed with all the good features well-known as Kāntī was his capital. It was the most excellent one of all cities with lofty ramparts and ornamental gates.

5. His beloved wife was well-known as Padmāvatī. She was honoured by the greatest people. She was endowed with exalted good qualities and beauty.

6. On the day of Vaiśākhī (full-moon day in the month of Vaiśākha) he used to come out from his abode accompanied by her and a limited number of soldiers.

7. O excellent Brāhmaṇas, he used to perform *Rātrijāgara* (keeping awake at night) in front of Lord Mahākāla. The king was always accompanied by his wife and he was ardently faithful.

8. He used to observe fasts. He meditated upon Maheśvara. There used to be delightful singing and dancing with instrumental music, narration of religious discourses by Brāhmaṇas and elaborate chanting of Vedic Mantras.

9. Getting up early in the morning, he used to take his holy bath and wear clean and washed clothes. With purity of mind and body, he used to make gifts to Brāhmaṇas and ascetics in particular.

10. He distributed gifts to the blind, the wretched and the miserable people in thousands. Every year that king used to come thus and perform the rite of *Jāgara* in front of that Lord.

11. As the king continued to peform this holy rite of *Jāgara* in front of Mahākāla, he became more and more prosperous.

12-13. All the enemies were destroyed. Fortune increased. Once when the king arrived there, he saw excellent Brāhmaṇas who had come from different quarters on that very day and had gathered before Mahākāla.

14. They were highly conversant with the Vedas. They were regular in the observance of vows. A few highly meritorious, excellent Brāhmaṇas narrated stories.

15. They narrated the stories of saintly kings. Others narrated the stories of ancient sages and Devas. Others enumerated the Tīrthas. Some of them told the stories of Brāhmaṇa-sages. The stories of Yajñas, oceans and continents were very charming.

16. The king bowed down to them in due order and sat in the middle of the assembly. He was heartily congratulated by all of them.

17. At the close of the discourse, those leading sages asked the king eagerly:

18-20. "O king, every year you regularly come here from very far on the Vaiśākhī day. You assiduously perform the rite of *Rātrijāgara* in front of the Lord even abandoning all the other rites such as *Snāna, Dāna* etc. mentioned by those who expound the scriptural texts. If this be no closely guarded secret, do narrate everything in full. Of course you know the benefit that accrues from *Rātrijāgara.*"

The king said:

21. Well, this is indeed a very great secret, O excellent Brāhmaṇas, that which you have asked me. Still I shall narrate everything unto you.

22. Formerly I was a merchant by caste in the city of Vidiśā. I was very poor and all my kinsmen abandoned and avoided me. At every step I met with discomfiture.

23. On one occasion, the Lord of rain, the Slayer of Paka, did not shower rain at all in Vidiśā city for twelve years.

24. On account of drought, all the people were oppressed by hunger. Due to the absence of food, some people died and some went to foreign lands.

25-27. I took my distressed wife with me and set off thinking about Saurāṣṭra (Kathiawad) (as my destination). The lady was emaciated in every limb through starvation and tears welled up in her eyes. She was faltering at every step. O excellent Brāhmaṇas, I had heard from people that there was plenty of food there. I duly proceeded ahead eating the food received as alms. Ultimately I arrived in the Ānarta country near Camatkārapura.

28. There a beautiful lake was seen by me. It was adorned with clusters of lotuses and filled with clear water. Aquatic birds hovered around it.

29. Distressed with hunger and thirst and particularly exhausted due to the fatigue of the journey, I went in and took my bath in the cool waters thereof.

30-31. Then I was told by my wife: " O Lord, collect some lotus flowers from the lake so that some may buy them and we will have food for the day. Yonder, an excellent city is visible. It is like the city of Indra. It behoves you to go there and sell them."

32. O excellent Brāhmaṇas, many lotus flowers were gathered by me for selling, as I desired food.

33. Going into the city of Camatkārapura, O excellent Brāhmaṇas, I wandered everywhere in the rows of houses and the crossings of three and four roads.

34. It was my bad luck that the people were averse to buying. No man took those lotuses.

35. Even as I became utterly tired with the throat parched due to hunger, the sun reached Astācala (the mountain behind which the sun sets) and it was evening.

36. Utterly disgusted, I placed the lotuses on the bare ground and lay down there in a ruined temple along with my wife.

37. When it was about midnight, the sound of music was heard by me and the thought occurred to me that this was the rite of *Jāgara* undoubtedly.

38. 'Should I go there; some man might buy the lotuses and I could have meal for the price those might fetch.'

39. After deciding thus I accompanied by my wife took the flowers and hastened to the place from where the sound of music came.

40. O leading sages, I went into the temple. There I saw Mahākāla, the Lord of chiefs of Devas, worshipped by excellent Brāhmaṇas who were engaged in singing and were seated in front.

41. Some were dancing and others were singing. A few were performing Japa. Some excellent Brāhmaṇas were performing Homa and others were engaged in religious discussion.

42. One of the assembled men was asked by me: "Is the rite of *Jāgara* being performed here? Who are these people engaged in the *Jāgara?* Do tell me quickly."

43-45. He said: "This is the *Jāgara* of Lord Mahākāla. It is devoutly performed by Brāhmaṇas who have been observing fast. It is the holy lunar day named Vaiśākhī. It is highly meritorious. One should perform the rite of Jāgara devoutly before Lord Mahākāla. Thereby he undoubtedly attains happiness.

O fair Sir, you have lotus flowers; give them to me and take the price thereof. For your food I shall give you three *Palas* of silver."

46-47. Then I began to think on these lines, O excellent Brāhmaṇas: 'Shall I worship Mahākāla, the Lord of Suras? No meritorious rites have been performed by me in the previous birth. Certainly that is why I have become very distressed in this manner.

48. But my sweet-speaking beloved wife has become very hungry and her throat is parched. Want of food may doubtlessly cause her death in the morning.'

49. Even as I was thinking thus my beloved wife spoke these sweet words after humbly bowing down to me:

50-53. 'O Lord, do not sell the lotuses for the greed of money. Do according to my words conducive to welfare.

We had to observe fast under compulsion doubtlessly because there was not even a bit of greens. In this state of hunger, we shall have the rite of *Jāgara* too. Both of us had our holy bath in the splendid lake during the day, because we were distressed due to fatigue and heat. We worshipped the deity as well. Hence let us now worship Lord Mahākāla by means of these lotuses so that we may have great welfare.'

The king said:

54. O excellent Brāhmaṇas, with a mind full of Sattva (purity) both of us joyously performed the adoration of Maheśvara by means of those lotuses.

55. Due to the pangs of hunger we could not sleep at all by

any means, as we continued to stay in the temple here in front of Hara.

56. Then, in the morning, when the disc of the sun rose up, I died due to the overwhelming hunger in this very same place, O excellent Brāhmaṇas.

57. Thereupon my wife took my body and with great delight entered the funeral pyre.

58. Thanks to the power thereof, I was born as a king and Lord of Kāntī. That chaste lady was born as the daughter of king of Daśārṇa with the power to recollect previous births.

59. Knowing me to be her own husband, she choose me in the *Svayaṁvara*. After knowing that she was my previous wife she was brought with me by me.

60-61. It is for this reason, O excellent Brāhmaṇas, that on the Vaiśākhī day every year I perform the rite of *Jāgara* of Mahākāla along with this beloved of mine, after worshipping Mahākāla with flowers, incense and unguents. It is the truth that I have mentioned.

62. At that time the rite of *Rātrijāgara* was performed by me, O Brāhmaṇas. Thanks to the power of this Lord, this merit has accrued (to me).

63. Now with great ardour and faith, I am performing this in accordance with the injunctions. I do not know what fruit (reward) he will grant me.

64. Thus, O excellent Brāhmaṇas, the entire truth has been related to you. May Mahākāla be pleased with the truth I have spoken.

Sūta said:

65. On hearing this, those excellent Brāhmaṇas with their eyes gleaming with wonder, exclaimed "Well done! Well done!"

The Brāhmaṇas said:

66. O king, the entire truth has been spoken by you. Nothing is difficult (to be achieved) on this earth if there is the favour of Mahākāla.

67. Hence, O king, we shall also ardently perform the rite of *Rātrijāgara* of this Lord every year.

*　　　　*　　　　*

68. Then that king and all those Brāhmaṇas performed the rite of Jāgara in the presence of Mahākāla.

69. Ever since then all the kings swayed by wonder performed the *Jāgara* rite with special gaiety, singing and playing on instruments in diverse ways. There were religious legends, dances, recitation of Vedic passages of different contexts.

70. When the day dawned clearly the king got up, worshipped Mahākāla and took leave of all those excellent Brāhmaṇas. Accompanied by his army, he joyously went to his city.

71. In due course the king met with his death and attained the greatest region devoid of death and old age.

72. Thus, O excellent Brāhmaṇas, the greatness of Mahākāla has been fully spoken to you. It is destructive of all sins.

CHAPTER FORTYEIGHT

Installation of Umā-Maheśvara[1]

Sūta said:

1. There itself in that very place is the hermitage of King Hariścandra. It is well-known and overgrown with various creepers and trees.

2. Penance was performed there by him after installing Umā and Maheśvara. Further he distributed different kinds of gifts to Brāhmaṇas according to their desires.

3. Formerly there was a king named Hariścandra, the son of Triśaṅku. The glorious king hailing from the solar race ruled over Ayodhyā.

4. While he was ruling virtuously there was no famine, no ailment and certainly no premature death. Nor was there any fear from thieves.

5. The clouds always showered rain at the proper time. The vegetation was luxurious. The waters were tasty and the trees bore fruits in all the seasons.

---

1. This story is a new contribution of this Purāṇa. The sonlessness of Hariścandra, the curse of Umā and establishment of an Āśrama etc. are not found in Mbh, Padma and other Purāṇas.

6. Daṇḍa (punishment; a staff measuring four Hastas) existed only at the place where dwelling place is built. There was *Gṛharodha* (closing of houses; attacking of houses) only in the game of dice. There was only one *Doṣākara* (storehouse of faults; the Moon, the cause of night) and it was the Moon. Only owls were *Priyadoṣas* (fond of faults; fond of nights).

7. There was *Snehakṣaya* (decrease in oil or affection) only in lamps. There was *Karagraha* (holding of the hands; levying of taxes) in marriages only. There was *Vṛttabhaṅga* (violation of Vṛtta i.e. prosody or decorum) only in prose. There was *Dānotthiti* i.e. elevation of *Dāna* (ichor; bribery) only in the face of an elephant.

8. Thus the king was endowed with all good qualities and he had imperial authority. There was one great defect, that he was sonless.

9. Therefore he installed a Liṅga devoutly in the holy spot of Camatkārapura and performed very great penance for getting a son.

10. He used to meditate on Maheśvara and practised austerities: He sat inside five fires in the months of summer; during rainy season he stayed under the open sky; he resorted to water-lakes in Hemanta (winter).

11. Then at the end of a thousand years Maheśvara was pleased with him. He appeared before him along with Gaurī and surrounded by groups of Gaṇas (attendants).

12. He said: "I shall bestow boons. Request for anything desired. I shall grant it to you even if it be very difficult to get."

13. Thereupon the king bowed down to him and eulogized through the Sūktas of the Vedas. With humility and palms joined in reverence he spoke:

14-16. "O excellent one among Suras, whatever there is worthy of being mentally cherished on the earth is in my house. My wives are beautiful. The kingdom is devoid of thorns. The enemies have been exterminated. My body is without ailment. Unlimited and vast is my wealth. I have only one source of unhappiness that I have no issue. Hence, O Lord Śaṅkara, if you are pleased, grant me a son.

Śrī Bhagavān said:

17. O excellent king, due to my favour, a son will be born to

you ere long. There is no doubt about it. Hence go home quickly.

Sūta said:

18. In the meantime Gaurī rebuked Mahādeva with eyes reddened due to anger. Then she spoke to the king:

19-20. "O big fool, since you did not bow down to me after Hara, I am going to curse you. You will beget a son as said by the Trident-armed Lord. But you will also meet with the sorrow arising from his death even in infancy."

21. After saying thus, the goddess vanished along with Śambhu and the attendants too.

22. After the acquisition of the boon and having received the curse as well, the king did not go home. He performed a great penance once again.

23. He installed Gaurī and Maheśvara in the same seat (pedestal) and then propitiated them together, with flowers and unguents.

24. The king offered special gifts to Brāhmaṇas. He lay on bare ground. He kept himself quite calm. He took food once in two days.

25. Then, at the end of a year the Bull-emblemed Lord appeared before him in the company of Pārvatī once again.

26. Thereupon the king bowed down before both of them duly and spoke these words humbly:

27-32. "Formerly, O goddess, my mind was overwhelmed with the flood of bliss. Hence I failed to bow down to you. It does not behove you to be angry on that account.

O goddess, you are always the occupier of half of the body of the Trident-bearing Lord. Hence, tell me how, when one of you is bowed to, you are not paid obeisance.

This is my opinion that you are always bowed to by one who bows to the Lord of Devas and when you are bowed to the Lord of Devas too is bowed to.

Still, you are also separately bowed to as together before. Now you have been mounted in the same seat. O goddess, you are worshipped along with him.

Hence be favourable to me. Let the boon given by the Enemy of the Puras earlier become fruitful immediately in regard to obtaining a son.

O goddess, it behoves you to do what is necessary to facilitate the birth of a son who will perpetuate the family line, who will be long-lived and whose valour will be steady with your favour."

Śrī Devī said:

33. O king, my words cannot be otherwise on any account. Hence your son will meet with death though yet a child.

34. After giving you the sorrow arising out of early death, he will regain life ere long, with my favour.

35. Thereafter he will live long; he will be victorious and perpetuate your race as an emperor of great eminence. He will be munificent and will perform Yajñas. He will be one conversant with virtuous rites.

36. So, O king, go home and rule over your kingdom as you desire. You will beget a son of great excellance as proclaimed by me.

37-38. If any other man worships me installed here in this form along with Lord Śaṁbhu, I will grant sons of his choice and other things also ere long. There is no doubt about this.

Śrī Mahādeva said:

39. O excellent king, once again beg of me whatever you desire. A visit of mine shall never be in vain. This is the truth that I speak.

Hariścandra said:

40. O Lord of Devas, I am blessed and contented. Excepting a son there is everything in my house. Now you have given me a victorious son capable of perpetuating the line.

41. Still I cannot disregard your behest at all. For this reason I shall request for a desired object.

42. I have been thinking of performing a Rājasūya for a long time. But all my ministers and friends dissuade me.

43. The reason is this. That Yajña is possible only when all the kings have been made to pay tribute. O Lord, they will not readily pay tribute without an actual fight.

44. When I opt for war they and my well-wishers oppose me though I am enthusiastic. They strictly abide by the path of good policy and ethics.

45. Hence, with your favour, may my *Makha* (Rājasūya sacrifice) be concluded without obstacles. I will not choose anything else.

Sūta said:

46-48. Hara said: "It shall be so", and vanished. After acquiring the boon, the king went to his abode. It was thus that Umā and Maheśvara were formerly installed by that king. Afterwards others too installed them. One who performs their adoration on the fifth lunar day for one full year, O Brāhmaṇas, with fruits placed on all the limbs of the idols of Umā and Maheśvara will get a son desired who will be capable of uplifting his race.

CHAPTER FORTYNINE

King Kalaśa Turns into a Tiger[1]

Sūta said:

1-2. There itself on the banks of the tank has been installed the highly meritorious deity called Kalaśeśvara. He is the destroyer of all sins. By visiting Kalaśeśvara, a man is rid of sins.

3. Formerly there was a king hailing from Yadu race, named Kalaśa. He performed Yajñas. He was vigilant and munificent. He was engaged in the welfare of all the worlds.

4. Once upon a time, the excellent sage Durvāsas came to his abode. He had adopted the vow of Cāturmāsya.

5. The king immediately got up and joyously came forward to him, respectfully saying "Welcome, welcome to you."

6. He devoutly bowed down to him, washing his feet himself. After offering *Arghya* he said with tears of joy welling up in his eyes:

1. Chapters 49-51 are meant for the glorification of Kalaśeśvara. King Kalaśa is cursed by sage Durvāsā to be a tiger, for feeding him with meat. But he assures him redemption when a cow, Nandinī by name, shows him the Śiva-liṅga adored by Bāṇa. When it took place and the king recovered his human form, he devoted himself to the adoration of that Liṅga which consequently came to be known after him as "Kalaśeśvara." He built a temple of Umā-Maheśvara with a splendid Kuṇḍa in front, of a meritorious efficacy.

7. "O sage, I shall give you all these things—this kingdom, these sons, these women, this wealth. Tell me your purpose (in coming here)."

Durvāsas said:

8. O great king, it is proper on your part to say thus to a Brāhmaṇa like us, a person of vows who has come to your abode.

9. O excellent king. I have nothing to do with your riches nor with your kingdom. I have adopted the Cāturmāsya (vow extending to four months) Vrata. Hence I am eager to perform the Pāraṇā.

10. Hence, O king, whatever food is ready in your house, give it unto me for eating. My hunger is very great.

Sūta said:

11. Then the king himself served him the food well-cooked as it was.

12. There were many types of sweet dishes and side-dishes of various kinds. There were four traditional types of food-stuff, viz. *Peya* (beverages), *Coṣya* (foodstuff worthy of being sucked), *Khādya* (food to be chewed) and *Lehya* (food worthy of being licked and lapped up). There were many meat dishes well sesoned with salt etc.

13. The hungry and distressed Brāhmaṇa hurriedly gulped everything in big morsels without relishing the taste. Yet he was joyous.

14. After getting satiated he realized that he had the taste of meat, O Brāhmaṇas. Thereupon the leading sage became furious and cursed him:

15. "Since you caused a violation in my Vrata by feeding me with meat, you will become a terrible carnivorous tiger."

16. The miserable king in utter fright, bowed down to the leading sage and said trembling with a distressed face:

17-18. "O sage, you had your throat parched with hunger. With great devotion I served you the meal cooked and ready. So why do you feel inclined to curse me? Be pleased with me, your humble devotee, O excellent Brāhmaṇa, by quickly changing your curse into a blessing."

Durvāsas said:

19. Excepting in a Śrāddha and Yajña no Brāhmaṇa shall eat meat. Especially so at the conclusion of a Vrata pertaining to Cāturmāsya.

20. If a Brāhmaṇa eats flesh after the observance of fast, certainly his Vrata becomes fruitless and the meat is futile.

21. Hence my Vrata pertaining to Cāturmāsya has been fruitless, O leading king. So you have been now cursed angrily by me.

The king said:

22. Still, O Brāhmaṇa, bring about the desired end to the curse given to me particularly since I am devout, wretched and blameless.

Durvāsas said:

23. When the cow Nandinī points out to you the Liṅga formerly worshipped by Bāṇa, your liberation shall take place immediately.

24. After saying thus, the eminent Brāhmaṇa went back to his hermitage. The king too assumed the highly terrible form of a tiger.

25. He soon lost memory (of his antecedents). On seeing animals in front of him, he killed them and was dislodged from that place by other animals. He then entered a great forest.

26. The ministers of the king, desiring that there should be an end to his curse, protected the kingdom duly.

CHAPTER FIFTY

Dialogue between the Cow and the Tiger

Sūta said:

1-3. Thus, O Brāhmaṇas, a great deal of time passed, when that king in the form of a tiger roamed about in the forest killing different types of animals.

Once upon a time, O excellent Brāhmaṇas a beautiful herd of cows with the full complement of cowherds and cowherdesses came to that region.

In that herd there was a cow named Nandinī with stout udders and large hind quarters. She was of the colour of a swan and yielded (milk) in potfuls.

4-5. With a desire for grass, she used to go ahead of the herd always. Then she saw the Liṅga of the Trident-bearing Lord within a bush. The refulgent Linga was present there by itself. It had the lustre resembling that of twelve suns. It was extremely delightful to the mind.

6. The cow stood above it and shed a great deal of milk for bathing it. She was endowed with great faith, O Brāhmaṇas.

7. No one in that forest with many trees growing all round, was aware of the fact that the cow had always been bathing the Liṅga thus.

8. On a certain day, a huge tiger of sharp fangs came to that spot. He instilled fear in all the creatures.

9. That cow Nandinī came there and fell within the range of the tiger's sight by chance, O excellent Brāhmaṇas.

10. Then she remembered her small calf that was tied in the cowpen. As she remembered that the calf could not eat grass and could be sustained only through milk, she lamented piteously:

11-12. "Alas, I have come here alone to this forest devoid of people, leaving my infant calf kept tied up in the cowpen by the cowherds! May there be my re-union with my calf by the power of that truth that I have come here to bathe Śiva."

13. While that cow Nandinī was lamenting thus piteously, the tiger smiled derisively and spoke in harsh words.

The tiger said:

14. Why do you lament in vain, O splendid cow? You have come within my grip. So you better remember your favourite Lord for the sake of heaven.

The cow said:

15. O tiger, it is not for my sake that I lament and feel miserable. My death is surely auspicious, in view of the adoration of Śiva (for which I came here).

16. My calf is being kept tied in the cowpen. It is eagerly waiting for my arrival. Its sole sustenance is my milk. How can it live without me?

17. It is for this reason, O tiger, that I lament and feel very miserable and not for the sake of my own life. I pledge myself truthfully (on my honour, I promise).

18. Hence, O great tiger, leave me immediately as I am fond of my calf. I shall entrust it to a companion of mine and return to you.

The tiger said:

19. How (can I believe) that after falling into the jaws of death and escaping somehow (from that) you will come back again? So I am going to devour you.

Nandinī said:

20. O tiger, listen to my solemn oaths uttered by myself whereby I undertake to come back to you again and then do what is proper.

21. If I do not come back again, let me incur that sin which is incurred on murdering a Brāhmaṇa or by deceiving parents.

22. If I do not come back again, let me incur that sin which befalls those who are eager to take bath in the nude and those who indulge in sexual intercourse in broad daylight.

23. If I do not come back again, let me incur that sin which accrues to those who pursue women in their monthly periods and to those who go to bed in the nude.

24. If I do not come back again, let me incur that sin which those who betray trust and are ungrateful, incur.

25. If I do not come back again, let me incur that sin which befalls those who defile and slander cows, virgins and Brāhmaṇas.

26. If I do not come back again, let me incur that sin that befalls those who cook in vain and eat meat in vain (just for the pleasure of it).

27. If I do not come back again, let me incur that sin which befalls those who violate holy vows and those who carnally approach their wives on the prohibited days of the menstrual cycle.

28. If I do not come back again, let me incur the sin of backbiters and talebearers as well as manufacturers of weapons.

CHAPTER FIFTYONE

Greatness of Kalaśeśvara

Sūta said:

1-2. On hearing those solemn oaths, the tiger became surprised. Considering that it was the truth, he said to Nandinī fond of her calf: "If it is so, go home and meet your calf. Entrust it to your companions and return soon."

Sūta said:

3. On hearing these words of the tiger, Nandinī of excellent conduct went homewards where her calf was tied.

4. The calf was surprised on seeing its mother coming back before the usual time in a frightened state of mind and lowing it said:

5. "Why have you come back before the time? Why are you upset and bewildered? Why is your face drenched and full of tears? O dear mother, speak out quickly."

Nandinī said:

6. If you want to ask me anything, first you suck the udders.

If you are fully satisfied after sucking the milk, I shall tell you everything.

Sūta said:

7. At her instance the calf sucked up as much milk as it was wont to do. Then the mother sniffed at its head. The calf thereupon said immediately.

8. "Tell all the news of the forest now. On hearing it, O dear mother, straight from you, I shall have some relief."

Nandinī said:

9. Dear son, I went to the great forest today and as I was roaming about as I pleased, I was held up by a tiger.

10-11. When that wild animal with claws as his weapon was bent upon devouring me, I requested him on oath, "I shall come back after meeting my calf in the cowpen."

I was allowed to come away after many solemn oaths had been taken. I shall go there again. I have met you and talked to you.

The calf said:

12. I shall go there where you are proceeding to. My death in front of my mother could be worthy of praise now.

13. If I am deserted by you I am sure to die in a short while being left alone and denied the sucking of milk.

14. Mother, if the tiger kills me too along with you, I am sure to attain the goal of those devoted to their mothers.

15. Or, O splendid mother, let those solemn oaths taken before him by you be held in abeyance for me. Do remain here in the cowherds colony.

16. To children sustained with milk there is no other kinsman on a par with the mother. There is no other leader and guide on a par with mother; there is no other place of resort equal to mother.

17. There is no other person worthy of adoration on a par with mother. There is no other friend equal to and on a par with mother.

18. With this consideration always excellent persons should evince ardent devotion to mothers. Those sons who follow this highest righteous rule ordained by Prajāpati, attain the greatest

goal.

19. Hence I shall go there. Do stay here in the cowherds' colony. Undoubtedly I shall save your life by means of mine.

Nandinī said:

20. On this day it is my death that has been enjoined, not yours, son. Hence, how will you save my life through yours?

21. Dear son, this is the ultimate and excellent message conveyed to you which you will assiduously carry out in pursuance of my direction.

22. While roaming about in the forest, dear son, do not commit any mistake. Both here and in the other world, ruin is bound to occur through greediness.

23. Persons deluded by greed enter ocean, great forest and battlefield. Here there is nothing which men do not undertake due to greed.

24. A person is doomed due to three things: covetousness, inadvertence and trust. Hence one should not covet, be inadvertent or trust blindly.

25. When you roam about in a deep forest with all efforts, dear son, your own self should be guarded by you always from the beasts of prey.

26. You should not stray away from the herd anywhere, dear son. Should the grass, fodder etc., be in a risky place, you must not go there alone.

27-28. Thus that Nandinī addressed her calf and licked it repeatedly. She was overwhelmed with great grief and her eyes were dimmed with tears. Then, O excellent Brāhmaṇas, in that very state of excitement and afflicted utterly by the grief for her son, she went to meet with all her companions.

29. She went to the great forest, O excellent Brāhmaṇas, where all of them were joyously grazing the grasses they liked and said to them:

30-32. (She addressed the companions individually:) "O Bahulā, O Campakā, O Dāmā, O Vasudhārā, O Ghaṭasravā, O Haṁsanāḍī, O Priyānandā, O Śubhakṣīrā, O Mahodayā and other cows present here belonging to your cowherds colony, listen to my words. Thereafter do accordingly.

Today I was roaming about not very far from our herd. Then I entered the thick jungle devoid of men. Roaming there for the love of the green grass I was waylaid by a tiger.

33. By means of solemn oaths (for a sure-return to the tiger) after seeing you all and talking to my calf I was able to make that claw-weaponed one relent with very great difficulty, and I have now come back.

34. I have met and talked to my son. He has been suitably advised and admonished. Now this dear son is being entrusted to the care of all of you.

35. O fair ones, it may be that I had committed some misdemeanour against you knowingly or otherwise. May that be forgiven with favour.

36. My weak and distressed child, still feeding on milk, will now be helpless and all the more grief-stricken due to separation from its mother. All of you should rear him up.

37. Should he stray into other herds or roam about in uneven places or be engaged in misdeed of any sort, all of you will always dissuade him with care.

38. I am going to that place where the tiger is present. This is my final adieu to all of you."

The cows said:

39. O Nandinī, you should not go there at any cost. You are not aware of *Āpaddharma* (misdeed condoned during distress). Hence you are keen to go there.

40. Utterance of falsehood on these occasion is not sinful: when death is imminent, when there is the likelihood of loss of all wealth, when indulging in a joke, when talking about castes among women, at the time of fixing up of marriages.

41. Hence, O fair one, you should not go there. In this you are not blameworthy. Bring up your calf. Come along with us to our adobe.

Nandinī said:

42. O splendid ones, such a course is proper to be undertaken for the sake of saving the life of others. But in the case of good people it is not commended when the aim is

saving one's own life or furthering one's own welfare.

43. The universe is well-established on truth. Piety is well-established on truth; the ocean does not transgress the limit on account of the truthful statement.

44. Bali handed over the earth to Viṣṇu and took refuge in nether worlds. The king of Daityas did not back out after making his promise.

45. If anyone promises anything but does not carry it out as promised, he becomes a thief of irresolute character. Has he not then committed a great sin?

The companions said:

46. O Nandinī, you are worthy of being bowed down to by all the Suras and Asuras for you have decided to give up your life for the preservation of truth. Life is not ordinarily given up easily.

47. What else shall we say, O auspicious one, to you already engaged in expounding pious themes, equipped with all the good qualities and always abiding by truth?

48. O highly esteemed one, do proceed ahead. Do not be worried for your child. What we have been told by you we shall carry out.

49. This we know fully well that a task undertaken by truthful men never goes to waste.

Sūta said:

50-51. After addressing all the companions thus Nandinī started towards the tiger. She continued to be afflicted with the grief for her son. Giving up the hope of seeing her son again she was extremely distressed by the fire of grief. She was like a ruddy goose separated from her beloved. She was like a creeper fallen from a tree.

52-53. Like a blind one devoid of sight, she faltered at every step. For the sake of her child she prayed to all the sylvan deities:

"May all the sylvan deities guard my infant calf whether he is asleep or in the act of roaming. May they do so at my instance."

54-55. Lamenting thus mentally, she reached the place where the terrible tiger with sharp fangs (curved teeth) was waiting for her. He was roaring like thunder with the throat parched due to hunger. He was displaying his fury and arrogance, licking the corners of the mouth.

Nandinī said:

56. O great tiger, here I am. Abiding by my true and solemn oath I have came back. Now you can gratify yourself with my flesh.

57. Though he was wicked-minded he experienced a state of highest detachment on seeing her because she had come back without any fear for her life, only because she was clinging eagerly to the truth.

The tiger said:

58. Welcome to you, O excellent cow of auspicious features and truthful speech. Nothing is inauspicious in the case of truthful ones.

59. O fair one, pledging solemn oaths you said, "I will come again." That provoked my curiosity as to what will this (cow) do?

60. Ruthlessly killing living beings, I have been very wicked in conduct. On account of this perpetual activity, I am bound to fall into terrible Naraka.

61. O highly esteemed one, it behoves you to do me the favour of imparting instructions to me though I am a sinner and utterly evil-minded.

62. Thereby I will have the greatest weal in this world as well as in the other one. I believe that there is nothing not known to you, thanks to the truthful conduct.

63. Hence you describe to me succinctly the essence of piety and virtue. Thereby I will reap the fruit of association with the good entirely.

Nandinī said:

64-65. They commend austerities in Kṛta Yuga and meditation in Tretā Yuga. In Dvāpara Yuga Yajña and Yoga are praise-worthy, but in Kali Yuga it is Dāna alone. One who gives freedom from fear to all living beings both mobile and immobile, becomes himself free from all fears and attains the greatest Brahman. Of all the types of Dāna there is nothing greater than this.

The tiger said:

66-67. O auspicious one, in the case of other living beings who sustain themselves through food (i.e. vegetation) without injuring anyone that type of Dāna may be relevant. On the other hand it is impossible for us to sustain ourselves without violence. Hence, O highly esteemed one, tell me something conducive to my happiness, an instruction in excellent piety though I am one who injures other living beings.

Nandinī said:

68. Here there is a great Liṅga installed by Bāṇa in this forest. Certainly it is the power of that Liṅga whereby I have been liberated by you.

69. Do get up early in the morning, circumambulate it everyday and then bow down to it. Thereby you will attain the desired fulfilment.

70. O claw-weaponed one, this is my opinion that you do not have the ability to perform other rites such as adoration etc. in view of the fact that you do not have hands.

71. O excellent Brāhmaṇas, after saying thus that cow stood before the tiger at the outskirts of the forest and showed that Liṅga.

72. Thanks to its sight, he instantly got rid of his tigerhood. He became a king as before.

73. The excellent king remembered the curse uttered by Durvāsas and his own kingdom along with his sons. Then he said to Nandinī:

74. "I am a king named Kalaśa, born of the Haihaya race. I was cursed by Durvāsas earlier for certain reasons."

75-76. When he was pacified he had said, "When Nandinī shows you that Liṅga you will become liberated." It is now known that you are certainly that Nandinī because my curse has come to an end. So, tell me, O excellent cow, what is this part of the land.

77. Thereby I can quickly go back to my abode, O highly esteemed one, after meeting some human being and finding out my way.

Nandinī said:

78. O king, this is the holy spot of Camatkārapura. It is destructive of sins. All the Tīrthas are present in it and it yields all desired benefits.

79-80. I had thought thus, 'There is no doubt about this that within a day one perfectly achieves that weal which ascetics get elsewhere in the course of a year.' After thinking thus, I went away from my herd always with my mind purified by devotion and bathed the Liṅga with my milk.

The king said:

81. O Nandinī, god bless you! Do go back to your calf, the herd, your companions and other friends.

82-83. I had heard about this holy spot from the report (speech) of some Brāhmaṇas earlier. I had wished to enquire about but I could not visit it, O Nandinī, because I was engaged in kingly duties or rather I was over-indulging in worldly pleasures. Since it has been achieved by myself I would rather not lose it.

84. It was a blessing to me that the lofty-minded sage cursed me, O splendid one. How could I have attained this holy spot otherwise?

Sūta said:

85. After saying thus and bidding goodbye to that Nandinī, the king stayed there itself meditating upon that Liṅga day and night.

86. He built a wonderful mansion (shrine) as lofty as the peak of Kailāsa and performed penance before it.

87. Then, O Brāhmaṇas, by its power within a few days he obtained the greatest fulfilment inaccessible even to those who regularly perform Yajñas.

88. One who lights and offers a lamp there in the month of Kārttika will be rid of all sins and honoured in the world of Śiva.

89. A man who makes arrangement for songs, dances etc. before it devoutly in the month of Mārgaśīrṣa attains the greatest goal.

90. Thus, O excellent Brāhmaṇas, the greatness of Kalaśeśvara, destructive of all sins, has been fully narrated in detail to you all.

91. One who is endowed with great faith and reads this devoutly becomes liberated from sins and is honoured in the world of Śiva.

CHAPTER FIFTYTWO

Greatness of Rudrakoṭi

Sūta said:

1-3. Umā and Maheśvara were installed there by that king after building a great mansion (shrine) that gave pleasure to the eyes of righteous people.

In front of it, an auspicious holy Kuṇḍa (pit, small pond) was made and filled with clear water and adorned by clusters of lotuses.

A man who devoutly takes his holy bath there and visits (the idols) then, with mental concentration and purity, on the fourteenth lunar day in the bright half of the month of Māgha, is not reborn.

4. To the eastern side thereof and near Agastyakuṇḍa, there is a highly meritorious tank that destroys all sins.

5. A man who takes his holy bath therein on the eighth lunar day in the bright half of the month of Phālguna and observes fast, obtains all desired benefits.

6. River Kapilā flows on its southern side. It was there that Kapila attained Siddhi (spiritual perfection) through the practice of Sāṅkhya philosophy.

7. The region to the east of Kapilā is glorified as Siddhakṣetra (Holy land of those who have attained spiritual fulfilment). Formerly hundreds and thousand of Siddhas had attained fulfilment there.

8. A man who cherishing any desire performs penance there, shall certainly realize it within six months.

9-10a. Beneath it, O Brāhmaṇas, there is a splendid, square, Vaiṣṇavī slab. It whirls and is destructive of all sins. It is perpetually washed by the waters of the great river. It bestows salvation on men.

10b-12. River Sarasvatī flows in between Gaṅgā and Yamunā. The Triveṇī (three rivers) thus flows in front of it. It yields worldly pleasures and salvation.

If Brāhmaṇas are cremated on its banks they will certainly obtain salvation. A Goṣpada (cow's foot) becomes visible in the ashes of their pyre. After seeing it, obsequies of dead Brāhmaṇas must be performed.

13. O excellent Brāhmaṇas, Rudrakoṭi is to the northern side thereof. It is adored by noble-souled southern Brāhmaṇas.

14-15. The excellent Brāhmaṇas of the south had heard that the Consort of Umā was himself present in the form of a great Yogin in the holy place called Camatkārapura. Endowed with great faith and urged by curiosity ten million of them rushed in with a desire to visit the Lord.

16. Everyone of them said, "I will visit Lord Hara first." They took oath thus on going there.

17. "The last person among these who visits the great Yogin Īśvara will become a sinner."

18. Lord Maheśvara understood their intention and he was pleased with their devotion. So for their convenience and benefit, he established himself there in ten million forms.

19. O excellent Brāhmaṇas, he was thus visited very easily by all of them. Ever since then, that holy spot became well known as Rudrakoṭi.

20. Nārada was delighted on seeing this circle (multiplicity) of Rudras, O excellent Brāhmaṇas. Then he recited a verse on that event.

21. "Only blessed people on the earth will obtain (a view) of Rudrāvarta (Rudrakoṭī) on the fourteenth day of the months of Āṣāḍha, Kārttika, Māgha and Caitra.

22. Even after committing sins on the earth in the course of hundreds and thousands of births, a man shall be freed from those sins on viewing Rudrāvarta.

23. A man who goes to Rudrāvarta and views Hára, the Yogin

Lord, on the fourteenth day in the bright half becomes certainly free from sins."

24. O Brāhmaṇas, one who performs Śrāddha at Rudrāvarta, the city of the great Yogin, obtains the merit of a hundred Yajñas.

25. A man who observes fast and keeps awake at night (i.e. performs Jāgaraṇa) goes to heaven in an aerial chariot that can go wherever one pleases.

26. One who gifts a tawny-coloured cow to a Brāhmaṇa who preserves the holy sacred fires (*Āhitāgni*) shall undoubtedly become a Gaṇa and a favourite of Hara.

27. If a devotee sits in front of the great Yogin and repeats the six-syllabled Mantra, he will get six times the merit of Rājasūya.

28. One who repeats *Śatarudriya* devoutly in front of the Lord, shall obtain the merit of reciting all the four Vedas.

29. A man who sings and/or dances in front of him (the Lord) shall undoubtedly obtain the merit of all Yajñas."

30. O excellent Brāhmaṇas, after saying thus the sage born of Brahmā (i.e. Nārada) stopped. Pleased much, he quickly proceeded on pilgrimage.

CHAPTER FIFTYTHREE

Greatness of Bhrūṇagartā[1]

Sūta said:

1. There itself is Ujjayinī Pīṭha that grants whatever men desire. It is extremely miraculous and is resorted to by many Siddhas.

2. O excellent Brāhmaṇas, Maheśvara himself is present in its centre in the form of Mahākāla.

3-4. A man who has mental concentration and purity, who performs Śrāddha there on the Vaiśākhī day, who visits the Lord of Devas remembered as Mahākāla and who adores the Lord as Dakṣiṇāmurtī redeems ten generations of his ancestors, himself

1. This chapter uses the legend of King Kalmāṣapāda in Mbh, *Ādi*, Chs 175, 181, to glorify the Tīrtha called Bhrūṇa-Gartā.

and ten generations of successors, O excellent Brāhmaṇas. He is honoured in Śivaloka.

5-6a. After adoring the group of Yoginīs and the group of virgins, a devotee should worship the Pīṭha with any desire mentally conceived. He attains everything entirely even if it be very rare.

6b-7. A man who is endowed with faith, mental concentration and purity, remains physically clean and observes fast on the full-moon day of the month of Vaiśākha as well as keeps awake at night (i.e. performs Jāgaraṇa) in front of the deity faithfully, attains the greatest region devoid of old age and death.

8. Of what avail are Vratas? Of what worth are futile Dānas? Of what (more) advantage are *Japas* and observances? All these are not worth even a sixteenth fraction of (devotion to) Mahākāla.

Sūta said:

9. O highly esteemed ones, the holy chasm well known as Bhrūṇagartā[1] is also there itself. It is very large in size and it destroys all sins.

10. King Saudāsa was liberated from the sin of Brāhmaṇa-slaughter at that place. Suṣeṇa, the overlord of the earth, was completely liberated from the sin of the murder of a woman.

The sages said:

11. How did that king Saudāsa who was a patron of Brāhmaṇas, incur the sin of Brāhmaṇa-slaughter? Do narrate it to us.

12. It is heard that the king was engaged in the welfare of Brāhmaṇas mentally, verbally and physically. How did he become a Brāhmaṇa-slayer?

13. How was he again liberated after resorting to Bhrūṇagartā? Further how did that *Gartā* (chasm) originate? Mention everything in detail.

Sūta said:

14. When the penis of the Trident-bearing Lord of Devas

1. As explained in vv 14-16, this Gartā or chasm was created by Śiva to hide himself after the loss of his phallus due to the curses of sages.

fell down, O excellent Brāhmaṇas, he was overcome with shame due to the loss of the penis.

15. He made a deep chasm and entered it. The Wielder of the Trident did not show himself to anyone.

16. It was thus, O excellent Brāhmaṇas, that the chasm was formed there. I shall tell you now how Saudāsa became liberated from sin therein.

17. There was an extremely righteous king named Mitrasaha. Saudāsa[1] was his son, a direct descendant of the solar race.

18. Elaborate Yajñas in which gold and other excellent things were gifted (as Dakṣiṇā) were performed by him. The great soul had performed numerous *Dānas* also.

19-20. Once, while a Sattra lasting for a period of twelve years was going on duly in accordance with the procedure laid down in the scriptural injunctions, two very powerful Rākṣasas came there for creating obstacles in the Yajña. It was the beginning of the night.

21. They were also accompanied by many Rākṣasas, others called goblins and vampires who could not be assailed and who were eager to destroy the Yajña.

22. Looking out for some opportunity and possible way of entry, all the Rākṣasas entered the sacrificial chamber and they spread all round.

23. They killed the Brāhmaṇas. They swallowed the holy *Havis* prepared there as well as other articles kept ready for the sake of Yajña.

24. While the Brāhmaṇas were being devoured by the more powerful Rākṣasas there was a great hue and cry.

25. Thereupon the royal son of Mitrasaha became enraged. He set aside his initiation and holy vows and kept them in abeyance, took his bow and arrows and began killing them.

26. He himself was fully safeguarded by Vasiṣṭha, the priest. He slew Krūrākṣa along with many Rākṣasas.

---

1. The following are the modifications of the Mbh story in this Purāṇa: Vasiṣṭha, out of misunderstanding and rashness cursed the king. The king was dissuaded from giving countercurse by Nārada (and not by his queen). As a demon, he killed Vasiṣṭha's sons and many Brāhmaṇas but he got cleared of all the sins by his inadvertent fall in Bhrūṇagartā. That is the efficacy of Bhrūṇagartā.

27-28. On seeing that his excellent brother was killed and that the tiger among kings could not be approached due to the refulgence of the Brāhmaṇa, Krūrabuddhi took the surviving Rākṣasas and fled in great fright. Along with his soldiers, he too became wounded by his arrows.

29. Cherishing enmity due to the death of his elder brother, the demon looked out for an opportunity to kill him (the king), day and night.

30. Even as vulnerable points of the noble-souled one were being watched, O Brāhmaṇas, the twelve-year long Sattra came to a close.

31. In the course of the Sattra, due safeguard was accorded to the king by Vasiṣṭha and not even a smallest vulnerable point was seen by that wicked one.

32. Then the king, after duly bidding farewell to the Brāhmaṇas after the due distribution of monetary gifts, spoke to Vasiṣṭha with the palms joined in reverence:

33. "O my venerable preceptor, I wish to feed you with my own hands. So be favourably disposed towards me and have food in my palace."

Sūta said:

34. Vasiṣṭha, the excellent sage, assented saying "So be it." The king washed the feet of the sage and sat down for the meal.

35. O excellent Brāhmaṇas, Krūrabuddhi observed the splendid meat prepared duly by the cooks and then consecrated in accordance with the injunctions for the sake of the sage.

36. He made an *ukhā* i.e. a saucepan or vessel which can be put on fire. It was similar to and of the same dimension as the original (used by the king's cook). He filled it with human flesh and served it as meat.

37. The tiger among sages knew that the morsel he ate was human flesh. Enraged thereat, he said angrily:

38. "O base one, since you forced me to eat human flesh like a Rākṣasa, you shall just today itself become a Rākṣasa."

39. The king met the cooks individually and tactfully tried to find out how human flesh had come therein.

40-41. The cooks said: "O king, such a piece of meat as this has not been cooked by us. Believe us. Nor could this have been done by another human being. O Lord, excepting a Rākṣasa, Piśāca or Dānava no one could have done this. Consider this, O Lord, and do what is proper."

42. In the meantime, Nārada, the excellent sage, came there and narrated everything perpetrated by the Rākṣasa.

43. On hearing it, King Saudāsa became furious. He took water in his hand and was about to curse Vasiṣṭha. On seeing him bent upon cursing, Nārada spoke these words:

44-45a. "O excellent king, Brāhmaṇas have to be bowed down to by one who wishes for his own welfare even if they were to strike, hate or curse. Moreover, this is your preceptor and he has to be honoured by you. So, it does not behove you to curse the excellent sage in return."

45b. Thus forbidden, the king let the entire quantity of water fall over his own feet from his hand.

46. His feet drenched with the water heated by the curse became burned. O excellent Brāhmaṇas, they instantly turned black.

47. Ever since then, O tiger among Brāhmaṇas, that king was specially called by the name Kalmāṣapāda.

Sūta said:

48-51. In the meantime, Vasiṣṭha, the Brāhmaṇa, became ashamed on realizing that he had cursed the king unreasonably. He said: "O king, this curse had been given to you without any reason. But my words cannot be otherwise on any account. O excellent king, you will be a Rākṣasa for some time. Then you will regain your original form. Listen when it shall happen. When you kill a Rākṣasa named Krūrabuddhi you will get rid of the hideous state of Rākṣasa."

Sūta said:

52. In the meantime the king became a Yātudhāna (demon). He had a huge body with hairs standing upright. His teeth were black. He was awful altogether.

53. In this state of Rākṣasa he killed leading Brāhmaṇas and destroyed Yajñas and hermitages of sages.

54. Once that Rākṣasa named Krūrabuddhi came to know that he had become a Rākṣasa himself and was without any

weapon.

55. He recollected their previous enmity due to the slaying of his brother. Thereupon accompanied by many Rākṣasas he arrived there to kill him.

56. Encircling him all round, the Rākṣasa said to the king angrily as his loud roar was reverberating in all the quarters:

57. "O excessively wicked-minded one, our elder brother was killed by you by the strength derived from Vasiṣṭha in the course of the Yajña. Reap the fruit thereof now."

The king said:

58. Only you of wicked behaviour, act according to what you say. Your roar, like the thunder of the autumnal cloud is futile.

59. After saying thus the king uprooted a tree and with the tree he rushed towards him roaring like a rumbling cloud.

60. He (Krūrabuddhi) too uprooted a tree. His eyes became red with rage. He knitted his eyebrows together into the shape of a trident and came face to face with him.

61. Thus both of those mighty heroes continued this fight with trees resulting in the destruction of many trees.

62. Noticing that Krūrabuddhi had become tired the king caught him by the feet and whirled him quickly into the sky.

63. Then with increased rage, he thrashed and dashed him on the ground. By pounding him repeatedly he turned him into a lump of flesh.

64. When the mighty Rākṣasa was killed the king got rid of the state of Rākṣasa and regained the physical form of a king.

65. Thereupon the remaining Rākṣasas surrounded him and struck him with huge trees and showers of stones and gravel.

66. O excellent Brāhmaṇas, armed with a huge tree the king laughingly and easily killed them also with full confidence.

67. After killing the Rākṣasas and regaining his earlier body the king became delighted. He reached his city experiencing horripilation.

68-69. Yet he was without the previous refulgence. He was stinking awfully. His ministers, sons, grandsons and others noticed these and various other sorts of signs of the sin of Brāhmaṇa-slaughter. So they did not come near the king as if they were afraid of contracting his sins.

70-71. They said: "O excellent king, since you have incurred the sin of Brāhmaṇa-slaughter you do not deserve to come into close contact with us. Invite Vasiṣṭha and perform the rites of expiation whereby your impure body may regain purity."

72. Thereupon the king quickly called Vasiṣṭha, the leading sage, and spoke these words standing humbly at a safe distance:

73-75. "O Brāhmaṇa, that Rākṣasa has been killed by me with your favour. I have got rid of the curse too. But, O sage, listen further: Stinking odour emanates from my body and spreads around. All my limbs appear to be very heavy, benumbed and stiff. What is this, O excellent Brāhmaṇa. There is loss of refulgence. Why do the ministers and sons not even touch me today."

Vasiṣṭha said:

76. O excellent king, many Brāhmaṇas were killed and Yajñas destroyed by you when in the state of Rākṣasa. Thus you have been assailed by the sin of Brāhmaṇa-slaughter.

The king said:

77. For that purpose, for the sake of purity, O Brāhmaṇa, tell me the requisite rite of expiation whereby I can be rid of sins and regain my own kingdom.

Vasiṣṭha said:

78. For this purpose, O excellent king, undertake a pilgrimage free from egotism and sense of possession. Thereby you will attain fulfilment.

79. Thereafter, the great king practised self-control, conquered the sense-organs and performed the holy ablution in Prayāga and other Tīrthas with great mental concentration and purity.

80. Still the stinking odour did not disappear; his refulgence did not increase, the body did not regain lightness and he was not rid of sluggishness.

81. Roaming about still further, O excellent Brāhmaṇas, once he happened to come to the holy place of Camatkārapura for the purpose of holy bath.

82. The king was already weak and tired. He was distressed due to hunger and thirst. At midnight, in pitch darkness, he slipped down into a Gartā (pit) full of water.

83. With very great difficulty the king came out of that Tīrtha. When he looked at himself, he found that he had the lustre of twelve suns.

84. On seeing himself bereft of the stinking smell, with the body light and active, he thought that he had become rid of sins.

85. At the very same time, there was heard an unembodied voice delighting the king rid of the sin of Brāhmaṇa-slaughter.

86-90. "O great king, by the power of this Tīrtha you are now relieved of all your previous sins. So do go back to your abode. Śaṅkara is always present here in the form of a Bhrūṇa (a very young child), O king, particularly on the fourteenth lunar day in the dark half. When the penis of the Trident-bearing Lord of Devas fell down due to the curse of Brāhmaṇas, he made this Gartā. He had become ashamed of the state of Bhrūṇa. He was very distressed due to separation from Satī. Therefore, O king, this Gartā is destructive of all sins. Named after the Lord (in the form of a Bhrūṇa) this Gartā became well known as Bhrūṇagartā in all the three worlds."

Sūta said:

91. After saying thus, that aerial voice stopped. That tiger among kings joyously went to his city.

92. On seeing him freed from sins and appearing like the sun in refulgence, the sons and other men became delighted and bowed down to him.

93. Vasiṣṭha, a tiger among Brāhmaṇas approached the king and said with a voice choked due to delight:

94-95. "O leading king, luckily you have been relieved of the terrible sins arising from Brāhmaṇa-slaughter. Fortunately you have come again to your city with the full complement of your original radiance. Hence do say, O king, which Tīrtha did you go to and get relief from the terrible sin arising from Brāhmaṇa-slaughter."

96. Thereupon he narrated all the events of the Bhrūṇagartā to the Brāhmaṇa-Sage in the manner he experienced.

97-98. Thereupon the elderly ministers, the king and the leading sage crowned the son named Pratardana in the kingdom. Instantly they went to Bhrūṇagartā, O excellent Brāhmaṇas, and performed penance meditating on Mahādeva day and night.

99. By worshipping Maheśvara in the form of a Bhrūṇa, they attained the greatest Siddhi in a short time, though it is very difficult to be obtained.

100. Ever since then, O leading Brāhmaṇas, that Gartā became well known over the earth as Bhrūṇagartā, which destroys all sins.

101. A man who performs Śrāddha there on the fourteenth lunar day in the dark half of a month redeems ten ancestors and ten successors in his family.

102. Hence, O excellent Brāhmaṇas, one should perform Śrāddha, Snāna (holy bath) and Dāna there in accordance with one's capacity.

CHAPTER FIFTYFOUR

Greatness of Carmamuṇḍā

Sūta said:

1-2. Goddess Carmamuṇḍā is also established in that holy spot. She was formerly installed by the noble-souled Nala himself.

One who devoutly worships her on the day of Mahānavamī (ninth day in the month of Āśvina) obtains desired benefits and attains the eternal state (i.e. Mokṣa).

3. Formerly there was a king named Nala[1]. He was the son of Vīrasena. He was endowed with all good qualities. He brought about the destruction of all enemies.

4. His wife was a chaste lady well-known as Damayantī. She was dearer to him than his own life. She was the daughter of the king of Vidarbha.

5. O Brāhmaṇas, haunted by Kali, the king played the game of dice day and night with Puṣkara, his Dāyāda (kinsman).

1. The Nala episode follows the Mbh story in general except vv 16-33 which are meant for the glorification of Carmamuṇḍā.

6. He indulged in this vice though forbidden by good people. He lost the entire kingdom consisting of seven Aṅgas, (constituent units such as arms) excepting his beloved.

7. Taking her with him he entered a forest devoid of people. He was overwhelmed with shame and utterly distressed with grief.

8-10. Thereupon he thought: 'If this gentle lady goes to the palace of Bhīma (her father), she can be relieved of painful sufferings due to the stay in the forest.

I have to maintain my prestige. So I should not go there at any cost. So I shall desert her at night and go very far. Abandoned by me, the chaste lady will go to his city Kuṇḍina.'

After deciding thus, he left her during sound sleep and went deep into the terrible forest infested by wild beasts of prey.

11. Early in the morning, the lovely woman got up but found a void in the place where Nala had been before at her side.

12. Distressed with misery, she lamented piteously in the forest. She slowly proceeded ahead along the path and reached the palace of her father.

13. King Nala roamed alone all over the forest always resorting to clusters of trees and bushes.

14. Then he left that forest and went to another great forest full of trees of various kinds and infested with many beasts of prey.

15. Roaming thus from forest to forest, the king ultimately reached the holy spot of Hāṭakeśvara.

16. In the meantime there occurred the advent of that great Navamī day (ninth day) when kings perform special adoration of the goddesss of Suras.

17. The king made a clay icon of Carmamuṇḍadharā. Thereafter improverished that he was, be propitiated the goddess with fruits and roots.

18. The king of Niṣadha endowed with great faith stood before the goddess with palms joined in reverence and eulogized.

Prayer of Carmamuṇḍā:

19. "Be victorious, O omnipresent goddess, O excellent Carmamuṇḍadharā. Be victorious, O splendid daughter of Dakṣa,

efficient in the annihilation of the race of demons.

20. Be victorious, O Kālarātri, O incomprehensible one, O goddess fond of Navamī and Aṣṭamī (9th and 8th lunar days). O three-eyed one, O beloved of the Three-eyed One. Be victorious, O goddess adored by Suras.

21. O terrible one, O beautiful one, O great deity of learning of great power, O goddess of huge body and great prosperity. Be victorious, O goddess of great Vratas.

22. O mother of the universe, of permanent form, O goddess fond of liquor and meat and suet! O Mahākālī of hideous form, be victorious, O goddess with Pretas as followers.

23. O beautiful goddess fond of corpse as vehicle. O goddess with serpents for ornaments! O goddess of huge hands armed with the noose, O goddess having flood of blood made as the place of residence.

24. O goddess splendidly shining with shouts and howls! O goddess shining with music of instruments and songs. Be victorious, O goddess without beginning. Be victorious, O goddess worthy of meditation, O goddess resorting to a half of the body of Bharga (Śiva).

25. Undoubtedly you are Rati, you are Dhṛti (fortitude), you are Tuṣṭi (satisfaction) O Gaurī; you are the goddess of Suras. You are Lakṣhmī; you are Sāvitrī and Gāyatrī.

26. O goddess, whatever is seen in the three worlds in female form is identical with you. Here I have no doubt at all.

27. On the basis of that truth whereby I believe so you shall be present here quickly. O goddess bowed down to by Suras and Asuras, pleased with my devotion, be present here."

Sūta said:

28. On being eulogized thus by King Nala, the goddess fond of her devotees appeared before him and said to him:

Śrī Devī said:

29. O my dear one, I am now pleased with this prayer of yours. So receive from me anything you desire as a boon.

Nala said:

30. Damayantī is my wife. She is dearer to me, more than my

life. She has been deserted by me in a desolate forest infested by tigers and serpents.

31. O goddess, immediately see to this that I regain her. She is faultless and is never cross at me. She cannot be called unchaste. With your favour, I shall get her again.

32. O goddess, if anyone were to pray to you reciting this hymn and standing before you, you must grant his wish on that day itself.

Sūta said:

33. Saying "So be it" she vanished. The tiger among kings obtained everything mentioned by her.

CHAPTER FIFTYFIVE

Greatness of Naleśvara

Sūta said:

1. The deity known as Naleśvara is near the shrine of Carmamuṇḍā. He was installed by Nala. By visiting Naleśvara, the Lord of Devas one is liberated from sins.

2. A man who visits the Lord on the sixth lunar day in the bright half of Māgha, O Brāhmaṇas, shall be free from all ailments and attain the highest status.

3. Itching sensation, scab, herpes and cutaneous eruptions, leprosy with round spots–all these are cured in the case of creatures of purified souls.

4. It front of it there is a holy Kuṇḍa filled with clear water. It is adorned with clusters of lotuses and the holy pit is full of fishes and turtles.

5. Even if one is afflicted by the fell disease of leprosy, one shall become fresh (and handsome) once again by taking the holy bath there at dawn on a Monday.

6. When Śaṁbhu was installed by King Nala, the Lord was pleased and he said to him, "Tell me what shall I do for you?"

Nala said:

7. O Lord Śaṅkara, you should stay here. You shall be present here always for the sake of the welfare of all the worlds and for the destruction (healing) of sickness.

Śaṅkara said:

8. O king, at dawn on any Monday, I shall be here within the palace at your request. There is no doubt about it.

9. O king, throughout the day and night on the eighth lunar day in the month of Māgha, especially in the bright half, I will be present here for the eradication of ailments of living beings.

10. If a devotee takes his holy bath in the pure holy Kuṇḍa and sees me stationed here on that day with excellent ardour and faith, all the ailments of his body will perish.

11. A man who takes the clay our of this Kuṇḍa and applies it over his body in the morning on Monday, shall become free from ailments. He will be strong too.

12. O excellent king, a man without any personal desire who worships me devoutly at that time with flowers, incense and unguents shall be rid of all sins. He will attain my world.

Sūta said:

13. O Brāhmaṇas, after saying thus, Lord Hara, the illuminator of all the three worlds, vanished instantly like a lamp.

14-16. Nala too became satisfied, The king propitiated the Lord for a long time. Then he invited all the Brāhmaṇas hailing from Camatkārapura and said: "This deity Śaṁbhu has been installed by me very near your city. By visiting this Lord, all the ailments shall be destroyed. O Brāhmaṇas, I shall now go to the city of Niṣadha (modern Narwar, Rajasthan) for ruling over my kingdom. This deity should be adored by all with mental concentration and purity."

The Brāhmaṇas said:

17-18. O tiger among kings, we shall do so with mental concentration and purity. Our sons and grandsons and others too yet to be born in our family shall devoutly perform his adoration. In such rites as religious procession etc., for the deity installed by you and his adoration we shall make all efforts to carry them out.

Sūta said:

19. On being told thus by those Brāhmaṇas the king became delighted. He was congratulated by them in loud voice. He bowed down to them and set off.

20. It was thus that Lord Śaṁbhu became established there for the sake of the welfare of all the worlds . He is the destroyer of all ailments.

21. Hence with all effort the Lord should be visited especially on Mondays by one who wishes for permanent weal.

CHAPTER FIFTYSIX

Greatness of Sāṁbāditya

Sūta said:

1-2. By seeing the Lord of Suras named Sāṁbāditya[1] who is not far from the previous shrine, a man obtains all the desires cherished in his heart.

A man who devoutly visits the deity on the seventh lunar day in the bright half of Māgha and on a Sunday, will never see hells.

3. Formerly there was a Brāhmaṇa named Gālava. That great sage was always engaged in the self-study of the Vedas. He was a master of the Vedas and Vedāṅgas.

4. He was devoted to excellent holy vows. He was quiescent. He was engaged in serving gods and Brāhmaṇas. He was well-behaved and grateful. He was an adept in the sacrificial rites.

5. Thus he continued till he attained very old age. It was then, O excellent Brāhmaṇas, that he fuly experienced the misery of being without a son.

---

1. The name of the deity is later explained in verse 13. This has no relation to Kṛṣṇa's son Sāmba, a devotee of the Sun-god.

6. Therefore, he left all domestic activities, and in this very holy spot he devoutly propitiated the Sun-god with mental concentration and purity.

7. Equipped with great ardour and faith, he installed the image of the Sun-god at the foot of a banyan tree as mentioned in the Pañcarātrika scriptures.

8. He abstained from taking food and kept his sense-organs under his control. During rainy season he stood under the open sky. During winter he remained in water and during summer he practised penance standing in the midst of five fires.

9. When the fifteenth year approached the Sun-god appeared on the banyan tree and spoke to him as he stood nearby.

Śrī Sūrya said:

10. Welfare unto you, O Gālava. Today I shall bestow boons on you. Do request for a boon. Even if it be very difficult to get, I shall undoubtedly grant it to you.

Gālava said:

11. O excellent one among the Suras, I am without a son and I have reached old age. Hence bestow on me a son who will make the family flourish (and continue it).

Śrī Sūrya said:

12. O Brāhmaṇa, your son will make the family flourish. He shall be brilliant, renowned, well-versed in scriptural texts and a master of the Vedas.

13. The image made by you in the vicinity of the Sun-god along with the goddess (*Sa-ambā*) shall become well-known on the earth by the name Sāmbasūrya.

14-15. A person who is endowed with ardent faith and abstains from food and devoutly worships the deity for twelve Saptamīs (seventh lunar days) coinciding with Sundays, O excellent Brāhmaṇa, shall undoubtedly obtain a son furthering the prosperity of the family.

16. After saying thus the Seven-horsed Lord, Sun, stopped. Delighted in his mind Gālava went to his abode.

17. Not long thereafter, a son marked with all characteristic features, as mentioned by the Lord, was born to him.

18. Since the son had been granted by the delighted Sun-god appearing on the banyan tree, the father himself gave the name Vaṭeśvara to the son.

19. O excellent Brāhmaṇas, Gālava saw the sons of Vaṭeśvara, his grandsons, performed very elaborate penance and attained identity with the Sun-god.

20. After realizing that the Sun-god was installed by his father, Vaṭeśvara erected a charming mansion for him.

21. Ever since then, that deity named Vaṭāditya became well-known all over the three worlds as the bestower of sons on those without them.

22. A person engaged in observing fasts, who worships the deity faithfully for twelve Saptamīs coinciding with Sundays (or/and twelve Sundays) in the proper order shall obtain an excellent son making his family prosper and flourish (in progeny).

23. A man who has no desire and who adores the deity devoutly, shall certainly obtain salvation rarely obtained by even gods.

24. Then there is a couple of verses sung by Nārada, the celestial sage, after visiting Vaṭāditya, the Lord of Suras and bestower of sons:

25. "Even if a woman is hundred years old, barren or widow, she will quickly conceive with the favour of Sāṁbasūrya.

26. Of what avail is *Dāna, Vrata, Japa* and fast for the sake of sons when Sāṁbasūrya, the Lord of Suras, is present?

27. A man who makes it convenient to stay in the holy spot for a year and devoutly visits the deity on Sundays, shall easily obtain an excellent son".

28. Hence, O Brāhmaṇas, for the sake of one's own weal and for prosperity and growth of one's own family, a devotee should assiduously visit the Lord.

CHAPTER FIFTYSEVEN

Bhīṣma's Pilgrimage[1]

Sūta said:

1. Further, O excellent Brāhmaṇas, the Sun-god was installed in that holy spot by Bhīṣma himself honoured by leading Brāhmaṇas.

2. Formerly there was a well-known dear son of Śāntanu by the name Gāṅgeya. He was the most excellent one among men. He was reputed as Ūrdhvaretas (one whose semen goes upwards instead of downwards in the form of discharge i.e. a celibate man).

3. A fierce fight has taken place between him and Bhārgava for a period of twenty-three days. It could be well compared with the fight between Devas and Asuras. It was with reference to Aṁbā[1] (Princess of Kāśī) that they fought with sharp weapons and arrows.

4. Thereafter Devas beginning with Brahmā were engaged in making them desist from fighting for the purpose of peace among all embodied beings. After making them cease to fight, they returned to heaven.

5. Having suffered the most humiliating discomfiture from Bhīṣma, Aṃbā, with her eyes reddened with anger entered well-enkindled fire.

6. Standing in the midst of fire, with her eyes bedimmed with tears, she rebuked the son of river (Bhīsma) i.e. the elderly grandfather of the Kurus and said:

7-8. "O Bhīṣma, O extremely evil-minded one. You discarded me who was love-stricken. So I will born again on the earth in order to kill you. You will certainly be defiled by the sin of murdering a woman, if the word of Smṛtis and other scriptural texts is authoritative."

9. Thereupon, overcome with disgust, Bhīṣma, the grandfather of Kurus, approached Mārkaṇḍeya, an excellent sage, and asked him humbly:

---

1. The aim of this chapter is to glorify ablution in Śarmiṣṭhā Tīrtha at Camatkārapura on Aṅgārakī Ṣaṣṭhī (6th lunar day on Tuesday).

10-11. "O holy Sir, daughter of the king of Kāśī prattles thus to me. 'The entire sin of causing my death will incur to you.' O excellent Brāhmaṇa, shall it be so merely because of her utterance, or not? I have a grerat doubt in this respect. It behoves you to clarify it duly."

Śrī Mārkaṇḍeya said:

12. If a woman or a Brāhmaṇa, on being insulted or beaten, were to cast off her or his life with direct reference to the person concerned, the sin thereof shall be that of the person so referred to.

13. Hence if one wishes for one's own good, one should not enrage a woman or a Brāhmaṇa even if the woman or Brāhmaṇa were intent on killing or cursing.

14. [1]In your case, the unfortunate pitiable girl was stricken with love. She had been won by you in (the battle following) the Svayaṃvara. Hence how can you escape being a sinner?

Bhīṣma said:

15. For the sake of that, O Brāhmaṇa, advise me as to the expiatory rite to be performed for the sake of purity, whether it be penance, or Dāna, Vrata or any special restraint.

Mārkaṇḍeya said:

16. O bull among the descendants of Bharata, if a woman is killed, the sin accruing is equal to the entire sin that has been proclaimed in the scriptures to be incurred for the murder of ten leading Brāhmanas.

17. Hence, excepting pilgrimage there is no other atonement such as Dāna, penance, Vrata and the like in this regard. So do undertake a pilgrimage.

---

1. Bhīṣma was guilty of a woman's murder as he refused to marry Aṁbā, princess of Kāśī, whom he abducted for his brother. She declared her love for Śālva and was allowed to go to him. But Śalva refused to accept her. She straightway asked Bhīṣma to marry her but he refused on the ground of life-long celibacy. She charged him with murder and entered a funeral pyre.

The Mbh story in *Ādi Parva* Ch. 102, and *Udyoga* chapters 174-78 is used by the author.

Sūta said:

18. On hearing his words, Bhīṣma, the elderly grandfather of Kurus, roamed over the entire sphere of the earth in the course of his pilgrimage.

19. Roaming over the earth, in due course, he reached the holy spot of Camatkārapura full of many Tīrthas.

20-26a. Then that noble soul visited Gayāśiras. Endowed with faith he took the holy bath and performed Śrāddha duly; but during its performance an aerial voice spoke these words:

"O Bhīṣma O mighty-armed one, you do not deserve to perform a Śrāddha. You are defiled with the sin of a woman's murder; you are not eligible to perform Śrāddha. Hence you listen to my words. Śarmiṣṭhā Tīrtha is well-known as destructive of sins. It is situated very near this spot. It is meritorious and is there to the west. A devout man should take his holy bath on Aṅgāraka Ṣaṣṭhī (sixth lunar day coinciding with a Tuesday) in a dark half. One who bathes thus is rid of the sin resulting from woman-murder. There is no doubt about it.

This day happens to be the same Ṣaṣṭhī coinciding with Tuesday, dear son. It is the meritorious Tithi. So go quickly to that place. Dear son, I am king Śantanu, your father. On coming to know that you have been defiled by the sin of woman-murder I hastened hither."

26b-28. Thereupon Bhīṣma went to that holy spot quickly with mental concentration. He took the holy bath and then performed Śrāddha with due faith. Thereat Śantanu came there again and said:

"O excellent one among the descendants of Kuru, you are free form the sin undoubtedly. So go home and carry on the administration of the kingdom."

29-31. On coming to know the excellence of the Tīrtha he became surprised. The most excellent one among Kurus made another image of Vāsudeva. Then he made an idol of the Sun-god with Pārijāta wood. The idol was characterised with all regular features, the dimensions were proportionate and the form was fascinating. He made this with his mind purified by faith.

Then he installed a Liṅga of the Trident-bearing Lord. He then with great devotion made the idol of Durgā in accordance with the injunctions.

32. Bhīṣma, the descendant of Kuru, invited all the Brāhmaṇas of that city. Standing humbly he said to them:

33-34. "O Brāhmaṇas, I have been urged by my divine ancestors already on the path to heaven and so have built four shrines in this holy spot of yours. Take pity on me and maintain these shrines. I am hastening back to my abode."

The Brāhmaṇas said:

35. O most excellent one among the descendants of Kuru, do go carefree and happily. We all will carry out what is conducive to the increase of your welfare.

36. O king, a number of deities have been made by you here. We shall perform all the rites such as adoration etc. of these always.

37. O king, we are pleased on seeing your humility. Hence do pray unto us all for any boon that you have cherished in your mind.

Bhīṣma said:

38. This alone is the excellent boon unto us that the excellent Brāhmaṇas have been pleased. Still I have now to carry out your instruction.

39. If any man on the earh faithfully worships in these shrines built by me, with any desire in his mind, he shall undoubtedly obtain that due to your favour.

The Brāhmaṇas said:

40. We shall organize the Yātrā (religious procession) of Āditya in the month of Bhādrapada with great mental concentration, when the seventh lunar day coincides with a Sunday.

41. Due to your love, we shall organize Śiva's Yātrā on the eighth lunar day in the bright half of Caitra.

42-43. When the twelfth day of Āṣāḍha and Kārttika arrives at the time of *Śayana* (sleep) and *Bodhana* (waking up) of Viṣṇu we shall organize Viṣṇu's Yātrā.

On the ninth day in the bright half of Āśvina, we shall organize the Yātrā of Durgā with songs and instrumental music. We shall have great festivities with dances and jokes of diverse kinds.

44. A man who is endowed with great faith always and performs the rites of *Gīta* (song) etc. shall attain the highest goal

45. We shall always be pleased with him, O king, and shall grant him all the desires cherished in his heart.

46. After saying thus those Brāhmaṇas went back to their respective abodes. Bhīṣma too was delighted and started back homewards.

CHAPTER FIFTYEIGHT

Greatness of Śiva Gaṅgā

Sūta said:

1-4. After installing the four deities of great merit, Gāṅgeya (Bhīṣma) installed Gaṅgā of triple path in the Kūpikā (holy well) to the east of Śivaliṅga.

The highly esteemed one then joyously honoured the excellent Brāhmaṇas and said:

"A person who takes his holy bath in this and visits me shall become liberated from all sins and go to Śivaloka. Similarly a man who makes his solemn oath untrue (i.e. breaks it) will go to Yama's abode quickly."

5. After saying this, Bhīṣma, the highly esteemed grandfather of Kurus, became extremely delighted and went to his city

Sūta said:

6. There was a boy born of a Śūdra and named Pauṇḍraka. During childhood, he used to play day and night.

7-8. Jokingly a friend's book was stolen by him. On being asked by his friends, Pauṇḍraka said: "It has not been taken away by me. The book should have been well pondered by you all with great endeavour. Look out for it somewhere here."

9. Taking his bath in the waters of Gaṅgā solemn oaths were taken by him. (Later) when he ceased to be a wicked fellow the book that had been stolen was returned by him.

10. Again he cracked many charming jokes with him Then

he became a leper and immediately he became a despicable person.

11. He was abandoned by all the kinsmen and even by beloved wives. Thereupon he became dejected and he committed suicide by hurling himself down from the precipice.

12. By its power he became rid of leprosy. That person indulging in jokes became mute due to the fault of the theft of the scriptural text.

13. Hence, O Brāhmaṇas, in front of this deity, even the slightest solemn oath should not be taken by one who wishes for his own happiness, even a jocular vein.

CHAPTER FIFTYNINE

Vidura Builds the Lord's Temple

Sūta said:

1-2. Formerly, O excellent Brāhmaṇas, Ravi, Śiva and Viṣṇu were installed by Vidura in that holy place. A man who worships them with great devotion attains the highest region, very difficult to be achieved even by Yajñas.

3. Formerly, O Brāhmaṇas, while Vidura was staying at Hastināpura he was visited in his house by Gālava, a tiger among sages. He (Gālava) was asked:

4. "Of what sort is the ultimate goal in the other world of one who has no son? Kindly be gracious to me and tell me even as I ask you this."

Gālava said:

5-6. There is no salvation unto one who has no son. On death he does not go to heaven if he has none of these twelve (types of sons): (1) *Aurasa* (bosom-born), (2) *Kṣetraja* (son born to his wife), (3) *Krayakrīta* (one who is bought on pay- ment), (4) *Pālita* (one who is brought up), (5) *Paunarbhava* (widow's son after remarriage), (6) *Datta* (adopted), (7) *Kuṇḍa* (son born in adultery), (8) *Gola* (widow's bastard), (9) *Kānīna* (son of an unmarried woman), (10) *Sahoḍha* (son of a woman pregnant at the time of marriage), (11) *Aśvattha* (banyan tree) (see verse 12 below), (12) *Brahmavṛkṣaka* (religious fig tree).

7. If men do not have any one of these, they will have to stay surely in the Naraka named *Puṁ*.

Sūta said:

8. On hearing the words of the noble-souled Gālava, Vidura became extremely distressed because he had no sons.

9-11. Vidura was dejected and Gālava said to him: "Do not grieve over it. At my instance make the tree named *Viṣṇu* (i.e. *Aśvattha)* your son quickly. Thereby you will obtain the entire benefit of having a son. Go to the holy place on the top of the mountain Raktaśṛṅga, to the holy spot named Hāṭakeśvara that is the cause of (i.e. which gives) all prosperity and auspicious well-being."

On hearing his words Vidura instantly started:

12. With great joy he went to the place indicated by Gālava. There he planted an *Aśvattha* tree and consecrated it as his son.

13. He became contented with that sort of marital rite. Thereafter he went round that holy place like engaged in pilgrimage.

14. He had heard the glorification of various wonderful holy spots connected with noble-souled saintly kings. Now he travelled and visited the different deities of those holy Spots.

15. He visited the glorified shrines of the noble-souled, elderly member of the Kuru clan (i.e. Bhīṣma) and intended to build places to the deities.

16. Then he installed the Liṅga of Maheśvara beneath the Vaṭa (holy fig tree). He then installed Viṣṇu beneath the Aśvattha tree.

17. After consecrating the deities he pleaded to the Brāhmaṇas: " These three deities have been installed by me in your holy place. All the affairs (services) of these should be considered and managed by you all."

The Brāhmaṇas said:

18-19. We shall perform all the rites such as the Yātrā (religious procession) etc. of these deities. Our sons, grandsons and others hailing from our families shall continue to perform all the requisite rites. Do go back home.

20. Thereupon Vidura joyously went back to his city and was contented. Those Brāhmaṇas too carried out the requests made by him.

21. A man who worships Bhāskara (the Sun-god) there on the seventh lunar day in the month of Māgha coinciding with a Sunday attains the greatest goal.

22. Or he should worship Śiva on a Monday particularly coinciding with the eighth lunar day in the bright half of the month. He should worship Viṣṇu with full faith at the time of *Śayana* (Āṣāḍha) and *Bodhana* (Kārttika) (on the eleventh days in the bright half of Āṣāḍha and Kārttika).

23. Hence with all endeavour that splendid trio of deities should be worshipped particularly by men desirous of attaining the goal of heaven.

24. Hundreds and thousands of sages of esteemed vows have attained Siddhi there formerly by propitiating Videreśvara.

25. Thereupon, realizing that the Liṅga is the bestower of Siddhi, the Chastiser of Pāka (i.e. Indra) filled it with dust particles so that none will come to know of it.

26. Once thereafter Vidura happened to come there. On seeing that the Liṅga had vanished he felt very miserable.

27-28. At the same time an unembodied voice spoke: "O Vidura, do not feel sorry now. Yonder there appears a sapling of *Vaṭa* tree. The divine Droṇī (tank) beneath it has been filled up with dust particles by the Lord of Suras."

29. Thereupon he brought much wealth from Hastināpura and renovated the entire place working day and night untiringly.

30. Then he saw the deities and was delighted very much. He built palaces befitting them and well constructed.

31-33. The great sage built a palace as lofty as the peak of Kailāsa for the Sun-god. He observed that Maheśvara had got entangled with the hanging roots of the *Vaṭa* tree. So he did not build a palace lest the Liṅga should be displaced. He built a big chamber befitting Vāsudeva. With great delight he offered means of sustenance to the Brāhmaṇas. He took leave of the Brāhmaṇas then and went to his hermitage.

CHAPTER SIXTY

Greatness of Narāditya

The sages said:

1. O Sūta-nandana, earlier you had mentioned the deity Māhitthā. By whom was the deity installed? Do describe every thing without leaving anything.

Sūta said:

2-3. The Vidyā (divine power) named *Śoṣaṇī* was propitiated by Agastya. The great goddess was propitiated through Ātharvaṇa Mantra. Then the ocean was dried up by the noble-souled son of Mitra and Varuṇa. He addressed the goddess standing before.

4-7a. "Since Māhittha (?) has been adopted by you, everything is auspicious unto me. Therefore you will become the deity named Māhitthā. In the holy place of Camatkārapura you will get excellent adoration. One who is endowed with devotion and adores with the Ātharvaṇa Mantras, you who are stationed there, shall obtain prosperity always. Hence hasten to that excellent city along with me. Be present there for ever in order to protect Brāhmaṇas."

7b. It was thus that the excellent deity Māhitthā happened to manifest there.

8. This mountain that had been moving was rendered immobile by that deity. It was here, O excellent Brāhmaṇas, that the mountain was pierced by Skanda with his Śakti (Tri-dent) formerly.

9. Another deity named Narāditya was installed by Nara. One who visits him on the sixth lunar day coinciding with a Sunday is liberated from sins.

10. Like Arjuna, he will never suffer defeat from enemies. A sick man is rid of his ailments. Poor people will attain wealth.

11. Similarly, O excellent Brāhmaṇas one who visits Lord Janārdana who lifted up the mountain Govardhana there, on the first day in the bright half of the month of Kārttika, will have many cows devoid of ailments.

12. Lord Hari himself directly in the guise of the Man-lion

and Vināyaka, the bestower of all desires and the remover of all obstacles, was installed by Arjuna.

13. One who devoutly worships him on the fourth lunar day through sweetmeats and other foodstuffs shall be liberated from all obstacles. He will get desired benefit. O excellent Brāhmaṇas, he is stationed there for the welfare of leading Brāhmaṇas.

14. One who worships him through Ātharvaṇa Mantras on the twelfth lunar day in the bright half of the month of Kārttika attains the greatest goal.

15-16. O excellent Brāhmaṇas, both the deities Nara and Nārāyaṇa are present there. One who is greatly rediant and visits them devoutly and worships them on the twelfth day, attains the highest place devoid of old age and death.

17. O excellent Brāhmaṇas, Dhanañjaya (Arjuna) who undertook his pilgrimage came to the holy place of Hāṭakeśvara.

18. On seeing that sacred holy spot full of many excellent Tīrthas, he installed Āditya in a very charming mansion (temple).

19. Lords Nara and Nārāyaṇa were installed afterwards in front of him (i.e. Āditya). Similarly the Lord holding the mountain Govardhana was also installed.

20. Another deity was also installed by him with great faith, namely Narasiṁha. Thus the son of Kuntī established five shrines.

21. Then he summoned all the Brāhmaṇas hailing from that city, gave them ample cash and spoke after duly bowing to them with devotion:

22. "The Sun-god, the destroyer of all ailments, has been installed by me and entrusted to you all. It is your duty always to look after the shrine.

The Brāhmaṇa said:

23. O excellent one among the sons of Pāṇḍu, do go home with full confidence. All of us will carry out what is conducive to what is good for you.

24. Thereupon Arjuna was delighted. He gave much wealth to them. He took leave of them, bowed to them and went to his city.

Sūta said:

25. Thus everything concerning the greatness of Narāditya has been narrated to you, O excellent Brāhmaṇas. It destroys the sins of the listeners.

CHAPTER SIXTYONE

Birth of Viṣakanyā

The sages said:

1-3. O highly intelligent one, you spoke of the Śarmiṣṭhā Tīrtha. O highly fortunate one, do tell us how it originate? What is its power?

Sūta said:

There was a king named Vṛka born in the lunar race. He was a patron of learned Brāhmaṇas, a person worthy of being a shelter on refuge, always engaged in the welfare of all the worlds.

His wife was a chaste lady dearer to him than even his own life. She was endowed with all good characteristics and a devoted, faithful and chaste wife.

4. In her late life, a daughter was born to her on a day condemned by all scriptural texts (i.e. considered inauspicious by them).

5. Thereupon, he summoned Brāhmaṇas well-versed in the Science of Astrology. He asked, "Of what sort will this daughter of mine be?"

The Brāhmaṇas said:

6. If a girl is born when the Sun is in the constellation Citrā or the Moon in the fourteenth lunar day, she will become a Viṣakanyakā (a poison girl).

7. A man who grasps her hand in marriage, O excellent king, will certainly meet with his death within six months.

8. She will render the mansion wherein she is born, even if it be that of Kubera, a place devoid of riches within six months.

9. Such is , O king, your daughter who is called a Viṣakanyakā. She will destroy the two families, viz. that of parents and that of her father-in-law.

10. Hence, do be happy, O king, by abandoning her if you have faith in our words, spoken by us for your good, O Lord.

The king said:

11. Whether I abandon her or keep her in the house my Karma of the previous body (of the previous birth) will certainly fructify.

12. Whether auspicious or inauspicious (evil), nothing can be prevented. With this Karma in view I will not abandon my daughter.

13. Any man doing anything with whatever body of his attains the entire fruit further with the same (or similar) body

14. Auspicious or inauspicious act may be done in different states or situations. Certainly the fruit thereof is experienced in the same or similar situation by men.

15. An action of the previous birth done by any of the organs does not perish. Nothing results from what has not been done. So I am not afraid.

16. Span of life, Karma, wealth, learning and dealth-these five are ordained even as the embodied being is in the womb itself.

17. Just as flowers and fruits on trees and creepers do not deviate from their fixed time, so also the previous Karma.

18. Only the doer experiences always the good (or adverse) result of his own good or bad act in the manner previously done.

19. Just as a calf finds out its mother cow among thousands of cows, so also Karma finds out the doer from among ten million doers.

20. No man on the earth can by means of his might or intellect alter a Karma done in the previous body.

21. A sensible man with intellect penetrating deep into the scriptural texts, is honoured otherwise. But the Karma previously done alters it like the master.

22. The happiness and misery of embodied beings depend on their own acts. He who is the cause thereof is bound to them by Ahaṁkāra (feeling of I and mine).

23. One's own action pursues one, even if one runs very fast: when one lies down the action too lies down and when one stands it too stands by.

24. Just as shade and sunshine are well inter-related, so also action and doer. No worry need be entertained in this regard.

25. If a man is destined to experience happiness or misery in any sphere, he is led there by force like one bound by ropes.

26. Karma is the authority to bring happiness and misery to living

beings even when they are watchfully alert or continue to sleep.

27. Just as a lamp goes out when oil is used up, so also a creature is liberated when Karma is exhausted.

28. Neither Mantras nor penance, neither Dāna nor Tīrtha nor even perfect self-control can be competent to save a creature afflicted by the previous Karmas.

29. An insentient drop of semen deposited in a womb by intercourse during the prescribed menstrual period by a man grows up in accordance with the previous Karma.

30. Why does not the foetus get dissolved in the very same belly where foodstuffs and beverages get digested, what is eaten gets dissolved?

31. Hence this is my decision once and for all that the merit and sin of embodied beings is the result of the action done.

32. What is apparently unprotected stands firm when protected by fate; what is well guarded perishes when struck by fate. A seemingly helpless person left in forest survives but one well protected in the house may not continue to live.

CHAPTER SIXTYTWO

Greatness of Śarmiṣṭhā Tīrtha

Sūta said:

1. That king decided thus, O excellent Brāhmaṇas. He did not abandon that Viṣakanyakā though advised by the astrologers.

2. She became well known by the name Śarmiṣṭhā as she was like spittle (Ṣṭhīvana) of happiness (*Śarman*) that had been thrown out by the father. She was being given by the king lovingly but none accepted her.

3. In the meantime the enemies of that king angrily attacked him and the kingdom from all sides.

4. The enraged king set off from his place surrounded by his army for a fight thinking that if he were to return it would be (no better than) death.

5. He fell upon the enemies and fought a great battle with his army consisting of four divisions and increased the population in the country of Yama (by killing enemies).

6. On the tenth day all his enemies encircled him and killed him.

7. The men of that king who survived the battle, were frightened and distressed. They fled to the city quickly.

8. All the hosts of the enemies were highly delighted. Desirous of gaining further victory they besieged the city in order to exterminate his sons.

9. In the meantime all the citizens in the height of their grief rebuked and reviled the wicked Viṣakanyakā with very harsh words.

10-13. "It was the result of the (ominous) defect of this sinful girl that the king died. The annihilation of the country will follow the ruin of the (capital) city. The king too had been told then by the learned Brāhmaṇas: 'Abandon this censured Viṣakanyakā who is full of many defects.' But the noble-minded, compassionate king was fettered by bonds of affection. So he did not abide by the advice even of those well-wishers. Hence, at least now, let this sinful girl be killed quickly or banished from the city lest the city should be ruined."

Sūta said:

14. She too heard the diverse kinds of derogatory remarks of the people. She became disgusted much and censured herself.

15. Filled with terror and grief, she went out at night and proceeded towards the forest where she had determined to die.

16. Then the great sacred place of Hāṭakeśvara was seen by her. It gave much solace to her mind as it was filled with sages.

17-18. Thereupon, she recollected the incidents of the previous birth: "As a Cāṇḍāla woman I had quenched the thirst of a cow. By its power I was reborn in the palace of a king. It was due to the power of this holy spot. Hence I shall stay here only."

Sūta said:

19. In the previous birth she was a despicable Cāṇḍāla woman distressed with poverty and overburdened with many children.

20. In the course of her ramblings she came to this holy spot. She was overcome with thirst. It was the time when the Sun

was overhead at midday in that terrible (very hot) month of Jyeṣṭha.

21. She saw a small well with very little water. Near it she saw a tawny-coloured cow standing by.

22. In the height of her compassion she left off all thoughts of love to her children and her own life. She made (allowed) the cow to quench her thirst.

23. Her mind had been swayed by devotion to the cow. Due to the lack of water she met with death along with the children.

24. Then, O excellent Brāhmaṇas, she was reborn in the palace of a king by the power thereof; but she was born as a Viṣakanyakā as an inevitable result of the previous Karma.

The sages said:

25. What was that Karma as the inevitable result of which she was reborn as a Viṣakanyakā? She had exterminated her own family. O Sūta, narrate everything to us.

Sūta said:

26. O Brāhmaṇas, even as she was rambling as a Cāṇḍāla woman, she went into a temple where there was a splendid gold image of Gaurī.

27. That being a deserted place, she got hold of the gold image joyously and went to another country. The despicable woman wanted to cut the image into pieces for selling. Even as she was engaged in it the officers of the king who had been searching for her overtook her.

28. On meeting her they rebuked her repeatedly and hit her with their fists, pelted with clods and struck her with sticks.

29. They seized the gold and left her in a pool of blood. Thinking that she (being a woman) should not be killed thus, they returned to the city.

30. She had touched (and defiled) the image of Pārvatī. Further she cut it into pieces. It was a result of this evil deed that she was reborn as a Viṣakanyā.

31. She then recollected the incidents of this previous birth. Pondering over the greatness of the gift of water drunk by the cow she now dug a big lake of clear water in the place of the earlier small well.

32-33. It was a big lake like a sea. It was beautifully embellished with clusters of lotuses. Fish and turtles abounded in it and porpoises added to its glory. Many swans, cranes and ruddy geese resorted to it all round. The water was unfathomable and the aquatic creatures took delight therein.

34. With great devotion she got a charming mansion lofty like a peak of Kailāsa erected near it pleasing to the eyes of the good.

35. Then she devoutly installed Gaurī and performed a penance. Before the goddess she observed the Vrata as laid down in the scriptural texts.

36. Even in *Hemanta* (early winter) she used to take bath in the morning and worship Gaurī devoutly with adoration and offerings of oblations and making gifts to Brāhmaṇas and the like.

37. That princess used to take bath both in the morning and in the evening during Śiśira (late winter) with great mental concentration and purity. She used to observe fast on alternate days.

38. During spring season the pious lady propitiated Pārvatī through dances and songs. She used to take food only once in six times (i.e. in three days). She was engrossed in making gifts of foodgrains.

39. The daughter of king Vṛka endowed with great faith performed penance in the midst of five fires during summer. Fruits alone constituted her diet.

40. During rainy season water constituted her intake. The Viṣakanyā abandoned her hut and lay down under the open sky.

41. Then she spent autumn by taking in only air. She was always engaged in *Japa* with her mind meditating on Pārvatī.

42. Even as she continued to propitiate thus, the goddess, the daughter of the Mountain, a long time elapsed; but she did not obtain any desired benefit.

43. Continuing her state of virginity, her face was full of wrinkles and her head was marked with greying hairs; but the Beloved of Hara did not get pleased (with her).

44. After some time had elapsed, once the goddess adopted the form of Śakrāṇī in order to test her. Thus she appeared before the princess.

45-46. She was seated on a great elephant with four tusks

and a very long trunk. It could be compared to the peak of Kailāsa. It resembled the Sun in lustre. It was as white as lime powder and in the state of rut.

She was surrounded on all sides by the wives of Devas. She was adorned with necklaces and bracelets and she wore a crown on her head.

47. A white umbrella was held above her head. She was attended upon by celestial damsels and was eulogized by Kinnaras.

48-50. She was sung about by Gandharvas. She then spoke respectfully, "O daughter, I shall grant a boon unto you. Request for whatever you desire."

I am the wife of the Lord of Suras and am glorified as Śacī in all the three worlds. Now I am pleased with this excellent penance of yours. Taking pity on you, I have myself come to you.

A great penance has been performed by you meditating on the Beloved of Hara. Yet the highly ruthless Bhavānī has not become pleased by your penance (so seek a boon from me)."

Sūta said:

51. On hearing the words of Śakrāṇī the Viṣakanyakā bowed down to her, standing with palms joined in reverence and spoke thus:

The Viṣakanyā said:

52. O goddess, I don't intend to request you for anything. Similarly, O Indrāṇī, I don't wish to request other deities too. There is no doubt about it.

53. O beloved of Indra, I may go to a hideous Naraka by the command of the wife of Hara; but I will not go even to heaven by your command.

54. I will choose a boon from that goddess who is adored by Devas, who has neither a beginning, nor a middle nor an end and who is endowed with glory and perfect knowledge.

55. I will choose a boon from that goddess whom Viṣṇu, Brahmā, Rudra and Vāsava propitiate. I will seek the object I desire from that goddess alone.

56. I will choose a boon from that goddess by whom the entire range of the three worlds consisting of mobile and immobile

beings, is pervaded by means of diverse kinds of female forms.

Śrī Devī said:

57. I am the wife of the Lord of Suras. I am dearer to him than his life. Devas, Dānavas and Pannagas obey my order.

58. Kinnaras, Guhyakas and Yakṣas too obey. Then why not those of mortal activities? So, O bad ascetic woman, why don't you receive a boon from me?

59-60a. Hence I shall certainly shatter your head with a blow of the thunderbolt.

60b-64. O Brāhmaṇas, on hearing her words the ascetic woman took enough courage to tell the goddess of Suras once again: "You are the mistress of Devas. This is undoubtedly true. I am propitiating that supreme goddess from whom you have received your power and glory. O goddess of Suras, even the least of a fault has not been perpetrated against you by me. Still, if you consider me as one deserving death, do hurl the weapon. O Śakrāṇī, do listen attentively to another word of mine also. On hearing it, you ponder over it fully and do what is beneficient. Neither you, nor your husband Śakra nor the other Suras and Asuras are capable of slaying me, as I have sought refuge in Pārvatī. So hasten to heaven kindly; do not waste your fury over me, O goddess of all Suras, as I strictly abide by the right path.

Sūta said:

65. After saying this to Śacī, the miserable Viṣakanyā decided to die and thought thus:

66-70. 'Since the goddess, the Daughter of the Mountain is not pleased with me, and if this Śakrāṇī too does not kill me, I shall certainly resort to the burning fire immediately.' Thereafter she saw presently the elephant Airāvaṇa turning all of a sudden into the Bull having complexon like milk, jasmine and moon. She saw Goddess Pārvatī seated on it along with Śambhu. The goddess had four arms. Her face was beaming pleasantly in her divine form. She was wearing white garlands and garments. The crescent moon adorned her forehead. Then the Viṣakanyā looked at her closely and realized that it was Pārvatī the unborn. Then she repeatedly bowed down and eulogized.

Prayer of Viṣakanyā:

71. "Obeisance to you, O goddess of the chiefs of Devas. Obeisance to you, O goddess abiding in everything, O truthful goddess devoid of old age and death, O bestower of everything desired.

72. O goddess, even Śakra and other gods do not know how to extol your real form. How can I, a mortal woman, do it?

73. You are the goddess from whose person was born the Cosmic Egg constituted of Earth, Ether, Water, Fire and Air and consisting of Devas, Asuras and human beings.

74. Brahmā is not competent to give birth to her; Maheśvara is not competent to destroy her; and Govinda is not competent to protect her. How can I adequately eulogize you?

75. You are the goddess who are the possessor of the highest eightfold perfection by your very nature; which has nothing superior to it in the world, and is always the most desirable thing.

76. You are the goddess whose diverse forms the sages engaged in perfect meditation think of devoutly and obtain what they desire.

77-78. The Yogins who are determined to attain salvation conceive your form in the heart and adore it by means of the flowers of genuine sentiments. Being a human being, how can I eulogize that Maheśvarī?

The Devī said:

79. O daughter, I am happy with you. O lady of excellent Vratas, choose your boon. I shall grant you certainly what has been cherished for ever in your heart.

Viṣakanyā said:

80. It was for the sake of (obtaining) a husband that I endeavoured thus, O goddess, by means of the penance. Now that I have been overcome by old age, what can I do with him?

81. Hence I shall have to stay here in this hermitage for ever along with you. O Pārvatī, at my instance and for the welfare of all women you must stay here always.

Śrī Devī said:

82. O fair lady, from now onwards, I shall make my hermitage in this excellent and auspicious penance grove of yours. (I Hope) this has been thought of by you within the heart.

83. A woman who takes her holy bath here on the third lunar day in the bright half of Māgha, shall, due to my favour, obtain the desired benefit.

84. Even after committing great sins, a woman or a man shall,with my favour, be free from sins after taking the holy bath here.

85. If men make gifts of fruit here, all their hopes and expectations shall become fruitful undoubtedly.

86. Even after killing a woman, a man who takes his holy bath here on the third lunar day in the bright half of Māgha, shall become free from sins.

87. O fair lady, a girl who takes her holy bath on that day with great devotion shall undoubtedly obtain an excellent husband.

Sūta said:

88. After saying this, Gaurī touched her with her hand. Thereby she instantly became one possessing a divine form.

89. Old age disappeared from her. She had divine garlands and unguents. With protruding thick bosom, she became a woman with the gait of an elephant in rut.

90. Then she made her own maid. Taking her she went to Kailāsa, the excellent mountain, along with Hara.

91. Ever since then that Tīrtha is called Śarmiṣṭhā Tīrtha. It is well-known in all the three worlds as one that destroys all sins.

92. Hence, O excellent Brāhmaṇas, one should duly take one's holy bath there assiduously on the third lunar day in the bright half of Māgha.

93. This narration of mine of the greatness of the Strītīrtha is sacred, conducive to longevity and destructive of all sins.

94. A man who gets up early in the morning always and reads this, shall obtain all desires of his mind.

95. Similarly a man who reads this or listens to this on festive occasions with devotion, shall go to Śiva's palace.

CHAPTER SIXTYTHREE

Greatness of Somanātha

Sūta said:

1-3. Now there is an excellent Liṅga there named Someśvara. It is well known in all the three worlds. It was installed here by the Moon-god himself.

One who makes it a point to stay there for a year and adores it on every Monday, becomes relieved even of awful ailments.

There is no doubt that he is relieved of even tuberculosis, leaving aside (smaller ailments, like) leprosy etc. Hence by all means a man distressed with ailments should worship it.

4. Formerly the Moon-god propitiated it when he was afflicted by the ailment of tuberculosis. He became one with a body free from ailments like King Pāṇḍya.

The sages said:

5. O Sūtaja, how did Soma, the Lord of the medicinal herbs, become afflicted by tuberculosis formerly. How did he get the relief?

6. O highly intelligent one, narrate this to us in detail. So also relate the auspicious story of that Pāṇḍya king.

Sūta said:

7. Formerly the Lord of night (Moon) married in the presence of Fire-god and Guru (Preceptor, Bṛhaspati), the twentyseven daughters of Dakṣa.

8. They are being glorified by excellent Brāhmaṇas well-versed in astrology by the name Nakṣatra (Star). Of them Aśvinī is the first. All of them are endowed with qualities like beauty, liberal-mindedness etc.

9. Out of them all, Rohiṇī was the most beloved to the Lord of night, dearer than his own life.

10. Hence he abandoned all the other daughters of Dakṣa and stayed with Rohiṇī day and night.

11. Hence all of them who had thus become unfortunate became all the more distressed with passion (love). They went to Dakṣa with faces drenched with tears and said:

12. "Dear father, we have been given by you to a sinner as his wife. He does not lovingly give us (enjoyment) even on the Ṛtu days (i.e. prescribed days after the menstrual flow, for cohabitation).

13. Hence we shall cast off our lives entering fire ere long. O highly exalted one, we are telling you the truth."

Sūta said:

14. On hearing their words, Dakṣa was also distressed. He himself took them all and went to Śaśin (Moon-god).

15. In the presence of all of them, Dakṣa, the Prajāpati (Patriarch), spoke to the Lord of night, rebuking him repeatedly with very harsh words:

16-18. "O base Lord of night, O foolish one, is this proper on your part to do. It is what is censured in the Dharmaśāstras (codes of ethics), O base one excluded by the good. Even when the Ṛtu days come, you do not speak lovingly to my daughters. Don't you know Dharmaśāstra? One who does not go to his wife after she has had Ṛtu bath undoubtedly incurs the awful sin of foeticide."

19. On hearing his words, the Lord of night became ashamed. With face bent down, he spoke to Dakṣa: "I shall carry out your behest."

20. Thereupon, Dakṣa became delighted in his mind. He left all his daughters to the care of the cool-rayed Moon, took leave of him and went back to his own abode.

21. But Candra did everything as before. He ignored all other daughters of Dakṣa and continued his passionate association solely with Rohiṇī.

22. Then all those miserable ones again went to their father and spoke to him with tears in their eyes, words befitting that occasion:

23-26. "O father, this is our greatest sorrow in our heart that a misfortune hated by all women has befallen us.

Your effort has been rendered ineffective by that lecherous fellow of wicked soul. Your authority has been flouted by him in our case.

We cannot bear in our heart that misery at all. That Candramas is diverting himself with Rohiṇī always.

Particularly despite the fact that he has been prohibited by your order, the Lord of night has done this. Permit us now to carry out our intention in this regard. Distressed by the misery of absence of conjugal felicity, we shall give up our lives."

Sūta said:

27. On hearing their words, Dakṣa became very angry. He went to the Lord of night and cursed him:

28. "O sinner, my advice of righteous import has not been followed by you. So the fell disease of tuberculosis will oppress you."

29. After saying thus, O excellent Brāhmaṇas, Dakṣa went away. Candra was instantly afflicted by tuberculosis and began to decline in strength day by day.

30. He became emaciated. Incompetent to continue the dalliance of love, he forsook Rohiṇī too and roamed all over the earth.

31. He began asking physicians about the ways and means of curing the disease of tuberculosis. Controlling his sense-organs, he had the medication of herbs of diverse kinds.

32. Still the Lord of night was not rid of the tuberculosis. Due to the terrible imprecation of Dakṣa he grew more and more emaciated every day.

33. Thereupon, he eschewed the excellent medication. He became endowed with ardent faith. In this attitude of disgust, he undertook pilgrimage to holy spots.

34. Roving over the tīrthas and shrines, O excellent Brāhmaṇas, he arrived at the excellent holy spot of Prabhāsa.

35-36. The Lord of night took his holy bath there and gained purity. After visiting the deity of Prabhāsa, he wanted to go elsewhere when he saw the sage named Romaka standing in front. The sage was a man of esteemed holy vows. He was endowed with vigour due to penance. He was one who took pity on all living beings.

37. On seeing him, O excellent Brāhmaṇas, Candra afflicted with the disease of tuberculosis bowed to him and spoke loudly and respectfully exhibiting the disgust he felt:

38-40. "O eminent Brāhmaṇa, I have become utterly exhausted as a result of the disease of tuberculosis. I seek refuge in you.

Kindly do something to cure this.

O highly esteemed one, many physicians have been consulted by me. I have taken medicines prescribed by them in diverse ways but I am getting weaker and weaker every day.

If you cannot give any suggestion for quelling the disease, I will cast off my body."

Romaka said:

41. O Lord of night, even the curse of an ordinary person cannot be altered; the curse of Dakṣa of immeasured splendour is all the more so.

42. So I shall give you an advice commonly accepted, whereby your tuberculosis can surely be cured.

43. There is nothing which cannot be given by the Trident-bearing Lord of Devas, if he is pleased. Hence propitiate him at my instance.

44-45. Satī stays (Read *satyā vāsaḥ* instead of *satyam vāsaḥ* in the Text) always in sixty-eight Tīrthas on the earth. Install the Liṅga in all of them, O Lord of night, for removing (the disease). Then propitiate the Liṅga every day with a mind sanctified by faith. There is no doubt, you will get relief from tuberculosis.

Sūta said:

46. On hearing his words, the Lord of night became delighted. He installed the divine Liṅgas of the Trident-bearing Lord in the holy place of Prabhāsaka marking them with his names. He devoutly worshipped them.

47. Thereupon the great Lord was pleased and appeared before him. He said, "I shall bestow boons. Request for whatever is desired by you."

Candra said:

48. O Lord of Devas, I am immensely tired and exhausted by the disease of tuberculosis. I have sought refuge at your feet. Save me from it. I do not request for anything else.

49. On hearing his words the Bull-emblemed Lord summoned Dakṣa there itself and spoke respectfully:

50. "This Candra, your son-in-law, has been cursed by you. This is not good. Hence at my behest do bless him now."

Dakṣa said:

51. He has a crooked mind. I gave him a sound advice of righteous import. After undertaking to abide by it before me he failed to do it and he became untruthful in his words.

52. So, O Bull-emblemed Lord, for the sake of my daughters I cursed him angrily. Even what I utter jokingly cannot become changed.

The Lord of Devas said:

53. At my bidding, this Lord of night will see all your daughters impartially from now onwards. There is no doubt.

54. Hence let him waste away for a fortnight and wax again for a fortnight. Thereby your words can be true along with my favour.

55. Then Dakṣa said "So be it" and went to his adode. Lord Śaṅkara said to the Moon again:

56. "O Moon, you can once again request for something desired. I shall grant everything even if it be rare."

Candra said:

57. O Lord of Devas, if you are pleased, if a boon has to be granted to me, you must be present always in the Liṅgas installed by me for the welfare of all the worlds.

The Lord said:

58. At your request I shall be present on all Mondays in the sixty-eight Liṅgas installed by you.

59-61. After saying thus the Lord of Devas vanished. Candra too joyously and impartially saw them all. He saw the daughters of Dakṣa impartially as he remembered the words of Śaṅkara. They also became delighted thereafter. It was thus, O excellent Brāhmaṇas, that Someśvaras came into being there in the sixty-eight Tīrthas and in the others thereafter.

CHAPTER SIXTYFOUR

Greatness of Camatkārī Durgā

Sūta said:

1-3. The great goddess Camatkārī is there itself, O excellent Brāhmaṇas. It was formerly devoutly installed by King Camatkāra.

It was by her that the demon in the form of a buffalo (Mahiṣa) was killed in battle. The demon who could wield thousands of Māyās was defeated by the goddess who adopted the Kaumāra Vrata (holy vow of celibacy).

When the noble-souled king built the city there, O Brāhmaṇas, she too was installed there for its protection.

4. She was there for guarding that city and to protect all the leading Brāhmaṇas, the inhabitants of that city, because they had purified their minds by means of devotion.

5-6. If any one adores her duly on the day of Mahānavamī, he will not have any cause of fear during the entire year from goblins, corpses, ghosts, vampires, enemies in particular, illness, thieves, wicked people or others.

7. A man should be pure in body and mind on the eighth lunar day in the bright half of the month. Whatever he thinks of at the time of worshipping devoutly, he attains it undoubtedly.

8. The truth has been averred by me that by the grace of the goddess a person (worshipping her) without any desire will undoubtedly attain liberation from Saṁsāra quite easily.

9. Formerly many kings, Brāhmaṇas, Yogins and others had propitiated the supreme goddess Parameśvarī and attained Siddhi.

10. One who is endowed with faith and scrupulously circumambulates her every day for a year, can avert being born in a brutish womb.

11. Listen attentively. I shall narrate unto you the great miracle that happened formerly in her shrine.

12. Formerly there was an excellent king named Citraratha. He was well-known as the overlord of the Daśārṇa country and as the slayer of all enemies.

13. Always on the eighth lunar day of the bright half of the month, he faithfully and devoutly circumambulated the goddess a hundred and eight times.

14. Thereafter, he used to bow down to the goddess and then go home surrounded on all sides by his army consisting of the four divisions.

15. Thus, a great deal of time passed by even as the leading king continued to be devoted to the goddess scrupulously making the circumambulations.

16. Once, when that king went there, he saw some excellent Brāhmaṇas resting in the shrine of the goddess.

17. Then the king circumambulated the goddess and bowed down with concentration to all the Brāhmaṇas stationed before.

18. Thereafter, he sat down along with them (listening to) the narration of splendid stories of saintly kings and ancient Brāhmaṇa-sages.

19. At the conclusion of one story-session, the king was asked as he stood there politely by those excellent Brāhmaṇas who were very curious (to know the king):

20-22. "O king, we are asking you out of curiosity. Hence recount in detail if there is no secret about your engagements. Always, in every month, on the eighth lunar day in the bright half, you come here from a very distant place and carry out your rite of circumambulation. You carefully avoid all other pious rites such as worship etc. Indeed you may be knowing the entire benefit that accrues from circumambulation."

The king said:

23. This is the truth, O excellent Brāhmaṇas; what you say is true. Even a secret has to be shared with you by narrating it to you.

24. Formerly I was a parrot in this splendid shrine of the goddess. I had built a nest in the western section of the temple and lived there.

25. Every day I went out of the temple and returned later. This constituted a circumambulation of the goddess, O excellent Brāhmanas.

26. In due course death overtook me here in the temple itself. As a result thereof, I was reborn as a king with the power to recollect the previous birth and activities.

27. That is the reason why, O excellent Brāhmaṇas, I come here over a long distance and circumambulate the goddess with concentration and mental purity.

28-29. Earlier I had no devotion at all, and I stayed in a nest. But I circumambulated the goddess. Thereby I became a king. Now I circumambulate with full faith but I do not know what (better) welfare is in store for me, O excellent Brāhmaṇas.

Sūta said:

30-31. On hearing it, the Brāhmaṇas' eyes widened with surprise. Joyously they congratulated the king. Then the king bowed down to all the Brāhmaṇas, received their assent and went homewards along with his army.

32. Now, one who is endowed with faith and performs the circumambulation, shall be liberated from all sins and obtain the desired benefit.

33-35. Ever since then, those Brāhmaṇas endowed with great devotion and others as well, circumambulated the deity for the sake of salvation. They did attain great Siddhi they desired, by its power. The *Siddhi* they attained in this world and in the other world has been rarely achieved even by gods. Hence by all means, one should resort to that goddess stationed in that holy spot bestowing all desires on men.

CHAPTER SIXTYFIVE

Greatness of Ānartakeśvara and Śūdrakeśvara

Sūta said:

1-3. Similarly there is another lake there dug by Devas. It was there that a king of Ānarta named Suhaya became a Siddha.

The same king installed a splendid Liṅga there named Ānarteśvara. It is the bestower of all Siddhis on men.

A man who performs his holy ablution there on a Tuesday coinciding with the sixth lunar day, there in the lake, attains Siddhi in the same way as it was by the Lord of Ānarta.

The sages said:

4. How was Siddhi attained by the noble-souled king of Ānarta. O Sūta, narrate everything. Undoubtedly you know everything.

Sūta said:

5. Formerly there was a king of Ānarta named Suhaya. He was attacked by all the enemies in battle and he fled. He became *Ucchiṣṭa* (polluted by partaking remnants of food) and was touched by a barbarian. He was alone and was surrounded by many.

6. Then a certain person following the vow of Kāpālikas seized his skull for the purpose of his black magic after knowing that he was born of a heroic warrior.

7-9. This (Kāpālika) stayed in a forest in the vicinity of Ānarteśvara. He used to fill the skull at night with the water of the lake where all the Devas are present and then used to pour it off (in the morning after use).

Formerly there was a Vaṇik (merchant) remembered by the name Siddhasena. He was very rich and accompanied by his servants, he always engaged himself in meritorious rites. Once, O excellent Brāhmaṇas, he set off towards the north accompanied by his caravan for doing business.

10. Going ahead gradually along with every one, he reached a desert area devoid of trees and water and abandoned as it were by all living beings.

11. At nightfall all the travellers became tired. Occupying different positions they all slept soundly.

12. At daybreak they all woke up quickly and started towards the north leaving behind there a Śūdra servant.

13. He had become too tired to get up from sleep. Even when the onward journey started with a lot of noise he did not wake up.

14. He was not remembered by the members of the caravan with whom he had travelled from the original home. The fact that he was on the banks was not noticed by any one.

15. Thus the caravan left the place and the sun began to rise up. The Śūdra felt the intense heat and woke up thereafter.

16. He looked ahead but could not see any member of the caravan at that place. In the desert region their footprints too could not be traced.

17. He became overwhelmed with grief. He ran here and there. At midday he was excessively distressed by hunger and thirst. He sprawled himself on the ground.

18. Despite his distress due to thirst, he somehow held on to his life lying on the ground. By that time the sun too set.

19-20. When the sun's warmth became reduced he regained consciousness somehow. He thought within himself. 'Where shall I go now? No pathway is seen. No one is to be seen. There is neither water nor shade. Indeed my death is approaching.'

21. When that Śūdra was mentally worried thus in the lonely desert region, night set in.

22. Soon he heard the sweet sound of music and the fascinating voice of the chanting Nandi Vṛddhas (elderly goblin attendants of Śiva).

23. In an instant he saw a *Preta* (ghost) who seemed to be the leader of the gang and he was surrounded by groups of *Pretas.*

24. Some of the attending *Pretas* began to dance. Others sang before him. Still others began to eulogize.

25. The (leader) said to the Śūdra: "O dear guest, have your meal. Drink water as you please so that it may result in my weal."

26. The hungry Śūdra had a hearty meal and drank water. At the bidding of the king of the *Pretas,* he became carefree and fearless.

27. Then all the *Pretas* endowed with the characteristic features of the *Pretas* took their food duly sitting in the order of their seniority.

28. Thus, O excellent Brāhmaṇas, all of them were engaged in games and sports with royal grace and charm till the night came to a close.

29. The day dawned clearly and the disc of the sun rose high into the sky. When the Śūdra looked before him there was nothing.

30-31. Then he thought, 'Was this a dream? My hallucination? Or some jugglery? Or rather is it something real? I was distressed with hunger and thirst but I am satisfied now.

32. Even as he mused thus the sun rose very high in the sky and scorched the surface of the earth.

33. He resorted to the foot of a tree which had but a small area of shade to offer. He was excessively distressed due to hunger and thirst and somehow spent the time till the close of the day.

34. At nightfall he saw the king of the *Pretas* of the same form as before and accompanied by the other *Pretas.*

35. In the same manner he took the food, the result of his hospitality. The Śūdra eschewed all fear. He was delighted much.

36. Thus the king (of the *Pretas*) came every day at nightfall. On coming he used to extend his hospitality.

37-38. Then one day, the ghost king was asked by the Śūdra: "What is this miracle seen every day at nightfall? O highly esteemed one, your riches come to an end when the day dawns. Do explain this position, if it is not a secret, O king of *Pretas.* On seeing this strange occurrence, my curiosity has been aroused."

The Preta said:

39. There is a great meritorious holy spot named Hāṭakeśvara. Gaṅgā and Yamunā have a confluence there.

40. Very close to both of them there is an auspicious temple of Śiva. There a *Sunaiṣṭhika* (a sage of continued celibacy) performs penance there adopting a great Vrata.

41-42. At night he keeps my skull filled with water intended for toilet purposes and kept near his bed. By its power at night, I get all these riches. During the day time the skull is kept dry and empty after the toilet is over at night. O highly intelligent one, all my riches vanish then.

43. Do a favour unto me. Go there and shatter the skull to pieces and cast them into the water.

44. Thereby I shall get rid of my hideous ghostly form.

45. Moreover, there is an excellent Tīrtha well-known as Gayāśiras to the east thereof. It can accord salvation from ghosthood.

46. O highly intelligent one, go there and perform the Śrāddha of all of us. O gentle Sir, a bundle of papers is seen there near you.

47. Write the names of all in these sheets in the order of seniority. Have great pity on us and perform the Śrāddha quickly.

48. O fair Sir, we shall easily carry you to that place and also show you a very big treasure to meet the expanses of Śrāddha.

49. The Śūdra agreed to it readily saying, "So it shall be." As promised they took the Śūdra to the holy spot after placing him on their shoulders.

50. They showed him the treasure containing ample wealth. The Śūdra took it and went to the place where the Naiṣṭhika was present.

51. He bowed to him devoutly and told him humbly the full details of the ghost-king.

52. The Śūdra received the skull. With great concentration he reduced it to powder and joyously cast it into the confluence of Gaṅgā and Yamunā.

53. In the meantime the *Preta* appeared before the Śūdra; he was seated in an aerial chariot in a divine form. Then he joyously told him:

54-55. "Thanks to your favour, I have been liberated from the hideous form of ghost. Hail unto you! I shall now go to heaven. Go to the sacred Gayāśiras now and performed the Śrāddha unto all these, so that they too can get salvation."

56. He was surprised. With great concentration and mental purity, he performed the Śrāddha unto all the ghosts severally.

57. All those *Pretas* went to heaven by its power. They joyously revealed themselves to the Śūdra in his dream.

58. The Śūdra realized that the holy spot contributes to the increase of merit. Therefore he did not return home. He stayed there itself performing penance.

59. The Liṅga named Śūdrakeśvara was installed by him near Gaṅgā and Yamunā. It is destructive of all sins.

60-61. A man who duly takes his holy bath in their confluence and worships the Liṅga named Śūdrakeśvara with great ardour and faith becomes liberated from all sins and goes to Śiva's palace riding in an excellent aerial chariot and being eulogized by Gandharvas.

62. A man who performs *Prāyopaveśana* (religious fast unto death) and casts off his life, is not reborn in this world.

63. One who stays there and drinks even a mouthful of its

water is liberated from the sins committed between birth and death.

64. If any one gives food to leading Brāhmaṇas there, (his) Pitṛs become satisfied for a period of three hundred Kalpas.

65. One who, with mental concentration and purity, makes a gift of a piece of gold of the size of an atom there, obtains the entire benefit of Rājasūya and Aśvamedha.

66. Hence, O Brāhmaṇas, a man who wishes for eternal Svarga shall resort to that excellent Tīrtha by all means.

67. On being pleasantly surprised at the sight of that power of Gaṅgā and Yamunā, a Gāthā (a conplet in this connection) was sung formerly by the great sage Gautama.

68. "A man with mental concentration, who takes his holy bath in the confluence of Gaṅgā and Yamunā and visits Śūdreśvara, shall immediately attain Svarga."

69. Thus, O excellent Brāhmaṇas, the greatness of Gaṅgā and Yamunā has been entirely narrated to you all. It is destructive of all sins.

CHAPTER SIXTYSIX

Murder of Jamadagni[1]

Sūta said:

1-2. Further there is a famous Tīrtha which is well-known and remembered as Rāmahrada (the tank of Rāma or Paraśurāma). It was here that his Pitṛs were propitiated by him (Rāma) with libations of blood.

1. The story of Paraśurāma is used in Chapters 66-69, to describe the efficacy of Paraśurāma Hrada for performance of Śrāddha. The Hrada was created by Paraśurāma to avenge the murder of his father Jamadagni by King Sahasrārjuna, a Kṣatriya. For this act of one Kṣatriya, Paraśurāma attempted, genocide of Kṣatriyas and filled a pit (pool) with the blood of Kṣatriyas and performed the Tarpaṇa of his father.

Just because the Hrada proved efficacious to Paraśurāma, it is recommended to others for Śrāddha. The exploits of Paraśurāma are described in Mbh, *Ādi.* 2.5-7. and in other Purāṇas.

He who devoutly offers libations to Pitṛs on the New-Moon day in the month of Bhādrapada shall obtain the benefit of a horse-sacrifice.

The sages said:

3-5. This is something very mysterious that you say, O highly intelligent Sūta, that the Pitṛs were propitiated with libations of blood by him (Rāma).

Sacred things have been prescribed by learned men for the purpose of offering libations to Pitṛs. Blood is prescribed in the case of the libations of Rākṣasas.

An action contrary to the dictates of Śruti and Smṛti, and despised by good people has been performed by the son of Jamadagni. Why did he do so? Tell us, O Sūta.

Sūta said:

6. It was done so by him out of anger, in order to abide by his promise and vow. That was why the Pitṛs were propitiated with the libation of blood.

7. His father Jamadagni, O Brāhmaṇas, who abided by his duty and was faultless, O excellent Brāhmaṇas, was struck down by a Kṣatriya.

8. Thereupon, when his anger was roused, the noble-souled sage (Paraśurāma) said: "My Pitṛs should be propitiated by me with the blood flowing out of the Kṣatriyas."

9. It was for this reason that the Pitṛs were propitiated with blood libations mixed with gingelly seeds by that noble-souled one with devotion.

The sages said:

10. Why was the great Sage Jamadagni killed by a Kṣatriya? What is the name of that king? O Sūta, narrate it in detail.

Sūta said:

11. The son of Ṛcīka is remembered as Jamadagni. Formerly he was in the holy spot of Hāṭakeśvara where all his sins were burnt.

12. He had four sons endowed with good qualities. Rāma was

the most junior among them, but he was most superior in good qualities.

13. Jamadagni continued to stay in a great forest. Once his sons had gone out to forest for gathering roots and bulbous roots.

14. In the meantime, the powerful king of Haihayas, who was well-known all over the earth as Sahasrārjuna, happened to come there.

15. It was the season of summer and the Sun was in the Zodiac of Taurus. Desirous of hunting deer, the king had been roaming here and there in the forest. At midday he became very distressed due to weariness.

16. On seeing the hermitage full of different kinds of trees, he entered it with his army having four divisions.

17. There he saw the great sage Jamadagni seated. He had concluded his bath and was engaged in worshipping the deities.

18. On seeing the king, the sage was pleased. He duly offered him *Arghya* and honoured him with due greetings.

19. He too bowed down to him with great humility; humbly enquired about his health and happiness when speaking to him, in return.

The king said:

20. O Brāhmaṇa, I hope you are hale and hearty in the company of your wife, sons, disciples and attendants. I hope you duly maintain the sacrificial fires.

21. Today my birth has become fruitful and the life meaningful since you, the storehouse of penance, bowed down to by all the worlds, are seen.

22. After saying thus the saintly king rested there for a long time. After drinking water, he bowed down to the great sage and said to him:

23. "If there be any job for me whereby your purpose may be served, it may be mentioned, O holy Brāhmaṇa. Permit me, I shall go home."

Jamadagni said:

24. You have come to my house at the time of the worship of

the deities. You are my guest and have been regarded as though (you are) the desire cherished. A guest is identical with all the Devas.

25. So, O excellent king, I am pleased much and I have great devotion unto you. Hence take the food offered by me with my own hands.

26. Whether it is a king or a Brāhmaṇa, or a Śūdra or one of low caste, if a guest comes at the conclusion of Vaiśvadeva rite, he is one who will take one to heaven.

The king said:

27. O holy Brāhmaṇa, I have here with me hundreds and thousands of soldiers. Without their being fed, is it proper for me to take food? Do tell me.

Jamadagni said:

28-29. I shall serve food unto all of your soldiers. In this respect, you need not worry at all, though I am a sage without any property. O leading king, the cow seen yonder, tethered very near me, yields whatever I desire, always on being requested.

Sūta said:

30. Thereupon, O excellent Brāhmaṇas, the king became full of curiosity. Saying "So be it", he stayed on in the hermitage itself.

31-33. After propitiating Devas and Pitṛs thereafter, he worshipped *Havirvāha* (Fire-god) and then Brāhmaṇas. Thereafter, he sat along with all the hungry servants and followers who were weary and distressed, O excellent Brāhmaṇas. They were overwhelmed with wonder for him (his spiritual power?) Then the excellent sage prayed to the cow, "O splendid one, give unto everyone whatever food he asks for."

34. Thereupon the cow yielded splendid food of various kinds. The sweetmeats in particular were highly pleasing.

35. Then there were foodstuffs that could be chewed, masticated, swallowed, licked and sucked. There were diverse kinds of side-dishes and pickles. Some tasted astringent, some sour and hot. There were sweet and bitter foodstuffs too and all of them were of good quality.

36. Thus that king became extremely satisfied on being fed with foodstuffs born of ambrosia. Thanks to the cow, he became pleased along with his servants and soldiers.

37. At the conclusion of the meal, the king who was pleasantly surprised, requested the great sage Jamadagni for that cow:

38-40. "O holy Brāhmaṇa, this Kāmadhenu does not deserve to be kept with sages of quiescent mind permanently residing in forest. So give it to me.

Thereby I can make people exempt from taxation. Depending upon its power, I can tackle all my enemies even if they are entrenched in fortresses and equipped with formidable armies.

If this is carried out it will be to your own credit and well-being in this world as well as in the other one. So do as I say."

Jamadagni said:

41. O king, this is my only *Homadhenu* (cow intended for the purpose of sacrificial rites). It is as dear to me as my own life. It is worthy of being worshipped always and so can not be given away. Hence it does not behove you to request for it.

The king said:

42. O Brāhmaṇa, in return for this cow I shall give you a hundred thousand other cows and also wealth as much as you wish for.

Jamadagni said:

43. O great king, even an ordinary cow is declared as one that should not be sold. It is much more so in the case of this *Homadhenu* which has powers like these.

44. A deluded Brāhmaṇa who sells a cow prompted by greed for wealth, undoubtedly sells his own mother.

45. Means of expiation has been laid down in the Smṛtis in regard to the Brāhmaṇas who imbibe liquor or kill other Brāhmaṇas. But there is no atonement in the case of those who sell cows.

The King said:

46. O Brāhmaṇa, if you do not give me this cow on being requested politely, I will take it by force. It is better if given when requested peacefully.

Sūta said:

47. On hearing it, O excellent Brāhmaṇas, Jamadagni became furious. He got up from the seat in the assembly shouting, "Weapon! Weapon!"

48. Thereupon the attendants who knew the mind of the king killed the Brāhmaṇa with sharp weapons even before he could lay his hands upon any weapon.

49. When the noble-souled Jamadagni was being butchered thus, his beloved wife named Reṇukā fell on his body in utter grief.

50. That lady of excellent complexion was hit and wounded by different kinds of sharp missiles but did not die, for she was destined to live yet there.

51. After thus killing Jamadagni, the leading Brāhmaṇa, the king drove the cow to the city of Māhiṣmatī.

52. Driven thus forcibly and observing killing of Jamadagni; the cow became enraged and so lowed piteously.

53. Even as she lowed thus, Pulindas, Medas and hundreds and thousands of other terrible fellows came out of her mouth.

54. They wielded different kinds of weapons. All of them were like another set of Yama's messengers. They respectfully said to the cow, "Command us quickly."

55. She said, "May this army of the king of the Haihayas be killed." Thereupon the terribly angry barbarians began to destroy the army with sharp weapons ruthlessly.

56. No man from among them came face to face with them, because everyone was afraid much, not to speak of a direct fight.

57. On seeing the army shattered by the terrible Pulindas, the ministers spoke to the king:

58-60. "O Lord, you have lost much of your refulgence due to this murder of a Brāhmaṇa. Hence let this cow be left alone. Be pleased to go to your own palace.

It is better you go away before his powerful son named Rāma returns. Otherwise, you will be killed along with all your soldiers here itself.

This Kāmadhenu of great power cannot be taken away by force. In the form of divine Śakti, she herself can create thus."

61. Thereupon, the king became afraid particularly at their words. With all his attendants killed, he left the cos there and went to his own abode.

CHAPTER SIXTYSEVEN

Sahasrārjuna Killed

Sūta said:

1-2. In the meantime Rāma came there to the hermitage accompanied by his brothers carrying fruits, roots and bulbous roots.

He saw the hermitage damaged and surrounded by a large number of Pulindas and the cow grievously hurt with stones and sticks.

3-5. He asked: "How has this catastrephe happened? The penance grove is surrounded by Ābhiras and Pulindas. By whom has this cow of mine been beaten and wounded? Why do these ascetic men and women weep? Where is my old father? Where is my mother fond of her sons? Why does she not approach me lovingly as before?"

6. Thereupon all those ascetics utterly grief-stricken narrated to him all the events in detail, all the acts of misdemeanour of Sahasrārjuna as witnessed by them.

7-8. All the brothers heard the stunning words that smote them like thunderbolt. On hearing it and seeing their father cut with weapons and their mother too grief-stricken with all the limbs injured, but somehow breathing alive, they began to cry in despair but not the all-powerful Rāma.

9. After crying for a long time and lamenting repeatedly, they performed the obsequies in accordance with the injunctions in the Vedas.

10. After the cremation, all the others except Rāma, made a befitting deep pit and offered libations to their father along with gingelly seeds.

11. The other ascetics asked Rāma, the most excellent one among wielders of weapons: "Why don't you offer handfuls of libation to your dead father?"

12. This son of Jamadagni was asked thus many times even as he was engaged in counting the number of wounds inflicted by sharp weapons on the body of his mother.

13-17. Then Rāma heaved a sigh and spoke to those leading sages: "You may now be pleased to hear why I refused to offer water libations. My father was killed by a Kṣatriya without any fault on his part. There are twentyone wounds on the body of my mother. Hence, O Brāhmaṇas, if I do not exterminate Kṣatriyas from the earth as many times as there are wounds (on my mother's body) I will incur all sins. In addition to the murder of my father and mother that sinful base Kṣatriya has perpetrated other foul deeds.

Therefore I shall fill this pit with his blood as well as that of other wicked-souled Kṣatriyas, though it is usually filled with libations of water. I shall propitiate my father with libations of blood, not of water."

Sūta said:

18. On hearing his dreadful vow, the excellent ascetics were struck with awe and were mystified. They did not say anything further.

19. Then, after the days of pollution (due to death) were over, the furious Rāma, seized his axe and proceeded in the direction of Māhiṣmatī.

20. He was accompanied by all those tribal people, the Pulindas and the Medakas. They had fastened their arms with alligator skin to prevent injury. They had similar finger protections too. They had excellent arrows and bows.

21-22. On hearing that the scion of the family of Bhṛgu was advancing accompanied by a great army after taking a vow, Arjuna was delighted. He too set out facing him for fighting, along with different kinds of warriors who could be compared to Devas and Asuras.

23. Thereafter, O excellent Brāhmaṇas, a great battle ensued between the Pulindas and the warriors of the king of Haihaya, who could be compared to Devas and Asuras.

24. Then all the followers of Haihaya were killed with arrows on a par with poison-breathing serpents, by the tribals who were repeatedly roaring while fighting.

25. Due to the sin arising from Brāhmaṇa-slaughter all of them were lustreless and fell on the ground.

26. No one was competent to show valour. As they fled, all of them were killed with sharp arrows.

27. On seeing his army broken up, the Lord of Haihayas became furious. Hurriedly he desired to string his bow, but could not do so although he tried the utmost.

28. Then he wanted to draw out the clean sword from its sheath; but he failed to do so. He felt a great discomfiture.

29. His club too fell down on to the ground in an instant. It was the club with which the terrible Rāvaṇa, who used to make people cry in despair, was defeated.

30. These were the very hands which once used to restrain the flooding current of Narmadā. All his splendid hands numbering a thousand became agitated with great tremor.

31. As ill luck would have it, they were too weak to life the weapons at all. Further all the Mantras of the divine missiles became forgotten.

32. In the meantime Rāma came there with his fury at its zenith. He lifted up his axe and said to him these harsh words:

33. "O sinner, king of Haihayas, quickly show me those hands with which my father was killed by you."

34. He too, already struck down by the Brāhmaṇical splendour did not say anything by way of reply though harshly taunted thus. He remained like one painted in a picture.

35. Then Rāma, the most excellent one among those who wield arms, rebuked him repeatedly and slowly cut off the row of his hands.

36. Then the scion of the family of Bhṛgu cut off his head with his axe. Assiduously he himself collected the blood from the wounds, O Brāhmaṇas.

37. He filled big pots and handed them over to the hunters. Then he respectfully spoke to the barbarians and the fowlers (hunters):

38-40. "A big pit has been dug by my brothers in the holy spot of Hāṭakeśvara. It was filled with water for the purpose of propitiating the Pitṛs. At my behest go there quickly and unhesitatingly pour therein the large quantity of blood of my sinful enemy. Thereby I shall devoutly propitiate my father in accordance with the injunctions. Thereby I shall be liberated from indebtedness to my father."

CHAPTER SIXTYEIGHT

The Sea Recedes

Sūta said:

1-3. Then those hunters carefully carried the blood taken out from the Haihayas to the place where the pit was dug for offering libations to the Pitṛs.

Bhārgava too after killing him (i.e. Sahasrārjuna) collected the entire blood and sent it to the place where the pit connected with his father was present.

Bhārgava did not spare any Kṣatriya whether a child, young man or an old man. In particular he did not leave off even a child in womb.

4. He killed the kings himself and others also on their sides. He caused the death of the soldiers as well in the height of his anger.

5. He eagerly collected the blood and made his attendants collect too. Then he used to send it through them to that place.

6. Thus the scion of the family of Bhṛgu made the entire earth devoid of Kṣatriyas. Thereafter he went to the holy spot of Hāṭakeśvara.

7. He took his bath in blood. He took up a large quantity of gingelly seeds and offered the libation pouring it anticlockwise.

8. In the presence of all Brāhmaṇas and other ascetics, he did thus and fulfilled his vow. Thus he became free from grief.

9. In the world thus deprived of Kṣatriyas he performed a horse-sacrifice and gifted away the entire earth to Brāhmaṇas along with monetary gifts.

10. After receiving all those excellent gifts the Brāhmaṇas said to the most excellent scion of the family of Bhṛgu: "You

cannot stay in our land because it has been laid down in the Smṛtis that there can be only one king."

11-12. Highly delighted he said, "So be it." Then he went to the end of the land and told the Ocean after stringing his very big bow and fitting an Āgneya missile (missile the deity of which is Fire-god) to it. He knitted his brows in great fury:

Rāma said:

13. The earth consisting of mountains and forests was rendered devoid of Kṣatriyas. Thereafter in the great horse-sacrifice, it was gifted to Brāhmaṇas.

14. After gifting the earth to the Brāhmaṇas I will not take it back from them. Hence you recede and give me some space of land.

15. In case, O Lord of rivers, you do not act according to my direction now, I will dry you up by means of the fire-missile and convert you into a piece of land (i.e. completely devoid of water).

Sūta said:

16. On hearing his words, the Ocean became frightened. He receded as far as he desired that he should.[1]

17. The scion of the family of Bhṛgu made his residence there performing penances (though) he continued to remember the murder of his father.

18. Then Bhārgava made all the Pulindas, Śabaras and Medas inhabit the mountains at the frontier of the earth.

1. The strip of land to the west of the Western Ghats from Gujarat to the southern end of Kerala is regarded as the land won from the sea: A mythological explanation of a geological phenomenon.

CHAPTER SIXTYNINE

Creation of Rāma Hrada

Sūta said:

1-3. Thereafter when the earth became devoid of Kṣatriyas, Kṣatriya women desirous of perpetuating their race had union with Brāhmaṇas and gave birth to excellent Kṣetraja sons (sons born from others in one's wives).

These Kṣetraja sons grew up and prospered. They came to be equal to Kṣatriyas. With their valour, they expelled the excellent Brāhmaṇas and took possession of the earth.

Thereby the Brāhmaṇas became distressed much on being thus utterly humiliated. They approached Bhārgava and said:

4-5. "O Rāma, O Rāma of powerful arms, the earth that was granted to us by you at the time of the horse-sacrifice, has been forcefully taken possession of by Kṣatriyas. Hence, if you have enough manliness left, kill those base Kṣatriyas and grant us the land once again. Increase our prosperity."

6. Thereupon the anger of Rāma was greatly roused. He once again set out along with those Śabaras, Pulindas and Medakas for the extermination of the Kṣatriyas.

7. There too he killed the Kṣatriyas, collected much blood, filled the pit dug already and offered libations to the Pitṛs.

8. In the horse-sacrifice performed again, he granted the earth to Brāhmaṇas. On being denied residence (therein) by them, he went back to the seashore.

9. Thus the earth was rendered devoid of all Kṣatriyas, twenty-one times by him, O eminent Brāhmaṇas. It was then granted to the Brāhmaṇas too.

10. Libation was offered to the Pitṛs by that noble-souled one through blood. The vow made was kept up and therefore he became free from anger.

11. After the libation was offered on the twenty-first time, there was heard an unembodied aerial voice originating from the Pitṛs:

12-14. "O Rāma, O highly exalted Rāma, put a stop to this despicable act. We are pleased with you because you kept your word.

What has been done by you, no one other than you, will do; it has not been done by anyone before as a result of the enmity arising from father's (murder).

So we are all pleased, O dear one. We shall grant you what has been cherished in the heart by you. Therefore, be quick in requesting for it even if it be inaccessible unto even the Devas."

Rāma said:

15. If the Pitṛs are pleased, if they give what is desired, may this meritorious Tīrtha become well known all over the world after my name. Let it be devoid of the defect of blood pollution. Let it be resorted to be excellent sages.

The pitṛs said:

16. This *Gartā* (Pit) made by you, where the libation to the Pitṛs was offered will become famous all over the three worlds as *Rāma Hrada.*

17. Those people endowed with devotion who offer to the Pitṛs the requisite libation here, will obtain the benefit of Aśvamedha and attain the greatest goal.

18-19. A man who devoutly performs the Śrāddha unto one killed by weapons on the fourteenth lunar day in the dark half of the month of Bhādrapada will cause the redemption of that ancestor even if he had attained the state of a *Preta* or fallen into Naraka. It does not matter if he was a sinner.

Sūta said:

20. After saying thus to Rāma, they ceased (to speak and disappeared). Thereafter Rāma eschewed his anger completely and performed penance there itself.

21. Hence by all means, one should perform Śrāddha with full faith, to the person killed by a weapon on the same day (occurring every year).

22. The Śrāddha on the concerned day is cited as that which yields salvation unto those dead due to violent injury, serpent bite, fire, eating poison or hanging.

23. One who performs libation rites to the Pitṛs even with water during the *Pretapakṣa* (dark half of Bhādrapada) becomes

free from indebtedness to them and he is honoured in Pitṛloka.

24. Thus everything connected with *Rāmaharda* has been entirely recounted to you. The greatness thereof is destructive of all sins, O excellent Brāhmaṇas.

25. A man who devoutly reads this himself at the time of Śrāddha shall undoubtedly obtain the entire benefit arising from Gayā Śrāddha.

26. One should read this in the presence of Brāhmaṇas at the time of *Parvans* (festive occasions). Thereby one obtains the entire benefit of *Pitṛmedha* (Yajña pertaining to Pitṛs).

27. A man who devoutly listens to this on being recited obtains undoubtedly the entire benefit of Sautrāmaṇi Yajña.

CHAPTER SEVENTY

Birth of Kārttikeya[1]

Sūta said:

1-3. Similarly there is another *Śakti* there that destroys sins. It is the *Śakti* (holy javelin) discharged by Kārttikeya after killing Tāraka in battle.

Further there is also a very great Kuṇḍa filled with clear water caused by himself (Kārttikeya). One who takes his holy bath there and performs the worship is immediately liberated from the sin committed ever since birth and until death.

The sages said:

At what time was that Śakti discharged by him? Tell us. Why was it discharged by the Lord? What is its efficacy? Do narrate it yourself.

1. Birth of Skanda or Kārttikeya and his exploit of killing the Dānava Tāraka are described in Mbh, *Vana* Ch. 226 and in other Purāṇas. It is adapted here to claim that the Śakti with which Skanda killed Tāraka is in Camatkārapura. Similar claim is made in the Revākhaṇḍa of Skanda Purāṇa for Bhṛgu Kaccha. The differences of the story in this Purāṇa and in Mbh are noticed at proper places.

Sūta said:

4. Formerly there was a very powerful Dānava named Tāraka. He was successor of Hiraṇyākṣa and he caused terror in all the three worlds.

5. After coming to know that his father had been killed by the powerful Viṣṇu, he went to Gokarṇa mountain and performed a very severe penance.

6. He sustained himself by consuming withered dry leaves and continued the meditation on Mahādeva for a thousand years mentally, verbally and physically.

7-8. He offered excellent articles of worship and different kinds of foodstuffs. Even at the end of those thousand years, Rudra was not pleased. This made the Daitya distressed and he performed still severer penance. He cut off pieces of flesh from his body and consigned them into the sacred fire.

9. Thereupon Mahādeva was pleased. Riding on his bull, the Consort of Umā appeared before him along with all his Gaṇas.

10. In words faltering with excessive delight, Mahādeva joyously rendered all the quarters resonant with his voice of high pitch and spoke:

11. "O Tāraka, I am pleased. Do not persist further in a risky venture like this. Request for anything you may desire, so that I can grant the same."

Tāraka said:

12. O Lord, thanks to your favour, let me be invincible unto all the Devas. Make it possible for me to defeat all in battle except you.

The Lord said:

13. With my favour, all this will happen. Undoubtedly, O Daitya, whatever has been requested for by you will become effective. You shall be the sole mighty warrior.

14. After saying this, Mahādeva went to his abode. The delighted demon Tāraka too went home.

15. Then, accompanied by a vast army of Dānavas, he went to Amarāvatī, the well-known city of Indra, for fighting with him.

16. Thereafter, a great battle of Devas with Dānavas ensued and continued for a thousand years when the god of Death never turned back.

17. The Devas faced destruction every day in the battlefield and the Dānavas gained victory with the favour of the Trident-bearing Lord.

18-20. For the purpose of ultimate victory, the Heaven-dwellers resorted to all possible means. Various kinds of armours, mechanical devices, trenches etc., for the sake of general protection were ardently prepared by them, O excellent Brāhmaṇas. Other things also they got ready for protecting the bodies of the principal warriors in particular. The chiefs of Suras created various things to guard themselves from Dānavas day and night.

21. At that time *Mudgaras* (hammer-like rods), *Bhindipālas* (a short javelin), *Śataghnīs* (cannon-like devices capable of killing a hundred at a time), excellent arrows, *Prāsas* (javelins), *Kuntas* (spears), *Bhallas* (spike-like weapons) etc. were prepared. They evolved strategic modes of special battle arrays also.

22. *Kūṭayuddhas* (deceptive warfare) of diverse kinds, threats, hoodwinking tricks and *Indrajāla* (wizardry) were made use of entirely.

23. Still, O excellent Brāhmaṇas, they did not gain any victory over the Dānavas. Smitten and shattered in the great battle they became distressed.

24-26. Then the frightened Thousand-eyed One (Indra) said to Bṛhaspati: "O excellent Brāhmaṇa, every day we are getting defeated by the Daityas. The more I get ready with better means of warfare, the greater is our defeat in the tremendous war. Hence, O preceptor of Suras, think of some intelligent means whereby I can win the war and you, a blameless reputation as its result."

Sūta said:

27. Then Bṛhaspati thought for a long time. After finding out the means of victory in the great battle, his face beamed with delight. Then he said to the Consort of Śacī:

28-34. "That means has been found out by me, O Śakra, whereby most of the enemies can be sportingly defeated in the great battle.

When the Slayer of the Three Puras was requested by him for the desired boon, the Daitya had repeatedly bowed to him and spoken these words:

'O Lord, let me be invincible unto all the Devas with your favour. Make it possible for me to defeat all in battle except you.'

Mahādeva himself will never slay him who is his disciple. Who thinks it fit to cut down even a poisonous tree, should he happen to be the one who had planted it?

'He who is the father shall be the son as well.' This Vedic statement is often proclaimed. So let Hara procreate a son who will slay him (Tāraka).

Then we shall appoint him as the commander-in-chief and fight a bitter fight with the Daityas and ultimately gain victory.

This is the means which I just explained, O Thousand-eyed One. There is no other means of victory in all the three worlds."

35. Thereafter the Slayer of Pāka went to Śaṁbhu along with the groups of Devas and requested him after bowing down to him humbly:

36-38. "O Bull-emblemed One, it behoves you to exert yourself for the procreation of a son, so that I can appoint him as the commander-in-chief of the Heaven-dwellers.

With your favour I shall gain victory in the battle after killing all the Dānavas including Tāraka.

There is no other means for my victory in the battle with the Dānavas. So says the highly intelligent Devejya (Preceptor of gods i.e. Bṛhaspati) after perfectly considering everything."

39-40. Thereupon Śaṅkara laughed boisterously and spoke to the Lord of Devas: "O Śakra, I shall soon do what you suggest. There is no doubt about it. I shall procreate a son who will destroy all the Daityas. You can make him the commander of your army and be crowned with success always."

41. After saying thus Mahādeva went to the Kailāsa mountain and started a befitting sexual dalliance with Gaurī.

42. It was fully accompanied by coquettish blandishments, emotional fervour, jocular remarks and other things of the sort. A period of a thousand divine years passed like a moment.

43. Here, all the groups of Devas, harassed by Tāraka and hence utterly terrified in their minds met together and had consultations with one another:

44-45. "A thousand years have elapsed and the Trident-bearing One is continuously engaged in the sexual dalliance. He has not carried out the task of Devas. Hence we shall go to the Kailāsa mountain where Lord Maheśvara is in union with Gaurī in a secluded spot."

46. In the height of their distress arising from the frustrated hope about (the birth of) an enemy of Tāraka, all the Devas including Vāsava went there itself.

47-48. They reached mount Kailāsa and attempted to go near Bhava. But they were prevented by Nandin saying, "You must not go beyond this. The Lord is present here in a secluded spot along with Pārvatī. Even we have no right to enter. Do not go."

49. Then all the Devas sent the Wind-god[1] there. They told him, "Let this be quickly found out what Mahādeva is doing there."

50. Then the Wind-god went to that spot where Lord Śiva was in the acme of bliss in the act of sexual dalliance with Gaurī.

51. There was an emission of the semen but it did not reach the vaginal aperture. At that time the Lord saw Vāyu standing not very far away.

52. Feeling abashed very much the Lord got up instantly leaving his beloved alone in the acme of excitement and emotion saying, "Oh, don't get up."

53. He then said to Vāyu who was standing humbly, "Why did you come here? I hope the Heaven-dwellers are all right."

Vāyu said:

54. Here Śakra and other Devas have been stopped by Nandin. All of them are dispirited and without enthusiasm. They are now waiting on the ridge of the mountain.

55. So, do talk to them and console them with encouraging words. Send them also immediately to the place occupied by the Dānavas.

56. Instantly the Slayer of the Three Puras summoned them.

1. According to Mbh; *Vana* 225. 16-18 Agni frustrated the sexual intercourse. Here Vāyu is the disturber.

With dejected face, he addressed them as they stood with palms joined in reverence:

The Lord said:

57. I started my endeavour for the procreation of a son for the sake of you all. The seminal fluid has been displaced from the organ of secretion but rendered ineffective by Vāyu (by his intervention).

58. It (seminal fluid) has been retained with great restraint by me within the penis. It cannot go in vain. Tell me where I can deposit it.

59. It is from that, that a great son who will destroy the Dānavas is to be born. He shall be the leader of your army. He will be irresistible in the battle by his enemies.

60. Except Vaiśvānara (Fire-god) no one else is capable of retaining it. It resembles the Kalpāgni fire. So let him come forward and retain this eternal fluid.

61. Then only can I release this intensely powerful seminal fluid lustrous like twelve suns (united together) for the sake of a son in order to win victory.

62. Then all the Suras praised Vahni (Fire) and eagerly said to him, "O Agni, do hold this seminal fluid of Bhava within your mouth."

63. Carrying out the behest of Śakra unhesitatingly Pāvaka (Fire) quickly opened his mouth.

64. Śaṅkara who had been afflicted by the arrows of Kāma thought of goddess Gaurī, experienced the bliss of orgasm and deposited the fluid there (in Agni's mouth).

65. Being scorched by that fluid that resembled fire appearing at the end of the universe, Pāvaka dropped it on the ground in the spacious grove of reeds.[1]

66. In the meantime the auspicious six Kṛttikās, the wives of the six sages who had been wandering here and there came to that place.

67-68. Śatakratu himself gave them this direction: "This seminal fluid of the Three-eyed Lord should be preserved

1. According to Mbh Agni transferred the semen to Gaṅgā who threw it among Śara reeds.

cautiously (by you). Herefrom will be born a son having the lustre of twelve suns. He will be almost a son unto ye all."[1]

CHAPTER SEVENTYONE

Installation of Skanda's Śakti

Sūta said:

1-3. Assenting "So be it", those ladies carried out the behest of Śakra. They performed all his post-natal rites to be performed in the lying-in-chamber.

The next day, the boy gained the lustre akin to that of twelve suns. He was born with two arms and a single face.

As soon as the auspicious child was born he miserably cried. On hearing his cry, all the Kṛttikās came to him.

4. On seeing those mothers approaching, Mahāsena became anxious and one with six faces, twelve eyes and twelve arms.

5. With great affection, he embraced each of them separately with two arms and sucked the milk from the breast of each.

6. In the meantime Brahmā, Viṣṇu, Śiva and all other Devas, Gandharvas, Apsarās came there along with Indra.

7. At that spot, great festivities were held without any restraint. The entire universe was filled with the sound of music and musical instruments.

8. Raṁbhā and other graceful maidens of Heaven-dwellers danced there. Gandharva chiefs such as Citrāṅgada and others sang.

9. Then all the Devas respectfully gave him the name Skanda because the seminal fluid was spilled on the ground.

10. Then the coronation of that boy as the commander-in-chief of the army of Devas was performed by Śaṁbhu himself.

11. A Śakti of miraculous appearance and unfailing forever was given to him by Vidhi (Brahmā) for gaining victory (of Devas) and the destruction of Daityas.

---

1. Mbh and other Purāṇas say that the wives of Seven Sages (Saptarṣis) felt cold in the early morning and saw fire in the reeds. Arundhatī told them not to resort to that fire. They refused to listen to her advice and sat round the fire for the sake of warmth and became pregnant.

12. A Mayūra (peacock) was quickly given by the Three-eyed Lord as the boy's vehicle. Divine weapons were given by Mahendra and the noble-souled Viṣṇu.

13. Thereafter the desired missiles were given severally by all the Devas and the groups of mother goddesses who were delighted.

14. Then keeping him in the forefront as the leader of the armies, the chiefs of Suras and their soldiers went to the place where Tāraka was present.

15. On observing that Devas themselves had come for fighting, Tāraka was delighted. Hurriedly he came face to face with them.

16. A great battle ensued between Devas and Dānavas. With their eyes redened with anger, they set at nought the fear of death.

17. On seeing Tāraka far away in the battlefield, Skanda challenged him and hurled the Śakti towards him to kill him.

18. The terrible Śakti pierced the heart of the Daitya and fell down at the outskirts of Camatkārapura. It was besmeared with blood.

19-20. Tāraka was doomed. In an instant his life became extinct. Then all the groups of Devas became delighted. They eulogized the mighty Lord Kārttikeya with hymns of diverse kinds when Tāraka fell dead. Free from fear, they went quickly to heaven along with Indra.

21. Skanda took up that Śakti and fixed it there in the excellent city whereby Raktaśṛṅga became firm and steady.

The sages said:

22. That Raktaśṛṅga which was already motionless was rendered firm by him? At whose instance? O highly intelligent one, tell us in detail.

Sūta said:

23. There was a terrible earthquake once when Raktaśṛṅga swayed from its position violently.

24-25. The earthquake was due to the fall of that Daitya. Like the other excellent mountains, Raktaśṛṅga too swayed. Further all the mansions in Camatkārapura crumbled down. When the mountain swayed to and fro the Brāhmaṇas became distressed. Most of them lost all their possessions and became poor. Others became afflicted by loss of consciousness.

26-27. The Brāhmaṇas who survived rushed to Skanda angrily and said, "O sinner, what is this done by you foolishly? We are all ruined along with our sons, kinsmen and cattle-wealth. So due to our excess of misery, we will curse you."

Skanda said:

28. This has been carried out by me for the welfare of all the worlds. The terrible Dānava has been killed. This could not have happened otherwise, O excellent Brāhmaṇas.

29-30. Be pleased therefore. Brāhmaṇas are always worthy of my honour. By resorting to Amṛta (Nectar) I shall resuscitate the dead Brāhmaṇas once again. There is no doubt about it. Similarly, with my Śakti I shall make the mountain very stable.

31. After saying thus, he took up the Śakti besmeared with blood and installed it on the top of Raktaśṛṅga.

32. Then he spoke joyously to the four deities viz. Āmbavṛddhā, Āmrā, Māhitthā and Camatkarī:

33-34. "This excellent mountain should be kept stable and motionless again by you all, so that this Raktaśṛṅga shall not move from its place even at the time of Pralaya. Let this excellent city be well-known forever after my name. All the Brāhmaṇas will adore you always."

35. Delighted by the words of Skanda, they said: "Of course". With the tips of tridents fixed in all directions, they steadied it further.

36. Then Skanda ardent in the devotion to Brāhmaṇas, took Amṛta and enlivened the dead excellent Brāhmaṇas.

37. The delighted Brāhmaṇas granted him the excellent boon. He said, "Let this excellent city become well known forever after my name. This is my desire."

The sages said:

38. O most excellent one among Suras, this excellent city now called Camatkārapura will be known also by the name Skandapura after your name.

39. We shall erect an excellent mansion (temple) and shall offer worship to you as well as the four deities supported by you.

40. We shall evince respectful reverence in all our rites, O most excellent one among the chiefs of Suras, we shall always worship this Śakti of yours faithfully on the sixth lunar day.

Sūta said:

41. Promised thus by the Brāhmaṇas, the mighty Mahāsena stayed there itself at their instance after realizing that it was an excellent holy place.

42. If any one devoutly worships him with great emotional fervour on the sixth lunar day in the bright half of the month of Caitra,[1] the Peacock-vehicled Lord will make him satisfied.

43. O Brāhmaṇas, a man who worships that Śakti with perfect faith with flowers etc., and then rubs his back against the Śakti shall never fall sick for a whole year.

44. Thus his Śakti was fixed there by the intelligent Skanda for the protection of Raktaśṛṅga and that city in particular.

CHAPTER SEVENTYTWO

Dhṛtarāṣṭra's Pilgrimage to Hāṭakeśvara Kṣetra[2]

Sūta said:

1-2. A Liṅga was installed there by King Dhṛtarāṣṭra and also by Duryodhana. Viewing it, one is rid of all sins.

The sages said:

O son of Romaharṣaṇa, when was the Liṅga installed there by King Dhṛtarāṣṭra? Do tell us.

---

1. This day is called Skanda-Ṣaṣṭhī.

2. Chapters 72-74 describe when and why Dhṛtarāṣṭra (Kauravas and Pāṇḍavas) installed Liṅga at Hāṭakeśvara. The story has no basis either in Mbh or in *Bhāgavata* but the author wishes to record the visit of these celebrities to Hāṭakeśvara.

Sūta said:

3. Formerly Balabhadra had a daughter named Bhānumatī. She was richly endowed with all the excellent features. She was endowed with good qualities, beauty etc.

4. The scion of the Yādava family consulted Viṣṇu (i.e. Kṛṣṇa) and gave her to Duryodhana, the intelligent son of Dhṛtarāṣṭra, as his wife.[1]

5. Then Bhīṣma, Droṇa and all the Kauravas started immediately for the city of Dvārakā from Hastināpura.

6. In view of their excellent fraternal consideration, all the five sons of Pāṇḍu and their attendants and followers joyously accompanied Duryodhana and proceeded towards Dvārakā along with their vast army.

7. Proceeding thus gradually, all the Kauravas and Pāṇḍavas reached the land of Ānarta prosperous with wealth and foodgrains.

8. It is the land where the excellent meritorious place of Lord Hāṭakeśvara is situated. It is well-known in all the three worlds as destructive of all sins.

9. Then (Bhīṣma) the elderly grandfather of pure soul, the grandfather of Kurus, laughingly said to King Dhṛtarāṣṭra accompanied by his sons:

Bhīṣma said:

10. Dear son, this excellent holy place of Lord Hāṭakeśvara has already been visited by me. It is destructive of all sins.

11. Further, in this holy spot, I was liberated from the sin of the murder of a woman.[2] Hence, O great king, we shall stay here itself for five days.

12. Thus we can visit all the Tīrthas and shrines situated here. They are the meritorious holy places of sages of purified souls.

---

1. It is a fact that the name of Duryodhana's wife is Bhānumatī. But the author seems to have made a confusion of names. According to Harivaṁśa, Viṣṇuparva (Ch.90), Bhānumatī was the daughter of Bhānu, a leader of the Yādava clan. But she was married to Sahadeva, a Pāṇḍava (P.E. p.116). Here the author regards her as the dauther of Balabhadra, Kṛṣṇa's elder brother, and states that she was given in marriage to Duryodhana.

2. The self-immolation in fire by Ambā on Bhīṣma's refusal to marry her.

13. Then, at his instance King Dhṛtarāṣṭra, the son of Aṁbikā, became interested therein. Accompanied by his sons numbering a hundred, he immediately started.

14. He soon went to where the excellent holy place is situated. It was full of splendid hermitages and groups of ascetics.

15. All the quarters reverberated with the loud chanting sounds of Vedic passages. The smoke arising from the adored sacred fire had rendered many trees therein black. Many antelopes sported about and ran here and there.

16-18. Afraid of harassment likely to be caused to the residents of the hermitages, the king stopped the entire army. He moved about in that holy spot accompanied by only the five sons of Pāṇḍu, his own hundred sons, Bhīṣma, Somadatta, Bāhlīka, heroic Droṇācārya, his son Aśvatthāman, Kṛpa, Saubala (i.e. Śakuni), Karṇa and a few princes without their attendants.

19. All the noble-souled Kṣatriyas stationed there, performed all sacred rites with minds sanctified by faith.

20. O excellent Brāhmaṇas, they duly took their holy baths in the Tīrthas of great merit where they wandered listening (to the chantings) of the Brāhmaṇas.

21. They made excellent gifts as desired. Others distributed gifts among the distressed and the wretched and also ascetics in particular.

22. Others devoutly performed Śrāddha rites with the Pitṛs in view. Still others offered libations to the Pitṛs with water mixed with gingelly seeds.

23. Other kings performed Homas. A few continously repeated holy names in Japa. Others endowed with faith and quiescence studied the Vedas of their respective Śākhā.

24. Others performed special Pūjā (worship) in the holy temples of exalted state, listening to the glory of previous kings.

25-26. O excellent Brāhmaṇas, the Brāhmaṇas there were rendered happy and contented by means of offerings, oblations, excellent garments, fragrant flowers, unguents, rubbings, gifts of banners, splendid spectacular shows, decorations with flower garlands and gifts of elephants, horses, chariots, cows, garments and gold.

27. After bathing and worshipping the deities and the Brāhmaṇas, the excellent kings accompanied by Dhṛtarāṣṭra entered their respective camps.

28. Struck with wonder, they praised the Tīrths, the shrines, the Brāhmaṇas and the ascetics of esteemed Vratas in that holy spot.

CHAPTER SEVENTYTHREE

Pilgrimage of Dhṛtarāṣṭra and Others

Sūta said:

1-3. All those brilliant sons of Pāṇḍu and Kauravas went from that holy place to the place where the city of Dvārakā was situated. After going there with delighted minds, they performed the marriage rite of king Duryodhana with Bhānumatī. On the occasion festivities were marked with the loud sound of different musical instruments combined with the sound of the Vedic chant, charming songs and recitations by thousands of bards.

4. The celebrations continued for eight days, which the Yādavas and Kauravas enjoyed together.

5. Sūtas, Māgadhas and Bandins (bards), Cāraṇas, leading Brāhmaṇas and other Tārkikas (Logicians) became satisfied.

6. On the ninth day, Kauravas and Pāṇḍavas including Bhīṣma spoke in a friendly spirit to the lotus-eyed Lord (Kṛṣṇa).

7. "O lotus-eyed one, we do not wish at all to leave the resort of yours as well as Rāma's. We are so much bound by the bonds of affection.

8. Still, O Mādhava, we have to go to our city. Hence permit us with the consent of Balabhadra."

Viṣṇu (Kṛṣṇa) said:

9. A year has not elapsed since you came to stay here, nor a month nor even a fortnight. Then why this eagerness to go?

10-11. Therefore, O Kauravas and Pāṇḍavas, you and we shall stay here together engaged in various pastimes of hunting and playing at dice, training and practising the use of missiles, taming and controlling elephants and other desirable activities. This is my suggestion if you entertain any love for me.

Bhīṣma said:

12. Proper indeed, O Viṣṇu, are the words uttered by you. But please listen to my words indicating why we are eager (to go).

13-15. While we were coming to you here, the wonderful holy spot of Hāṭakeśvara was visited by us in the land of Ānarta. There the Liṅgas were seen installed by the noble-souled kings born in the Solar and the Lunar dynasties as well as others. So also the Liṅgas installed by Devas, Dānavas and more particularly by sages. They are refulgent and shapely enshrined in different kinds of suitable palatial temples.

16. Hence, O Mādhava, we have felt inclined to install Liṅgas there on behalf of the chiefs of Kauravas and Pāṇḍavas.

17. We shall therefore go there and install separately several Liṅgas in accordance with our desire and capacity.

18. It is for this reason, O Acyuta, that we are in a hurry to move. In fact even after staying with you for hundreds of years, we cannot be fully satisfied.

19. Therefore O Lord, make up your mind and allow us to proceed. We shall come again as we too shall be eager to see you.

Śrī Bhagavān said:

20. I know that highly meritorious holy spot that destroys sins. It is being glorified everyday by ascetics and other pilgrims in my presence.

21. Hence we shall also accompany you there for the purpose of installing the Liṅgas and fulfilling the desire of visiting the holy spot.

Sūta said:

22. On hearing it all the Kauravas, the sons of Pāṇḍu and all other kings who were present there became highly delighted.

23. All the Kauravas and Pāṇḍavas started together making the earth quake with the heavy pressure of the elephants and horses.

24. They reached the holy place. After making the army encamp at a distance the Kauravas and Yādava chiefs entered Camatkārapura.

25. There they invited all the Brāhmaṇas. After offering them presents of ornaments and garments of diverse kinds, they spoke to them politely:

26. "All of us wish to perform the rite of installing Liṅgas. In addition we wish to erect grand palaces according to our capacity.

27. Take a sympathetic and favourable view, O excellent Brāhmaṇas, and give the necessary instructions quickly so that the work can start.

28. Further you alone should be the Hotṛs in all the rites (but) no other Brāhmaṇa from outside even if he be Bṛhaspati.

29. For, in this connection an ancient legend has been heard by us narrated by Viṣṇu (Kṛṣṇa) in regard to the *Pretaśrāddha* of a saintly king.

30-31. The Śrāddha of his departed father was carefully performed by him in front of other Brāhmaṇas as well as the Brāhmaṇas duly specified. O Brāhmaṇas, on the Nāga Pañcamī day, this was performed in the Tīrtha in accordance with the injunctions in the month of Śrāvaṇa. Yet his father was not liberated.

32. The father was not liberated from the state of Preta due to *Sarpadoṣa* (the defect of serpent-bite), O excellent Brāhmaṇas.

When the Śrāddha was performed respectfully in the presence of Deva Śarman, O Brāhmaṇas, the father was liberated from the awful state of *Preta.*

33. Whatever may be the religious rite performed here, O excellent Brāhmaṇas, if that were to be performed with external (priestly) help, it cannot but be futile. This we know very clearly.

34. We are feeling miserable. Hence we make this special request. Please do us this favour and kindly order (the concerned persons) without delay."

Sūta said:

35. On hearing their words, those Brāhmaṇas had mutual consultations to decide what would be the best procedure in the matter.

36-37. Some said, "We will not grant a plot of land for the construction of a palace (temple) to even one person among these. Let them go away at once. This holy spot is extended to an area of only five Krośas. Further it is full of the palaces of the earlier deities."

38-39. Others said, "You are arrogant on account of your affluence and happy life. You do not know the distress due to poverty. That is why you say so much. So we shall surely grant these the required plot of land so that we will get some cash and the place shall also be beautified (with temple)."

40-42. Others of impartial view said: "When Janārdana himself requests for a plot of land, how can it be denied? So, now that the Kauravas, Pāṇḍavas and Yādavas have assembled together, let them and others as well erect palaces in accordance with their importance. When Gāṅgeya himself requests, so also Dhṛtarāṣṭra in the company of his sons and the very powerful Pāṇḍavas make this request for the installation of Liṅgas, refusal is not proper."

43. On hearing their words the proposition was accepted by the excellent Brāhmaṇas irrespective of the fact whether they were rich or poor, greedy or disinterested.

44. Then they came back. All the Brāhmaṇas told the excellent Kauravas, Yādavas and Pāṇḍavas about their decision after consulting one another.

The Brāhmaṇas said:

45. Indeed this holy spot is very small in area. It is already filled with the temples of all sorts of kings all round. What shall we say now?

46. So, you may build fascinating palaces in accordance with your importance, wish, seniority and excellence in this holy spot.

47. Then Dhṛtarāṣṭra and others became delighted. They arranged for the erection of a series of palaces according to seniority and excellence.

CHAPTER SEVENTYFOUR

Installation of Liṅgas by Kauravas, Pāṇḍavas and Yādavas

Sūta said:

1-5. O Brāhmaṇas, one hundred one Liṅgas were installed by king Dhṛtarāṣṭra in the company of his hundred sons at that place.

Similarly five Liṅgas were installed by all the Pāṇḍavas. Four idols of Gaurī were installed by Draupadī, Kuntī, Gāndhārī and Bhānumatī according to their wish. One Liṅga was installed by each of the following: Vidura, Śalya, Kaliṅga, Yuyutsu, Bāhlīka with his son, Karṇa with his son, Śakuni, Droṇa, Kṛpa and Aśvatthāman severally, Thus the excellent Liṅgas were installed with great devotion along with excellent palaces to house them in.

6. So also a Liṅga was installed there by the highly powerful Viṣṇu (Kṛṣṇa) after erecting a palace with lofty turrets.

7-8. Sāttvata, Sāṁba, the intelligent Balabhadra, Pradyumna, Aniruddha and other important Yādavas also installed the Liṅgas. Ten important Liṅgas were installed with devotion by ten sons of Rukmiṇī beginning with Cārudeṣṇa.

9. After installing the Liṅgas thus, all the Kauravas and Pāṇḍavas and Yādavas became delighted and contented.

10-13. They stayed there for a long time, made many gifts and rendered the Brāhmaṇas hailing from Camatkārapura wealthy. They gave them cash, excellent elephants, horses of the finest breed, diverse kinds of holy spots and fertile fields including excellent villages, good cows, huge bulls, good garments, plots of lands, places of resort, male and female slaves, servants, and different kinds of gifts. Thereafter all of them bowed (to the elders) repeatedly, took leave of one another and joyously went to their respective places.

Sūta said:

14-16. Thus everything has been narrated to you about how a sin-destroying Liṅga was installed by that king Dhṛtarāṣṭra (and others), by the Pāṇḍavas and Yādavas separately arrayed in accordance with their prominence.

A man urged and sanctified by devotion, who worships those Liṅgas well, shall attain all things desired in their minds.

CHAPTER SEVENTYFIVE

Greatness of Yajñabhūmi

Sūta said:

1-4. In an earlier Kalpa this excellent holy place was given to Brahmā, O excellent Brāhmaṇas, by Lord Rudra who was delighted. When the Liṅga named Hāṭakeśvara was installed by Devas what had been given to Brahmā by the delighted Rudra, viz. this holy place, was then given to Ṣaṇmukha for according protection to the Brāhmaṇas from the defects of Kalikāla (period of Kali etc.) when he was requested by Brahmā. On being commanded by his father Gāṅgeya (i.e. Ṣaṇmukha) stayed there, in the primordial excellent holy spot.

5. He who visits the Lord on the Kārttikī day when there is the conjunction of Kṛttikā constellation shall be born as a Brāhmaṇa in seven successive rebirths. He will be wealthy and a master of the Vedas.

6-8. Vibudhas (Devas) heard that the palace of Lord Mahāsena was fascinating and it stood very high as though it was desirous of protecting the sky. All of them, out of curiosity, hurried to the city and visited the holiest city. Through Brāhmaṇas they made preparations for the sacrificial rites in the manner stipulated on the northern as well as eastern side of the palace.

9-10. All the Vibudhas (Devas) performed the sacrifice and offered monetary gifts to them. Thereafter they joyously went to heaven after obtaining the benefit arising from that holy spot.

Then its name came to be *Devayajana.* By means of a single *Kratu* (sacrifice) here, with the due monetary gifts, one shall get the same benefit as is obtained elsewhere by means of a hundred sacrifices.

CHAPTER SEVENTYSIX

Installation of Muṇḍīra, Kālapriya and Mūlasthāna

Sūta said:

1-4. Further there is a splendid set of three Bhāskaras. If they are pleased in the worlds, one shall attain salvation.

There the first one is Muṇḍīra; the next one is Kālapriya and the third is Mūlasthāna that is destructive of all ailments.

When the night ends, the Sun passes on to Muṇḍīra, to Kālapriya at mid-day and to Mūlasthāna at nightfall.

A man who devoutly visits even one at any time after getting the requisite opportunity undoubtedly attains salvation. This is true.

The sages said:

5-6. Verily it is heard that Muṇḍīra is on the eastern side of the earth. Lord Kālapriya is in the middle and Mūlasthāna is beyond them. Well, O Sūta, how did those three Bhāskaras happen to rise there, on the holy spot of Hāṭakeśvara? Do narrate everything in detail.

Sūta said:

7. There is that excellent Viṭaṅkapura on the seashore. It is embellished with high rampart walls washed by the waves of sea.

8. There was a Brāhmaṇa there who became afflicted by leprosy at the advent of his youth as a result of the previous Karmas.

9. His wife was a chaste lady of noble birth. She was endowed with good behaviour. Despite the fact that he was in such a state, she used to look upon him like the god of love himself.

10. For his sake, she used to bring costly medicines of various kinds, ointments to be smeared with, and wholesome foodstuffs of diverse kinds.

11. Further she brought excellent physicians respectfully for his sake. Still there was no good effect on his body.

12. O excellent Brāhmaṇas, the more he continued the

treatment, the more the fell disease of leprosy continued to spread over all his limbs.

13. Even as that excellent Brāhmaṇa continued to suffer in the house, a certain weary traveller came there as his guest.

14. On seeing a Brāhmaṇa as a guest in the house, his chaste wife rendered good service to him and delighted him though he was previously unknown.

15. When he saw that the excellent Brāhmaṇa had concluded his bath, holy sipping of water, and meal and had due rest in his bed, the Brāhmaṇa host, the householder, said:

16. He said to the other one who was refulgent like the Sun, endowed with handsome features and exalted qualities, and in the prime of his youth like another god of Love incarnate:

The leper said:

17. O Brāhmaṇa, where do you come from? Where will you go now? Tell me, though you are endowed with handsome features thus, why you are alone like a distressed one.

The traveller said:

18. There is a city named Kāntipurī. It is like the city of Indra. It is always inhabited by persons of good status and endowed with righteousness and holy vows.

19. I was staying there leading the life of a householder, O excellent Brāhmaṇa, then I was afflicted by the fell disease of leprosy like you.

20. Then I heard that it is mentioned in the *Skandapurāṇa*[1] that the trinity of Bhāskaras in this world is destructive of all ailments

21. I was disgusted with medicines of all sorts taken for a long time—all salty, pungent, sour, astringent and bitter.

22. Then I resolved mentally, took with me much cash and went to Lord Muṇḍīra and stood before the deity.

23. Thereafter, I regularly got up early in the morning and visited the Lord. I used to perform rites of adoration within my capacity and bow to him.

---

1. Does this *Skanda Purāṇa* refer to some other version of the *Skanda*?

24. Particularly on Sundays I used to observe fast and control all sense-organs. I kept awake at night singing and playing on instruments.

25. Then at the end of the year I bowed down to that Lord of the day :

Thereafter I went to Kālapriya, endowed with great faith.

26. With the mind sanctified with faith, I performed, in accordance with the same procedure (as with Lord Muṇḍīra), the rite of adoration of the Lord of day too at mid-day.

27. Further at the end of the year I bowed down to that Lord with concentration. Then I went to Mūlasthāna, the Lord stationed in the west.

28. The rite of adoration for that Lord too was performed by me in accordance with the procedure as before during the dusk. O excellent Brāhmaṇa, thus I stayed there for the whole of the year.

29. Then at the end of the year, O Brāhmaṇa, Bhāskara appeared before me in dream. With a delighted mind, he laughed and spoke to me:

30. "O Brāhmaṇa, I am pleased with you by your devotion and this rite. Hence let your leprosy vanish as a result of this rite of propitiating me.

31. O excellent Brāhmaṇa, you are tired. Go home quickly and meet all your relatives. See, they are waiting for you anxiously.

32. Formerly, gold belonging to a noble-souled Brāhmaṇa was stolen by you. As a result of that commission of sin, the disease of leprosy has afflicted you.

33. That has been eradicated by me for your sake. O Brāhmaṇa, I am pleased with you. Realize this and stop indulging in stealing gold hereafter.

34. All the men seen in this world as afflicted and distressed by the disease of leprosy had been previously great sinners and had stolen gold.

35. Hence gold should never be stolen by sensible persons. It should be given away as gift if people wish for permanent happiness of their bodies."

36. After saying this the Thousand-rayed One vanished. I got up hurriedly from my bed with a great but pleasant surprise.

37. Lo, I beheld my body free from the foul disease of

leprosy. It had the divine lustre of twelve Suns, O Brāhmaṇa, as you see now.

38. Hence, O leading Brāhmaṇa, you too visit the trio of Bhāskaras in accordance with the same procedure, so that your leprosy may subside and be healed.

39. When this trinity of Sun-gods—Lords competent to quell ailment, is present, of what avail are medicines and pungent and astringent foodstuffs taken in?

40. Hail unto you, O Brāhmaṇa! I have relaxed myself today in your house as though in my own. I shall now go to that city.

41. On being told thus by the traveller, the Brāhmaṇa afflicted by leprosy cast a miserable glance at the face of his wife.

42-43. She said: "O my dear, the traveller has given you the most appropriate advice. So do go to that place where the trio of Bhāskaras is present. I shall also, no doubt, accompany you and be engaged in serving you. O Lord, do hurry along."

44. On being urged thus by her, the Brāhmaṇa took with him a lot of cash and set off along with his wife to Lord Muṇḍīra.

45. He told himself, "I vow that I shall go to visit the trio of deities viz. Muṇḍīra, Kālanātha (Kālapriya) and Bhāskara named Mūlasthāna."

46. Then, O excellent Brāhmaṇas, the person afflicted by leprosy reached the holy place of Hāṭakeśvara with great difficulty.

47. On seeing the great holy spot resorted to by groups of sages, the Brāhmaṇa afflicted by the disgusting disease of leprosy and fatigued by the journey, said to his wife:

48-49. "I have become dejected and disgusted due to this disease and the enormity of hunger. I find it impossible to go so far to Lord Muṇḍīrasvāmin. O my beloved, I shall cast off my body here itself undoubtedly. You go home along with some good caravan."

The wife said:

50. O my Lord and beloved one, O highly esteemed one, I have never taken food when you were hungry nor have I gone to sleep while you were awake.

51. Having come to this great holy place, how can I leave you alone to proceed to the other world and myself go home?

52. How can I show my face to my kinsmen and elders and friends after going there alone without you?

53. Hence this is my solemn oath that I would rather enter fire along with you, my Lord, as I have been so bound with you with the cords of affection.

54. O highly intelligent one, I have kept all those fasts you have observed. How can I then go home?

55. On coming to know of her determination the Brāhmaṇa built a pyre for self-immolation and entered it along with her.

56. Meditating on Bhāskara, he set it on fire when he saw in front of him a highly refulgent set of three persons.

57. On seeing them, he was struck with wonder. 'Who are these three persons? Persons with such refulgence and splendour have never been seen by me.'

The persons said:

58. O Brāhmaṇa, do not tread the path of death out of your excitement and dejection. Turn back and go home along with your wife.

The Brāhmaṇa said:

59-60. Earlier I left home with the solemn vow that I will take food there after seeing Muṇḍīrasvāmin, Kālavallabha and Mūlasthāna. Hence without seeing them how can I go home? How can I take food? Hence I shall cast off my life.

The persons said:

61. O holy Brāhmaṇa, we are those three Bhāskaras come here attracted by your devotion. Tell us what shall we do (for you).

The Brāhmaṇa said:

62. If you three Bhāskaras have come here yourselves, let this leprosy disappear

63. Further, you all should stay here itself forever keeping

your presence in the three worlds as well as before.

Bhāskaras said:

64. O Brāhmaṇa, we shall do so. We shall stay here for ever. You too shall be free from ailments and gain excellent happiness.

65. O Brāhmaṇa, arrange for three (temples) palaces for our sake, so that we can be present on three occasions (times) a day.

66. After saying thus all of them vanished. He too saw that his body had become free from the ailment.

67. His body had the refulgence of twelve suns and marked with all the (auspicious) characteristics. He then told his wife who was standing there modestly :

68-69. "O lady of excellent eyebrows, see that my body has become as beautiful as before with the favour of Bhāskara, the Lord of Devas. I shall stay here and adore Bhāskara always. I will never go home. This is the truth uttered by me."

70. After saying thus, that leading Brāhmaṇa endowed with devotion built three beautiful palaces in that splendid holy place.

71. All of them were embellished with excellent banners; one for Muṇḍīrasvāmin, another for Kālapriya and still another for Mūlasthāna.

72-73. He installed excellent images for all the three Bhāskaras as explained in the scriptures, on a Sunday when the Sun was in the Hasta constellation. Then the Brāhmaṇa adored them with flowers, incense etc., for a long time thrice a day. On death he went to the region of Bhāskara.

Sūta said:

74-75. Thus, O excellent Brāhmaṇas, those three Bhāskaras came to be present there as the destroyer of all ailments of devotees. One who visits them at their respective periods of time on a Sunday specified above, shall all cherished desires inaccessible to men.

CHAPTER SEVENTYSEVEN

Importance of Harāśraya Vedikā

The sages said:

1-4. O Sūta, with reference to the installation of Umā and Maheśvara performed by King Hariścandra you say that they resorted to the middle of the *Vedi* (Altar). Is it so? Or another set was installed at Camatkārapura? This is what is heard by us always that they are in the middle of the altar as their marriage took place in Oṣadhīprastha, the favourite spot of Himālaya. Here we are in doubt. In fact your words deserve credence. Are we confused even after hearing your words? Or you have committed a slip? Clarify this kindly.

Sūta said:

5. O excellent Brāhmaṇas, there is no confusion in me (my speech) but it is yours. However know the reason of it as I explain to you fully.

6-7. Formerly it was in the Vaivasvata Manvantara[1] that the fascinating marriage of Umā and Trineetra (Śiva) took place in Oṣadhīprastha delighting all the Devas. O excellent Brāhmaṇas, this seventh Manu is well known and you all know the same.

8. But their marriage which took place in Hāṭakeśvara Kṣetra was celebrated with great fanfare in the Svāyaṁbhuva Manvantara of the first Manu.

The sages said:

9. O Sūta, the marriage of Pārvatī and Hara that took place earlier in Oṣadhīprastha has been heard by us in detail.

10-11. The marriage of the Bull-vehicled One which took place in the holy spot of Hāṭakeśvara during the charming Yajña of Dakṣa occurred in the Svāyaṁbhuva Manvantara[1]. O scion of the family of Sūta, that should be duly narrated to us by you in detail just in the way it had occurred. This is our great curiosity.

---

1. This is the usual Puranic way of resolving contradictions by referring the matter to a different Manvantara when certain different happening took place.

Sūta said:

12. Here I shall completely narrate the sin-de-stroying marital function of the Trident-bearing Lord of Devas.

13. O Brāhmaṇas, Dakṣa, the Prācetasa, was born from the right thumb of Brahmā. A hundred and five daughters were born to him.

14. The eldest of those daughters was Satī by name. The chaste lady of splendid smiles and long eyes was endowed with all good qualities.

15. No girl either from Deva or Gandharvas or Asura or Nāga clans was as beautiful as that girl of excellent waist.

16. Dakṣa gave her to the Trident-bearing Lord as his wife. She had been repeatedly requested by him. He was desirous of her and she of him.

17. He thought of the holiest of holy spots befitting the rite of *Kanyādāna* (marriage) and came there along with his daughter, ministers and servants.

18. Then he brought in great quantity different kinds of articles all highly auspicious and especially befitting marriage celebrations.

19. Maheśvara came there on the thirteenth lunar day in the bright half of Caitra coinciding with a Sunday and the constellation Pūrvāphālgunī.

20. He was accompanied by all the groups of Suras with Lord Viṣṇu at their head, Ādityas, Vasus, Rudras, Āśvins and others.

21. Groups of Sādhyas, Siddhas, Bhūtas, Pretas, Vināyakas, Gandharvas, groups of Cāraṇas, Guhyakas, Yakṣas and Rākṣasas were also with him.

22. In the meanwhile, Dakṣa whose hair stood on end due to excessive joy, accompanied by his friends and relative came forward to receive him personally.

23. Great musical instruments were being played by Sūtas, Māgadhas and Bandins (all different kinds of bards). Many people recited Mantras. Many musicians sang songs.

24. All the Suras were duly honoured by Dakṣa himself in accordance with their seniority and importance. They were seated in due order all round the *Vedi* erected within the pavilion.

25-26. Dakṣa bowed down to Pitāmaha with great pleasure and requested: "O Lord, all the rites in connection with the celebration of the marriage should be performed by you. Bless her yourself so that my daughter shall be fortunate, beautiful, loyal, well-behaved, dear to her husband and blessed with sons and grandsons."

27. "So be it," said he with a delighted mind. Getting up he performed all the rites beginning with the honouring (of the elders).

28. He performed the rite of Saṁpradāna (giving away the daughter in marriage) there itself in accordance with the injunctions. In front of *Mātṛs* (Mothers) Vedhas (Brahmā) made Satī and Īśa grasp each other's hands in the proper manner.

29. Then he came to the *Vedi* (Altar) and performed all the rites in the fire as mentioned in the Gṛhya Sūtra texts in full detail.

30. As he eagerly and enthusiastically looked at the beautiful limbs of Satī, Pitāmaha became delighted and distressed with lust.

31. Excepting her face hidden behind the veil, all the other limbs were glanced at by that lascivious one in a manner unknown to anyone else.

32. He did not look directly at Śaṁbhu's face out of shame. She too was very bashful and hence did not reveal her face.

33. Then Brahmā began to look for ways and means to see the face (of Satī). He thought of doing so through smoke as he became more and more distressed with lust.

34. He put many wet sacrificial twigs into the fire repeatedly. The clarified butter was reduced in quantity when poured. Thus the wet things became prominently used.

35. In the meantime columns of smoke enveloped the place all round. The foot of the Altar became completely enveloped in darkness.

36. With eyes distressed with smoke Tripurāntaka (Śiva) and all members present covered their eyes with hands.

37. The lascivious Brahmā lifted the veil of Satī and looked at her face delightedly.

38. As a result thereof there was an emission of the semen of Brahmā which fell on the ground like a mass of snow drops.

39. The Lotus-born One (Brahmā) immediately covered that mass of semen with sand-particles lest anyone should see it.

40. Lord Śambhu knew it through his divine perception. Being angry at the emission of semen, he said:

41-44a. "O sinner, what a despicable act has been committed by you! It does not behove you to look at my wife's face lustfully. You seem to think that all these activities were not noticed by Śaṅkara. O Vidhi, is there anything concealed from me in all the three world? How can they be?

O foolish one, I am in the interior of everything in all the three worlds whether it is mobile or immobile, like oil latent in a gingelly seed. Hence give up this your head, O Brahmā, undoubtedly."

44b. As this transpired, Brahmā touched his head with his hand (The root *√Spṛś* means 'to touch', 'to give up' etc.). Presently the Bull-vehicled One stood there in his own form.

45. Then, O Brāhmaṇas, he was completely overwhelmed with shame and stood there with face cast down. Further, all the Devas beginning with Indra were standing around.

46-47. The bashful Pitāmaha bowed down to Maheśvara, eulogized and said, "Do forgive. Do forgive. Do tell me, O Lord, what shall be the expiation for this sin? Mete out to me the punishment befitting it so that the sin may be quelled."

Śrī Bhagavān said:

48. With this form held on your head perform penance. Meditate on me with eagerness to propitiate me.

49. You will become well-known under the name Rudraśiras all over the earth. You will be the accomplisher of all tasks of the Brāhmaṇas endowed with refulgence.

50. Since this act has been perpetrated by you—an act befitting only human beings—you will become a man and roam about on the earth.

51-52. One who sees you in this form and enquires: "What is this? Lord Tripurāntaka over the head of Brahmā?" and eagerly hears about your act, shall become rid of the sin of cohabiting with another man's wife.

53. The more people go on narrating this act of yours, the more your sin will get dissolved and you will become purified.

54. O Brahmā, this alone is spoken as the atonement for you, as people of the earth will laugh at you and ridicule you very

much.

55. Your semen that dropped down in the middle of the Vedī as you were distressed with lust, has been noticed by me. It shall not go in vain.

56. As many particles of sand came into contact with the semen so many sages of esteemed holy vows will arise from it.

57. All of them will be of the size of a thumb and be famous as Vālakhilyas. They will be capable of cursing and blessing. They will be endowed with the power of penance.

58. In the meantime, O excellent Brāhmaṇas, eighty-eight thousand sages of sanctified souls, all of the size of a thumb, came out of the centre of the *Vedī*.

59. They bowed down to Lord Pitāmaha and spoke to him loudly, "O father, show us a place devoid of Kali (quarrel) for performing austerities."

Pitāmaha said:

60. O dear sons, perform penance in this holy spot along with me. Thereby you will attain the greatest Siddhi rare in the world.

61. All those Vālakhilyas promised to do so. They erected a splendid hermitage, performed penance and attained the greatest Siddhi.

62. Brahmā too duly completed himself the rites of the marriage in the way in which it has been enjoined in the Śruti.

63. Showers of flowers fell around from the sky. Musical instruments were played and songs were Sung.

64. Eminent Brāhmaṇas chanted the Vedic Mantras. The celestial damsels beginning with Raṁbhā began to dance passionately fascinating the eyes of the Devas.

65. Thus a great festival went on there even as Tuṁburu and others sang in the manner they used to sing in heaven earlier.

66-67. At the conclusion of the celebration of marriage, Lord Tripurāntaka devoutly said to the Lotus-born One: "O excellent one among Suras, what monetary fee shall I give you for this celebration of marriage? Tell me quickly, even if it be too high, O highly esteemed one, there is nothing which cannot be given my me."

Pitāmaha said:

68. O Lord of Suras, you should stay in this *Vedī* in this very form always, for the purification of the sins of men.

69. O Moon-crested Lord, I shall make my hermitage in your vicinity and perform the penance for the destruction of this sin.

70. A man who visits the deity devoutly on the thirteenth lunar day in the bright half of Caitra coinciding with Sunday and the constellation Pūrvāphālgunī, will find his sins dissolved at the very same time.

71. A woman who is unlucky, barren, squint-eyed and ugly shall become beautiful by visiting you. Undoubtedly she shall become fortunate, enjoying excellent pleasures and giving birth to good children.

Maheśvara said:

72. O Vidhi, at your true instance I shall remain in the *Vedī* accompanied by my wife for the welfare of all the worlds.

Sūta said:

73. Thus the Bull-bannered Lord stands in the centre of the Vedī along with his wife, destroying the sins of all people.

74. Thus, O Brāhmaṇas, it has been fully narrated to you how formerly in the Svāyaṁbhuva Manvantara the marriage of Vṛṣanātha took place.

75-76. If on the occasion of a marriage or at the beginning, anyone listens to this narrative after adoring calmly the Bull-bannered Lord, all the rites of the marriage celebration shall become unhindered. The bride shall become endowed with happiness, conjugal felicity, good qualitic and conduct; she shall be chaste and loyal and give birth to sons.

CHAPTER SEVENTYEIGHT

Greatness of Rudraśīrṣa

The sages said:

1-3. At what place there, O Sūta, was the penance performed by Brahmā along with the sages (named) Vālakhilyas of esteemed holy vows?

Sūta said:

O excellent Brāhmaṇas, penance was performed by Brahmā with proper devotion and endeavour on the north-western side of the Vedī of Hara. Vālakhilyas engaged themselves in Japa and holy ablution and performed the penance on the western side. Now I shall narrate to you, O excellent Brāhmaṇas, the wonderful thing that happened in the hermitage of the Four-faced Lord.

4. A certain woman of loose conduct, though hailing from a Brāhmaṇa family, always used to dally with her paramour named Devadatta, at the place.

5. She used to come to this place with a happy mind during the nights of the dark half without the knowledge of her husband, mother and other relatives.

6. Once, O Brāhmaṇas, someone saw her in the company of the paramour and intimated it to her husband.

7. The husband became furious. He rebuked her with very harsh words and also thrashed her with blows.

8. She shamelessly shed tears profusely in accordance with her womanly nature and said in piteous tones with palms joined together:

9-10. "O my Lord, I am blameless. I am one bowing down at your feet. Still why do you beat me harshly and ruthlessly solely relying in the words of some wicked man? I can convince you of my innocence by taking solemn oaths, by drinking poison or by entering blazing fire."

11. Thereupon the Brāhmaṇa said to her, "If you are sinless then take up *Divyagraha* (ordeal through fire etc.) in front of the deities and Brāhmaṇas."

12. Bold and venturesome that she was, she consented saying

"So be it" and took up *Divyagraha* (the ordeal) in accordance with the convention.

13. Though really a sinner, she came out unscathed after the ordeal in front of all the kinsmen, elders, Brāhmaṇas and the deities.

14. In the meantime (as a result of this) she was admiringly congratulated and the husband was roundly condemned and despised with words like "Fie upon you!"

15. "Alas, this wicked and base Brāhmaṇa is the real sinner! He has falsely accused his virtuous wife free from sins."

16-17. O excellent Brāhmaṇas, thus, he was rebuked by all the people. He became very miserable and was furious with the Fire-god. In his great misery he felt inclined to curse the Fire-god. Censuring him (Fire-god) repeatedly, he spoke these harsh words:

18-19. "She has been seen by myself in a very compromising situation in the company of her paramour. O Vahni, she is a great sinner; why is she not reduced to ash by you? Hence you are an abettor of her crime. You are partial to an indecent one. Now I shall curse you undoubtedly with a terrible imprecation."

Sūta said:

20. On hearing those words of the furious Brāhmaṇa, the Fire-god became terrified. He said to him with palms joined in reverence.

Agni said:

21. O Brāhmaṇa, it is not my fault that your beloved wife was not burnt in spite of her sinful offence. In this connection listen to my clear statement.

22. Sexual intercourse is being conducted by this woman with her paramour. O excellent Brāhmaṇa, it has been so for a long time, though you knew it only this day.

23. But, O Brāhmaṇa, I shall tell you the reason why she has not been burnt and why she is declared pure. Listen attentively.

24. Brahmā with Rudra on his head is stationed in that shrine, O Brāhmaṇa, where this woman's contact with the paramour has been going on.

25. After the various kinds of dalliance with her paramour, she used to see the deity Rudra stationed on the head of Brahmā.

26. Thereafter she used to wash her limbs in the holy pit present in front. Thereby this woman of sparkling smiles attains purity despite her sinful crime.

27. It was here that formerly Brahmā, the grandfather of the worlds, became liberated form his sin. His sinful offence was that he looked at the countenance of Goddess Satī after being overwhelmed by lust.

28. Hence, O excellent Brāhmaṇa, I cannot be blamed in the least. It is the power of Rudraśīrṣa and the holy water of the sacred pit.

29. Hence, O excellent Brāhmaṇa, take this woman home. She has become sanctified and so she is free from sins. What has been said by me is the truth.

The Brāhmaṇa said:

30. O Hutāśana (Fire-god), I will not take her home though she might have become pure. I did see myself, her in the company of her paramour, in her rash action!

31. After saying this, the excellent Brāhmaṇa of pure holy vows, abandoned her also and went home later. The people too went to their respective abodes.

32-33. Abandoned thus by her husband, she became highly delighted in her mind. After knowing the greatness of that Tīrtha directly uttered by Vaiśvānara, she continued her dalliance with the paramour with added zest in the same shrine and later took her plunge in the holy Kuṇḍa.

34-36. Thereafter, even men with their faces averted from other men's wives, and women with strict adherence to the vow of fidelity used to come to that holy shrine from places very far off. They were scrupulous in everything because of their fear of what was in store for them in the other world. They indulged in sexual intercourse in that shrine called Rudraśīrṣa. Thereafter, they used to take their holy bath in that Kuṇḍa destructive of sins. They were liberated from their sins by seeing Rudraśīrṣa.

37. In the meantime all virtuousness of men in regard to their fidelity towards their wives and that of women in regard to

their faithfulness to their husbands got lost.

38. (There was shameless promiscuousness in sexual relations, O excellent Brāhmaṇas.) Whoever sets his eyes on a comely woman, be she of a noble family, he used to take her to that holy spot for joyous indulgence.

39. Similarly if any woman finds any handsome man anywhere, she used to take him over there for joyous sexual enjoyment.

40. Neither the man nor the woman was contaminated by the sin thereof even in the least, thanks to the power of that Tīrtha.

41-42. Once there was a king named Vidūratha in the land of Ānarta, who became old in due course. Though he was old, he had a young maiden of excellent beauty as his wife whom he loved more than his own life, even though he had reached old age.

43. The king affected by senile atrophy never found a place in the heart of that woman. She used to come to this holy shrine and divert herself with any man of her choice.

44-45. After coming to know of her misconduct, the king became very furious. He went to that splendid shrine and quickly filled the holy Kuṇḍa with dust particles and broke the palace to pieces. Thereafter he spoke these terrible words:

46-47. "If anyone digs again this Kuṇḍa now filled with dust particles and renovates this temple, he will fully incur the sin of coming into intimate contact with other men's wives as in the case of men deluded by lust who will indulge in sinful conduct."

Sūta said:

48. After declaring thus the king took his beloved back to his abode. He was evidently pleased much in his heart.

49. The king knew that his beloved wife thought of other men previously but had ceased to be so. Yet he guarded her with effort and alertness and did not fully believe in her.

50. One day the lady of excellent complexion concealed a very small weapon in her plaited hairs and went to bed with the intention of killing him.

51. She indulged in sexual dalliance and jocular remarks with him as befitting the emotions of a Kṣattriya along with conquettish manner and sensuous movement of limbs.

52. When the king fell into a sound sleep the ruthless beloved of the king took off the weapon from her braid of hairs and killed him.

53. Thus the Lord of Ānarta immediately reaped the fruit of his act of destroying the Tīrtha. The act was indeed violent and despised by all people.

54. O excellent Brāhmaṇas, the king was afraid of shattering the Liṅga. Hence Lord Rudraśīrśa was not broken by him. The deity stands even now.

55-59. One who remains pure, stands in front of the deity and recites *Rudraśiras Mantras*[1] on the fourteenth lunar day in the bright half of Māgha after the adoration with garlands etc. obtains immediately all desired benefits by the power of the Lord.

One who stands in front of the deity and chants Rudraśīrṣa one hundred eight times attains the greatest goal undoubtedly.

One who recites it once in front of the deity everyday, O excellent Brāhmaṇas, gets rid of the sins of that day.

Thus everything connected with the greatness of Rudraśīrṣa has been narrated to you. It destroys all sins immediately. It is highly auspicious and increases fame. Hence the greatness of Rudraśīrṣa should be listened to respectfully.

CHAPTER SEVENTYNINE

Greatness of Vālakhilyāśrama

Sūta said:

1-3. To the south itself thereof is the well-known Liṅga installed by Vālakhilyas. It is destructive of all sins. It is by propitiating that Liṅga that those who were extremely furious with Śakra created Garuḍa, the bird who became the well-known vehicle of Viṣṇu here.[2]

---

1. Mantras of Ātharvaṇa Rudra-śīrṣa
2. Vide Mbh, *Ādi*, 30-40.

The sages said:

O Sūtaja, how did Vālakhilyas become angry with Śakra and how was Garuḍa born?

Sūta said:

4. Formerly Dakṣa, the Prajāpati (Patriarch), duly performed in that splendid holy spot a Yajña with profuse distribution of monetary gifts.

5. Therein Śakra and other Devas, sages and pure saintly kings, were invited for assistance by Dakṣa.

6. So also were invited Brāhmaṇas fully conversant with the Vedas and clever in the rites of Yajña, those who were in the stage of householders and those who were permanent residents of forests.

7. Then Vālakhilyas, the sages of esteemed holy vows, started towards the sacrificial hall for assisting Prajāpati. They were carrying a single sacrificial twig all by themselves but still they were distressed due to its burden.

8. Due to the advent of untimely rains, a pit created by cow's foot that was on their path, got filled with water.

9-10. As they were eager to cross it and were straining themselves under the weight of the sacrificial twig; the king of Devas who was also travelling by the same path towards the sacrificial place of Dakṣa, the Prajāpati, happened to see them. He looked at them out of curiosity for a long time and then smiled. In the height of his arrogance on account of his affluence, he went ahead crossing over them.

11. In view of this disrespect shown by Śakra, they became very angry. They turned back to their hermitage and took counsel with one another with a final decision:

12-14. "On getting the position of Śakra, this sinful one has crossed over all of us! He should be pulled down from his excellent post. Another Śakra should be created by the power of Mantras, the great Sūktas from the Atharva Veda, after applying them for *Abhicāra* rites (Black Magic).

This Śakra, haughty and intoxicated with power, endowed with greatness due to the sacrifices (performed by him for getting Indrahood) should be overthrown. His intellect and exploits are meagre."

15-16. Thereafter, they remained pure mentally and physically and performed Homa in the holy fire day and night. With great earnestness, those excellent Brāhmaṇas recited *Skandasūkta* as mentioned in the *Kṣurikā* section, *Garbhopaniṣad, Nīlarudra* passages, charming *Rudraśīrṣa* etc., along with *Viṣṇu Sūkta.*

17. They placed a pot filled with water in the centre of the Maṇḍala. At the conclusion of the Homa they touched (all Homa articles with) that sacred water.

18. In the meantime Śakra saw frightening, evil-foreboding omens arising all round pointing at his own destruction.

19. His left arm and left eye throbbed. He could not see the tip of his nose or tongue or the chin.

20. He saw his own shadow bereft of the head and two Suns in the sky. He was unable to see Arundhatī star and Dhruva (Pole Star) or portions of the firmament.

21. Hari (Indra) could not see the planet Saturn and the heavenly river stationed in the sky. While sleeping he used to dream of a woman of dark complexion, armed with weapons.

22-24. She was hideous and frightening and naked, she has dishevelled hairs and black teeth.

On observing these omens of great magnitude, the King of Devas asked Bṛhaspati in great fear: " O my preceptor, what is this? Terrible ill omens and scenes foreboding evil occur severally. O wise one, will destruction overtake just now? Do tell me. Will my kingdom of the three worlds be affected? Will my fortune etc., suffer?"

Bṛhaspati said:

25. You have been arrogant. The great sages, Vālakhilyas, who had been held up on the way in their intention to cross the *Goṣpada* (Puddle of water caused by cow's foot) were transgressed by you.

26. O Consort of Śacī, they have performed a perfect Homa by means of the Mantras of *Atharva Veda* against you. The waterpot has also been charged with the Mantras.

27. There is no doubt about it that another Hari (Indra), the Lord of all the Devas, will spring up as a result of these *Ātharvaṇa Mantras* in order to bring about your destruction.

28. On hearing his words, the Thousand-eyed One became afraid. He went then to Dakṣa with a sad face and said to him:

29-30. "O Prajāpati, the Vālakhilya sages have endeavoured to destroy us and create another Śakra. Do go there yourself and prevent them before another Śakra is born for destroying us. There is nothing that they cannot do."

31. Accompanied by the Devas beginning with Śakra, Dakṣa hurried to that place and spoke to them laughingly yet with humility:

32. "O Brāhmaṇas, why is this most terrible act being done by you whereby the entire range of the three worlds has become upset."

33. On seeing Dakṣa coming to their place of residence, they hurriedly proceeded towards him with *Arghya* in their hands.

34-35. After duly offering the *Arghya* and adoring him devoutly they bowed to him and said: "O Prajāpati, welcome to you. May we be commanded at once. Why have you come here? Even by offering our lives we shall do what is pleasing to you."

Dakṣa said:

36. This highly terrifying rite that has instilled fear into Devas should be discontinued by you all unexcitedly. I have come here for this purpose.

The sages said:

37. We were coming devotedly to attend your Yajña. But, in his height of arrogance, Śakra repeatedly indulged in laughing at us and transgressed us.

38. In order to exterminate this Śakra, we, the agitated angry ones, began to create another Śakra by means of the Mantras of great power. The Homa too has been concluded.

39. Hence, tell us, O Lord. How can the power of the Mantra be rendered ineffective after it has been created by the Vedas?

40. O Lord, if you yourself are competent to alter it, do it. We are powerless in this respect.

Dakṣa said:

41. O highly esteemed ones, what has been said by you all is true. The power generated by the Vedic Mantras cannot be rendered otherwise.

42. Homa has been performed by you all by means of the Vedic Mantras. For the purpose of (creating) a king of Devas, the water-pot has been charged with Mantras by you all in a cool and calculated manner.

43. At my instance, he shall become the king of birds. He will be endowed with refulgence and vigour. He will be superior even to Śakra.

44. Again at my instance, what has been perpetrated by this king of Devas should be forgiven. He has done this foolishly.

45. After saying thus, Dakṣa pointed to the fear-stricken Thousand-eyed One standing humbly.

46-47. On seeing the Thousand-eyed One standing with palms joined in reverence and trembling much, they said: "O Śakra, do not transgress Brāhmaṇas hereafter.

Do not do so again if you wish for the overlordship of the heaven-dwellers. Even a stupid, foolish Brāhmaṇa who does not regularly perform his sacred rites should not be insulted by sensible persons desirous of attaining the pleasures of the two worlds."

Indra said:

48. This misdemeanour of mine knowingly or unknowingly committed by me should be forgiven by all the Brāhmaṇas especially at the instance of Dakṣa.

49. May a boon cherished in the heart always, be received from me. I shall undoubtedly grant it. There is nothing which I cannot give.

The sages said:

50-52. If any man endowed with faith worships this Liṅga and performs Homa in this Kuṇḍa let him get what he desires.

Indra said:

He who adores this Liṅga and performs Homa in the Kuṇḍa shall immediately attain the desired benefit.

One without desire who worships this auspicious Liṅga will attain the greatest Siddhi inaccessible even to Devas.

Sūta said:

53-54. After saying thus to the Vālakhilya Sages, the Thousand-eyed One (Indra) mounted his Airāvata and took (them?) to the Yajña of Dakṣa.

O excellent Brāhmaṇas, Dakṣa too duly performed the Yajña while the delighted Vālakhilyas sat near.

CHAPTER EIGHTY

Importance of the Sight of Viṣṇu[1]

The sages said:

1-2. It has been mentioned by you that Garuḍa endowed with refulgence and vigour was born from the Homa performed by the sages (Vālakhilyas).

How was he born there? Tell us this in detail. We have heard that he was born of Vinatā.

Sūta said:

3-4. The water-pot was charged with the Mantras of *Atharvaveda* by Vālakhilyas swayed by great indignation. They were

1. Chapters 80-85 contain the story of Suparṇa i.e. Garuḍa. Here the author skilfully weaves the future events in Kṛṣṇa's Avatāra. Garuḍa lost both his wings due to his baseless derogatory remarks against women in general. The celibate old Śāṇḍilī did not like it. Her mental disapproval deprived Garuḍa of his wings. This episode is therefore the glorification of the local deity Suparṇeśvara, at Camatkārapura.

The birth of Subhadrā with a horse's face and Kṛṣṇa's penance to make her beautiful again is attributed to the curse of Lakṣmī who however, though cursed with an elephant's head, frees herself from it by performing penance instead of depending on Viṣṇu.

restrained by Dakṣa and the Lord of the birds was indicated by him. Thereupon Kaśyapa took that *Kalaśa* (pot) and went to his abode.

5-6. Then he joyously said to his beloved wife Vinatā: "O fair lady, drink this holy water highly sanctified by Mantras. Thereby a son will be born to you, who will be stronger than the Thousand-eyed One. He will be refulgent and famous. He cannot be conquered by all the Dānavas combined.

7. On hearing his words, that beautiful lady drank that water instantly and conceived immediately.

8. It was thus that Garuḍa who strikes terror into all the serpents was born to Kaśyapa but through the imbibing of that holy water.

9. It was he who defeated Purandara heroically and carried away Amṛta (Nectar). Endowed with devotion to his mother, he offered it to the serpents.

10. It was he who became a great favourite of Viṣṇu after attaining the (high) status of being his vehicle. He is always present on the flag at the top of his chariot.

11. It was he who performed penance formerly and the Three-eyed Lord was propitiated by that noble-souled one who became sensible after losing his wings.

12. Similar wings were acquired by him once again with the favour of the Lord of Devas. Actually they were made better.

The sages said:

13. How did the noble-souled Garuḍa lose his wings? How did he get them back? How was Maheśvara propitiated? O son of Sūta, narrate this in detail as it had occurred.

Sūta said:

14. Formerly, O excellent Brāhmaṇas, ever since his childhood, Garuḍa had a Brāhmaṇa friend hailing from the family of Bhṛgu.

15. This friend had a daughter named Mādhavī who was endowed with exalted qualities of beauty etc. and marked with all (auspicious) features. She was honoured by all.

16. Neither a Deva lady, nor a Gandharva woman, neither

an Asura lady nor a Pannaga woman had such a beauty of form as that of the highly esteemed slender-waisted one.

17. That intimate friend humbly requested the Lord of birds to assist him in getting a bridegroom for her:

18. "O Lord of birds, find out a suitable bridegroom for this daughter of mine so that I can offer her in marriage to him."

Garuḍa said:

19. O excellent Brāhmaṇa, take this daughter with you and ride on my back. Thus roam over the entire range of the world.

20. Then you yourself select a suitable husband endowed with good qualities for this girl. This is an act of friendship on my part.

Sūta said:

21. O excellent Brāhmaṇas, on being told thus that Brāhmaṇa rode on the back of Garuḍa along with his daughter in search of a bridegroom for her.

22. Whatever young men the Brāhmaṇa saw none of them appealed to him.

23. The features of a son of someone were very handsome but his family was not spotless. One whose family and features were good did not have good qualities.

24. One who had all good qualities did not possess excellent handsome features. Nor did he have the other essential features of a good bridegroom, such as wealth and inclination (towards good men).

25. Thus for a thousand years the Brāhmaṇa and the Lord of birds roamed about the earth for the sake of a suitable bridegroom, O excellent Brāhmaṇas.

26. In the course of their wanderings they were tired very much. They reached this very holy spot (of Vāsudeva). They had a desire to meet Vāsudeva.

27. They had already visited Śvetadvīpa, the splendid Badarī, the Milk Ocean, Vaikuṇṭha and other habitual resorts of Vāsudeva.

28. Then Sage Nārada, the son of Brahmā, was seen by them. The gently asked him about Viṣṇu, the eternal Brahman:

29. "O Sage, where is the Lotus-eyed Lord now? All the abodes of Viṣṇu have been visited joyously by us both. But Keśava was not seen."

Nārada said:

30. He always stays in the holy spot of Hāṭakeśvara Kṣetra for a period of four months in the form of *Jalaśāyin* (one who lies down in water).

31. Hence go immediately to that place for meeting him. The Discus-bearing Lord may come within the range of vision of both of you.

32. I too have started for the purpose of meeting him in connection with a certain task of Devas. I shall now accompany you.

33. Both of them, the prominent bird and the leading Brāhmaṇa as well as the sage, the son of Brahmā, all these reached the place where Janārdana was present in the form of *Jalaśāyin.*

34. On seeing the great refulgence of Viṣṇu from afar Garuḍa and the leading sage Nārada spoke to that Brāhmaṇa:

35-37. "O excellent Brāhmaṇa, stay here itself along with your daughter far away from the refulgence of Viṣṇu that is on a par with the fire appearing at the end of a Kalpa.

Otherwise you will be reduced to ash like a moth that falls into fire, deluded during the night.

This unbearable splendour has been endured by us both due to his favour. So it does not cause distress to our bodies or any other similar adverse effect."

38. After leaving the Brāhmaṇa thus along with his daughter very far away, both of them went to that place where Janārdana was asleep.

39. Placing the palms joined together in reverence on their heads, they engaged themselves in the divine eulogy. Hairs stood on ends all over their body. Tears of joy welled up in their eyes and drenched their faces.

40. After circumambulating thrice, they bowed down to Hari and prostrated before him. They saw the Daughter of the Ocean (i.e. Lakṣmī) seated near the feet.

41. She was joyously engaged in massaging his feet with her eyes riveted to the face of Viṣṇu. They saw another lady too, an

elderly one with a white veil covering her face.

42. She was also seated near her, engaged in deep meditation. She had slender limbs with horripilation manifest on them. She possessed the lustre of twelve suns.

43. Both the visitors were delighted when Viṣṇu joyously engaged himself in conversation with them asking them why they called.

Śrī Nārada said:

44. I have come to you on an errand from Devas. Garuḍa has come for the sake of a Brāhmaṇa. O Keśava, this is the reply for what you ask. (What else do you ask?)

Śrī Bhagavān said:

45. I hope, O excellent sage, all the Heaven-dwellers are happy and well. I hope there is no situation fearful to Indra caused by Dānavas.

46. I hope, all the Devas including Vāsava are regularly receiving their due share in the Yajñas. I hope, there is no powerful Dānava coming into predominance on the earth.

Śrī Nārada said:

47. Now, recently the (goddess) Earth came to the presence of the Four-faced Lord. Distressed with the burden and afflicted much by Dānavas she lamented much before the Lotus-born One to whom she said feeling greatly by miserable:

Dharaṇī (Earth) said:

48. The great Asura named Kālanemi who was killed by the powerful Viṣṇu is now born as Kaṁsa, the son of Ugrasena.

49-50. Ariṣṭa, Dhenuka, Keśi, Pralaṁba, the extremely terrible Pūtanā — all these and other terrible ones run about here and there causing me unnecessary pain.

51. People of the mortal world have raised up their arms for succour. On account of their multiplicity, they cannot be accommodated on my surface.

52. O Lord, if you do not reduce the burden immediately, I shall undoubtedly sink into Rasātala (nether world).

[*Nārada continued:*]

53. On hearing her words, Brahmā, the creator of the worlds, held consultation with Devas and he has now sent me to you.

54. (His message is:) "The Lord should be told by you thus: 'Lord Janārdana should take an incarnation on the Earth and reduce the burden (completely).'"

55. Hence, O powerful Lord, take up your birth on the Earth and reduce the burden of the Earth. It is for this purpose that I have come here.

Śrī Bhagavān said:

56. O sage, it shall be (done) so, I shall consult Brahmā along with Devas including Vāsava and reduce the burden of the Earth.

57. After saying thus to Nārada, the leading sage, Viṣṇu said to Garuḍa: 'Why have you come here?'

CHAPTER EIGHTYONE

Fall of Suparṇa's Wings

Śrī Garuḍa said:

1-5. I have a very close friend, a Brāhmaṇa hailing from the family of Bhṛgu. The name of his lotus-eyed daughter is Mādhavī. A husband befitting her could not be found by that noble-souled one. Therefore, he said to me: "O excellent bird, bring a husband suitable to her, if you consider me worthy of honour." Then the entire earth was searched by me for a bridegroom befitting her. But no bridegroom endowed with all good qualities could be obtained. Then, O Lotus-eyed One, you were re-collected by me in my mind as a befitting husband for her. You are endowed with all good qualities. Hence, O Lord of Suras, accept her. Hold her hand in marriage. She is very beautiful. I pray to you with this appeal of mine.

Śrī Bhagavān said:

6. O excellent bird, bring that lotus-eyed girl here. On seeing her myself, I shall do as spoken by you.

Garuḍa said:

7. It is on account of our fear from your refulgence that the girl and the father had been kept far away by me. How can I bring her here?

Śrī Lord said:

8. My refulgence will not scorch her and her father here. Hence, O excellent bird, bring her quickly.

9. On being told thus by that powerful Viṣṇu he brought her and also the Brāhmaṇa, a descendant of the family of Bhṛgu.

10. The Brāhmaṇa bowed down to Madhusūdana and came to the side of Viṣṇu, near Garuḍa, like Lakṣmī herself.

11. Due to child-like innocence the blameless beautiful girl sat at the end of the bed to the right of the Enemy of Mura.

12. Thereat, Lakṣmī who had the status of the chief queen became extremely furious thinking her to be her co-wife and cursed the girl:

13. "Since, verily in my very presence, O sinful girl, you set aside all bashfulness and joyously took your seat on the bed of my husband, you will become a hideous Aśvamukhī (Horse-faced)."

14. When the curse was thus uttered by Śrī, there was a great hue and cry among all those present there. The Brāhmaṇa became angry.

The Brāhmaṇa said:

15. A thousand persons have been requested on behalf of the girl. Not even a single one among them has accepted her even verbally, let alone grasping her hand. How can she have the status of a wife?

16. As long as she has not been handed over with a prior resolve, in accordance with the injunctions of the Gṛhyasūtras

and in the presence of the holy fire, Brāhmaṇas and elders (she has no status of a wife).

17. Hence she is blemishless. But you regarding her on a par with your co-wife, have made her horse-faced. O sinful one, you will also be elephant-faced.

18. After saying thus the leading Brāhmaṇa spoke to Keśava: "A befitting hospitality has been extended to me by your wife! Hence I shall go to that place where such a daughter shall be born."

Śrī Bhagavān said:

19. In this matter, O excellent Brāhmaṇa, do not be so enraged. Never can inauspiciousness befall those who come to my vicinity.

20. Hence she will not become horse-faced in this birth. Take her and go home. Give her to a desirable person.

21. It is the left side in the bed that has been assigned to wives and the right side to kinsmen who may lie for the nonce.

22. Here, your daughter, O Brāhmaṇa, has occupied the spot reserved for kinsmen. So she will be born as my younger sister in the next birth.

23-24. I will incarnate then on the earth on account of some task of Devas. Since she has been cursed to become a horse-faced one by my wife, I will perform great penance along with her and transform her into one of splendid face, O Brāhmaṇa, I will make Lakṣmī too so.

25. After consoling that Brāhmaṇa with his words, the Lord continued the narration of charming stories of diverse kinds in the company of Garuḍa.

26. At the close of the narration, Garuḍa looked at the aged lady endowed with refulgence and spoke to Puruṣottama:

27. "O Janārdana, O most excellent one among Suras, this elderly lady sitting near you seems to be someone not seen before. Do tell me who she is. Where has she come from? Why has she come?"

Śrī Bhagavān said:

28-29. O most excellent one among birds, this is the

elderly maiden well-known in this world by the name Śāṇḍilī.[1] She is omniscient and strictly adhering to celibacy. She is endowed with the power of penance. She is venerated by all the Devas. O leading bird, there is no woman like her in all the three worlds.

Sūta said:

30. On hearing his words, O Brāhmaṇas, the Lord of the birds looked at her for a long time, then laughed and ultimately spoke to Vāsudeva:

Garuḍa said:

31-32. It is not unusual that a very great penance is performed. Similarly if gifts are made it is not a wonder. Further if a battle is fought by able warriors, what is surprising in that? But, O Puruṣottama, this is unusual that one maintains celibacy especially during the prime of youth.

33-35. More so in the case of women. I do not have any faith in this respect. Emotional outlet is essential in the case of lower animals. Youth is not for supression of rights. If women do not get access to men anywhere, they will indulge in mutual sexual alliance when afflicted by the arrows of Kāma. In the absence of suitable men, they will consider a leper, a sick one, and an old man and one short of a limb or two on a par with the Five-arrowed One (Kāma).

36. Fire is never satiated completely with fuel, nor the great sea with the rivers flowing into it. The god of Death cannot be surfeited with all living beings nor a woman with men.

37. If women keep a limit, it is not due to the fear of the other world. Except the fear of the king or that of the elders (there is nothing to restrain them).

Sūta said:

38. On hearing these words of his, Śāṇḍilī[1], the celibate woman, had in her heart the surging emotion of anger, although she was under the vow of silence.

---

1. This Śāṇḍilī is different from the other Śāṇḍilī who carried her disabled husband on her head and prevented sunrise lest her husband might die. This Śāṇḍilī is a celibate old woman.

39. In the meantime both the wings of the Lord of the birds got destroyed and he became mutilated in shape.

40. Though he was really ferocious and devoid of all ailments, he could not go ahead even a step. He was no better than a mass of flesh.[1]

CHAPTER EIGHTYTWO

Greatness of Suparṇeśvara[2]

Sūta said:

1-4. On seeing the condition of Garuḍa, the Lotus-eyed One was wonderstruck. He thought: 'What could be this present situation? Even when struck with Vajra not even a single hair from his body fell down! How then did his wings fall on to the ground all of a sudden?

Indeed, the fact that this noble-souled one censured women in general and derided their celibacy after casting a meaningful glance at Śāṇḍilī has made her strike down the wings by the power of her penance. In the whole of the three worlds, no one else has such a power.'

5. Thereupon, O excellent Brāhmaṇas, the Garuḍa-emblemed One (Viṣṇu) humbly propitiated Śāṇḍilī on behalf of Garuḍa, after smiling a little.

Śrī Bhagavān said:

6. O highly esteemed one, only a general statement was made by him about all the women. So, why was he made thus by you?

Śaṇḍilī said:

7. O Janārdana, he looked at my face and smiled. O preceptor

1. Mbh, *Udyoga* 113.8-17 notes that this incident—dropping and recovery of wings by Garuḍa due to Śāṇḍilī's favour took placed on Ṛṣabha mountain.

2. The story of Garuḍa's loss and restoration of wings is adopted from Mbh, *Udyoga* 113 to glorify Suparṇeśvara at this sacred place.

of the universe, a censure of woman-folk was also made by him wantonly.

8. It is for this reason that he has been thus chastised by me. O Keśava, it is not mental, verbal or physical attack.

Śrī Bhagavān said:

9. Still, O sinless one, O auspicious lady, if you honour me, do a favour unto this fellow at my instance.

Śāṇḍilī said:

10. O Lord, whatever is conceived by me in my mind, good or otherwise cannot become otherwise, especially if my anger is aroused.

11. Hence at my behest, let him propitiate Śaṅkara for the restoration of the wings. No one else has enough competence vested in him to grant him (the wings).

12. Otherwise, O Lotus-eyed One, he will have to go permanently like this in the world. I am telling you the truth.

Sūta said:

13. On hearing her words Janārdana said to Garuḍa who continued to be in that wretched plight akin to a mass of flesh.

14. "O excellent bird, this alone is the boon granted by this lady, the greatest one among bipeds i.e. human beings. She has told you to propitiate Śambhu for the acquisition of the wings.

15. Hence with a concentrated mind, quickly apply yourself day and night energetically to the propitiation of the Moon-crested Lord who is immutable.

16. Thereby, O Kaśyapa's son, by the greatness of that Lord and his power, your body shall ere long be as it was before."

17. On hearing it, Garuḍa immediately adopted Pāśupata Vrata after installing Lord Īśāna and then propitiated him. He thereby caused delight to him.

18. He performed the rites of Cāndrāyaṇa, Kṛcchra, Sāntapana, Prājāpatya and Pārāka thereafter.

19. He took holy baths thrice a day. Thereafter he smeared ash all over his body by way of *Bhasma Snāna* and performed the Japa of Rudraśiras, Rudra verses and other Nīlarudra passages.

20. He himself performed the worship after bathing him duly. Then he offered oblations, and gifts of offerings, and adoration in accordance with the injunctions of the scriptural texts.

21. Thus he continued performing the Vrata rites, Japa and Pūjā. Then at the end of a thousand years Maheśvara became pleased. He said, "O most excellent bird, I shall grant boons. Choose whatever is desired."

Garuḍa said:

22-23. See my plight, O Īśāna, brought about by Śāṇḍilī. My wings have been caused to fall down. This is what I request you further, O Hara, that you should stay here always in the Liṅga at my instance, unhesitatingly, if you are to grant me what is desired by me.

Śrī Bhagavān said:

24-25. From today onwards my stay shall be here in this Liṅga. You will also be endowed with that original form, particularly possessing special strength and speed. This shall undoubtedly take place with my favour, O bird.

After saying this to him, the Lord himself touched him with his hand.

26. At the very instant beautiful wings grew. So also divine hairs comparable to gold appeared thereon.

27. Then the delighted bird bowed down to the Lord. Afterwards he took leave of Maheśvara and went to his abode.

28. At his request, Lord Hara always resided in that Liṅga during the three Sandhyās (dusks and midday).

29. A devotee shall adopt Prāyopaveśana (fast unto death) rite in that meritorious shrine and cast off the life through Yoga. He is never reborn.

30. He may be a man of regular sinful conduct, a Kaula, a ruthless fellow (perpetrator of great sins), a Brāhmaṇa-slayer, liquor-drinker, thief or one guilty of foeticide (he is redeemed).

31. One who worships thrice a day with the mind sanctified by faith and stays here for a year is honoured in Śivaloka.

32-33. Or a man who seizes an opportunity and visits the

year, O Brāhmaṇas, shall undoubtedly go to Śiva's palace riding on an excellent aerial chariot and waited upon by groups of celestial damsels.

34. Hence particularly in Kali age, the Lord named Suparṇa (Suparṇākhya) should be visited by persons endowed with faith with all efforts.

35. In front of that deity, people should adopt the Prāyopaveśa vow and cast off their life, if they desire Śiva's proximity. This is the truth uttered by me.

CHAPTER EIGHTYTHREE

Greatness of the Deity Suparṇa

Sūta said:

1-3. O excellent Brāhmaṇas, I shall narrate to you a miracle that occurred there formerly. It has been cited in the Purāṇa.

Formerly there was a king of the Solar dynasty named Veṇu. He was a person of vicious mind, always afflicted by lust and engaged in committing sins.

Royal charters and grants awarded to noble-souled Brāhmaṇas by other leading kings formerly were forfeited by him.

4. Many women and widows in particular were ruined by him. So also beautiful virgins as well as those belonging to his own family.

5. That sinful king never allowed anyone to propitiate deities or adore them. Neither Yajña, nor Homa, nor Vedic Studies (*Svādhyāya*) were permitted by him.

6-7. He used to tell all the people: "Worship me always. There is no one superior to me, whether a Deva or a Brāhmaṇa. If I am pleased, everything that all of you cherish in your hearts whether good or bad, shall become realized in this world undoubtedly."

8. Unarmed persons with implicit faith in him, were killed by him. Those who sought refuge in him were forsaken. All persons became overcome with fright.

9. On seeing the groups of enemies assembled for a great fight, he forsook the duty of a Kṣatriya and he used to flee to save his own life.

10. Persons other than thieves were held captive by him and thieves were given protection. Good people were always subjected to torture and their wealth and property were confiscated.

11. He did not observe any Vrata with a mind sanctified by faith. He did not offer anything to Brāhmaṇas nor did he perform any Yajña at any time.

12. Thus, O excellent Brāhmaṇas, while the king continued to be engaged in sinful activities, a severe fell disease of leprosy attacked him resulting in the ruin of the family itself.

13. As he was assailed by the disease and as he had no son or grandson, the cousins suddenly attacked him and seized his kingdom.

14. He became isolated and abandoned by all the groups of friends. Then they banished him from the kingdom. He was forced to go out on foot.

15. He was abandoned thus by all due to his sinful activity, even by his wives and close relatives, remembering his past (mis) deeds.

16. Caught in this grievous plight he wandered alone and ultimately weary with hunger and thirst, he reached this place in the holy spot.

17. He came near the palace (shrine) of the deity (called Suparṇa) and in that state of starvation itself he ceased to live.

18. Thereupon he assumed a divine body. Seated in an excellent aerial chariot, he went to the world of Śiva that is rarely attained even by righteous persons.

19. Attended upon by celestial damsels, eulogized by Kinnaras and sung about by Gandharvas, he got stay near Śiva.

20. On seeing him very near, Gaurī asked respectfully: "Who is this meritorious person, O Lord, who has come to your palace? What excellent deed has he performed that he has come here in all glory with holy ash smeared over?"

Śrī Bhagavān said:

21. This is a king named Veṇu who had been committing sins on the earth. He was afflicted by the fell disease of leprosy.

22. Abandoned by his wives and all close relatives, he was attacked by groups of his enemies. Wandering everywhere he ultimately came to the palace of the deity Suparṇākhya (Suparṇa by name).

23. Exhausted by starvation, he reached the shrine sanctified by my presence. Ultimately he breathed his last in that auspicious shrine.

24-26. He reached this place on account of that. What I say is the truth. O lady of excellent complexion, anyone else who observes fast and gives up his life there shall attain a glory and prosperity superior to everything else.

You see here, O goddess, all these Gaṇas of mine standing at my sides. All these had performed *Prāyopaveśana* there. Even worms and moths, animals, birds and beasts, liberated from their vital airs, come near me.

Sūta said:

27. On hearing the statement made by Lord Śaṁbhu, Pārvatī was overwhelmed by wonder in her heart. She said, "Excellent! Excellent!"

28-30. Ever since then all the persons on the earth desirous of salvation came there from far-off countries and gave up their life there by means of *Prāyopaveśa.*

Endowed with great faith, they attain the greatest Siddhi, although they might have been sinners.

Thus everything regarding the greatness of Suparṇākhya has been narrated to you. It was heard by me from my father. It is destructive of all sins.

CHAPTER EIGHTYFOUR

Mādhavī Born as Subhadrā

The sages said:

1-2. O Sūta, you said that Viṣṇu, the Lord of Devas, had told that when Mādhavī became his sister in her next birth as a horse-faced one he would perform penance and turn her into one of splendid countenance. How was she rendered thus? How was the penance performed? Describe everything in detail. Our curiosity is indeed great.

Sūta said:

3. On hearing the message of Suras from Nārada, Viṣṇu went to heaven and held consultation along with Suras.

4. It was for the purpose of reducing the burden of the earth and killing Dānavas that the glorious Lord Hari took birth in the house of Vasudeva towards the end of Dvāpara.

5. The Lord, the destroyer of the arrogance of Daityas, was born of the womb of Devakī. He (Vasudeva) had another wife named Rohiṇī.

6. Of her was born the valorous son named Balabhadra otherwise known as Plough-wielder (*Halin*). A third wife, the beloved of Vasudeva was known as Suprabhā.

7. Mādhavī was born of her assuming the form of a horse-faced one. One seeing the daughter born with such a hideous form, Suprabhā and Vasudeva became grief-stricken.

8-9. Then all the Yādavas performed the *Śāntika* (pacificatory) and *Pauṣṭika* (nourishing) rites. In their excessive terror, they said, "*Svasti, Svasti,* may it be vell!". "In our family growing up as a young woman, she is sure to be unhappy. On seeing a girl with horse-face, no one will marry her."

10-11. Lord Viṣṇu, on coming to know that his sister was like that and the parents were highly distressed, took her with him. Accompanied by Baladeva he quickly went to the holy spot of Hāṭakeśvara for performing a great penance.

12. Properly engaged in Yajña, he propitiated Brahmā through different kinds of Vrata and Dāna and propitiations of Brāhmaṇas.

13. At the end of a year, Brahmā was pleased with the

Śārṅga-armed One. He said "I shall grant boons. Request for the desired thing."

Viṣṇu said:

14. O Lord, this sister of mine is born as a horse-faced one. Let her be one of excellent countenance. This is my desire.

Śrī Brahmā said:

15. With my favour this good lady shall be one with excellent countenance. She will become well-known by the name Subhadrā. A beloved of her husband, she will give birth to a heroic son.

16-17. A man who devoutly worships her in this form here, O Viṣṇu, along with you and also this Sīrin (Balabhadra) on the twelfth lunar day in the month of Māgha with sweet scents, flowers and unguents shall attain undoubtedly what is cherished in his mind.

18-19. A barren woman or one abandoned by her husband, who devoutly worships her, O Keśava, on the third lunar day, shall become fortunate, happy and blessed with good sons. She will be always rich and prosperous and endowed with all good qualities.

20. After saying thus, the Four-faced One ceased to speak. Delighted in himself, Vasudeva went to the city of Dvārāvatī.

21. He took leave of Pitāmaha. Accompanied by Baladeva, he took the large-eyed lady with the countenance resembling the lunar disc.

Sūta said:

22. It was thus that Mādhavī who was afflicted by the curse of Lakṣmī was born on the earth (and later) attained the beautiful form of a Subhagā (a fortunate lady).

23. Pārtha, the son of Pāṇḍu, married that lady with charming smiles. A heroic son well-known as Abhimanyu was born to her.

24. Thus, O excellent Brāhmaṇas, everything connected with the birth of Mādhavī has been narrated to you as incidental to the narrative of Lord Suparṇākhya.

25. A man who devoutly reads or listens to this becomes rid of sins incurred only on that day.

CHAPTER EIGHTYFIVE

Greatness of Mahālakṣmī[1]

The sages said:

1-2. Everything connected with the sequence and result of the curse uttered by Padmā in the case of Mādhavī has been heard by us today.

Kamalā was cursed by that noble-souled Brāhmaṇa. How did she become elephant-faced and then get transformed into one of splendid countenance?

Sūta said:

3. By the curse of that Brāhmaṇa, O Brāhmaṇas, she (Lakṣmī) became instantly an elephant-faced one, causing great wonder.

4-5. She was told by Hari: "O splendid daughter of the Ocean, stay in this very form for some time till the close of the Dvāpara Yuga. Then I shall incarnate on the earth. By the power of my penance I shall make you splendid-faced once again."

6. She ignored those words of the wielder of Śārṅga bow. She joyously performed a very severe penance for the sake of a splendid face.

7. She came to this holy spot and took the holy bath thrice a day. She was active and alert day and night and propitiated Brahmā.

8. Becoming pleased with her at the close of a year Brahmā said to her: "O beloved of Keśava, I am pleased with you. Request for a boon."

Lakṣmī said:

9-10. For some reason, O Lord, I have been transformed into an elephant-faced woman by an extremely furious Brāhmaṇa by uttering a terrible curse. Hence, O Pitāmaha, if you are

1. This is not the deity Mahālakṣmī of Kolhapur. Here the adj. 'Mahā-' is applied to glorify Lakṣmī (see v.12).

pleased, change me back again into the old form. I do not choose anything else.

Brahmā said:

11. O fair lady, with my favour, your face will undoubtedly become splendid all the more. So go home.

12. O splendid lady, *Mahattva* (greatness) has been granted to you by me from today. Hence your name here will be Mahālakṣmī.

13. A man who devoutly worships you as elephant-faced, shall become a king on the earth and Lord of elephants.

14-15. On the second lunar day, O goddess, one who calls you Mahālakṣmī and devoutly worships you through *Śrīsūkta* will never become poor during seven successive births.

After saying this the Four-faced God ceased (to speak).

16. That goddess joyously went to the place where Keśava was staying.

CHAPTER EIGHTYSIX

Greatness of Saptaviṁśatikā[1]

Sūta said:

1-3. There is another deity named Saptaviṁśatikā. She is the goddess installed by the constellations (stars). She bestows everything desired.

Formerly twenty-seven daughters of Dakṣa were married by Soma (the Moon). Among them Rohiṇī was his sole beloved, more than his very life. He remained attached to her and always stayed near her.

4. Distressed due to their unfortunate plight all those

1. This numerical name is given to Goddess Durgā as she was installed by the twentyseven daughters of Dakṣa (see vv.1 and 23).

daughters of Dakṣa became highly disgusted with worldly life. They began to perform penance in this holy place.

5. Endowed with great faith, they installed the deity Durgā. They worshipped the goddess of Suras with oblations, adorations and holy presents.

6-7. After a long time she became pleased with them and said: "O my daughters, I am delighted and I shall grant you a boon. So let what is cherished in your minds be requested for. Undoubtedly I shall grant whatever is present in your heart."

8-10. Then all of them said: "O goddess, with your favour we have everything desirable in all the three worlds excepting one thing, namely, the happiness from our husband, that which is the outcome of conjugal felicity. Hence O Caṇḍikā, if you are pleased, give us that (bliss). Due to adverse fate all of us have undergone great hardships. We are unable to retain our vital airs in our body by any means"

Śrī Devī said:

11. By my grace from today onwards you will have conjugal bliss from your husband, enhancing your happiness undoubtedly.

12-14. Another woman, also abandoned by her husband, who staying here always worships me with great devotion and observes fast on the fourteenth lunar day, shall become blessed with conjugal felicity and good sons. She should take only one meal everyday for the period of a year. If the woman worships me abstaining from astringent or saline item in her diet, she will never have any trouble from her husband nor adverse luck.

15. If the woman observes fast on the ninth lunar day in the bright half of the month of Āśvina and worships me at midnight her conjugal felicity will always be at its best.

16. After saying thus that goddess ceased (to speak), O excellent Brāhmaṇas. All of them (the Constellations) of stars became delighted and went to the palace of Dakṣa.

17. In the meantime Dakṣa was summoned by the Trident-bearing One and was asked: "Why was Moon caused to be afflicted by the disease of tuberculosis? O Dakṣa, an improper act has been committed by you as he is your son-in-law."

Dakṣa said:

18. My daughters, numbering twenty-eight in all have been married by him. All of them are of unbroken fidelity and blemishless. Yet they were abandoned by him, O Lord, except one namely Rohiṇī, though he had been warned by me many times (for his negligence of others).

19. He proved himself as one prattling falsehood, a slow-witted one under the full control of the god of Love. So I have angrily caused him to be afflicted by the disease of tuberculosis.

Śrī Bhagavān said:

20. From today he will behave with all of them impartially at my behest. There is no doubt about it. What I have uttered is the truth.

21. Of course, the words uttered by you can never be untrue. So he will wane for a fortnight and wax for the next.[1]

22. Dakṣa too said, "So be it" and went home. Candra thereafter began to treat all the daughters of Dakṣa alike for ever.

23. He goes on increasing and decreasing in alternative fortnights, O excellent Brāhmaṇas. That goddess therefore was called *Saptaviṁśatikā* on the earth. She was established in that holy spot. She bestows all conjugal felicity on women.

24. One who remains pure and reads this in front of the deity with devotion on the eighth lunar day shall attain all good fortune.

1. This myth—Dakṣa's coming to the Moogod — is created to explain the waxing and waning of the moon.

CHAPTER EIGHTYSEVEN

Greatness of Soma's Shrine

Sūta said:

1-2. Similarly, O leading Brāhmaṇas, there is the splendid shrine of Soma there. By visiting it alone, a man is liberated from sins.

Even a man of sinful deeds who visits the deity on a Monday or at the time of lunar eclipse will never see Naraka.

The sages said:

3. In a holy place only the resorts of all the Devas are usually seen. How did it happen that a resort of Candra too has been created here?

4. O Sūta-Putra, this is a very surprising thing that lurks in our mind. Hence, O highly esteemed one, do explain this. You know everything entirely.

Sūta said:

5. O excellent Brāhmaṇas, the entire universe is proclaimed as *Somamaya* (identical with and influenced by Soma). When Soma is well established, all the three worlds too will be (automatically) well established.

6. All these medicinal herbs, all these beginning with *Sasya* (vegetables and foodgrains) on the earth are also *Somamaya* (permeated by Soma). All creatures are alive due to them.

7. Since, O Brāhmaṇas, Devas beginning with Brahmā attain the greatest satisfaction after duly getting Soma and become joyous, therefore he is considered excellent here.

8. Similarly the Yajñas beginning with Agniṣṭoma are dependent on Soma because the excellent Brāhmaṇas derive satisfaction by imbibing it.[1]

9. For this reason Soma is proclaimed as superior to all the Devas and Dānavas. Indeed he is the most worthy of being worshipped by them.

---

1. Soma is identified here with the Soma plant.

10. Men erect palaces on the earth for the Lord of the night in the same manner as they are erected for other leading Suras.

11. All those men by whom palaces (shrines) were made for the Lord of the night on the earth have accumulated a lot of merit and attained liberation.

12. By means of a single mansion of the Moon, men obtain that merit which is attained by a thousand mansions (temples) of Maheśvara.

13. O excellent Brāhmaṇas, on coming to know the greatness of a mansion (shrine) raised for Candra, Brahmā and other Devas became frightened in their minds. They resorted to the top of Meru and said thus in order to put obstacles in its erection:

14-18. "All the following (astrological) events beginning with *Sa* should coincide on a single day: (1) *Saumya-Ṛkṣa* i.e. Mṛgaśīras, (2) *Somavāra* (Monday), (3) *Saumyatithi* (?full-moon day) and (5) *Somagraha* (lunar eclipse). One who erects a palace on that (juncture) in a single day and instals Candra shall obtain the excellent benefit of erecting palaces (temples) for all the deities.

If the mind is sanctified by perfect faith, the benefit shall be thousand-fold. If one erects the palace of Candra otherwise he meets with the ruin of his family and falls into Naraka.

It is for this reason, that, O excellent Brāhmaṇas, men are afraid and so do not construct a shrine of the Lord of the night, though it is highly meritorious.

19. A mansion of the Lord of the night that has been erected here in this holy place was raised by Aṁbarīṣa, the king who somehow found such a time as has been enjoined by those who ponder over scriptural topics.

20. To the northern direction thereof, a second Candramas was installed by Dhundhumāra. Like the other one he too is well established.

21. Therefore, O Brāhmaṇas, both the kings attained the greatest Siddhi, by his power unaffected by birth and death.

22. Another palatial shrine, the third one, is in the holy place of Prabhāsa. It was erected by the great king Ikṣvāku endowed with faith.

23. Excepting these three palaces there is no other palace on the earth pertaining to Candra. What I have uttered is the

truth. There is however one on the banks of Narmadā on the meritorious confluence of Revā and Ūri.

24. Thus everything connected with the excellent greatness of Candra has been narrated to you completely. It is destructive of all sins of those who read and those who listen.

CHAPTER EIGHTYEIGHT

Greatness of Aṁbāvṛddhā

The sages said:

1-3. O son of Sūta, four deities were enumerated by you, viz. Camatkārī, Mahitthā, Mahālakṣmī and another deity, the fourth one Aṁbāvṛddhā.

Of them, three have been described in detail. The fourth one Aṁbāvṛddhā has not been described. O son of Sūta, state the power of this deity. Who instituted her Yātrā (religious procession). Mention everything in detail.

Sūta said:

4. This goddess of Suras, namely Aṁbāvṛddhā is the divine power of austerity. May it be listened from me how she came to be established here formerly.

5. When this city was built by King Camatkāra, a man of meritorious soul, he installed these four deities in consultation with and advice of Brāhmaṇas for the protection of the city.

6. This king had two daughters, one by the name Aṁbā and the other named Vṛddhā. Both of them were endowed with beauty and excellent virtues.

7. Both of them were married to the king of Kāśī, in accordance with the injunctions laid down in the Gṛhyasūtras and in the presence of Devas, Brāhmaṇas and the holy Fire, O excellent Brāhmaṇa.

8. Once upon a time the king of Kāśī had to fight a great battle with the Kālayavanas (dark-complexioned Barbarians).

9. Though the king of Kāśī was endowed with great prowess,

he was killed in the battle along with his servants, armies and vehicles by those terrible ones who had obtained boons from Hara.

10-11. Aṁbā and Vṛddhā were reduced to the miserable state of widowhood. They went to the holy place of Hāṭakeśvara, the bestower of all desired things. They endeavoured to propitiate the goddess. They observed auspicious Vratas for the destruction of the enemies of their husband.

12. For more than a hundred years, the goddess of Suras did not become pleased. They got disgusted and detached from the world. They wished to destroy their bodies.

13-14. O Brāhmaṇas, they recited the Mantras of the *Kṣurikā Sūkta* of the *Ātharvaṇa Veda.* They cut off their flesh devoutly inspiring and sanctifying them with the Mantras and performed Homa in the well-kindled holy fire.

Thereupon a deity with four arms and splendid countenance rose up from the fire-pit.

15. The lady was clad in white garments and she resembled the early morning sun in lustre. Another lady of excellent eyes and countenance also rose up. She resembled molten gold in lustre.

16. She rose up from the fire-pit holding a sword. She was terrifying. This other lady too was a highly frightening Śakti.

17. They said, "Let the boon cherished in the heart be requested for, even if it be very difficult to attain."

The two (queens) said:

18. Our beloved husband, the valorous king of Kāśī, has been killed in battle by the ferocious Kālayavanas.

19. O great goddesses, something should be done so that their destruction can be effected undoubtedly with your favour.

20. Further, both of you should eagerly stay here for the protection of your own city. This is the task (boon) thought of by us.

21. On hearing their words, both the deities said "So be it" and merged into that pit.

22. In the meantime, innumerable mothers (goddesses), thousands of them of many forms, rose up from that Kuṇḍa.

(The different kinds of beings that arose from that fire-pit are described below:)

23. One set had the faces of elephants and another had those of horses. Others had the faces of dogs and still others those of birds and goats.

24. Others had human faces but the bodies were those of lower animals. Some had three heads, some five heads and others even ten heads.

25. The faces of some of these beings were in different parts of the bodies. Some had faces in their privy parts; others in their breasts; yet others stood with faces at the sides; a few others had faces on the back.

26. Some had only a single hand; others two hands; still others had five hands; a few others had even twenty hands; others were devoid of hands.

27. There were beings with many feet as well as those devoid of feet; there were single-footed and half-footed ones; some were terribly hideous with faces down.

28. There were single-eyed ones, two-eyed and others many-eyed. Some of them rode on elephants and others on horses.

29. Still others were riding on bulls, monkeys, .lions, goats, tigers and pythons. Similarly some were seated on alligators, horses, donkeys etc. There were some seated on birds.

30. There were thousands seated on tortoises, cocks, serpents etc. They were gesticulating, howling and singing. Laughing, dancing and sporting about mutually, they proceeded ahead.

31. There were many beings with hairs raised up, hairs covering the bodies and some having no hair at all. Others had long hairs, some with hairs like those of horses and a few with various peculiar types of hairs.

32. There were terribly hideous beings with short teeth, long teeth and peculiar types of teeth. Others were frightening with elephant teeth and teeth like steel.

33. There were many beings with ears hanging loosely down; others with peculiar ears; still others with ears like a winnowing basket. There were spike-eared, many-eared, ugly-eared and excellent-eared beings.

34. There were single-clothed and many-clothed beings; others were without clothes; still others had hides as coverings or rags used to cover nakedness.

35. There were terrible beings with swords, arrows and javelins

in their hands. Others had nooses in their hands and a few others with spears and bows in their hands, beings with tridents, mallets and Bhuśuṇḍīs adorning their hands.

36. Then these beings heard the commands of the two goddesses and were highly delighted. They proceeded towards the place where dark-complexioned ones were staying.

37-38. On seeing the army of the goddesses with hideous forms and ugly countenances (advancing) all those (Kālayavanas) became afraid with gloomy faces. While they fled here and there, they were ruthlessly swallowed by those deities.

39. The entire kingdom of those wicked-souled ones including children and old people as well as women were quickly swallowed by those deities.

40. After de-populating and exterminating the entire territory, O excellent Brāhmaṇas, all of them joyously returned to their original abodes.

41-42. Then they bowed down with humility to those two deities and requested loudly: "All those Kālayavanas have been killed along with their sons, kinsmen and cattle. The entire realm though vast has been rendered waste. Now some food may be given to us for our satisfaction. Similarly some place may be assigned to us for residence.

The Devīs said:

43. The foetus of those pregnant women in the mortal world who go to sleep in dim light at the time of dusk may be taken by you quickly as your prey.

44. The foetus of these women too have been given to you all: Those who cry and lament and rush to places where three roads and four roads meet. Let it be eaten by you.

45. If women move about, sport about or sleep after being Ucchiṣṭa (i.e. without washing the mouth after taking food), the foetus of all those women have been assigned as food unto you all.

46. If there is a case of *Ucchiṣṭa* (rennants of food etc.) in the lying-in-chamber, that child has been assigned to you as food.

47. If Ṣaṣṭhījāgara (i.e. worship of Durgā and remaining awake on the sixth day after nativity) is not performed for any child, that child is undoubtedly given to you as food.

48. If the fire kept in the lying-in-chamber becomes extinguished, the child therein shall be assigned to you as your meal.

49. If the lying-in-chamber is left devoid of auspicious things, the boy who stays there is assigned to you for your meal.

50. All the children who sleep under the open sky at dusk are given over to you as prey.

51. If at the end of a year when the birthday falls no auspicious rites are performed, the body of that child has been assigned to you.

52. If after anointing the body with oil a man does not take bath, he is undoubtedly given over to you as food.

53. If a man is *Ucchiṣṭa* (polluted by remainings of food) and he stands in the centre of the quadrangle, he should be eaten by you all unhesitatingly.

54. A man who is deluded by lust and cohabits with a woman in her monthly course, one who goes to bed naked or takes bath in the nude, should be eaten quickly.

55. A man of deluded intellect who takes his bath at night facing the South and one who lies down on the bed thus should also be eaten quickly.

56. One who urinates or defecates with face towards the North at night and towards the South during the day should be eaten.

57. One who eats fried flour mixed with curds at the beginning of night or carnally approaches a low caste woman should be eaten quickly.

Sūta said:

58. On being told thus by the two goddesses those beings surrounded them with delighted minds and stood thus.

59. In the meantime the valorous king Camatkāra built for them a palatial mansion similar to the Kailāsa peak.

60. Ever since then those two holy deities of great prosperity, known as Aṁbā and Vṛddhā are always alert in guarding the city.

61. A man who gets up early in the morning and sees their countenances does not meet with misfortunes for the period of a whole year.

62. On happy occasions and festivities, a devotee should worship them at the beginning or at the close of the same. He never faces misfortune on the earth.

63. During pilgrimages, a man should perform the rite of adoration for those two. He attains the desired benefit and returns home quickly.

64-65. One who always offers oblation on the eighth or fourteenth lunar day to them, shall attain the desired things here and good goal hereafter.

One who is endowed with faith and worships them on the Mahānavamī day shall be free from risks and difficulties.

CHAPTER EIGHTYNINE

Greatness of the Pādukās of Śrīmātā

Sūta said:

1. Thus when the group of mother-goddesses stayed there, the incidence of child-mortality took place in every household.

2. All those goddesses roamed about in the city of Camatkārapura, in search of lapses and flaws in (the conduct) particularly of young men.

3. All those Brāhmaṇas came to know that the child-mortality (or destruction of children) was due to the blemishes and lapses and that it was created (caused) by those goddesses.

4. They approached Aṁbā and Vṛddhā, worshipped them assiduously and approached them humbly in the height of their misery:

5. "This excellent and charming palatial shrine has been built by King Camatkāra unto you two, for the sake of according protection to all the Brāhmaṇas.

6-7. But thousands of children are being carried away at night by these deities and beings belonging to you two after detecting some blemish or other everywhere.

Favour may be shown, therefore, to the noble-souled Brāhmaṇas. Otherwise we shall leave the city and go elsewhere on the earth."

8. On hearing their words, Aṁbā became compassionate. She kicked the ground with her foot and created a cave.

9. She placed her sandals in the cave and spoke to the deities, the beings who were standing there humbly with their bodies stooping law:

10-11. "These two divine sandals of mine kept in the interior of the cave should be served always by all of you. None should go out anywhere. One who, out of covetousness and delusion, goes out, shall be stripped of her divine nature. She will become a vixen."

The Devatās said:

12. O great goddess, who will perform our adoration in this spot? What shall be our food? Hence speak out, O goddess of Suras.

Aṁbā said:

13. Liberated Yogins devoted to meditation and contemplation shall come here and perform your worship with great devotion.

14. At the outset they will worship my sandals with flesh, liquor etc., in due order. They will attain great Siddhi inaccessible even to immortals.

15. All of them said, "So be it" and remained in the interior of the cave surrounding those excellent sandals that yield salvation.

16. Thereafter, men from even far-off places came there, duly worshipped the sandals and then the Mātṛs (Mother-deities) and attained the highest Siddhi (i.e. salvation) devoid of birth and death.

17. In the meantime Agniṣṭoma and other rites became defunct. So also pilgrimages, holy vows, mental control, restraint etc., came to a standstill.

18-19. Even those quiescent Brāhmaṇas who used to decry liquor began to offer libation of liquors of various kinds with their own hands. They eschewed all sacrificial rites. They propitiated the sandals with meat, wine and unguents in the company of the Mātṛs (Mother-deities).

20 In the meantime, all the Devas including Vāsava noticed, to their utter dismay, the destruction of Yajña riteṣ They became agitated with hunger and thirst.

21. They approached Maheśvara and stood before him humbly. After eulogizing Maheśvara by means of different kinds of Sūktas from the Vedas and the *Śatarudriya* passages they said:

The Devas said:

22. The sandals of Aṁbā are kept in the holy place of Hāṭakeśvara. They are well-guarded by the Mātṛs collectively in the centre of a cave.

23. Even Brāhmaṇas, O Lord of Devas, perform the adoration thereof with liquor and meat. They attain the highest Siddhi too.

24. All religious rites in the human world have become defunct now. O Lord, by the absence of our share in the Yajñas, we have been doomed.

25. Hence, O Lord of Devas, kindly do something to bring about the decline of the sandals. Let the Makhas (sacrifices) flourish on the earth. May we attain the greatest joy.

Śrī Bhagavān said:

26. She who is well-known as Aṁbā is the Śakti of the great Lord. She is the everlasting mother of the universe. She is my direct mother too.

27. So how can her decline be brought about by anyone even mentally. So also is the special case of the sandals.

28. But, O great Suras, in this respect I shall employ an easier means whereby the greatness of the sandals is not impaired and that of yours is maintained.

29. After saying thus, Lord Maheśvara began his meditation opening up the eight-petalled lotus within the heart along with its pericarp.

30. He then looked at the subtle and splendid being seated within. It has the size of the top of the thumb and the lustre of twelve suns. It was his own soul.

31. Even as he meditated thus, a pure and splendid girl clad in white clothes emerged from (his) third eye.

32. Then she bowed down to Lord Maheśvara and said, "O Lord, why have I been created? May the relevant command be given."

Śrī Bhagavān said:

33. The splendid sandals of Śrī Mātā of the worlds are present in the holy place of Hāṭakeśvara. They are very important, important ones of the worlds! Do perform their worship.

34. If anyone performs her adoration except a virgin brought up and nurtured in your family, he shall be the food unto the Mātṛs.

35. Their adoration should be performed by you maintaining celibacy from girlhood onwards. If not, you will be ruined too.

36. Those men who worship you with great devotion, shall be the persons getting the approbation of the Mātṛs. They shall always be happy.

37. After saying thus he explained to her the procedures of the utterance of the Mantras as well as the details of the procedure of adoration in particular.

38. Then, Maheśvara gave her the umbrella and other ornaments as well as right knowledge and sent her off along with all the leading Suras.

The Kumārī (virgin) said:

39-40. O Lord, this was mentioned by you that the girls hailing from my family would be adoring those splendid sandals. How can a family come into existence if one resorts to celibacy ever since childhood? It behoves you to explain all this in detail.

Śrī Bhagavān said:

41-42. If you are pleased with any virgin and if you impart this series of Mantras properly to her, she will be emotionally linked with you. O highly blessed one, in this manner other girls also can be trained successively. They will be considered as girls hailing from your family on the basis of the Mantras.

43. Thereafter she went to the cave containing the sandals and performed the adoration duly as explained by the slayer of the Tripuras.

Sūta said:

44. A man who with purity and mental concentration performs the adoration of the sandals through the hands of a virgin hailing from her family, shall attain happiness in this world as well as in the other

45. Hence by all means the sandals should be worshipped through the hands of a virgin. That worshipping virgin too should be duly worshipped.

46. This worship should be carried out by those men who desire perpetual happiness in this world as well as in the other. They should be endowed with devotion, so said Maheśvara.

47. Thus the greatness pertaining to the sandals of Śrīmātā has been narrated to you completely. Incidentally, O excellent Brāhmaṇas, the greatness of Aṁbādevī too has been narrated.

48. One who devoutly listens to this with mental concentration and purity on the fourteenth lunar day as well as on the eighth day in particular attains the greatest region.

CHAPTER NINETY

Greatness of Vasordhārā

The sages said:

1-2. O highly intelligent one, Agnitīrtha and Brahmatīrtha have been mentioned by you earlier, but their origin and greatness have not been told. Hence describe each one separately and in detail. We are not fully satiated by listening to your nectar-like words.

Sūta said:

3. In this context I shall relate to you a story that is destructive of sins. It refers to Agnitīrtha. It is auspicious and contributes to the happiness of everyone.

4. Formerly there was a king named Pratīpa. He hailed from the lunar race. He was endowed with heroism and was expert in the knowledge of Brahman.

5. He had two sons having all (good) features. Of them, O Brāhmaṇas, the first was Devāpi and the second was Śantanu.

6. When the excellent king Pratīpa went to the region of Śiva, Devāpi abandoned the kingdom and went to forest for performing penance.[1]

7. Thereupon Śantanu, his younger brother, was immediately installed in the hereditary kingdom by all the ministers.

8. In the meantime, while he was ruling the kingdom, Śakra who had become angry, did not shower rain for a period of twelve years.

9. So the entire world was afflicted by hunger and experienced great difficulties and sufferings. One who did not meet with death was like Cāmuṇḍā (ferocious).

10. Women were abandoned by their husbands; sons by their own fathers: mothers were abandoned by their sons. Others need not be mentioned.

11. By good luck or by chance, if at all any vestige of vegetation could be seen at any one's place, be it raw or cooked, it was carried away forcibly by others.

12. All the trees became parched and all the water reservoirs became dried up. Even Gaṅgā and other rivers contained only very little water.

13-14. When there was the absence of rain thus and religious observances vanished, the entire world was filled with heaps of bones and columns of ashes. No one performed Yajña, Svādhyāya (self-study of the Vedas) and Vrata. Those who were agitated through hunger simply gazed at the sky for rain.

15-16. At that time the great sage Viśvāmitra became so distressed with hunger that only skin and bone remained in his body. Wandering here and there he reached a certain village from which everything had been completely drained and extracted. All round the entire region was covered with heaps of bones of dead men.

17. Wandering about in the desolate region filled with stinking small and covered with bones of cows he reached the hut of a Cāṇḍāla.

---

1. Vide Mbh, *Ādi* 94.61-62, also *Udyoga* 149.15-28. It is stated there that Devāpi was disinherited because of his skin-disease and hence he became a sage. Naturally Indra punished people for their illegal act (vv 8-15 below).

18. There he saw near the residence a dog long dead, dry and rigid and odourless.

19. The sage resorted to a practice only befitting an occasion of excessive calamity and gathered it. He washed the dead animal with water and cut it up later.

20-22. Overwhelmed with hunger he cooked it over a well-kindled fire for the purpose of eating. He took a bit of the cooked meat, propitiated the Pitṛs and consigned it to the sacred fire. Instantly the fire left the entire earth and vanished from the view of all the inhabitants of the earth with a great anger in the mind against Śakra.[1]

23. In the meantime, when fire went out of the mortal world, those who remained on the earth were all the more troubled.

24. In the meanwhile Devas with Brahmā and Viṣṇu as their leaders wandered all over the earth in their search for the Fire-god.

25. While they were wandering thus, a great elephant was seen by them. Scorched and distressed by Vahni (Fire) he fell on the ground and breathed heavily.

26. On seeing the elephant, the Devas hurriedly asked it, "O elephant, we hope Fire-god was seen by you in the forest."

The elephant said:

27. The Fire has entered this thickly grown cluster of bamboos now. I have been almost burnt by him. With some difficulty I have come out of it.

28. Hutāśana (Fire) was thereupon surrounded by the Devas in the cluster of bamboos. He cursed the lordly elephant and came out of it later.

29. "O base elephant, since you pointed me out to the Devas, the tongue in your mouth will be inverted."

30. After cursing the elephant thus, Vaiśvānara (Fire) vanished instantly. The Devas closely followed him to find him out.

31. Then a parrot was seen by them as they were wandering

1. Mbh, *Śānti* ch. 141 records this but there the sage 'steals' the dead dog and after offering some of its part to Pitṛs, he gets good food. Here the Fire-god abhorred the oblation of a dead dog and disappeared completely as a reaction against it.

further in the great forest. They asked, "O parrot, if Vahni is seen by you, do tell us"

The parrot said:

32. Yonder is seen a Pippala tree, O excellent Suras, in the midst of the Śamī grove. Vahni is present within this Aśvattha.

33. My nest was amongst its branches. It has been completely burnt along with my young ones. I was able to escape with great difficulty.

34. On hearing it Pāvaka (Fire-god) stationed within Śamī was immediately surrounded by all the Suras. He cursed the parrot and went away:

35. "O sinner, my presence was divulged to the Devas (by you). Hence, O Śuka (parrot), your voice will never be clear."

36-37. After saying this Jātavedas (Fire) desired that he should not be seen by the Devas. He saw a deep water pond situated on the north-eastern side of the holy spot Hāṭakeśvara of lord Parameṣṭhin. He entered it and remained there quietly.

38. In the meantime the fishes, turtles and frogs thereof were scorched by the heat of Vahni. Hundreds of them were found dead.

39. One of the frogs partially burnt because he was destined to survive, came out of the water and it was seen by the Devas from afar.

40. "O Bheka (frog), tell us whether you have seen Hutāśana. It is for that purpose that all the Devas including Vāsava have come here."

The frog said:

41. Now Vahni is staying in this water pond. On account of him many aquatic animals are dead under water itself.

42. O excellent Suras, our families have been destroyed. It was with very difficulty that I was able to escape from this watery expanse.

43. On hearing it, all the Suras surrounded that water pond. Thereupon Vahni cursed the frog:

44. "Since, O foolish frog, I was pointed out by you to the

Devas, you shall become one without a tongue on this earth"

45. After saying thus Vahni came out of that spot. He was then addressed by the noble-souled Brahmā himself:

46-51. " O Vahni, why do you run away on seeing the Devas. Originally you have been their very mouth. If an Āhuti is duly offered to you it goes to Āditya (Sun). From Āditya is born rain, from that the foodgrain and from it subjects arise. Hence you have become Dhātā (creator) and Vidhātā (dispenser) of the universe. If you are pleased the universe is sustained. If you are angry it will perish.

All the Yajñas beginning with Agniṣṭoma are established in you. Then all the living beings sustain themselves through your support.

O Agni, you move about always within all living beings. Thereby the food and beverage taken is become digested.

Hence be pleased with all the Heaven-dwellers. Speak out the reason for your anger whereby you leave them and move out."

Sūta said:

52. On hearing those words of Lord Parameṣṭhin, Agni pretended to be angry because of his love, bowed down to the Lotus-born One and said:

Agni said:

53. I was angry with Śakra, O Lotus-born One, and so left the universe and vanished. Listen to the reason thereof.

54. Since Mahendra held back the downpour of rain, it resulted in damage to vegetation and medicinal herbs. As a result thereof I was offered the flesh of a dog by Viśvāmitra.

55. For this reason I vanished, not out of capriciousness or because of any mistake. I was afraid of eating the forbidden stuff. The truth has been told by me.

56. On hearing it the Four-faced One said to Śakra "What Śikhin (Fire) says in cogent? Why don't you send down rain?"

Śakra said :

57. O Pitāmaha, Śantanu has been installed in the hereditary

kingdom out of turn by transgressing his elder brother (Devāpi).

58. It is for this reason, O Lord, that the rain has been held back by me. Do tell me what shall I do now? O Pitāmaha you are the ultimate authority.

Pitāmaha said:

59. The sin of that irregularity has been already incurred and the result experienced by that king by way of the drought. Now do shower the rain quickly.

60. Do everything at my behest, O Devendra, lest the three worlds perish ultimately through the want of vegetation and the attack of hunger.

61. In the meantime Śakra hurriedly ordered the Puṣkarāvartaka clouds to pour down rain on the earth.

62. At the bidding of Śakra they began to rumble and display lightning. In an instant, they filled the entire earth with water.

63. Then Brahmā along with the Devas spoke again to Hutāśana: " O Pāvaka, be visible to the Brāhmaṇas in the course of the Agnihotras. Now, do request me for any desired boon."

Agni said:

64. O Four-faced One, may this watery expanse become meritorious and well-known all over the earth as Vahnitīrtha after my name.

65. If any devotee endowed with faith gets up early in morning, takes his holy bath, recites *Agnisūkta* and sees you respectfully, O Lord, you should be pleased with him. Do this kindly at my instance.

Śrī Brahmā said:

66-67. If a Brāhmaṇa, conversant with the Vedas, gets up early in morning, takes his holy bath, recites *Agnisūkta* and then sees me, he will obtain the entire benefit of Agniṣṭoma Yajña. O Pāvaka, sins originating from many births will perish.

Sūta said:

68. After saying thus, Lord Pitāmaha stopped, Pāvaka too stationed himself in the *Agnihotras* of Brāhmaṇas.

69. Thus the highly miraculous Vahnitīrtha originated there. A man who takes his holy bath (therein) in morning is liberated from all sins.

Agni said:

70. O Lord of the worlds, I remained unpropitiated for twelve years. As the mortal world was afflicted by hunger, I never got *Havis* anywhere.

71. Of course, Yajñas will be performed in future, O lord, in the course of a long time with herbivorous and other types of animals which afterwards will be born on the earth.

Śrī Brahmā said:

72-73. O Hutāśana, the few Brāhmaṇas who reside here will offer *Vasordhārā* (continuous flow of Havis etc., into the fire) day and night for ever. They will propitiate you and you will get nourished. They too will be requitted with all desirable things when their wishes are realized.

74-75. O Anala (Fire-god), when Homa is being performed at the time of Saṅkrānti (transit of the Sun), those who offer *Vasordhārā* may be sneezing. The sins of such persons committed knowingly or unknowingly ever since their birth and until the death, will be destroyed.

76. When you are satisfied all this will take place. Later on a well-known king named Śibi will be born in the land of Uśīnara.

77. He will be endowed with perfect faith. He will be performing a Sattra lasting for twelve years. He will offer you *Vasordhārā* day and night through the mouth of a waterpot with continuous flow of the current.

78. Thereby you will be fully satisfied and get completely nourished. You will be worshipped on the surface of the world by all the most excellent of those conversant with the Vedas.

79. From now onwards, whatever holy rite may take place either *Śāntika* (contributory to peace) or *Pauṣṭika* (nourishing) should be accompanied by *Vasordhārā*. All those will cause great satisfaction unto you.

80. The *Vaiśvadevīya* holy rite of the Brāhmaṇas will be futile if it is devoid of *Vasordhārā.*[1]

81. Since Yajña and other rites, the *Śāntika, Pauṣṭika* and *Vaiśvadevīya* become perfect and complete it is called *Pūrṇāhuti.*

82. One who is endowed with faith and offers *Vasordhārā* shall entirely attain his desire mentally cherished.

CHAPTER NINETYONE

Creation of Agni Tīrtha

Sūta said:

1-3. After saying thus and consoling Fire-god who was angry, O excellent Brāhmaṇas, Lord Pitāmaha stopped.

Then he went to Brahmaloka along with all the Suras including Śakra, Viṣṇu and Śiva. The Devas went to their region.

Pāvaka stationed himself in the *Agnihotras* of leading Brāhmaṇas. He duly accepted the Havis issuing from *Vasordhārā.*

4. It was thus that the excellent Agnitīrtha originated there. A man who takes his holy bath there in morning is rid of the sins accrued that day.

5. On seeing those Devas set off to their abodes, those leading elephant, parrot and frog spoke in their great misery:[2]

6. "O leading Suras, was have been cursed by Pāvaka because of you. Hence think about the means for restoring our tongues."

The Devas said:

7. O excellent elephant, though your tongue as in the case of others is inverted, it shall be especially efficient in its work. There is no doubt about it.

8. Further, all of you residing in the palaces of leading kings will be honoured duly and you will eat sweet food in plenty.

1. The above legend is an explanation of the origin of the rites 'Vasordhārā' on *Pūrṇāhuti,*

2. The story of Agni cursing the animals detailed in vv 25-45 of the last chapter is found in Mbh, *Anuśāsana* 85.28-40.

9. O parrot, though your tongue has been made dull by *Havirbhuj* (Fire-god), still it shall be worthy of the praise of kings.

10. Further, with our favour, you shall be worthy of the praise of other rich and glorious persons too.

O frog, though you have been rendered devoid of a tongue by Vahni, your croaking voice shall be long and loud.

11. After saying thus and blessing them sympathetically the Devas proceeded to their abode.

CHAPTER NINETYTWO

Greatness of Brahmakuṇḍa

[Importance of Bhīṣma-Pañcaka Vrata]

Sūta said:

1-5. Thus the greatness of Agnitīrtha has been narrated to you. Now the origin of Brahmakuṇḍa may be listened to, O Brāhmaṇas.

When Brahmā was installed by the noble-souled Mārkaṇḍa, a Kuṇḍa was also created there with crystal-clear water.

This was also proclaimed that in the month of Kārttika, when the Moon is in the constellation Kṛttikā a devotee should observe the *Bhīṣmavrata* properly, take his holy bath here in the auspicious waters and worship the Lotus-born Lord thereafter. Even if he is a Śūdra, he will attain Brāhmaṇa womb (i.e. will be reborn as a Brāhmaṇa) after casting off this body. A Brāhmaṇa who, after properly observing the *Bhīṣmavrata,* takes his holy bath there in the Kuṇḍa, will go to Brahmaloka.

6. Even as the excellent sage Mārkaṇḍeya was narrating thus, the entire speech was heard by a certain cowherd.

7. Then the *Bhīṣmapañcaka Vrata* was dully observed by him with great ardour and faith in the Month of Kārttika.

8. Thereafter on the full-Moon day when the Moon was in conjunction with Kṛttikā, he adored (at first) the Lotus-born Lord and afterwards Puruṣottama.

9. Then, as time passed on, he died, O Brāhmaṇas and he was reborn in this city itself in the house of a Brāhmaṇa. Endowed with great lustre, he gave his father and mother great pleasure. Further he could remember the previous birth too.

10-12. He grew prosperous thus in that excellent city. He entertained the same affection towards the father of the (previous) Śūdra birth as he had towards the parents (of this birth). The reborn Brāhmaṇa who was rich rendered all help to him and did everything approved by him. One day, as the span of life came to a close, the Śūdra father of the previous birth died.

13. The Brāhmaṇa son lamented much over this and performed all the rites due to the departed one without omitting anything. He had such a great devotion.

14. On noticing such an act on his part, he was asked by his father, mother, son and others (of this birth) out of curiosity:

15-16. "Why are you always extremely friendly to this low-born cowherd although he seemed to expect nothing? Do tell us. Why did you perform the obsequies when he passed away? Kindly explain this entirely if it is not a great secret."

17. On hearing their words he became slightly abashed. He told them, "Listen. I shall certainly narrate it.

18. In the previous birth, I was his duly honoured son dearer to him than his own life. I was well-versed in the art and craft of cattle-breeding.

19. Once, even as the great sage Mārkaṇḍa was speaking, I heard his statement referring to Brahmakuṇḍa:

20-21. 'A man endowed with perfect faith, who observes the *Bhīṣmapañcakavrata* on the full-moon day in the month of Kārttika when the Moon is in conjunction with the Kṛttikā constellation, takes his holy bath here, visits Lord Pitāmaha and worships Janārdana shall become a Brāhmaṇa in the next birth even if he happens to be a Śūdra.'

22. That observance was done by me after taking the holy bath in the sacred Kuṇḍa in the month of Kārttika. Hence I was reborn as an excellent Brāhamaṇa.

23. I was born in the well-known family of Candrodaya, a Brāhmaṇa-sage. I could recollect the previous birth. Hence I became excessively affectionate towards that Śūdra too without any inhibition.

24. Therefore (even now) I fully realize and devoutly perform the excellent *Bhīṣmapañcaka Vrata* on the full-moon day in the month of Kārttika when there is the conjunction of the full-Moon with the Kṛttikā constellation.

Sūta said:

25. On hearing his words, they and other excellent Brāhmaṇas observed the *Bhīṣmapañcaka Vrata* with perfect ardour and faith.

26. Ever since then that Kuṇḍa became well-known as Brahmakuṇḍa all over the earth. It is situated on the northern side.

27. A Brāhmaṇa who always takes his holy bath there, is reborn as a leading Brāhmaṇa frequently.

CHAPTER NINETYTHREE

Greatness of Gomukha Tīrtha

Sūta said:

1-3. Then, there is another excellent Tīrtha named Gomukha. It is destructive of all sins. The name was obtained on account of (its resemblance to) the face of a cow.

Formerly there was a Brāhmaṇa cowherd in Camatkārapura. He was afflicted with leprosy and was utterly emaciated.

Once upon a time, a herd of cows came that way at midday when the Moon was in conjunction with the Citrā constellation.

4. It was the eleventh lunar day. The Sun was in the zodiac of Taurus. The herd was extremely thirsty. One of the cows saw from a distance a blue spot excessively dark in colour. She was highly delighted.

5. She dug it up with her teeth, O Brāhmaṇas, and pulled it (the grass) quickly. A current of water flowed through the passage of the roots.

6. The cow grazed the grass and confidently drank the tasty water that was like milk.

7. Even as the cow drank the water rapidly, a deep and wide pit took shape on the ground. It was filled with water.

8. Thereafter, O excellent Brāhmaṇas, hundreds of other cows also drank the pure nectar-like water as she did when distressed with thirst.

9. As the cows went on drinking the water, the pit grew in size due to the contact with the mouths of the cows.

10. As the entire herd of the cows quenched their thirst, the thirsty cowherd too entered the water-pond.

11. He washed his body, drank the water and quickly came out of the water. He then saw his body as lustrous as a group of twelve Suns.

12. He was wonder-struck. After going to his abode he mentioned the incident fully to all the people.

13. He told them how the clump of grass was pulled out by the cow with force, how the water gushed out and how he plunged therein.

14. On seeing the divine water-pond, all men, especially those who were diseased, took their holy bath with great mental concentration and purity.

15. They were rid of their ailments and sins instantly. Freed from sins, they went to heaven at the same moment.

16. Ever since then that Tīrtha became well-known by the name Gomukha, O excellent Brāhmaṇas, because it originated through the mouth of a cow.

17. Thereafter, the Thousand-eyed One observed that it yielded heavenly pleasures to men without any pain or exertion on their part. He became afraid thereby and filled it with dust particles.

The sages said:

18. What was the cause of such a flow of water from that place? O son of Sūta, do narrate it to us.

Sūta said:

19. Here king Aṁbarīṣa had performed a penance. Formerly when he was overwhelmed by the bereavement of his son, the Garuḍa-emblemed Lord was propitiated by him.

20. O excellent Brāhmaṇas, somehow he begot a son during his old age. This son was very well-known as Suvarcas.

21. Even as a child that son was afflicted with the foul disease of leprosy as a result of his previous Karmas. He caused much distress to his father and mother.

22. Thereupon, the king went to that holy spot that yielded desired benefits. On behalf of his son, he performed a great penance to get rid of his ailment.

23. Janārdana became pleased. He himself granted his vision and spoke graciously these words:

24. "O dear one, I am very much pleased with you. Request for whatever is disired by you in your heart. Dear son, undoubtedly I shall grant you the boon."

The king said:

25. O Keśava, this well-esteemed son of mine has become afflicted with leprosy, though he is still a young boy. Do get his leprosy cured completely.

Śrī Bhagavān said:

26. He was formerly a king named Meghavāhana. He was a person who esteemed Brāhmaṇas. He was grateful. He had mastered all the scriptural texts.

27. Once a Brāhmaṇa entered his female apartment for adultery. He was therefore killed (by the king).

28. When he saw him in the morning after the sunrise, with a sacred thread, he realized that he was a Brāhmaṇa.

29. He was certain that he was a Brāhmaṇa. He got distressed and became disgusted with his own action. He went to the city of Kāśī later and performed a penance with great concentration and mental purity.

30. He installed his son in the kingdom. After becoming utterly disgusted with worldly life, he observed all restraints and restricted his diet to the alms he received by begging.

31-32. In due course of time he reached Yama's abode. Though he was otherwise sinless, he had all the signs of having committed Brāhmaṇa-slaughter. So the king in his rebirth became a leper even in his childhood. In the case of men who appear in the world suffering from leprosy, it is certain that Brāhmaṇa's slaughter was committed by them in the previous birth.

33. One who goes to the holy place of Hāṭakeśvara and performs Śrāddha unto all the Pitṛs shall be free from indebtedness to them.

34. The fell disease of leprosy afflicts none except those who committed the slaughter of a Brāhmaṇa. Even as I say this, O king, know that this is the truth.

Aṁbarīṣa said:

35. It is for this, O Lord of Suras, that you have been worshipped by me. If you are pleased, O Lord of Devas, there is nothing which cannot be achieved on the earth.

36. On being told thus by him, Lord Madhusūdana remembered through his mental absorption the water of the Jāhnavī of netherworlds.

37. On being meditated upon thus by the powerful Viṣṇu, she suddenly made a subtle crevice and gushed through it instantly.

38-39. Then the Four-armed Lord spoke these words to Aṁbarīṣa: "Let your son dive into this extremely meritorious water of the Jāhnavī. Thereby he shall instantly be rid of the leprosy as well as the major and minor sins of Brāhmaṇa-slaughter."

40. At the same time, the king brought his son and made him bath in the waters thereof in the very presence of the Lord having Śārṅga as his bow.

41. Then, O excellent Brāhmaṇas, immediately after his bath, the boy was rid of the fell disease of leprosy. He attained the refulgence of the morning Sun.

42. Thereafter, O Brāhmaṇas, he bowed down to the Lord with great joy. Then he went to his abode along with his son.

43. When the king went away along with his son Hari instantly filled up that hole lest anyone should see it.

44. It is for this reason that the water that had formerly dispelled all sins became manifest once again through the mouth of the cow.

45. Even today, if anyone on the earth gets himself sanctified by touching that water and takes the holy ablution on a Sunday at the time of sunrise, all ailments of his such as goitre (enlargement of the thyroid etc.) become destroyed.

46. Other ailments of very terrible symptoms, such as scabies, itches etc., swellings etc., arising from contact etc., become destroyed.

47. A man having no desire, who takes his holy bath devoutly there shall go to the world of the Discus-bearing Lord of Devas.

48-50. The day on which Gaṅgā was brought by Viṣṇu coincided with the transit of the Sun to the zodiac of Taurus; the Moon was in the Citrā constellation. It was the eleventh lunar day, that of the Śārṅga-bowed Lord of Devas. On the day (i.e. eleventh day in the bright half of Vaiśākha) when the clump of grasses was pulled out by the cow's mouth, the Yoga (combination) of the Planets etc., was the same.

Hence, anyone who takes his holy bath there on any similar day with great devotion shall obtain the benefit thereof.

CHAPTER NINETYFOUR

Greatness of Lohayaṣṭi

Sūta said:

1-2. There is another holy object in that holy spot, namely the splendid *Lohayaṣṭi* (iron staff) Which was abandoned by Paraśurāma after breaking his *Kuṭhāra* (axe). O excellent Brāhmaṇas, a man who perfectly observes fast and sees it, is rid of his sins at the very instant.

The sages said:

3. Why was his axe broken by Paraśurāma? Why was the iron staff made? Why was it left there?

Sūta said:

4-5. Rāma made the *Hrada* (whirlpool of blood) and offered oblations to his Pitṛs. Thereby his anger vanished. Then he donated the entire earth to leading Brāhmaṇas in the course of a Yajña.

He was extremely delighted in his mind. He started towards the ocean for his holy bath. At that time he held his axe too that had the lustre of the Sun.

6-8. Then he was told by all the sages of very quiescent nature, who were the inhabitants of that holy spot and always desired his welfare:

" O Rāma, O highly esteemed Rāma, it is not proper on your part to retain the weapon in your hand even when you have completed that task for which you had taken a vow. With this (weapon) held in your hand, the anger lurking in your physical frame will never go. Hence leave this off."

9. On hearing their words, Rāma joined his palms in reverence and humility. He spoke laughingly to those excellent Brāhmaṇas:

10-14. "O leading Brāhmaṇas, this axe was formerly made by Viśvakarman out of the steel arising from Rudra's splendour and is indestructible. Therefore, O excellent Brāhmaṇas, how can I abondon it and go elsewhere since I have been doing the duties of a Kṣatriya?

O excellent Brāhmaṇas, if any one else lays his hand on this axe left by me, he shall deserve to be killed by me. I shall be unable to brook this offence even if it be that of a Brāhmaṇa chief, to say nothing of another (non-Brāhmaṇa) man.

So, O excellent Brāhmaṇas, I shall have no peace even if it is left or taken by me. Therefore it should be guarded assiduously by you all."

The Brāhmaṇas said:

15-16. O highly esteemed one, if it is decided that you will hand it over to us for preservation, do break it and make a lump of it before giving it to us so that all of us can carefully guard it. Even after lapse of time, no one will seize it.

17. On hearing their words, Rāma, the foremost among wielders of weapons, broke the axe and made it a staff of steel.

18. Then the most excellent one among the scions of Bhṛgu's family handed it over to the leading Brāhmaṇas eagerly and stood aside bowing down humby.

The Brāhmaṇas said:

19. O Rāma, we shall guard this steel staff fashioned out of the axe, or rather we shall worship it.

20. Just as the glory of Skanda has been established here in the form of his Śakti, O Rāma, so also your glory will be established here in the form of this steel staff.

21. A king ousted from kingdom who propitiates this shall become extremely valorous and shall ere long regain his kingdom.

22. A Brāhmaṇa who worships this always for the sake of the acquisition of learning shall attain the greatest lore and become omniscient.

23. A man or a woman without a son, who adores this steel staff of yours shall get sons.

24. One who observes fast and worships this particularly on the fourteenth lunar day in the dark half of the month of Āśvina, will always acquire the desired objectives cherished in the mind always.

25. After listening to the words of those Brāhmaṇas Rāma bowed to them and went quickly to the abode at the ocean.

26. Those Brāhmaṇas erected an excellent palatial shrine for that steel staff, installed it therein and performed the adoration with mental concentration and purity.

27. They obtained from it within a very short period, all the desires cherished in their hearts and rarely available even to Devas.

CHAPTER NINETYFIVE

Greatness of Ajāpāleśvarī[1]

Sūta said:

1-2. Further, there is another goddess also there who bestows desired things on men. She was installed by King Ajāpāla and is destructive of all sins.

A man who worships Ajāpāleśvarī on the fourteenth lunar day in a bright half (Śukla Pakṣa) with devotion by means of incense, flowers and unguents shall obtain all desired things inaccessible to all other men.

3. He acquires (everything) with that favour of that goddess. It is the truth that has been uttered by me. Formerly there was a king named Ajāpāla, greatly honoured by good people.

4-5. He was one who did what is beneficial to all the people like their mother and like their father. After acquiring the splendid kingdom from his father and grandfather the noble-souled king mentally thought to himself thus: 'Such work should be done by me as has not been done by other kings and will not be done by those who are to be born later.'

6. Perpetual protection of the subjects and safeguarding their all-round happiness alone has been cited as the greatest virtue of kings.

7. The more greedy kings levy taxes and tributes on their subjects, inevitably, the more agitation is provoked in their hearts.

---

1. Chapters 95-105 gives the version of Rāmāyaṇa. The author has skilfully welded the incidents (may be imaginary) in the Rāma story around the sacred spots (deities and Tīrthas) in Camatkārapura.

Ajāpāla in this chapter is Aja, Daśaratha's father. He transformed all the ailments into goats and kept them locked up for preservation of the health of his subjects (vv 42-45). He propitiated the Devī who became known after his name (Aja). After the complaint from Yama, Śiva assumed the form of a tiger and began to eat the goats. The king fought unarmed with that tiger and Śiva manifested himself and took him and his queen with him without giving him any time to crown Daśaratha.

Rāmāyaṇa does not know this. Kālidāsa describes how he fought for the sake of Nandinī, Vasiṣṭha's cow.

8. Without taxation kings will not be able to maintain an army consisting of elephants, horses etc. and also infantry in particular.

9. Without levying taxes a king is likely to be overcome easily and quickly by base (enemies). It is for this reason, that kings levy taxes on the people.

10-11. Hence my kingdom should be rendered free from thorn-like enemies by me solely through the power of penance, without having recourse to elephants and human beings (infantry), without levying taxes, but always keeping the public in good humour. That will keep me distinct from other noble-souled kings.

12. After deciding thus in mind, he sent for the leading sage Vasiṣṭha, his priest, and then said to him respectfully:

13-14. "O Brāhmaṇa, tell me quickly, which is the most excellent of all the Tīrthas on this earth? It should be a place where Maheśvara, Vāsudeva or Brahmā may be pleased within a short time.

O excellent Brāhmaṇa, I solely pledge myself that I am not after selfish interests. I will perform a.penance for the sake of the welfare of all the world."

Vasiṣṭha said:

15. O tiger among kings, there are thirty-five million Tīrthas on the earth. All of them are highly powerful.

16. There are sixty-eight holy places on the earth where Maheśvara is always present.

17-19. Further, Brahmā, Viṣṇu, Śiva and all the Suras are pleased with them.

But, O king, the holy place of Lord Hāṭakeśvara yields Siddhi very quickly to men. It is destructive of the sins of all the Devas too.

Caṇḍikā becomes pleased quickly if propitiated by men endowed with perfect ardour and faith on the earth.

Hence, O highly esteemed one, go to that holy place and propitiate that goddess with perfect faith. You will attain Siddhi within a short time.

20. On being told thus by him (Vasiṣṭha) he went to that excellent holy spot, installed that goddess and worshipped with devotion.

21. He strictly adhered to the vow of celibacy. He observed all vows. He remained pure. He observed restraints in everything and particularly in the matter of the intake of food. He took holy bath thrice a day.

22. While he continued the propitiation thus with sweet scents, flowers and unguents and performed the adoration, the goddess became pleased with him.

The Devī said:

23. O dear one, I am well pleased with your continued Vratas and the performance of adorations and oblations in this manner.

24. Hence, O king, tell me so that I can grant you what you have in your heart, immediately, be it very difficult of obtaining even to Devas.

The king said:

25. This *Vrata* has been eagerly taken up by me with a desire for the welfare of the worlds so that, with my favour, they will attain excellent happiness.

26. Hence, O highly esteemed goddess, grant me missiles along with perfect knowledge. They must be able to move all round unimpeded. They should be of diverse kinds.

27. Though they may be staying at my side, they should be aware of all crimes such as ravishing other people's wives etc., wherever they are committed on the earth or anywhere in the world.

28. They must be able to mete out befitting punishment for the said sins so that there will not be inter-mixture of castes.

29. Further, O goddess, grant me different kinds of Mantras whereby I can immediately restrain and control ailments and beings that cause them.

30. Thereby all men in my kingdom shall be happy, well nourished, free from ailments and also devoid of fright and grief.

31. O goddess, I am not gathering together elephants, horses and chariots because they can be sustained only through money and money can be collected through taxes levied on all the people. So I do not like this.

Śrī Devī said:

32. O king, highly wonderful is your undertaking which has not been practised by anyone else nor anyone is likely to undertake.

33. Still I shall do this. I shall grant you weapons and missiles along with perfect knowledge and the requisite Mantras too.

34. By these all terrible ailments can be curbed. But, they should be well preserved always along with my Mantras.

35. If perchance they stray away from the range of your vision, they will be afflicting men who may get more of the calamities.

36. When you ascend to heaven from the earth, they should be deposited in the watery expanse existing before me.

37. All the Mantras and the missiles should, at this bidding of mine, be undoubtedly deposited in the Tīrtha so that all the activities of kings shall be carried on as before.

Sūta said:

38. When the king said "So it shall be", O excellent Brāhmaṇas, many divine missiles manifested themselves.

39. All of them were appended with the full complement of perfect knowledge (of Mantras) in the manner requested for by that noble-souled king. So also there were the Mantras for ailments.

40. By these, the ailments can (could) be curbed and released always as one pleased. Kept within the range of vision they can (could) be easily maintained.

41. Thereupon, after acquiring the favour of Caṇḍikā, he gave away to Brāhmaṇas everything including elephants etc.

42-45. He gave away everything excepting his wife and his only son Daśaratha.

After assiduously controlling all the ailments in the form of goats through the Mantras himself pursuing them with a staff in his hand, he protected the land (This is the significance of his name Ajāpāla).

As the king maintained all these things on the earth here was no offence or crime stealthily perpetrated. How could there be open offence?

If anyone perpetrated any sin on the earth, a befitting punishment followed instantly, in the form of death, bondage or sufferings at the hands of enemies.

46. These invisible missiles did everything instantly. Of course in the dominions of other kings men committed many secret crimes. In those places Vaivasvata (Yama) carried on the task of restraining and punishing.

47. There the people were too frightened to perpetrate crimes openly, especially due to the fear of the weapons.

48. Therefore, the people devoid of sins became sanctified in their bodies. When the ailments were curbed, they attained excellent happiness.

49. When the worlds thus became rid of sins and ailments, all the Narakas in the abode of Yama became empty.

50. No one fell into Naraka. No man traversed the path of death. Even in Tretā Yuga everything was a though in Kṛtayuga.

51. All the activities of Yama's world came to a standstill. All living beings free from death, attained happiness on a par with Svarga.

52. Vaivasvata went to the abode of Brahmā in great distress. He bowed down to Pitāmaha and said:

53-56. "Formerly, O Lord, I was entrusted by you with the task of punishing and blessing for the purpose of keeping watch on Dharma (virtue) and Adharma (vice).

Everything has been nullified by King Ajāpāla, O most excellent one among the Suras, through the power of his penance, acquired by propitiating Goddess Caṇḍikā.

As in Kṛtayuga, no one commits sins and no one falls sick or feels mental anguish.

Hence, of excellent one among the Suras, do something so that all the activities in my abode can be revived as before."

57. On hearing those words of his, Brahmā, the grandfather of the worlds, glanced at the face of Śiva who was sitting by his side.

58. On hearing the highly mysterious news conveyed by Yama, Three-eyed Lord laughed and said to the Four-faced One.

Maheśvara said:

59. How can one restrain or punish a king of excellent conduct pursuing the path of righteousness?

60-61. Since an unusual and unprecedented path has been shown and perfect righteousness has been established by that noble-souled one, O most excellent one among the Suras, an unusual and unprecedented favour should be shown by me, lest righteousness might be defiled.

62. After saying thus to the Four-faced One Śiva said to Yama: "Tell me how much of the span of life of King Ajāpāla yet remains so that when the time arrives I can take him to my abode. "

Yama said:

63-64. Five thousand years of his life have passed. Fifty-five thousand years yet remain. How can I wait till then? By that time my abode itself will become a void. So undertake some means immediately to destroy him.

65. When this was stated by Yama, Śiva sent him off to his abode. He assumed the form of a tiger and went near the king himself.

66. The king was stationed there engaged in his duty of according protection to the subjects. He (Śiva in the form of tiger) roared repeatedly in the loud rumbling sound of clouds.

67. The goats saw the tiger's aweful form and became frightened. They shought refuge in Ajāpāla.

68. Notwithstanding the carefulness of the king in guarding them, those goats were devoured by Śaṅkara in the form of a tiger.

69. On seeing the destruction of the goats, the king threw away the staff from his hand and took up a sharp weapon.

70. That fierce weapon had the lustre of the hot-rayed sun and was given to him by the goddess who was pleased with him. Śaṅkara, the great Lord, slowly grasped with his mouth that weapon as well as the other missiles given by the goddess.

71. The king had no weapon left with him. Though he was held back by his beloved, the king fought a duel with the tiger.

72. At the contact with the body of the king, the Lord cast away the form of the tiger and resumed his own form embellished with the moon and smeared over with holy ash.

73. The divine form had a garland of headless trunks

(skulls?) along with serpents. It had the Khaṭvāṅga weapon. On seeing it the king and his wife bowed down to him.

74. He stood humbly drenched with tears of joy. After eulogizing the Lord, he spoke with words choked with great joy:

The king said:

75. O Lord, I have hit you out of ignorance. I have insulted you. O Lord, may this be forgiven by you.

Śrī Bhagavān said:

76. O dear son, all your misdemeanour has been pardoned by me for I have witnessed with delight your superhuman exploit.

77. No other king administers the kingdom nor will ever do so in the manner done by you. The subjects have been protected by you very well.

78. Hence, O excellent king, accompany me to the nether world in this very body along with your virtuous wife.

79. Henceforth you shall never stay in the mortal world, since your activities are against the interests of all the Devas.

The king said:

80. O Lord, I shall do so after going to the great city of Ayodhyā, informing the ministers and installing my son as king in the kingdom.

81. Further I was particularly instructed thus by the delighted goddess who granted the series of Mantras and diverse kinds of weapons:

82. "O highly intelligent one, when you leave the mortal world ordinarily very difficult to get rid of, all these (Mantras and missiles) should be thrown into my holy Kuṇḍa."

83. O Lord of Suras, do hand over them again (to the goddess) so that, with your favour I shall be free from indebtedness to the goddess now.

84. On being told thus by the king, Lord Tripurānataka commanded them (weapons etc.) and gave them (to the goddess) quickly after going there.

85-89. The Lord said this also: " Your son shall himself be the king. He is endowed with heroism and exaltedness. He is capable of uplifting the race.

Do come to my palace this day itself after diving into the meritorious waters of Devīkuṇḍa.

O excellent king, on this day, i.e. the fourteenth lunar day in the bright half of the month of Māgha, if anyone else worships this goddess with great devotion, enters this water and casts off his life, he will go to the place in Pātāla where Hāṭakeśvara is present.

O excellent one among kings, a man who regularly takes his holy bath there will never contract hundred and eight kinds of ailments."

90. After saying thus Parameśvara took the king along with his wife, the goats and the weapons. He entered the waters of Devīkuṇḍa.

91. O excellent Brāhmaṇas, with the same human body and his wife the king was led to his (Lord's) own palace.

92. Even today he stays there without old age and death. He continues to worship Lord Hāṭakeśvara in Pātāla.

93. It was thus that Goddess Parameśvarī was installed by that king with his mind sanctified with faith.

CHAPTER NINETYSIX

Dialogue between Daśaratha and Śanaiścara[1]

Sūta said:

1-3. When King Ajāpāla went to Rasātala thus his son being honoured by the ministers became the king.

It was he who later regularly visited Svarga and enabled

1. This chapter and the next (97) record events in Daśaratha's life not known to Vālmīki. In this chapter, Daśaratha confronted Śani (Saturn) as Śani's attempt to cross the Rohiṇī Śakaṭa would have resulted in a long famine. Vālmīki tells us about Putrakāmeṣṭi performed by Ṛṣyaśṛṅga whereby he got four sons. Our Purāṇa tells that Daśaratha performed penance at Hāṭakeśvara and created a Tīrtha called Rājavāpī. Due to his penance Daśaratha got the sons.

Vāsava to enjoy himself always. Śanaiścara who was about to cross the orbit of Rohiṇī was conquered by that king.

It was in his abode that Viṣṇu joyously incarnated in four forms for the purpose of killing Rāvaṇa.

4. He came to this excellent holy place and propitiated Madhusūdana. After erecting a (a palace-like temple) of splendid features, he installed Madhusūdana therein.

5. A famous tank was dug by him. It became well-known all over the world as Rājavāpī.

6. One who performs Śrāddha on the fifth lunar day particularly in the *Pretapakṣa* (dark half of Bhādrapada) shall become a favourite of good people.

The sages said:

7. How did the son of the Sun (Saturn) break the cart-like figure or Rohiṇī, conquered by him? How was Nārayāṇa propitiated by him? Tell us.

Sūta said:

8. When that king, a knower of Dharma, was ruling over the earth righteously, the entire world was always very happy.

9. Cows yielded milk profusely. Vegetation (foodgrains) was luxurious and of good quality. Parjanya (god of rain, cloud) showered as much as desired. Trees bore fruits befitting the seasons.

10-11. Once Daivajñas (Astrologers) told that king: "The son of Ravi (Saturn) will cross the orbit of Rohiṇī. Immediately thereafter there will be a great famine. A terrible drought will come lasting for twelve years whereby the entire earth will become devoid of men."

12. [1]On hearing their words, the king became very angry. He got into an aerial chariot and marched against Śanaiścara.

13. Formerly, Indra who was pleased with that king had given him that chariot that could go anywhere one wished.

14-15. He left the path of the Sun and then that of the Moon. After reaching the path of the stars and stringing the

---

1. This confrontation of Daśaratha with Śani is found in the *Padma Purāṇa* (Uttarakāṇḍa ch. 34).

great bow, the king fitted an arrow therein and attacked Śanaiścara. He stood in front of Saturn (the son of the Sun) who stood with his face stooped down, and said:

16-17. "At my bidding, O Śanaiścara, leave the orbit of Rohiṇī now. Otherwise I will despatch you to the abode of Yama with this sharp-pointed arrow with flat joints and charged with divine Mantras. I am speaking the truth."

18. On hearing his words of extremely terrible import, *Manda* (Saturn) was stunned with wonder and spoke thus:

19. "O esteemed one, who are you? Why do you obstruct my path which is very difficult to approach even to all the Suras and Asuras of the world?"

The king spoke:

20. I am a king named Daśaratha, hailing from the Solar race. I am Aja's son. I have come here in anger to restrain you adequately.

Manda (Saturn) said:

21. O king, I have no relation at all with you that necessitates your wrathful obstruction of my path.

The king said:

22-23. Daivajñas (Astrologers) have mentioned this to me that now you will break the cart-like figure of the constellation Rohiṇī. O Manda, when it is broken by you, Śatakratu (Indra) will not shower rains. Thus say the Daivajñas (expert in the science of Astrology).

24. When rainfall is stopped food crops will not grow on the earth. Due to the absence of food the whole population on the earth will be ruined.

25. When people are ruined, such rites as *Agniṣṭoma* etc. will never be performed on the earth. That will result in complete destruction.

26. It is for this reason, O Saturn born of the Sun, that your path has been obstructed as you were desirous of proceeding against Rohiṇī. The truth has been uttered by me.

Śani said:

27-28. O dear son, go home. You do appeal to me. O king, I am pleased with your heroism. No one else has done anything which you have done. Nor will anyone do so, be he a Deva or a human being.

29. I do not see anything at all with my eyes raised up, O king, since everything will be reduced to ashes after being burned by my eyes.

30. As an infant, soon after the birth, my father's feet were looked at by me. Suddenly they were burnt. Thereupon, I was prevented by my mother (to look up):

31. "If the virtue of obeying your mother's words of advice in considered valid by you, nothing at all should be looked at by you, dear son."

32. O most excellent one among kings, a great deed like this, very difficult to be carried out, has been done by you. You have warded off from afar the fear (evil consequences) of mine from your subjects.

33. Hence, out of deference to you, I will not break the cart-like figure of Rohiṇī at any cost even for hundreds of Yugas.

34. So choose a boon from me, O king. Today the desire cherished in the heart by all embodied beings will be realized.

The king said:

35. One who offers you oil bath on Saturday will not be troubled by you till the next Saturday.

36-39. If anyone makes the gift of gingelly seeds or iron on your day (Saturday) in accordance with his capacity, he should be protected by you in the course of difficulties and great sufferings for the period of a year.

O highly esteemed one born of *Arka* (Sun-god), should you deem it proper to grant me a boon, you should accord full protection to a person for the period of your term of influence for seven years and half of your transit, if the person with devotion performs *Śāntika* (pacificatory) rites and Homa with gingelly seeds along with sacrificial twigs and raw rice grains on Saturday.

Sūta said:

40. Then Śanaiścara said: "Let it be so" and stopped, O excellent Brāhmaṇas. He granted everything in accordance with the request of the king.

41. Thus, everything has been told by me in detail about which I was asked by you, viz. the dialogue between Śanaiścara and Daśaratha, which happened when the breaking of the figure of Rohiṇī was imminent.

42. If anyone reads this everyday and listens to this in particular, the affliction brought about by Śanaiścara disappears.

CHAPTER NINETYSEVEN

Daśaratha's Penance

Sūta said:

1-2. Ever since then, O Brāhmaṇas, Saturn never broke the cart-like figure of Rohiṇi due to the deference for the words of King Daśaratha.

On getting the news of the incident, Śakra became delighted. Approaching that king, he spoke to him respectfully:

3-4. "O king, a wonderful act has been done by you. It is what cannot be even mentally conceived by any other man. For this reason, I am highly pleased with you. Receive from me the desired boon, cherished in your heart."

The king said:

5. O most excellent one among Suras, I solicit absolute and permanent friendship with you in respect of all tasks to be accomplished in the world.

Indra said:

6. O leading king, let it be so, A friendship, permanent like that of Vasu will always be maintained with you.

7. You must always come to the presence of the Devas and remain at my side, so that the friendship can flourish.

8. After saying thus, the Thousand-eyed One went to heaven. The king too joyously went to his own palace.

9. He had saved the entire universe from the fear of Saturn. He earned excellent glory not usually obtained by others. He was eulogized by bards.

10. Ever since then everyday he concluded his evening rites when the time of dusk arrived and then went to the palace of Śakra.

11-12. He used to stay there for a long time listening to the sweet songs of Gandharvas, seeing the charming dances of splendid quality, hearing the stories of diverse import and themes uttered by divine sages and glorifying them himself. He then used to return to his abode.

13. While proceeding to and fro, he used to ride in an excellent chariot reverberating with the sounds of swans and peacocks and well-adorned with charming banners.

14. Whenever he left the place of Śakra for his own abode, his seat was regularly sprinkled with water.

15. It was at the bidding of Śakra and the king was not at all made aware of it. On another day, Nārada, the excellent sage, told him about this sprinkling of his seat.

16. The matter was communicated to the saintly king by the sage who had come to his abode in the course of his pilgrimage. The sage had the ulterior motive of provoking hatred of the king.

17. On hearing the words of Nārada, the king did not take them to heart although the utterance of the sage was considered trustworthy. The king thought that it was unrighteous of him to do so.

18-19. But he was moved by curiosity. On another day he went of Śakra's abode as usual, stayed there for a long time and then rose to leave. In his curiosity he went to another building and observed his seat from afar. He took care in particular that this was not directly perceived by anyone else.

20. As usual, at the bidding of Śakra, the celestial attendant stood up and sprinkled the seat occupied by the king, with water.

21. On seeing it the king got angry. Approaching Vāsava he said: O Śakra, why is my seat sprinkled with water?

22. Were Brāhmaṇas killed by me? Were they censured by me? Was any charter or document connected with any Brāhmaṇa annulled by me?

23. Did I run away from a battlefield on seeing the enemies arrive? Did I cry wretchedly and piteously before them with great fright in my mind?

24. Or, O Śakra, is any weak subject in my kingdom oppressed by more powerful persons. Is anyone robbed by thieves and others, or defrauded by cheats?

25. Does a rape take place in my kingdom? Is there any mixture of castes and utter disorderliness due to the abandonment of holy rites?

26. Or, O Lord of Devas, is any innocent person abused at the instance of wicked persons? Is he punished by anyone in my kingdom?

27. Or, is any thief, sinner or criminal who has been caught, or anyone else of contemptible conduct released (by a responsible officer) due to greed for money?

28. Or, O Lord of Devas, was anyone afraid for his very life, who had sought refuge in me abandoned by me, because I too was frightened for my very life?

29. O Lord of Devas, was the flesh of anyone's back eaten by me? (Was anyone slandered and calumniated by me behind his back.) Did I act as a backbiter of any Brāhmaṇa?

30. Did I regret at any time after making any gift to a noble-souled Brāhmaṇa? Did I neglect any of my good duties.

31. Do the tears of wretched people in great distress continuously fall in my kingdom whether at night or during the day?

32. O Devendra, does any rite pertaining to the Devas or the Pitṛs suffer from omission or negligence in my abode? Is any rite performed disregarding the injunctions thereof?

33. Tell me quickly whether any sin has been committed by me for which my seat is being sprinkled with water on every occasion.

Indra said:

34. O great king, there is no sin (at all) in your physical form, abode, family, group of attendants or in the kingdom.

35. But listen, I shall explain. A sin is likely to occur, for which your seat is always sprinkled.

36-41. One without a son has no salvation. He does not go to Svarga. O king, a man who has not paid off the debt due to the Pitṛs becomes reprehensible to Devas and Pitṛs in particular.

When a man sees the face of a son, O king, he certainly becomes free from the indebtedness to the Pitṛs.

O king, you have never been free from the indebtedness I refer to. You are not free from the indebtedness to the Pitṛs. Hence the seat is always being sprinkled.

If you wish for salvation, make efforts to get a son in order to save yourself from the Naraka named *Put*, O king.

On being told thus by Śakra, King Daśaratha became overwhelmed with excess of shame. He stood facing down.

He took leave of the Thousand-eyed One and went to his city of Ayodhyā. Immediately he handed over his kingdom to the ministers.

42-43. Then he spoke to them all: "Penance has to be performed by me now.. Undoubtedly the penance has to be continued until I get a son. At my bidding this kingdom has to be duly guarded by you all assiduously till I come back."

The ministers said:

46. O great king, this endeavour for the sake of a son is proper indeed. Of what avail is the kingdom or wealth for a man without a son?

45-46. We shall protect your kingdom. Be free from worry and perform the penance for the sake of a son. It shall be more or less in the same manner as in the case of your father who went to Kārttikeyapura formerly, performed a penance and attained the Siddhi desired by him mentally.

CHAPTER NINETYEIGHT

Greatness of Rājavāpī[1]

Sūta said:

1-4. Then bidding farewell to his ministers, King Daśaratha joyously went to the holy spot of Hāṭakeśvara.

After his arrival, he worshipped the goddess installed earlier by his father. With great devotion he had already had his bath in the holy Kuṇḍa of splendid waters.

Thereafter, he had his holy ablutions in many Tīrthas. He visited all important shrines and made gifts of many kinds. He constructed a palace-like temple of the Discus-bearing Lord of Devas and installed the splendid icon of Viṣṇu there.

5. In front of it, he got a big tank full of clear water made with rows of flights of steps. All good men praised it duly.

6. The water thereof was respectfully made use of by him in the regular propitiation of the Lord. He performed severe penances of various kinds.

7. Seeing the severe penance performed by that king, Lord Janārdana was pleased with him after the lapse of a hundred years.

8. Seated on the King of Birds (Garuḍa) and surrounded by many groups of Devas, the Lord appeared before the king and spoke in a majestic voice like the rumbling of a cloud.

Śrī Viṣṇu said:

9. O dear one, I am pleased with you. O king of excellent holy vows, choose your boon. Even if your desire is very difficult to be fulfilled, I shall grant it entirely.

---

1. Chapters 98 (Rājavāpī),99 (Sage Durvāsā's Curse) sum up Rāma's life upto the death of Lakṣmaṇa. Then instead of returning to Ayodhyā, Rāma asks his ministers to crown Kuśa. Rāma goes to Sugrīva and then to Vibhīṣaṇa. He instals three Liṅgas on the Setu, but at Vibhīṣaṇa's request he breaks Setu in the middle.

Chapters 100-101. He returns with Vānaras and Rākṣasas to Ayodhyā but on the ways his aerial chariot Puṣpaka stops at Hāṭakeśvara. He builds Śiva temples in the name of his brother and Sītā (Chapter 102). Monkeys and Rākṣasas instal their Liṅgas.

The king said:

10. The whole of this undertaking of the penance by me is for the sake of sons. Grant me sons who will perpetuate my family.

11. O Overlord of Suras, everything else if of course present in the house. Thanks to your favour, I have some power and glory.

Viṣṇu said:

12. Undoubtedly, O king, I shall assume four forms and take incarnation in your abode.

13. For the sake of Devas, I shall undertake this task. Hence, O king, do go home and rule over your great hereditary kingdom duly.

14. The tank got dug by you that is full of pure water shall become well-known in the world as Rājavāpī (Royal Tank).

15-16. A man of great devotion should take his holy bath in this tank and worship this goddess with great ardour and faith on the fifth lunar day.

Thereafter, O king, he should perform Śrāddha for a year. If he has no sons he will beget sons who will perpetuate the family.

17. After saying thus, the Lord vanished. With his face beaming with delight the king too went to his abode.

18. Within a short time thereafter, he begot of his three wives four sons who became well-known in the world.

19. His splendid eldest queen was well-known by the name Kauśalyā. His first son named Rāma was born of her.

20. The youngest of his wives was Kaikeyī by name. Her son was famous by the name Bharata.

21. Another wife of his, the middle one, was Sumitrā by name. Śatrughna and Lakṣmaṇa were her very powerful sons.

22. He had a daughter of excellent complexion. She was given as the adopted daughter of King Lomapāda who had no sons.

23. King Daśaratha thus attained freedom from the indebtedness to the Pitṛs, O Brāhmaṇas. With contentment, he went to Svarga.

24. Rāma became the king and an emperor later. Rāvaṇa, the unassailable thorn of Devas, was killed by him.

25. Rāmeśvara, Lakṣmaṇeśvara and Sītā the goddess in a visible image—all these deities were installed by him.

CHAPTER NINETYNINE

Sage Durvāsa Visits Rāma[1]

The sages said:

1-5. O Sūta, you say that by Rāma the deity Rāmeśvara was installed there; similarly, that Sītā was also installed and further that a resort was made by him for the sake of Lakṣmaṇa. These words of yours entirely appear to be contradictory.

O Sūta, earlier you said thus: "Accompanied by Lakṣmaṇa and Sītā, Rāma who was travelling through forests reached this holy spot. After performing Śrāddha in Gayāśīrṣa he had some dispute with Lakṣmaṇa. Angry with him, he went again to the forest." There was mentioned by you, "Maheśvara was installed by him." There is a doubt in this, O Sūtanandana, kindly clarify it fully.

Sūta said:

6. In this regard I have no doubt; but you have. Hence I shall explain everything completely. May it be heard, O excellent Brāhmaṇas. This is the primordial holy spot. It does not perish at all.

7. It was on a different day that Raghunandana got into dispute with the son of Sumitrā.

8. But this day when Rāmeśvara was installed by him was a different day altogether. The noble-souled one in a miserable state of mind installed Rāmeśvara himself devoutly.

---

1. The episode of Durvāsā's interference in the Devadūta's conference with Rāma is based on VR, VII sages 103-105.

The sages said:

9. At what time did Raghūttama come there on a certain day? What was the misery he was in? Do narrate this.

Sūta said:

10. Afraid of the popular (scandalous) talk against him, the lotus-eyed Rāma abandoned Sītā, but continued to rule the kingdom.

11. The highly esteemed one did not take another wife. For the proper performance of the Yajña, he made a gold icon of Sītā and placed it in the position of his wife.

12. Uprooting all enemies like thorns he ruled for eleven thousand years, observing full celibacy.

13. At the close of the eleven-thousandth year, O Brāhmaṇas, a messenger from the Devas come to Rāma's abode.

14. He said: "I have been deputed to you by the king of the Devas. Hence do meet me in an isolated place."

15. On being told thus by the messenger, Raghunandana came to a very secret place and then took counsel with him.

16. Although he came and sat in the place of discussion, there was still no privacy because there were too many close relatives.

17. Seeing the throng of people in what was expected to be a secluded spot, the messenger (of Indra) laughed a little at the outset. But immediately he became very angry and spoke thus vehemently:

18-19. " Like a serpent with the poisonous fangs extracted or an elephant devoid of ichor, a king who cannot implement his own command, is treated with contempt by men. O most excellent one among the scions of Raghu, I have understood that you have ceased to exert your ability to command. It has come to this that you cannot listen even to the message of Śakra in adequate privacy."

20. On hearing his words, Rāma's eyes turned red due to anger. With knitted eyebrows he said to Lakṣmaṇa:

21-23. "While I am seated here in conference with this gentleman, O Lakṣmaṇa, If any man becomes so deluded as to interrupt, I will slay him soon with my own hand undoubtedly. Should I fail to slay him even when he comes here and falls within the range of my vision, let me not attain the excellent goal of a virtuous one.

After realizing this you should be alert yourself at the royal entrance, without hesitation or doubt. Let there not be an occasion when someone is slain by me now at the royal entrance itself."

24. Lakṣmaṇa said "om" (Yes) by way of assent. Marked with all excellent features, Lakṣmaṇa came to the royal entrance and turned away all the people therefrom.

25. The messenger of the Devas held the discussion with Rāma as ordered by Śakra and other inhabitants of Svarga.

The Devadūta said:

26. It is for the annihilation of Rāvaṇa that you have taken the incarnation on the earth. That wicked one, the sinful thorn of the three worlds, has been slain.

27. Everything connected with the task of Devas has been concluded by you, O highly esteemed one. So let the Devas with Śakra as their leader get their *Nātha* (Lord) (i.e. yourself) once again

28. Do this favour unto Devas if you like. It is not proper on our part to press our importunity. Leave this highly despised mortal world and come quickly to the heavenly world.

Sūta said:

29. In the meantime Durvāsas, the excellent sage, reached the place. Assailed by hunger he asked loudly: "Where is he? Where is the most excellent one among the descendants of Raghu?"

Lakṣmaṇa said:

30. O leading Brāhmaṇa, kindly wait here for a short while. Our excellent king is engaged in some task of Devas.

31. I humbly bow down and beseech you. Take pity on me. Please wait till Rāma satisfies the messenger of Śakra.

Durvāsas said:

32. If Raghūttama does not grant me audience (lit. come

within the range of my sight) immediately I shall no doubt reduce the entire family to ashes by burning.

33. There is no other task weightier than meeting me. O foolish Lakṣmaṇa, why do you prattle something else?

34. On hearing it, Lakṣmaṇa thought within his mind rather miserably. 'Better that I alone die. Let not the whole family be ruined.'

35. After resolving thus, he rushed to Rāma and feel at his feet on the ground like a log of wood. He then said with palms joined in reverence with a humble bow:

36. " O Lord, Durvāsas, the tiger among sages, stands at the entrance. He is hungry and wishes to see you. What shall I do, please command me."

37. On hearing his words Rāma said to the messenger: " At my instance go back to the Lord of Devas and tell him unhesitatingly that I will come to him by the end of a year."

38. After saying thus he despatched the messenger. Then he said to Lakṣmaṇa, "Dear one, do usher in Sage Durvāsas immediately."

39. Rāma, the Lord then happily took *Arghya* and *Pādya* and proceeded welcome the sage joyously. He was accompanied by the ministers.

40-42. After duly offering the *Arghya* and bowing down repeatedly Rāma, the Lord, spoke with words choked due to delight: "Welcome, O excellent sage. Welcome unto you. This kingdom, these sons, and the riches are yours, O holy Sir.

Do this favour unto me, O excellent sage. Accept this. I am blessed and contented that you came to my abode. You are worthy of being worshipped by the three worlds. You are the storehouse of all austerities."

The sage said:

43-46. O Raghūttama, I have been fasting after concluding my Cāturmāsya Vrata. In my hunger I have now come to your abode for food. O Raghunandana, feed me quickly. I am a recluse. I have nothing to do with anything else such as ready cash etc.

Rāma stood in front and faithfully caused him to be fed with excellent dishes of various kinds of lambatives, chewables, and other types of foods to be swallowed and licked up till the sage was fully satisfied. Foodstuffs of various kinds were also served.

CHAPTER ONE HUNDRED

Śrīrāma Goes to the City of Sugrīva

Sūta said:

1. Thus the saintly Brāhmaṇa eagerly took food in Rāma's palace. Then he showered benedictions on Raghunandana and taking leave of him, departed thence.

2. When Sage Durvāsas had gone from the vicinity of Rāma, Lakṣmaṇa took the sword and spoke to Rāma:

3. "O my Lord, take this sword and slay me quickly so that your earlier vow may be fulfilled."

4. Rāma later recollected the vow he himself had taken earlier that a person who interrupted would be killed.

5. His mind became agitated as he began pondering. His eyes became dim with tears. Like a serpent he began to heave sighs.

6. On seeing him sad-faced and heaving repeated sighs, the Son of Sumitrā who was politely standing by spoke again:

7-10. " This alone is the greatest virtue, especially in the case of kings, that words are unhesitatingly kept true. O Lord, in front of me as well as of the messenger of Devas, you had uttered thus angrily and loudly: 'O son of Sumitrā, if I do not myself kill a person who comes near me and the messenger. I will be a greater sinner than he.' O dear brother, I came in because I was afraid of Sage Durvāsas, though you had expressly prohibited it. Hence kill me soon."

11. The king then consulted his ministers for a long time along with the Brāhmaṇas well-conversant with Dharmaśāstras and others who had mastered the Vedas.

12. Afterwards he spoke to Lakṣmaṇa who was standing by humbly. Rāma was then heaving sighs repeatedly. His face was drenched with tears. While he spoke, he faltered in his speech:

13-14. " O Lakṣmaṇa ,you have been abandoned by me, go

to another land immediately. In the case of good persons banishment and killing both are equal. I should not see you again on any account. If you wish to do what pleases me, you shall not stay in this land any more."

15. On hearing his words, Lakṣmaṇa bowed down to him and went out of that city instantly.

16. He did not talk to anyone in the palace, either with mother, wife, son or friend.

17. Then he went to River Sarayū and entered the waters thereof. After purifying himself, he sat on the banks in a secluded but very splendid spot.

18. He adopted the posture of Padmāsana; concentrated the soul within the supreme Ātman. Thereafter he discharged (himself in) the form of *Tejas* (splendour) through the Brahmadvāra (cerebral aperture).

19. Rāghava saw that great *Tejas* going up into the sky. He was surprised and thought: 'What could be this?'.

20. O excellent Brāhmaṇas, that fourth part of Viṣṇu, the *Tejas*, abandoned the mortal sphere.

21. At the very instant, Lakṣmaṇa's physical body fell down on the ground on the splendid banks of Sarayū, devoid of all glory, like a piece of wood or a lump of clay.

22. On hearing that Lakṣmaṇa had ceased to live and his body had fallen on the river bank, Rāghava lamented miserably.

23. Along with his ministers and friends, he himself went to that place. Seeing Lakṣmaṇa fallen he lamented piteously:

24-30. "Alas! My dear one, why have you proceeded to heaven forsaking me, your dearest and most excellent brother who always abided by your suggestions?

When I proceeded to the great forest from the city I was followed by you who upheld me.

When the highly powerful Rākṣasa named Kabandha attacked at night, my wife and I were protected by you from the terrible plight.

Here he lies fallen lifeless on the ground—he by whom a Rākṣasa of such a terrible form, namely Indrajit, had been killed in battle.

He by whom the terrible demoness Śūrpaṇakhā was assailed as if for sport, at my order, has come to this state.

My brother whose might helped me to destroy demons, has fallen down here as though helpless.

Alas! My dear one, where have you gone leaving your own eldest brother who has been like your very vital airs? Has your love and affection strayed away elsewhere?"

Sūta said:

31. Thus in the company of his mothers, Raghunandana, being afflicted with great grief, lamented much.

32. On seeing the most excellent one among the scions of Raghu's family thus lamenting in the company of the women-folk, the ministers spoke to him:

The ministers said:

33. O great king, do not be grief-stricken like an unenlightened one. Make arrangements so that the obsequial rites may be performed.

34. Those who bewail what is lost, dead or past are foolish and silly. Bold and intelligent men treat what is lost as lost and what is dead as dead.

35-37. After saying thus the ministers got the dead body of Lakṣmaṇa smeared with sandal, Uśīra (*Khus*, ta frgrant root) and saffron. These were mixed with camphor, Aguru (Agallochum) and other sweet scents. The dead body was then decorated in excellent cloths and embellished with splendid flowers. A broad pyre was then made with sandal and Aguru wood. They then placed the body on it facing the South.

38. In the meantime, O excellent Brāhmaṇas, something miraculous and mysterious took place. Do listen to it even as I narrate.

39. While they placed the body on the pyre and were about to kindle the fire, the body vanished.

40. In the meantime a voice rose up in the firmament after a shower of flowers. All the quarters reverberated with the sound:

41-43. " O Rāma, O Rāma, O mighty-armed one, do not be distressed. It is not at all proper to apply fire to him (Lakṣmaṇa).

Cremation by the application of fire is not proper in regard to one endowed with the knowledge of Brahman, particularly in the case of one who has renounced the world. Burning the bodies of all Yogins is improper.

O Rāma, your brother has gone to the abode of Brahman. The highly renowned one has released his soul through the cerebral aperture."

44-45. On hearing the aerial voice, those ministers said: "O great king, Lakṣmaṇa has attained the greatest Siddhi. He should not be grieved over. Hence, O Lord, hurry homewards.

The affairs of the state should be attended to, consult the excellent Brāhmaṇas and discuss the procedure of the obsequial rites. Do everything befitting your love for him."

Rāma said:

46. I will not go home now without Lakṣmaṇa. I will give up my life here in the manner it had been done by that noble-souled one.

47. This honoured son of mine named Kuśa has been entrusted to you all. If you like, he may be crowned as king of the state.

48. After saying thus, Rāma felt the desire to go to heaven. But, on remembering his friend Vibhīṣaṇa he reconsidered it.

49-56. 'I was exceedingly pleased with his great devotion. So I gave him eternal rulership over Laṅkā lasting as long as the sun, moon and stars shine.

It is generally remembered that the community of the Rākṣasas is exceedingly cruel, especially of those richly endowed with boons on the earth.

It is possible that even the noble-souled Vibhīṣaṇa may, like Rāvaṇa, antagonize Suras, as a result of his inborn Rākṣasa nature.

As in the case of his Ten-headed Brother who verily was a thorn unto all the three worlds, Devas may bring about his death through Sāma and other expedients. In that case my words will be futile and untrue. So I shall go to him and advise him that he should not offend Devas.

Further there is a second great friend, the monkey named Sugrīva. Another one is the highly esteemed Jāmbavān. Then there is that attendant, the son of Vāyu along with the son of Vāli; the monkey named Kumuda, then Tāra. There are other monkeys also.

So I will have eager dialogues and consultations with them too. Thereafter, I shall go home fully satisfied that the task of Devas has been completed.'

57. After reflecting thus for a long time, he summoned Puṣpaka, the aerial chariot, got into it and hurried to the city named Kiṣkindhā.

58. The monkeys saw the remarkable splendour of Puṣpaka and knew that Rāghava had arrived. They came face to face with him.

59. From a long distance they bowed down to him and knelt before him on the ground. Then they repeatedly shouted "Be victorious."

60. Accompanying him they entered the great city of Kiṣkindhā that had been embellished all round with excellent banners.

61. Rāma alighted from the excellent aerial chariot and hastily entered the splendid and well embellished abode of Sugrīva.

62. Seeing that Rāma was seated calmly, the monkeys duly honoured him with *Arghya* etc; and later asked him:

The monkeys said:

63. O Raghunandana, you appear devoid of all your remarkable splendour! You are very lean and you seem to be distressed. Wh hope, everything is all right there in your abode.

64. We hope, you are physically all right. Lakṣmaṇa, your borther, who used to follow you closely is not seen near you now? What has happened to you, O Rāghava?

65. Further, your favourite wife, as dear to you as your very vital air, is not seen at your side? We are very much anxious.

Sūta said:

66. On hearing their words, Rāghava heaved a long and heavy sigh. With tears in his eyes he told them everything:

67. O excellent Brāhmaṇas, he told them why Sītā was banished and brother Lakṣmaṇa abandoned. He told them why he himself had come.

68. On hearing it, all the monkeys with Sugrīva as the chief became highly miserable and they cried. They embraced each other for consolation.

69-70. After lamenting loudly thus for a long time, they said to Raghūttama: "O king, let us be commanded. What shall be done by us?

All over the earth we are the most blessed ones, O most excellent one among the descendants of Raghu, since you have come to our abode so full of affection!"

Rāma said:

71. O Sugrīva, I will stay in your place for a night. In the morning I will be going to Laṅkā where Vibhīṣaṇa stays.

72. O most excellent one among monkeys, you should also come with me to the abode of Vibhīṣaṇa. Take the chief minister also with you.

CHAPTER ONE HUNDRED ONE

Installation of Rāmeśvara in the Middle of the Setu

Sūta said:

1-4. Thus Raghūttama spent that night there after being duly attended upon with great devotion by all the excellent monkeys.

When the day dawned and the solar disc rose up in all its splendour, he concluded his religious rites of the morning and summoned Puṣpaka. He got into Puṣpaka along with the ten monkeys, viz. Sugrīva, Suṣeṇa, Tāra, Kumuda, Aṅgada, Kunda, the intelligent son of Vāyu, Gavākṣa, Nala and Jāṁbavān.

5. Then at the proper time, Rāma started towords Laṅkā in that highly resplendent aerial chariot having the velocity of mind.

6. Instantly he reached the great city named Laṅkā and saw all those places where the battle had taken place before.

7. On seeing the remarkable splendour of Puṣpaka, Vibhīṣaṇa knew that Rāma had arrived. He joyously came to receive him along with all the ministers, servants, and sons.

8. Even as he saw Lord Rāma from a great distance, Vibhīṣaṇa prostrated on the ground like a log of wood and uttered the words "Be victorious."

9. He (Rāma) closely embraced Vibhīṣaṇa with great eagerness even as he arrived. Later accompanied by him, he entered Laṅkā.

10. After entering the abode of Vibhīṣaṇa, he sat on the splendid throne with the monkeys surrounding him.

11. Then Vibhīṣaṇa dedicated unto him everything—the kingdom, his sons, wives etc., and everything else.

12-13. Then he stood with palms joined in reverence and humility and said: "O Lord, let the command be given. Tell me, what work I shall carry out. O Lord, say why you came all of a sudden. Why did the son of Sumitrā not come with you? Nor Jānakī?

Sūta said:

14. Rāghava heaved a sigh with his face covered by tears and told everything to him in faltering words.

15. Raghunandana addressed Vibhīṣaṇa who was also highly distressed and spoke to him truthful words conducive to his good:

16. "O most excellent one of the Rākṣasas, soon I will also leave the kingdom and go to heaven where Lakṣmaṇa has already gone.

17. O tiger among the Rākṣasas, I am not eager to stay behind even for a short while in the mortal world without my noble-souled brother.

18. It is with the intention of advising you that I have come to you, O Vibhīṣaṇa. Hence listen without excitement in the mind and carry it out.

19. This prosperity and power arising from the rulership of the kingdom may generate arrogance in men of meagre intellect like liquor. So it shall not be adopted by you.

20. All the immortal ones including Śakra are worthy of being honoured and venerated by you always, so that your own kingdom will be always intact.

21-23. My statement should remain true. Therefore, I have come. Although your exceedingly mighty brother was well entrenched in his kingdom, he suddenly met with destruction. Hence Suras should always be honoured. If somehow a human being comes over here, he should be seen as one with my physical form by all the night-stalkers (Rākṣasas). O Vibhīṣaṇa, all the demons should be kept restrained by you. No one should proceed to the mainland transgressing my bridge."

Vibhiṣaṇa said:

24. Undoubtedly, I shall carry out your directions, O Lord. But when the mortal world is abandoned by you my very life may depart.

25. So, it behoves you, O Lord, to take me too along with you where Lakṣmaṇa having departed earlier is present.

Śrī Rāma said:

26. O most excellent one among Rākṣasas, an everlasting kingdom has been already promised for you by me. Hence it does not behove you to make me one with false conduct (untrue utterance).

27. For the sake of my lasting reputation, I will instal three idols (or Liṅgas) of splendid features on my own Setu (Bridge). They should be worshipped by you always with great devotion and determination as long as the moon, the sun and the stars shine.

28. After saying thus to Vibhīṣaṇa, the Lord of the Rākṣasas, the most excellent one among the descendants of Raghu stayed there in Laṅkā for ten days along with the monkeys.

29. He spoke about the diverse incidents of the battle that had been fought already and visited the different sites of the battle.

30. He praised those heroic Rākṣasas of superior strength such as Kumbhakarṇa, Indrajit and others who met him face to face in the battle.

31. On the eleventh days, Raghunandana got into that Puṣpaka and proceeded towards his city.

32. He was accompanied by those monkeys and Vibhīṣaṇa went ahead. Then he installed Maheśvara on the Setu at the end.

33-34. With the mind sanctified by faith, he installed the deity in the middle and in the beginning too. Thus he came actually to the site of the Setubandha and then proceeded towards his own home. Then Vibhīṣaṇa bowed down to him repeatedly and said:

Vibhīṣaṇa said:

35. Men will be coming along this Setu with a desire to visit Rāmeśvara either out of curiosity or keenly endowed with faith.

36. The community of the Rākṣasas is considered cruel, O great king. On seeing a man coming, they may feel a desire for human flesh.

37. If any Rākṣasa begins to eat any human being it will necessarily be disobedience and breaking of the command on my part, although I continue my devotion.

38-40. In Kali age, mankind in general may be poor. They will be coming here everyday under the pretext of visiting the deity but really motivated by the greed of gold. They may not be afraid of the Rākṣasas.

If any one among the Rākṣasas were to kill him it will be an act of disloyalty to my Lord on my part, O Lord. Hence think of some wayout, lest I should incur the sin of disobedience.

41. On hearing his words, the most excellent one among the descendants of Raghu said: "Of course, it may be so." Then he got his bow ready with string.

42. Then Raghūttama cut off with sharp arrows the monumental form of his renown in the middle region extending to ten Yojanas.

43. Thereby the peak where Śaṅkara had been installed by himself fell into the waters of the ocean along with the Liṅga.

44. In this manner the pathway over the Setu was rendered impassable. He then went home along with the monkeys and Rākṣasas.

CHAPTER ONE HUNDRED TWO

Erection of Five Palatial Shrines for Lakṣmaṇa and Others

Sūta said:

1. O excellent Brāhmaṇas, listen to the mysterious incident that occurred on the way as Rāma set out towards his abode.

2. The aerial chariot Puṣpaka that was moving along the path of the firmament stood still unaccountably all of a sudden mystifying the men.

3. On seeing Puṣpaka motionless in the sky Rāma who was surprised spoke to the son of Vāyu:

4-5. "O Māruti, go to the ground below quickly and find out the cause of this Puṣpaka having come to a standstill in the middle of the sky. This huge-bodied Puṣpaka created by the eyes of Brahmā has never been restrained in its movement by anyone at any place."

6. "So it shall be", said Hanumān and went to the ground quickly coming back. He bowed down to Raghūttama and said:

7-9. "Beneath here is the holy spot named Hāṭakeśvara where Brahmā, the creator of the universe, himself abides.

Ādityas, Vasus, Rudras, the two Aśvins who are the physicians of Devas as well as other Siddhas and Kinnaras—all these stay there.

It is for this reason that Puṣpaka does not go beyond that holy spot. It has become motionless. The truth has been spoken by me."

Sūta said:

10. O hearing his words, Rāghava became curious. He directed Puṣpaka towards that holy place.

11. He got down along with all the monkeys and Rākṣasas of various types. He joyously moved about in the holy place all round.

12. He saw the Tīrtha and visited the holy shrines. Thereafter he visited Cāmuṇḍā installed by Pitāmaha. Then he took his holy bath in the Kuṇḍa that bestows all desired things.

13. Then Rāma saw the Lord of Devas installed by his father. He then visited the Four-armed Lord who was he himself.

14-16. He took his bath in the Rājavāpī and became pure. He then offered libations to the Pitṛs. Thereafter he thought thus: 'In this holy spot here that yields much merit, I shall instal a Liṅga in the same manner as Keśava was installed by my father. Further, my dear brother has resorted to heaven. I shall instal a Liṅga named after him. I shall also instal an image of him along with a splendid image of Sītā. In this highly sacred and pure holy spot, I shall instal myself in the form of a stone idol.'

17. After deciding thus, Rāma the foremost among those who wield weapons, erected five palatial temples with great devotion.

18. Then all those monkeys and Rākṣasas in particular installed severally their own Liṅgas.

19. They all stayed there itself for a long time with great faith. Then they went to Ayodhyā riding on the excellent aerial chariot.

20. Thus everything has been narrated to you all about how the great deity of Rāmeśvara along with Lakṣmaṇeśvara was installed in that highly splendid Tīrtha.

21. A man who always gets up early in the morning and visits both of them shall attain the entire benefit which one gets when Rāmāyaṇa is listened to.

22. Further, one who reads Rāmāyaṇa before those two deities on the eighth and fourteenth lunar days shall attain the entire benefit of Vājimedha (horse-sacrifice).

CHAPTER ONE HUNDRED THREE

Greatness of Ānartaka Tīrtha Kūpikā

The sages said:

1. O Sūtaputra, you have said that Liṅgas were installed by the Rākṣasas as well as the monkeys. This is indeed surprising.
2. Hence do narrate it in detail where and how the (particular) Liṅgas were installed by them. What were the holy spots where they installed these?

Sūta said:

3. Sugrīva wandered over the entire holy spot and reached Bālamaṇḍanaka. There he took his holy bath with great mental concentration and purity. He installed the Mukhaliṅga of the Trident-bearing Lord there.
4. Similarly, O excellent Brāhmaṇas, Mukhaliṅgas of the Trident-bearing Lord were installed by all the other monkeys as they wished, as their respective tokens.
5. One who applies Ghṛtakaṁbala (coating the Liṅga with ghee) to those Mukhaliṅgas with the Sun in the zodiac Capricorn, goes to Śivaloka.
6. Then, O Brāhmaṇas, in the western area of that holy place four-faced Liṅgas were installed by the Rākṣasas.
7. In the eastern area, five palaces (temples) were erected with great devotion by Rāma. They are destructive of all sins.
8. Similarly a Kūpikā (small well) was dug by him in the southern area near the Ānartīya lake. It is destructive of sins.
9. One who performs Śrāddha there in the course of Dakṣiṇāyana (southern transit of the Sun) obtains the fruit of a horse-sacrifice and is honoured in the world of Pitṛs.
10. O Brāhmaṇas, one who offers oil-lamps there in the month of Kārttika never sees the twenty-one dreadful Narakas. Wherever he is reborn, he never becomes blind.

The sages said:

11. By whom was that Ānartīya lake made there? what is its power? O Sūtaputra, narrate this completely.

Sūta said:

12. O excellent Brāhmaṇas, the greatness of Ānartiya lake cannot be described adequately by means of a single mouth even in the course of hundreds of years.

13. With great mental concentration and purity, one should take his holy bath on the fourteenth lunar day in the bright half of the month of Āśvina and duly offer libations to Devas and Pitṛs.

14. Then on the day of the Festivities of Lamps, he should perform Śrāddha with concentration, worship Dāmodara and Yama and then devoutly offer the lamp.

15. Dharmarāja should be worshipped with sweet scents, flowers and unguents. Pulses and gingelly seeds should be offered saying "May Govinda be pleased."

16. By the offering of gingelly seeds and pulses and by the propitiation of Brāhmaṇas, Lord Puruṣottama along with Yama is pleased.

17. O Brāhmaṇas, one who does like this at the Tīrtha named Ānarta obtains the benefit of a horse-sacrifice and is honoured in the world of Brahmā.

18. On the day when Rāma very joyously reached that place, excellent Brāhmaṇas approached him. All of them respectfully said to him:

19. "O Raghunandana, the excellent Sage Agastya stays here. Do go and see that leading Brāhmaṇa born of Mitra and Varuṇa."

20. On hearing their words, the lotus-eyed Rāma joyously went there immediately along with the monkeys and Rākṣasas.

21. Raghūttama bowed down to him and made *Aṣṭāṅga* (prostrating with eight limbs touching the ground) obeisance to him. The delighted noble-souled sage embraced him closely.

22. With palms joined in reverence, he sat on the ground humbly, not far from him.

23. On being asked by the sage, Rāma narrated in detail all the events connected with himself and his departure to heaven.

24. He narrated everything about how Sītā was banished by himself, how Lakṣmaṇa gave up his life on being exiled by himself.

25. He told him how he went to Sugrīva and Vibhīṣaṇa; how he conversed with them; how they arrived there and how Puṣpaka became motionless.

26. Then Sage Agastya told him diverse wonderful stories of ancient saintly kings (who ruled) before him; citing many examples.

27. At the end of the narration, the sage observed that Raghūttama was emotionally upset. He then gave him an excellent ornament studded with jewels.

28. Such a jewel was never in the possession of even Devas, Yakṣas, Siddhas, Vidyādharas, Nāgas and leading Rākṣasas. No question of its being with humans arises.

29. From that ornament rainbow-like clusters of refulgence emerged in the thousands. Even during the night of the dark half its lustre resembling the solar light could be seen.

30-31. Rāma took it and gazed at it with eyes wide open with wonder. Out of curiosity he asked: "Where did you get this from, O sage? This necklace made of very wonderful jewels dispels darkness. There is no similar thing anywhere in all the three worlds. Tell me where you got this from."

Agastya said:

32. O most excellent one among the descendants of Raghu, this excellent lake which you see near my hermitage is created by the Lord of Devas.

33. I shall tell you, O Raghunandana, a mysterious thing seen by me on its banks. Listen.

34. Once, O Rāghavaśreṣṭha, I got up at midnight and saw a sun-like refulgence passing through the sky.

35. It was an aerial chariot shining with groups of celestial damsels. There was a young main in the centre thereof. A blind king it was, riding therein. He was being eulogized by Kinnaras.

36. In physical charm he was like another Kāmadeva. He was wearing this pure jewel-studded ornament shining like twelve suns.

37. Getting down from the excellent aerial chariot, O Raghūdvaha, with the support of the shoulders of a divine messenger, he came down to the water level.

38. He pulled up from the water a corpse of a man and immediately began to chew it with his teeth.

39. O Rāghava, even as he continued to eat the human flesh the body regained its original form once again.

40. After a long time, he became satisfied. Gladly he purified himself, got out of the water and was about to get into the Vimāna (aerial chariot).

41. By that time, I hastened to him out of curiosity. Even as he continued to be attended upon by the Gandharvas with keen intellect all round, I asked him:

42. "O excellent one among the travellers of aerial chariot, wait for a while. I am a Brāhmaṇa named Agastya, the son of Mitra and Varuṇa."

43. On hearing it he faced me and bowed down to me along with all those attendants in the aerial chariot, Kinnaras and others.

44-45. The king bowed down and stood before me when I asked: "Who are you with such a glorious body, seated in an excellent aerial chariot? You are being attended upon by the celestial damsels, Gandharvas and Kinnaras. You have come to this lake and have eaten the human flesh! How did you get blind in the eyes?

The Vaimānika (Aerial Passenger) said:

46. Well! Well! O excellent sage. It is good that you have come to me. indeed Vidhi (Fate) is favourable to me as you have come.

47. The sight of saintly men (meeting with good men) is meritorious. Good men are indeed better than Tīrthas. The benefit of a Tīrtha is achieved in due course, but a contact with good men yields the fruit instantly.

48. Hence, O great sage, I shall narrate my story, how my diet came to be a despised thing despite such affluence and splendid riches.

49. O great sage, I was formerly a king named Śveta, the ruler of Ānarta. The sinner that I was, I harassed all the people.

50. Nothing was given as religious gift by me earlier. I never performed Homa in the sacred fire. Nor did I accord protection to people. Those who sought refuge in me were not saved by me.

51. Whenever I saw any jewel on the earth, I took possession thereof forcefully. I took away everything belonging to any embodied person.

52. After a long time I became overwhelmed with old age. My kingdom was seized with force by my own son. I became despised and was banished.

53. Overwhelmed with old age, I became disgusted with the world. O leading Brāhmaṇa, I wandered here and there and ultimately reached this place.

54. Parched in my throat with hunger and thirst, I took my bath in the auspicious water here. Afflicted with hunger I died as soon as I entered the water.

55. Since I entered the holy, meritorious water and died, an aerial chariot came there at the very instant.

56. The divine servants took me with them investing me with another body in the aerial chariot. They then proceeded towards the abode of Brahmā.

57. I wore divine garlands and clothes. I was smeared with divine scents and unguents. I had divine ornaments and I was eulogized by Kinnaras.

58. Thereafter, blind as I was, I was presented in front of Brahmā by those attendants of Devas in the centre of the assembly of Brahmā, without eyes, in the same form as before.

59. I was looked at with evident surprise on their faces by all those who were in the assembly. They looked at one another too. A few others censured me and uttered the word *Dhik* ("Fie upon you!").

The Kinnaras said:

60. This is Lord Brahmā of four faces. This is his assembly. All the groups of Devas are here. Let him be bowed down to.

61. Then I made an humble bow to that Lord accompanied by Devas. I set in the middle of the assembly with the head lowered due to shame.

62-63. O Pot-born One, as the discourses of the Devas, Brāhmaṇas and kings on Dharma (righteousness) continued on the floor of the hall of the assembly, my hunger too kept on increasing. I knew I was even ready to gobble up stone or wood.

64. I gave up the feeling of shame, O excellent sage. After bowing down repeatedly, I said aloud to Prapitāmaha:

65-66. "O Prapitāmaha, hunger overwhelms me now. I am unable to see anything. Hence give me something to eat. There are no weaknesses like hunger and thirst felt by you here. How then do they harass me though I am stationed in Svarga?"

Pitāmaha said:

67. O evil-minded one, you never gave anyone any bit of food down there on the earth. Therefore you hunger goes on increasing here too.

68. Further, whatever gem or jewel you set your eyes on, you used to seize it. Hence you have become blind, though you have come to my world.

69. Listen to it attentively. I shall explain how you could come to my palace despite being very sinful.

70. The Lord of Śvetadvīpa is present in the water where you cast off your life. O sinner, The Lord abides there because he is afraid of Kali.

71. Since you touched that water, you are rid of all your sins. But one not giving food (to the hungry) gets afflicted with hunger.

72. Further due to the seizure of gems and jewels you incurred blindness. There is no other cause thereof. The truth has been mentioned by me.

73. Then, O excellent Brāhmaṇa. Brahmā was again addressed by me: "This Brahmaloka is no better than Naraka. Hence, O Lord send me there. What is here in this Brahmaloka?"

Brahmā said:

74. So you should have gone there! Why were you sent here? You cannot have a stay in Naraka even because of this Śvetadvīpa (where your sin is removed).

75. The greatness of the Śvetadvīpa would have perished. The scripture would have become untrue. Hence you remain here itself in the beautiful aerial car.

76. From here you go to that water tank riding in the aerial chariot—to the water tank where you had cast off your life. Then eat as you please your own body.

77. At my bidding that body within the water shall be everlasting. You will gain vision (visual ability) as long as you continue to eat.

78. Ever since then, at his instance, I regularly come here at midnight on the day of the Festivity of Lights and eat my own body.

79. Then, remaining in this form, I feel satisfied for a divine day, that is to say for a human year.

80. O excellent sage, the storehouse of waters, the ocean, was turned into a handful of water and was drunk by you. There is nothing in all the three worlds, which cannot be accomplished by you.

81. Hence, O sage, take great pity on me and save me from this misdemeanour despised by all the worlds.

82. So, O excellent sage, grant me the gift of vision. I am disgusted with the state of blindness. I have no other place of refuge than you.

83. O Raghūttama, on hearing his words my mind melted with pity. Then I spoke these words:

84. "You give me this necklace in exchange for food. Thereby the hunger in your stomach will disappear.

85. Further, O wise one, from now onwards give the lamps of jewels of pure rays to Dāmodara on the banks of this very lake.

86. Thereby, at my instance, your vision shall be free from defects and permanent undoubtedly. I promise this solemnly on oath.

The king said:

87. O excellent sage, take pity on me and receive this excellent necklace studded with jewels.

88. Therefore, though I am a sage devoid of desire and I reside in the forest I accepted his gift because I was moved with pity.

89. Then he washed my feet and gave me this jewel in exchange for food, with great devotion. His soul became purified by good thought.

90. Then, O king, his hunger disappeard instantly. A satisfaction as though resulting from the divine nectar occurred within him.

91. His earlier body which became old and dried and later became everlastingly renewed in the water, disappeared forever.

92. Then, O most excellent one among the descendants of Raghu, he erected an excellent palace with great devotion, and installed Dāmodara at that holy spot.

93. With great faith, he offered regularly oil-lamps and his eyesight became clearer day by day.

94. Then within a month the king regained divine eyes. He became the most excellent king and the most likable one to good ones.

95. Then joyously he started towards heaven. He bowed down to me and with palms joined in reverence he spoke words choked with delight:

96-97. "O excellent Brāhmaṇa, with your favour the dreadful insatiable hunger of mine has vanished and I have regained divine vision. Permit me, O excellent sage, so that I can go to Brahmaloka, thanks to the power of this Tīrtha."

98. Then he was sent away by me. After repeatedly bowing down to me he joyously went to the eternal Brahmaloka.

99. It was thus that his ornament came into my hands earlier. Realizing that this is worthy of you in every respect it has been given to you.

100. Ever since then, O great king, men regularly come here, take their holy bath here in the splendid waters in the month of Kārttika, offer lamps studded with jewels generously and go to the abode of Devas after death.

101. O Raghūttama, those with mental concentration and purity, who discard their life herein, go to Brahmaloka although they may be sinful.

102. On seeing the power of the holy water there the Thousand-eyed One (Indra) became agitated with fear and got it filled with dust particles.

103. Today happens to be the day of the Festivities of Oil Lamps. It is highly meritorious. At my bidding dig an excellent Kūpikā (well) here.

104. O Rāghava, take your holy bath therein and offer

libations to the Pitṛs. Give excellent Ratnadīpas (jewel-studded oil-lamps) in front of the deity.

105. Thereby you will attain the Siddhi of reaching Brahmaloka with this very body. The truth has been told by me.

106. Then at the bidding of Rāghava all those Rākṣasas and monkeys dug Kūpikās containing waters devoid of impurities in that region.

107. They spent the entire month of Kārttika there, taking holy baths, offering libations to the Pitṛs and placing *Ratnadīpas*. Then they started back to Ayodhyā.

108. Then by the power of that Tīrtha all of them except Vibhīṣaṇa and Hanumān, the monkey, went to Brahmaloka.

Sūta said:

109. Even today, one who makes the gift of oil-lamps respectfully in the month of Kārttika after taking the holy bath in the auspicious waters there shall be rid of all sins. He is honoured in Brahmaloka.

110. It was thus that the auspicious lake of Ānartīya and the splendid Viṣṇukūpikā happened to be there.